GROWTH AND STRUCTURE IN
THE ECONOMY OF MODERN ITALY

GROWTH AND STRUCTURE

IN THE ECONOMY

OF MODERN ITALY

GEORGE H. HILDEBRAND

PROFESSOR OF ECONOMICS AND OF INDUSTRIAL
AND LABOR RELATIONS, CORNELL UNIVERSITY

HARVARD UNIVERSITY PRESS

CAMBRIDGE, MASSACHUSETTS   1965

TO MARGARET

PREFACE

One of the remarkable facts about the postwar years has been the astonishing economic resurgence of the lands that suffered crushing military defeat. Much has been written about the miracle of West Germany, but until quite recently little attention has been paid to the Italian case. In its way it is all the more impressive, for Italy has always been poor in natural resources, and on the eve of the Second World War she was far less developed industrially in every way. In view of her mediocre and erratic record of economic advance during the eight decades before her entry into that conflict, there was little reason to expect what actually occurred in the postwar years.

During 1948–1961, Italy achieved one of the highest and best-sustained growth rates in the world, and became a strong and solvent international competitor, rebuilding her obsolete and badly damaged industries, and raising per capita incomes very substantially. The great boom was set off and kept going for over a decade under a monetary policy that was quite traditional and orthodox in several ways. More than this, currency convertibility and trade liberalization were adopted as goals from the start and were steadily put into practice, to culminate in the Rome Treaty of 1958, by which Italy joined the Common Market.

But there is a darker side of the picture. Throughout these years, Italy has had to struggle with a formidable problem of internal economic imbalance, most easily envisaged as the dichotomy between the technically advanced and prosperous north and the traditionally retarded and impoverished south—a failure of economic fusion that is centuries old and that still stubbornly persists despite very costly efforts at unification. Of equal gravity and not unrelated to this problem of dualism has been the continued unemployment and underemployment through the end of the fifties, despite a very rapid rate of growth.

Unfortunately, too, by late 1961 the great boom finally gave way to serious inflation, which gathered speed during 1962–1963. In consequence, the current balance of payments turned sharply negative, capital flight set in, and the nation's net short-term reserve position rapidly deteriorated. In part these adverse developments reflected the exhaustion of formerly unlimited supplies of industrial labor. However, the main source of the trouble can be traced to growing excesses in fiscal, monetary, and wage policies. Not until the summer of 1963 were efforts initiated to bring the rapid expansion of money and credit under tighter control. These tardy steps were both hesitant and inadequate. Early in 1964 they were supplemented by measures to check consumer demand and to shore up the lira, and studies were begun to find ways to check the advance of wages and of government spending. By mid-year, the payments deficit had been overcome, at least temporarily. However, it is still too early to tell whether full stability has been regained, and the growth rate adequately maintained.

Although the economic situation has shown some improvement during 1964, Italy continues to be beset by the problem of a weak national consensus regarding economic policy and institutions—a debility that manifests itself in an ominous growth of the protest vote and in a continuing dependence upon shaky and comparatively ineffective coalition governments. For the same reason, the nation has been unable so far to obtain political leadership of the quality so brilliantly supplied by Alcide De Gasperi and Luigi Einaudi during the even more difficult early postwar years.

This book is addressed to the postwar record of economic events. Although it centers upon this period, the approach recognizes at many points that historical and institutional perspective is imperative for understanding and explaining what has happened. Thus the guiding principle is that economic affairs are part of a larger system of behavior whose determining forces are broad in compass, including as they do the nation's history, its culture and institutions, and even its geography. Economic theory can do much to illuminate portions of this obscure terrain, and other factors can supply indispensable guidance to the economist who attempts to chart the area itself.

Part One reviews the story of the great boom: what immediately preceded it, how it began, and the diverse ways in which it has found expression. Part Two examines the labor market, to provide comprehension of the unemployment problem, to set forth the behavior of wages, and to connect up the institutions and policies of that sphere with the continuing duality of economic structure. Part Three considers the problem of dualism itself, the different ways in which the phenomenon has manifested itself, and the factors—real and spurious—that may be adduced to account for its protracted presence in the Italian scene. Then in the final chapter attempt is made to explain the boom, to evaluate the recent marked deterioration of economic conditions, and to explore possibilities for the future.

In part, I owe this book to the Guggenheim Foundation for two opportunities to do research in Italy, to the Conference Board of Associated Research Councils for a Fulbright Fellowship, and to the Ford Foundation for a year's leave at Ithaca to complete the study. To Cornell University I am deeply indebted for providing an ideal environment and opportunity in which to work. I also acknowledge with much appreciation the valuable help and criticism supplied by my colleagues, in particular Professors George P. Adams, M. Gardner Clark, Robert Kilpatrick, Ta-Chung Liu, Robert L. Raimon, and George Staller. Professor John T. Dunlop of Harvard University, and Mrs. June Hill, his editorial assistant for Wertheim Publications in Industrial Relations, have provided invaluable assistance in preparing the manuscript for publication. In addition, Dr. Vera S. Lutz, of the Banca Nazionale del Lavoro in Rome, has been an unwitting source of much inspiration, through her several superb papers about certain aspects of the Italian economy. Two research assistants, Drs. John C. Elac and Giovanni Torelli, have been of valuable help. My secretary, Mrs. Verma W. McClary, deserves my profoundest gratitude for faithfully discharging the tedious task of typing the manuscript. Miss Grace Locke has performed the job of typing revisions with equal competence. Finally, I owe a great debt to my wife for enduring with fortitude the discomforts attendant upon my preoccupation with this study.

G. H. H.

Cambridge, Massachusetts
February 2, 1965

CONTENTS

TABLES

PART ONE: THE ITALIAN MIRACLE

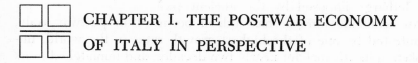 CHAPTER I. THE POSTWAR ECONOMY
OF ITALY IN PERSPECTIVE

There is admittedly a certain risk in writing about the problems of a foreign country, almost as great as in dealing with one's own. In this case, the risk is worth it, because the economy of postwar Italy, in its problems and achievements alike, commands an interest and an importance beyond its comparative position on the international scale.

In many ways, that economy is a puzzle, a thing of paradoxes and contradictions. Historically, it was the weakest of the major western systems and never more so than at the end of the Second World War. Political unity was not achieved until a century ago, and then only by stitching together in a fragile and incongruous combination the vigorous commercialism of bourgeois Piedmont and the almost oriental, parochial, and tradition-bound culture of the south. Few countries have ever been formed from such disparate materials. In consequence there emerged a nation with immense reserves of energy and creative power, but hobbled from the outset in its half-conscious quest for industrial advance by a niggardly endowment from nature and a monumental legacy of regional backwardness. If logic could have had its way, the Italy of the *Risorgimento* should have remained at the economic level of Greece, Spain, and Portugal. But it did not, and this is the key to its undeniable fascination for the economist.

More than three decades had to elapse after 1861 before well-sustained growth could get underway. In the hundred years following unification, real product per head was only tripled, but the curious fact is that nearly half the gain was won in the brilliant advance between 1950 and 1961. Even so, the industrialization of modern Italy, from its inception until today, has been a classic case of uneven development—heavily concentrated in the northern triangle formed by Genoa, Turin, and Milan. In depressing contrast, the south and the islands continued in their torpid economy for another ninety years after unification. Only now, with a good deal of prodding from the outside, are they beginning to be roused from the lethargy imposed by the ancient past.

An economic miracle has indeed occurred in postwar Italy, manifested by one of the highest growth rates in the world, unbroken in its advance for nearly two decades, and unmatched in its vitality by any previous period in its industrial history. More than this, it was achieved without forcing, without direct central controls, without heavy defense expenditure, and, for the most part, without inflation. No doubt the underlying circumstances were favorable. But it cannot be denied that this remarkable performance was fostered by an extraordinarily astute monetary and fiscal management, augmented by firm adherence to a policy of progressively freer international trade, and by a determined national effort to incorporate the backward regions of the economy in a program of national development.

If a miracle is something that seemingly defies naturalistic expectation and explanation, suggesting divine intervention, then the postwar Italian experience can easily qualify for such designation. How could a country so modestly endowed by nature, so ill-used by two decades of Fascist rule, and so ruined by war, have found a way to burst forth in so notable an economic refloresence, more than quadrupling its real output in only sixteen years?

Here was a land that emerged from the Second World War on the edge of starvation, surviving only by generous injections of foreign aid, with its total production down almost to the abysmal level of 1900. By mid-1946, it entered upon open inflation, with known unemployment in excess of two million at the same time. Its industries were worn out, obsolete and inefficient, ravaged by war, and badly distorted by ten years of Fascist autarchy. Obviously, they were wholly unsuited to the exacting demands of reviving international competition. Yet, more than ever before, the country had to export to live, for its reserves of foreign exchange were approaching exhaustion, while foreign aid was at best an uncertain and transitory means of support.

At this point the puzzle grows even more complex. In the autumn of 1947, the government decided to break the inflation, but not by suppressing it through direct controls, nor by attempting to create a budget surplus—neither of which had a ghost of a chance in that particular setting. Instead it applied the classical remedy

—a strong dose of quantitative credit control. All then currently fashionable precepts were against it; nonetheless the policy worked. Indeed, it succeeded even beyond the expectations of its proponents. It did not produce a credit deflation; nor was this its intent. With the introduction of obligatory reserves (September 30, 1947), the free balances of the commercial banks were not wiped out. Their advances increased, although at a much slower rate—which was the immediate objective. Furthermore, note issue continued to expand, which was also expected. Particularly important, the policy did not invoke a serious decline of production— industrial output dropped 11 per cent over the two quarters just following the monetary reform, but this movement was partly seasonal. By the fourth quarter of 1948 this index stood nearly 6 per cent over its 1947 peak. Also relevant, real gross domestic product increased 5.8 per cent in 1948, and 7.5 per cent in 1949. Although unemployment rose to 2.4 million by early 1948, for which credit restraint was mistakenly blamed, it was no worse at that time than at the worst of the inflation.

Equally interesting, the wholesale price level achieved a stability in 1948 that, except for the Korean bulge, has been maintained through 1961. Moreover, the new credit policy was able to work despite a rise in the deficit in 1948. In fact, although carefully controlled for their monetary impacts, deficits in both the cash and administrative budgets have been the rule even since, until 1961 without impairing price stability—a fact of some significance for current political debate in the United States.

The monetary decisions taken in 1947 have a classical flavor that they have never really lost, granted that in the fifties they were blended with some of the newer doctrines of state-guided and promoted economic development. Perhaps the initial absence of these latter ideas was simply because they were unknown at the time. More likely the reason is that the monetary authorities, while mindful of the country's deep-seated structural problems, courageously chose to put first things first.

The immediate and by far most urgent necessity was to stop inflation. Everything depended upon it if the nation were again to become a solvent economic unit. In electing the policy of credit control, the government turned to the most promising device at hand, indeed, the only one. In making this choice, it was undoubtedly guided by some well-conceived objectives and some basic conceptions of economic policy. One aim was to stabilize the lira at a realistic official rate, so that exports could revive and replenish the exchange reserves, in this way permitting imports to expand to bring the balance of payments into eventual equilibrium. The government also reasoned that only if the rise in the price level were stopped would capital flight yield to repatriation, and would the rate of voluntary saving recover to make possible a high rate of noninflationary investment for reconstruction, future growth, and effective attack upon the problem of the south. In all this, the central idea was to keep Italy within the orbit of the free market economies, relying upon private incentives to achieve renewed growth and increased competitive efficiency. If one wishes, it was the Piedmontese economics of Count Camillo Benso di Cavour, given new life and direction at the masterly hands of Luigi Einaudi and Donato Menichella.[1]

There was a certain non-Keynesian quality to their approach that was not lost upon their critics, and that again underscores the inherent interest of the Italian case. To be sure, their thinking did not run counter to the Keynes of 1942, or even to those parts of the *General Theory* that emphasize the importance of business expectations, the state of confidence, and the connection between prospective profits and private investment. But clearly Einaudi and Menichella feared no oversavings problem. They looked for no cyclical shrinkage of investment opportunities, let alone secular stagnation. Quite the contrary. In their view, there was no trouble at all about the demand for new capital. The real problem was to provide an adequate flow of noninflationary savings, for which price stability was the essential prerequisite. While they were implicitly at one with Keynes in taking great pains to prevent credit restraint from deliberately depressing effective demand, not for a moment did they yield to the idea that demand deficiency was the cause of the country's massive unemployment, or that full employment could be quickly overcome simply by a large increase of total spending. Admittedly, they entertained no prospects of forcing down money wages as a way to depress real wages and thus to increase employment, but neither did they look to inflation as an alternative means to the same end.

Instead they regarded unemployment as both an immediate and

a long-term problem, curable neither by deflation nor inflation. In 1947 the first order of business was to bring urgently needed raw materials into the country and to rebuild plant and equipment—in the power industry, on the railways, and in manufacturing generally. If monetary stabilization could succeed, the foreign balance would be relieved, output could recover to prewar levels, and employment could expand to some extent. Here the balance of payments was strategic, and monetary stability decisive to its desired behavior. But this was only a partial solution to the unemployment problem. For the longer run, the critical factor was capital formation, that curiously neglected element in so much of postwar economic thinking. If the Italian economy were ever to modernize and to unify itself, and to grow again, the prime essential was investment, in large and well-sustained amounts—thus the government's old-fashioned emphasis upon a reprise for saving. If, too, the Italian workers were to persevere in their insistence on a level of real wages too high for full employment—an understandable, inevitable, but disruptive objective—then the one sure way to high employment lay in rapid capital formation to build up the stock of capital relative to man-power. This way was taken, despite all initial doubts, and after 1959 the hitherto refractory problem of mass unemployment at last began to yield to the strong forces of persistent expansion.

By 1961, the number of registered unemployed had fallen to 1.4 million—6.7 per cent of a labor force of 21 million. Absorption of the remainder was proceeding quite rapidly, aided by repeal legislation (February 1961) now allowing much freer internal migration toward the northern industrial centers. In broader respects as well, the policy of indirectly controlled, noninflationary expansion of effective demand achieved astonishing success, granted that it very likely enjoyed the supreme good fortune of happening to coincide with a strong upward trend in real investment. In real terms (prices of 1954), gross domestic product rose 90.1 per cent between 1950 and 1961, while gross investment jumped 163.7 per cent, and exports soared by 291.6 per cent. Within this buoyant context, barriers to foreign trade were progressively lowered, and Italy joined the Common Market. Yet the balance of payments found equilibrium and by the late fifties even returned a surplus on trade account for the first peacetime year since 1932. In consequence of this, official holdings of gold and foreign exchange reached $3.4 billion by the end of 1961.

There is, however, a darker side to Italy's postwar experience—the still intractable problem of structural imbalance, or unification of the entire country as a modern industrial system. To be sure, all industrial societies reveal elements of geographic, economic, and technological dualism, and all of them suffer in varying degree from underdevelopment as well as maldistribution of labor supply. But probably none can compare with Italy in the intensity and persistence of such problems.

At bottom, structural disequilibrium within the Italian economy came with political unification in 1861, and the south and the islands were foredoomed to be the weaker partners in this new union. The backlash of industrial advance in the north further enfeebled these regions. Beyond this, until very recently a chronic shortage of national capital left little room for maneuver for generations, even if economic transformation of the south had been seriously contemplated, which it never was.

Under Mussolini, scarce capital was dissipated in wasteful autarchic programs and destroyed in war. By a series of restrictive laws enforcing fixed settlement upon the population, starting in 1926 and, surprisingly enough, not revoked until 1961, southern labor was dammed up on the land and in urban slums, and thereby denied all opportunity to better itself. As a result, these measures perpetuated the backwardness of the south, at the same time foreclosing to the whole nation the income-yielding benefits of an orderly but substantial redistribution of the population.

Postwar wage and price policies in the technically advanced sector of industry have also exerted a strong thrust toward maintaining the barriers of a divided economy. The unions in this field have pushed aggressively for ever higher real wages, sacrificing opportunities for increased employment in this highly paid sector, thus slowing the absorption of the unemployed, and confining most of the labor force to activities yielding much lower incomes. Industrial management in the advanced sector has also contributed to the dichotomy in the postwar Italian economy. Aided by product markets that commonly are either monopolistic or oligopolistic, it followed a policy of not cutting prices, although since 1948 gains in productivity per man-hour have consistently and strongly out-run those for hourly labor costs. Instead, the customary practice has been to retain the savings of increasing productivity within the sector itself, dividing them with its unionized workers while using much of its increased profits to finance further internal improvements. As a result, the weaker parts of the economy have not shared the gains through lower prices for capital goods, while some of them have even had to pay wage increases comparable to those awarded in the favored sector, although their offsetting gains in labor productivity have been much lower. This process, too, has accentuated structural imbalance within the country.

In addition, the continuous and expanding reinvestment of substantial retained earnings within the most progressive sector has led to ever greater geographic concentration of industry within the northern triangle. In turn, this has provoked a barrage of criticism of the apparent reluctance of dominant enterprises to invest in branch plants in the south, despite special incentives. Out of this debate have emerged some drastic proposals for direct state control over private investment, and schemes—now partly embodied in law—for increased investment in state-controlled industrial enterprises in the south.

Geographically, the focus of the structural problem lies in the south—starting with lower Lazio—and in the islands, although it also shows up in parts of central Italy (the Maremma region) and even in the north (Alto Adige and the Trentino).

As the traditional home of peasant agriculture, the latifundia system, handicraft industry, and petty trade, the south brought to unification a weak economy with very little thrust for development. What mainly kept it going was its extreme dependence upon subsistence agriculture—a self-sustaining system in which the market and money economy played little role at all. While it did have a small amount of industry and even some export trade, these activities were well-insulated by a protectionist policy. In joining the national union, the south exposed itself to competition from the north. Many of its nascent industries gradually died away, and there were no new ones to take their place. Despite the optimism of the Piedmontese, who had learned their Adam Smith and who awaited the benign effects of opening up what they supposed to be a vast internal market, the south simply failed to respond. For the next three generations, its difficulties steadily approached a desperate state.

Apart from sporadic studies and occasional efforts by the government to introduce local improvements, the malign proportions of the southern problem were not fully recognized until after the overthrow of fascism, when candid examination and discussion of a host of pressing national problems at last could be had. But in the early years of freedom, the vast resources required for effective action in the south were just not available. Indeed, at that time the most urgent national imperative was to make a badly crippled economy at least ambulatory once more, however halting its initial steps had to be.

By 1950, the twin objectives of monetary stabilization and basic reconstruction had been achieved, thanks to what Bruno Foa properly terms Einaudi's "financial masterpiece." Although continued growth and its underlying essential—rapid capital formation—remained as mandatory as before, now there was some room for maneuver, hence opportunity at last to give serious thought to economic development in the broad sense of introducing progress into the long-stagnant south.

The problem of the south lay almost entirely concealed by the highly encouraging aggregative statistics of national income and output. Moreover, in its direct requirements, the task itself largely exceeded the reach of a policy that put such stress upon monetary measures and private initiative, granting that these instruments could provide much mediatory support. The reason was simple. For generations, the south had been virtually a separate compartment of the Italian economy. To bring it into an effective and enduring economic union with the rest of the country demanded a thoroughgoing modernization of its obsolete economy, not to mention its entire cultural outlook. Because of its strategic prominence, the reorganization of agriculture had first priority: substantial direct investments, reduction of the man-land ratio, and alterations in the scale of farm enterprise. Closely allied to those measures were improvements of infrastructure—flood control and organized water supply; the building up of road and rail transport, and communications; provision of credit facilities; technical aid; reduction of illiteracy and greatly increased vocational training of the labor force.

Here, then, was not the American case of industrializing in open country, but the sharply contrasting one of effecting the complete transformation of an ancient way of life. This goal was to become a political commitment, shared in principle by all sections of the country. The real issues turned on questions of what specific lines of action to take, how rapidly and extensively to prosecute them, and by what primary means—the market economy or central planning and state enterprise.

The first massive effort in this direction began in 1950, when the Fund for the South (Cassa per il Mezzogiorno) was created by law, and granted $1.6 billion to be spent over the 1951–1960 period for "extraordinary works of public interest." [2] Of this sum, 89 per cent was assigned to infrastructure, with the rest as subsidies to private owners to effect land improvements. By 1959, when the cumulative appropriation had slightly more than doubled, substantial subsidies to private industry were now introduced (12 per cent of the total), as well as subventions to education and professional training.

At the outset of the *Cassa*, it was recognized on all sides that government intervention would be required on a broad scale, that financial costs would be large, and that the program would have to be pursued with great vigor over a lengthy period. Also, there was a general measure of agreement that the *Cassa* should proceed upon a schedule of priorities, emphasizing in order agriculture, transport and communications, aqueducts and sanitation, and tourism. Regarding land reform, subsidies to industrial enterprise, and the selection of local sites for the *Cassa's* undertakings, the consensus was much less strong. Also, as the program unfolded, heated controversies emerged over whether the *Cassa* in part was merely replacing "ordinary" government expenditures in the south, and over bureaucratic delays, lack of coordination among the several parallel government programs, and dissipation of efforts over too wide a geographic range.

In its original conception, the *Cassa* proceeded in a pragmatic and piecemeal fashion, rather than from a central plan. Viewed as a whole, the entire array of government efforts on behalf of the south have continued to take this form, although efforts have recently been made to achieve better coordination among programs. However, at the end of 1954, when the unemployment problem was still acute, an attempt was made to formulate a framework plan for a "scheduled" development of the national economy, within which the *Cassa* and other southern projects would be incorporated—the so-called "Vanoni Scheme" (Schema di sviluppo dell'occupazione e del reddito in Italia nel decennio 1955–1964). Named for Budget Minister Ezio Vanoni, who died early in 1956, this was a ten-year plan, based on certain econometric projections, to eliminate all un-employment above frictional minimum, to raise the savings rate to 25 per cent of gross product, and to achieve equilibrium in the balance of payments—all by the end of the period, and all resting upon a stable price level, annual increases of 5 per cent in real gross product, and some precise quantitative expectations regard-ing increases in population and labor force, consumption, tax yields, imports and exports.

Most relevant in the present connection, the scheme depended heavily upon an ingenious combination of public investment and private incentives. It never contemplated abandonment of the market economy, which its critics on the left were quick to point out. Nonetheless, one of its main ingredients was a program of pub-lic and private investment in the south, partly under the aegis of the *Cassa*, to raise per capita income there from 50 per cent of the north at the outset to at least 75 per cent by the end of the period (so-called "approximate parity").

The Vanoni Plan never became operative, although the sheer exuberance of the boom in exports and in capital goods during the fifties and early sixties thrust the economy well beyond the scheme's targets both in amounts and in timing, so far as saving and investment, consumption, exports and imports, and the foreign balance were concerned. By equal good fortune, between 1954 and 1961 real gross product rose by no less than 7.9 per cent per year, instead of the projected 5 per cent, while wholesale prices held steady and the implicit price deflator for gross product advanced by less than 1.8 per cent yearly. As of 1961 the income gap of the south had not yet begun to close. Since the close of the fifties, an impassioned debate has raged over policy toward the south. The issues are complex and can merely be cited at this point, and even then only superficially.

Probably the central questions concern the extent to which the south is an economically viable home for competitively efficient and therefore self-sustaining manufacturing industry; and whether the forces of the marketplace, suitably "guided," are the appropriate means for development, or should be supplanted by a system of direct central planning. Both questions pose the issues at the extremes, but the controversy itself has been joined in this admittedly oversimplified form.

Regarding the development of manufacturing, a typical question is whether the new steel complex at Taranto can survive without subsidy against rugged foreign competition. Viewed more broadly, should investment in southern industry be "forced" by the state all along the spectrum of manufacturing commodities? Should such forcing be undertaken, perhaps through a larger amount of state-controlled enterprise, even if the cost should require some sacrifice in the rate of increase in national income—a loss that hopefully might be recouped over the longer term? If manufacturing is to be introduced over a broad range of products and pushed vigorously without further delay, can it reasonably be expected that the parallel development of many lines of production will generate those reciprocal external economies (of which so much is made these days) that would make the new plants internationally competitive? Will they prove capable of absorbing the bulk of the surplus labor that must be transferred from agriculture as an integral part of the program to raise productivity and incomes on the land, or should more reliance be placed upon accelerating migration to the north—Luigi Einaudi's "natural solution" for the problem of structural disequilibrium?

And whatever the projected scope of manufacturing, are special incentives for private enterprise both economically sound and practically adequate—reduced duties on imports, special credits at low rates of interest, lower freight rates, tax concessions, and prescribed shares of government procurement orders? Or is there need of an over-all government plan for central control over all investment, by product line and by location throughout the country, presumably at whatever cost? Would it be wiser to adhere to the original schedule of priorities, concentrating still upon agriculture and related infrastructure, confining industrial development for some time to come to agricultural processing and light industry at carefully chosen sites; and only much later considering the introduction of broader types of industry?

These, then, are the main issues. Underlying them all is the fundamental question: will private initiative, supplemented but not supplanted by the state, be adequate to modernize this obsolete and ramshackle economic region, in time or at all? Or is a large dose of public enterprise, perhaps including central planning, in order?

Obviously, the central issue is only in lesser degree one of comparative efficacy of institutional means. Unquestionably, the root of the matter is ideological and therefore political. Clearly, the stakes are great, for it remains to be seen whether Italy's postwar experiment with mass political democracy will prove to be a lasting success. Certainly her ability to resolve the pressing problem of regional imbalance will provide a decisive test, for within the country today there exist the same severe income gap, the same growing impatience with the interminable sacrifices enforced by that gap, and the same revolution of rising expectations that together divide the rich lands from the poor ones throughout the world itself.

At the same time, the outcome of that test will also depend upon whether the country can maintain adequate and uninterrupted growth, free of much inflation and troubles with the foreign balance—a prospect that now stands in some doubt. The reason is that inflation broke out late in 1961, gaining speed in the two years following, and bringing with it an adverse balance of payments and a sharp deterioration of the country's net short-term foreign position. Behind these troubles, which mark the terminus of the long boom, lay excesses in policies affecting money supply, government spending, and wages. As of late 1964, depletion of the exchange reserve has been checked, and the pace of the inflation slowed down. However, wages have not been brought under control, and stabilization policy remains halting and uncertain. At bottom the basic difficulty is Italy's now perennial dependence upon weak coalition governments, which on the one hand reflects lack of national consensus, and on the other leads to enfeebled economic policies.

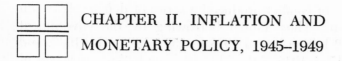 CHAPTER II. INFLATION AND
MONETARY POLICY, 1945–1949

The years immediately following the war were indeed difficult for Italy. Output had fallen 50 per cent by 1945. There was a critical shortage of foodstuffs. Equipment and inventories in industry were badly run down. Fiscal affairs were in hopeless disorder. Deficits were enormous and were largely covered by printing notes. The banks were far too liquid, while the central bank lacked effective control over the volume of credit.

Two problems had top priority after liberation in April 1945. Until they could be resolved, all talk about long-run programs was idle speculation. The first was to bring about an early recovery of agricultural and industrial production. The second was no less critical but proved far more difficult: to put the lira on a stable footing. By 1947, much had already been accomplished in production. However, the rapid depreciation of the lira continued until drastic measures initiated between May and October of that year finally took effect. They proved to be lasting. Undoubtedly they laid the basis for the long boom that began soon after their introduction. This chapter reconstructs this bit of monetary history.

THE INFLATIONARY PROCESS

The wartime inflation and its legacy. Between 1938 and 1945, Italy underwent a very severe price inflation. Underlying it were enormous increases in deficit spending and in note issue, and a disastrous decline in real output. After liberation, there was a brief period of adjustment in which the price level rose somewhat. Mainly this movement was in response to the reuniting of the northern and southern regions, whose price and wage levels had diverged sharply with the preceding division of the country under German and Allied military control. Between the end of 1945 and June 1946, price stability prevailed, although inflationary storm clouds were already gathering. In part these were a delayed impact of the war itself.[1]

First, the costs of conflict produced a series of deficits that soon became enormous. Thus annual borrowing by the government soared from 11.2 billion lire in 1938 to 152.3 billion by 1943, and 572 billion by 1944–1945. After the war's end, three quarters of these credits were in floating debt, and three quarters were supplied by the banking system.

The inevitable consequence was an astronomical rise in the liquidity of the public and of the banking system. The propulsive mechanism lay in the dependence of the treasury upon the *Banca d'Italia,* the central bank, for most of its funds. These the Bank supplied by advances on treasury account and by purchase of short-dated treasury bills. Together these volatile forms of credit stood at 10.6 billion lire in 1938. By June 1945, they had jumped to 470.1 billion. As the government drew on these credits, the Bank's note issue also soared. At the same time, this explosive type of deficit financing drove up the reserves of the other banks at the Bank of Italy from less than one-half billion in 1938 to 120.1 billion by June 1945.[2]

Since there was no effective system of required reserves at the time, this rise in the banks' liquid resources enormously expanded their lending potential, although exercise of this leverage upon money supply was largely delayed until 1946. Another interesting point is that the increase in the reserve base during the war did not come from enlarged credits from the Bank of Italy to the rest of the banking system. It was the indirect result of the huge advance in government expenditure, which bloated the public's holdings of notes and government checks. Both of these flowed back in part to the banks to become deposit credits and in turn were partly re-deposited by the banks with the Bank of Italy to become increased reserves.

Between 1938 and 1945, note circulation rose 18 times, while demand deposits increased 9.6 times. By 1945, notes accounted for 71.6 per cent of money supply (currency plus demand deposits), as against 57.2 per cent in 1938. After liberation, this huge stock of currency supplied much of the fuel to stoke the fires of the early postwar inflation. A catastrophic fall of production provided the rest.

By 1945, real gross domestic product was exactly half that of 1938. By contrast the total stock of money had swelled fifteenfold.

Interestingly enough, the price level had advanced by just over fifteen times in the same period (measured by the implicit GNP price deflator in prices of 1938). Since the increase in the money supply was slightly less than twice the rise in GNP at current prices, money velocity had fallen sharply. In short, the public was hoarding currency, and there was no flight from the lira at that time. Furthermore, the liquidity of the public, as well as that of the banks, had reached dangerous levels by the time of liberation. Table 1 presents the relevant figures.

TABLE 1. Movements in production, prices, and money supply, 1938–1945 [a]

Year	Current GNP	Real GNP	Implicit price index	Money supply [b]	Money supply to current GNP (per cent)
1938	100.0	100.0	100.0	100.0	28.5
1943	245.4	84.2	291.4	601.2	69.9
1944	448.7	62.4	719.2	1111.5	70.7
1945	820.8	50.1	1637.9	1443.5	50.2

[a] GNP refers to domestic product. Prices are for 1938.

[b] Includes government coins and notes, Bank of Italy notes, AMG lire, circular checks (assegni circolari and vaglia cambiari); checking accounts (conti correnti di corrispondenza con clienti), a small part of which are time deposits; and conti correnti in the postal savings system. Excludes all savings deposits (depositi fiduciari). Figures are on a year-end basis.

Source: GNP and price index computed from data in Istituto centrale di statistica, Indagine statistica sullo sviluppo del reddito nazionale dell'Italia dal 1861 al 1956, series VIII, vol. 9 of Annali di statistica (Rome: ISTAT, 1957); money supply from Banca d'Italia, Adunanza generale ordinaria dei partecipanti, 1949 (Rome: Tipografia Banca d'Italia, 1950).

Since price control was completely ineffective after 1940 except for rents and utility rates (although a price freeze was attempted at that time), the process was the classical one of open inflation deriving from excess creation of paper currency. Its ultimate sources were two. Soaring government demand for real resources, based upon deficit financing through the central bank, greatly bloated the money supply. Against this rapidly enlarging money demand, the supply of real output began falling, ultimately reaching disastrous levels. Clearly, demand-pull was at work with a vengeance. Furthermore, there was no feasible way for the government to extricate itself from the coils of the process. It could not eliminate its deficits, nor its extreme dependence upon central-bank financing, and it could not check the deterioration of production as the war went on.

Renewed inflation, 1946–1947. Between January and August 1946, the sole monthly index available for the national price level —for the cost of living—fluctuated around 27 times that of prewar, without upward movement or great variation. The index for foods alone actually fell, touching 29 times the prewar level by August. As of June 1946, the index of wholesale prices (resumed in May) stood at 25.9 times the 1938 level. Thereafter it began to shoot up. At the peak of the new inflation, September 1947, wholesale prices were 62 times that of prewar, rising an average 9.4 per cent a month from July 1946, when the inflation started. Within the same period, the indexes for foods and for the general cost of living went up 9.2 and 7.7 per cent monthly.[3] Since wages were tied to these indexes, they also rose, exerting a feed-back effect upon costs and prices.

By spring 1946, the external value of the lira also began to slide. At the outset of the year, the official rate was still pegged at the 1945 level of 100 to the dollar (19.0 in 1938). On January 18, the government authorized importers to offer 225 on certain goods. By May, the average daily free rate stood at 364.28, rising to 599.5 by October. At the end of 1946, the official rate was raised to 225. In March 1947, the free rate climbed to 605, soaring to 906 by May. In August the official rate was raised again, to 350. However, after the May peak the free rate began a steady decline, averaging 667 in September, when inflation reached its turning point.[4]

As in wartime, renewed inflation during July 1946–September 1947, was of the open type. However, there were some important differences. Deficit financing with the central bank was no longer the primary factor in building up the money supply. This time private demands for credit were very strong. Through loans and advances the banks rapidly expanded deposit credit, which now ran well ahead of note issue in rate of increase, reflecting the extreme liquidity bequeathed by war finance to the commercial banks. Also, production over the period was now increasing, although there was a bad harvest in spring 1947, and over-all output was still seriously below the prewar level.

Table 2 summarizes the ways in which net credit extensions by the Bank of Italy and the rest of the banks flowed into the government and private sectors, building up both note issue and checking deposits.

TABLE 2. Net extensions of credit by Bank of Italy and other banks to domestic economy, July 1946– September 1947 [a] (in billions of lire)

Debtors	Creditors		
	Bank of Italy	Other banks	All banks
All banks [b]	36.6	−36.6	
			0.0
Public sector [c]	109.6	49.4	
			159.0
Private sector [d]	11.0	420.1	
			431.1
Total	157.2	432.9	
			590.1

[a] Excludes foreign sector for lack of data.

[b] For Bank of Italy as creditor, includes loans and advances to other banks (36.6 billion), which are an off-setting debit for them. Excludes 4.0 billion required bank reserves at Bank, which were assumed not to change; and drawings of banks (67.3 billion) against free reserves, which were considered a switch of assets to cash.

[c] For Bank of Italy as creditor, includes 66.5 billion discount of wheat bills to credit of government, and 43.1 billion loans and advances to government. For government as debtor, excludes 48.6 billion drawings against deposits at Bank, treated as a switch to cash. For other banks as creditors, includes purchase of 7.9 billion in government bills for required reserves, plus 41.5 billion portfolio investment in government securities.

[d] For Bank of Italy as creditor, represents loans and advances. For other banks as creditors, represents 420.1 billion in loans and advances. This sector includes local government.

Source: Adapted from data presented in Paolo Baffi, "Monetary Developments in Italy from the War Economy to Limited Convertibility (1938–1958)," Banca Nazionale del Lavoro, Quarterly Review, no. 47 (December 1958), pp. 440–441.

Table 2 well reflects the altered sources of the new inflation. True, the Bank of Italy pumped in 109.6 billion in new credit through the treasury, as in the war years. However, the bulk of this sum represented compulsory discounts of wheat bills, emerging under a price support program. Although the government continued to run a substantial cash deficit, this was covered mainly by drawing cash against existing deposits at the Bank and by new borrowing from the other banks (both a potential source of new reserves), plus direct sale of new issues to the public. More important for the whole monetary setting, nearly three quarters of estimated total net extensions of new credit by the banking system took the form of investments and advances by the subordinate banks for private sector account. This, then, was the principal mechanism for creating new money. In turn, it rested upon the earlier huge increase in free reserves and reflected soaring demands for private credit as investment, production and imports began to recover, and as speculation in inventories and on the stock market became feverish with the rapid rise in prices.

To underscore the explosive nature of bank credit expansion in this period, consider the reserve position of the commericial banks.[5] At the end of December 1946—the earliest date for which figures were available for this study—their total primary reserves (deposits with the Bank of Italy and the treasury) stood at 145.8 billion (25.7 per cent of customers' deposits). Of these, 105.7 billion was available on demand (*liberi*). As for the over-all total, only 2.2 billion was tied up in required reserves (0.39 per cent of deposits), leaving 143.6 billion as free reserves against potential new deposits.[6] The only operative check against the expansion of private loans and deposits was the old rule that a bank must keep a certain proportion of cash to deposits. As deposits expanded, a currency drain began, and this compelled the banks to draw down their primary reserves, which fell to 115.4 billion by September 1947.[7] However, they still afforded ample margin for further inflation of deposits, without official intervention to halt it.

The inevitable reflex of rapid credit expansion was a speedy rise of demand deposits and currency in circulation—in other words, the money supply. Table 3 presents the essential data. In considering these figures, it should be borne in mind that increases in the public's holdings of currency can derive from two sources: deficit

TABLE 3. Movements in components of money supply during the inflation and after monetary stabilization, 1946–1948 (in billions of lire, month-end)

Year and month	Currency [a]				Demand deposits [b]			Money supply	Quarterly rates of increase		
	Bank of Italy notes	Circular checks	Less vault cash	Total in hand	Banks	Postal deposits	Total		Currency	Demand deposits	Primary money supply
1946: June	394.7	71.9	−26.0	440.6	219.9	18.7	238.6	679.2			
September	432.0	77.5	−28.5	481.0	296.8	21.7	318.5	799.5	40.4	79.9	120.3
December	505.0	99.8	−48.8	556.1	353.2	25.3	378.5	934.6	75.1	60.0	135.1
1947: March	524.0	88.3	−44.0	568.3	365.6	24.0	389.6	957.9	12.2	11.1	23.3
June	577.6	100.1	−53.0	624.7	440.1	30.9	471.0	1095.7	56.4	81.4	137.8
September	667.7	104.3	−64.5	707.5	471.1	34.5	505.6	1213.1	82.8	34.6	117.4
December	788.1	111.5	−72.6	827.0	485.4	33.0	518.4	1345.4	119.5	12.8	132.3
1948: March	797.9	107.0	−62.2	842.7	527.7	38.9	566.6	1409.3	15.7	48.2	63.9
June	816.0	105.8	−65.3	856.5	609.8	41.8	651.6	1508.1	13.8	85.0	98.8
September	862.5	115.3	−61.5	916.3	664.6	43.1	707.7	1624.0	59.8	56.1	115.9
December	963.0	128.7	−80.9	1010.8	714.8	51.0	765.8	1776.6	94.5	58.1	152.6

[a] Bank of Italy issue includes *biglietti, titoli provvisori,* and AMG notes. Circular checks include *assegni circolari* and *vaglia cambiari;* values interpolated between adjacent months for certain months. Vault cash refers to banks only; for 1947 and after, vault cash of Bank of Italy is excluded in its figures. For June 1946, vault cash of banks estimated by interpolation from published figures for December 1945 and September 1946. State coins and notes excluded from currency totals. For 1946–1949 they were negligible, ranging between 6.9 and 7.9 billion.

[b] For banks, refers to *conti correnti di corrispondenza con clienti,* which are predominantly demand deposits (*liberi*), but also involve a small amount of time deposits (*vincolati*). For postal deposits, refers to checking accounts only (*conti correnti*). Savings deposits excluded from these series as a form of secondary liquidity.

Source: Bank of Italy notes, circular checks, vault cash except as noted below, demand deposits of banks, and postal deposits after 1947 from Banca d'Italia, *Adunanza generale* (annual), for 1946–1948. Vault cash for September 1946 through September 1947, and postal deposits for 1946–1947 from Istituto Centrale di Statistica, *Bolletino mensile di statistica,* 1947–1949. For comparable dates the *Bolletino* series conform to those of the Bank.

financing by the treasury at the central bank, and drawings by the other banks against their reserve deposits at the Bank to cover their depositors' cash withdrawals. During the inflation, both processes were at work. Thus, referring back to Table 2 on net credit extensions during the period, the treasury borrowed 109.6 billion from the Bank of Italy, and 49.4 billion on short-term notes from the other banks. In addition, the latter advanced 420.1 billion to the private sector. By contrast, customers' deposits at the other banks rose only 267 billion. The explanation for the gap is that these deposits were leaking into note issue—a typical instance of the familiar cash drain during credit and price inflation.

Turning back to Table 3, we see that the big injections in money supply came in the third quarter of 1946 and in the second and third quarters of 1947. Granted, a huge increase occurred in the last quarter of 1946 as well, but this reflects a strong year-end seasonal bulge. Thus the average for this and the following quarter was only 79.2 billion, while in the others the range of advance was between 117.4 and 137.8 billion.

Of far greater significance, the net increase in demand deposits over the fifteen-month period came to 267 billion, which compares with 266.9 billion for note circulation outside of the banks. At the start, note issue constituted 64.9 per cent of money supply. By the end, it had fallen to 58.3 per cent. In small part this change reflects a secular shift toward deposit currency, which has gone much further since. In the main, it underscores the predominating role of credit inflation.

The figures for demand deposits are also highly revealing in another way. Again recalling the year-end seasonal distortion, if we strike an average for this and the following quarter, the quarterly advance was only 35.5 billion. Clearly, the most massive credit injections occurred in the third quarter of 1946 and the second one in 1947, with increases in deposits of 79.9 and 81.4 billion each. With the third quarter of 1947, the rate of advance dropped to only 34.6 billion. Table 4 clearly reveals this slowing down of deposit expansion. In the second quarter of 1947, the monthly rate of increase was running strongly ahead of the comparable period in 1946. However, in the third quarter of 1947, the monthly rate of gain fell far below July–September 1946.

After June 1947 there was a gradual tightening of credit at the

TABLE 4. Monthly changes in demand deposits and Bank of Italy notes, second and third quarters, 1946 and 1947 (in billions of lire, month-end)

Month	Demand deposits		Bank of Italy notes	
	1946	1947	1946	1947
April	+10.5	+21.9	+1.0	+17.4
May	+11.9	+35.1	+2.4	+16.4
June	+13.0	+17.5	+9.1	+19.8
July	+28.7	+18.5	+12.8	+34.9
August	+19.5	+3.1	+10.2	+27.0
September	+28.7	+9.4	+14.3	+28.2

Source: See notes to Table 3. Monthly data for circular checks not available. Vault cash of banks not deducted because of lack of monthly data.

banks, coupled with an accelerating shift from demand deposits to cash. There was no slackening in the demand for credit, because the flames of speculative inflation continued to rage right through to the end of September. By contrast, during the September quarter, loans and investments of the banks rose somewhat less rapidly, advancing by 90.4 billion as against 119.8 billion in the preceding quarter.[8]

It might be supposed that the banks were compelled to tighten up on credit because they were losing liquidity, given the unchecked flow of withdrawal of notes and a steady decline in their free reserves. The potentially debilitating cash drain stands out clearly: it was far more rapid in the two big quarters of 1947 than in their counterpart for 1946, and it grew much worse during July–September 1947. This was the main reason for the slowing down in the rate of deposit expansion at the same time.

It is also true that the banks' free reserves were steadily falling. In December 1946, they stood at 143.6 billion. By June 1947, they had dropped to 121.2 billion, and by the end of September they had contracted to 111.4 billion—reflecting the swelling cash drain. However, even at this date free reserves were still adequate to sustain a substantial expansion of loans and investments.

It follows, therefore, that the increasing credit stringency that emerged with the third quarter of 1947 did not result from voluntary action on the part of the banks. It came from quiet but steadily intensifying official pressure toward this end.[9]

The new monetary policy. During 1946–1947, Governor Einaudi was well aware of the credit inflation problem, but the Bank was unable to cope with it. In essence, the country had no effective system of required bank reserves. At this time, the Bank began to study reserve systems abroad and to determine the effects of various methods of fixing reserve requirements. Its guiding principles were that (1) the system adopted should start from the level of investments and deposits prevailing when it took effect, to avoid a credit deflation; (2) since liquidity varied among banks, provisions would be needed for the less liquid ones; and, (3) the authorities must have control of a mechanism for making the total volume of credit flexible.[10] However, the time for practical action was still not ripe.

Given the powers at hand, one gesture could be made. On January 29, 1947, Governor Einaudi formally notified the banks that thereafter they would be required to observe the "patrimonial" reserve requirements imposed by the law of 1926. Under that statute, loans and advances in excess of a certain multiple of the bank's net worth (*patrimonio*) were to be covered 100 per cent by government securities for deposit as an offsetting reserve—a device to check credit formation. After the war, the multiple was set at thirty. However, the rule had become a dead letter because loans and deposits had been allowed to get so far out of hand relative to net worth that strict enforcement would require an enormous deflation of credit—clearly in conflict with the principles of stabilization then under contemplation at the Bank. As the *Adunanza generale* suggests, Einaudi's real purpose was to try to get the banks to slow down on credit formation, using this rule as the only weapon then available. Both as a means of building up required reserves and of checking credit expansion, Einaudi's effort failed. In December 1946, effective required reserves were only 2.2 billion lire. By the following June they stood at 2.3 billion. In the meantime, the banks' investments jumped 198.3 billion lire. Clearly, more drastic powers were required to halt the inflation, but they would depend on the emergence of more resolute political leadership.

On May 30, 1947, Premier Alcide De Gasperi succeeded in reconstructing his cabinet, obtaining a much stronger ministry, and quite deliberately the first without Communist participation. De Gasperi was undoubtedly one of Italy's most distinguished premiers since Count Cavour—a man of the utmost principle and rectitude, tolerant in outlook, but strong and wholly dedicated to the rebuilding of his country according to the tenets of liberty and democracy.

The new cabinet represented a political shift fraught with great significance for monetary policy, since it made possible for the first time an effective attack upon inflation. Before then, while the Communists had collaborated nominally in forming the several preceding postwar cabinets—initially at the urging of the Allied occupation authorities—their real policy was one of disruption, within the government, in parliament, in union-employer relations, and by demagogic appeals for still more spending for the relief of the unemployed. Their purpose was clear: to bring the Italian economy to ruin under the new parliamentary regime, and so to prepare the way for a revolutionary crisis and seizure of power. For this objective, rampant inflation was a useful tool.

Nonetheless, the turn to monetary and fiscal responsibility can be dated from this time. It was no better emphasized than by the inclusion of Luigi Einaudi as deputy premier and budget minister —a distinguished liberal economist and expert in public finance in the Italian classical tradition, to whom sound money was the decisive ingredient of the free society to which he was intellectually and spiritually committed, and for which he had endured exile during the latter years of the Mussolini dictatorship. Einaudi was the principal architect of the new monetary design. In its technical execution, he was powerfully aided by a much stronger cabinet and by the very competent professional support of his successor as governor of the Bank of Italy, Donato Menichella.[11] Moments of crisis sometimes produce strong men. It was Italy's singular good fortune to have at hand leaders of the stamp of De Gasperi, Einaudi, and Menichella to take the helm, guided as they were by an almost puritanical devotion to principle, especially in matters of money and public finance; and possessed as they were of the intellect and strength of character to see what had to be done and then to do it.

The new government's first move was to reactivate the long-extinct Inter-Ministerial Committee on Credit and Saving (Comitato interministeriale per il credito ed il risparmio), which had been authorized in cabinet, on April 23. Considerable time had to elapse before the proposal could be passed through the temporary constitutional commission, and it did not become law until July 17, 1947,[12] to take effect on the day after its publication in the *Official Gazette*—Saturday, August 2. On the following Monday, the committee began its first session, under the leadership of Deputy Premier Einaudi.

The new measure gave the committee the formidable task of designing a workable system of credit control for defense of the people's savings—in short, it had to find a way to stop the inflation. Equally important, the statute put the technical resources of the government at the committee's disposal, and made the Bank of Italy the latter's executive instrument, with its governor to be present at all meetings. Once a policy for credit control had been formulated, the Bank would become its official custodian, and as such a central bank in the fullest sense of the term.

At its first meeting the committee began secret discussions regarding the problem of obligatory commercial bank reserves. By August 20, it was ready to call in the representatives of the banks, to lay out and explore the alternatives with them. The main choice lay between some version of the old principle of patrimonial reserves and one requiring a percentage relationship between tied reserves and deposits. After two days of deliberation in which the banks' own views could be considered, the committee adopted the percentage-of-deposits principle, formally communicating it to the banks on August 22. Under it, the bulk of the banks' free reserves would be frozen at the end of September; efforts would be made to prevent a contraction of credit; and the less liquid institutions would have over five weeks to get ready to meet the requirements. Beyond this, all banks were put on notice that credit restraint was finally on the way. Now an effective defense of the lira could be undertaken at last.

At this point, before considering the full scope and details of the new monetary policy, it is well to review for a moment the main options theoretically open to the new government as it began to address itself to the inflation question.

First, it might have striven to create a very large cash surplus in its budget, slashing expenditures and raising taxes drastically. This approach would have imposed new and politically intolerable hardships and would have required too much time. Also, it would have necessitated a tightening of private credit. Second, an attempt might have been made to suppress the inflation with a full panoply of direct controls, these also to be aided by a tightening of private credit and by much less reliance on the Bank of Italy for deficit financing. However, direct controls had already failed early in the war. Neither the requisite administrative machinery nor the necessary supporting public psychology was at hand, while the whole approach was thoroughly repugnant to the economic philosophy of the new cabinet. All this was indeed the country's supreme good fortune as matters turned out, for imposition of a tangle of price controls might well have frustrated the onset of the subsequent boom.

Third, the government might have decided simply to allow open inflation to go on longer, permitting the lira to continue in its fearful depreciation, while awaiting arrival of the strategic moment to put through a drastic program of currency reform and credit control. The basic trouble with that was that it would have risked the very survival of democracy itself. More than this, the government realized that the decisive opportunity was already near at hand. Reserves of gold and foreign exchange were close to exhaustion, and foreign credits were unobtainable. Yet the country had to maintain its imports to provide foodstuffs, together with the raw materials and capital goods essential to recovery and reconstruction.

Finally, an all-out fight to save the lira might have been undertaken, striking directly at the forces that were accomplishing its destruction, using weapons offering the best chance of prompt success. This was the option actually decided upon.

In designing the counterattack, Einaudi recognized that the source of the inflation was twofold: excessive creation of private credit by the lending banks, and excessive dependence of the treasury upon the central bank for the financing of its unavoidable deficits. Both were swelling the money supply, building up total demand far faster than the rate of increase in the supply of physical output. Because of this imbalance, by the third quarter of September 1947, wholesale prices of raw materials were soaring skyward by 6.9 per cent a month; over-all this index was going up 5.5 per cent per month, while the cost of living was following close behind. And as E. S. Simpson pointed out in a perceptive analysis at the time, all this was going on despite a massive burden of unemployment (1.87 million in September)—a fact of some interest in view of later attacks upon Einaudi's policy of sound money as the supposed cause of this human tragedy.[13]

Proceeding from Einaudi's diagnosis of the root causes of the continuing depreciation of the lira, the government unfolded a comprehensive program for breaking the inflation, beginning with the reserve regulations announced to the banks on August 22, to take effect at the end of September. Other measures, summarized below, were adopted in the months following.

(1) The Bank of Italy became the executive arm of the Inter-Ministerial Committee for Credit and Saving. In addition to new powers for enforcing reserve requirements, the Bank was to advise the committee on approval of proposed private capital issues, and to pass on private advances by the banks if in excess of certain ceilings. Also, the Bank retained its traditional authority over the banks in matters involving rediscounts, advances, and overdraft rights. Regarding these, it warned the banks in August not to expect these privileges automatically to be honored when the new reserve requirements took effect. Control was also given the Bank over the financing of acquisitions of foreign exchange by the official Foreign Exchange Office (Ufficio italiano dei cambi), enabling the Bank to influence the amount of foreign exchange available to the lending banks.

(2) Effective October 1, 1947, the rediscount rate was raised from 4.0 to 5.5 per cent. This move was of rather limited importance because of the comparatively small amount of rediscounting except for the wheat bills. Nonetheless, it bolstered the committee's effort to cut down on the banks' free reserves.

(3) Effective September 30, 1947, a required reserve had to be provided by the commercial banks against their total deposits of that date. This was fixed at 20 per cent of deposits *in excess of* ten times the net worth of the bank. However, this tied reserve was not to exceed 15 per cent of *total* deposits outstanding on the control date. Further, the reserve required could be provided either by deposit of cash with the Bank or the treasury, or by deposit of government or government-guaranteed securities either in a special tied account at the Bank or in an interest-bearing tied reserve at the treasury. Such securities could be bought for the purpose or transferred from the bank's portfolio. Whatever its form, imposition of

the reserve sharply reduced the liquidity of the banks. Another effect was to shift deficit-financing toward the banks, and away from the central bank.

(4) Effective October 1, 1947, the commercial banks were required to provide even higher margins of reserve against further increases in their total deposits above the level at the close of business on September 30. This requirement was set at 40 per cent of *additional* deposits, to hold until the *total* required reserve reached 25 per cent of *all* deposits, net of interbank and foreign exchange accounts. As noted above, the bank could cover the total required reserve by deposit of cash or of government paper, with the Bank or the treasury. Since the banks already held substantial free reserves, the effect of the requirements cited in (3) and (4) was to freeze these, and for certain banks whose coverage was now inadequate, to force them to contract credit. In whole, therefore, the new reserve policy greatly decreased the liquidity of the commercial banks.[14]

(5) Decree laws of December 1947 and May 1948, backed up by Ariticle 81 of the new constitution, restricted recourse of the treasury to financing by the central bank. The treasury was forbidden to seek such advances unless authorized by statute to do so for specific sums. It retained overdraft rights at the Bank, but these were limited to 15 per cent of current expenditures. Under Article 81, any law entailing new or increased expenditure now had to set out the means by which this spending was to be covered; the omnibus finance bill no longer could impose new taxes nor provide for new spending.[15]

(6) In the months after October 1, a serious effort was made to reduce government spending. This was to prove impossible, but the rise in expenditure was slowed down. Furthermore, aided by the devices cited in (5), the weight of public spending was shifted away from the Bank of Italy, to the banks; and to some extent to the capital market, where it could be financed by voluntary saving —to hold down the creation of free reserves.

(7) Efforts were started looking eventually toward strengthening the balance of payments, liberalizing foreign trade, and making the lira freely convertible. For these purposes, the government desired a more uniform system of exchange rates for the lira— ultimately to wipe out the hodgepodge of multiple official rates,

legal and illegal free rates, and cross rates, which had grown up in
the initial postwar period, disrupting trade patterns and cost-price
relations.[16] It also wanted to end the overvaluation of the lira,
made much worse by the inflation, and which had been largely responsible for emergence of an elaborate system of foreign exchange and trade controls. On August 2, the official dollar rate was
raised from 225 to 350. Licensed imports were broadened August
12. Despite continued inflation until the end of September, the
inflow of foreign exchange promptly increased. On November 28,
the official rate for dollars and Swiss francs became a floating rate,
fixed monthly by averaging the free rates prevailing during each
month preceding. This reduced effective import costs, by eliminat-
ing the former gap between the official and free rates, which had
raised the costs of foreign exchange for nongovernment imports.
The effect was to reduce prices for imported raw materials from
the free currency countries, and this benefited prices of manufactured exports, also helping the balance of payments.

THE IMPACTS OF MONETARY STABILIZATION

Immediate effects. Before stabilization, the control over the
money supply exercised by the Bank of Italy was slight. True, it
had the conventional full discretion over loans and advances to the
banks, and, excepting the wheat bills, over rediscounts. But it had
no control over the banks' free reserves, nor over treasury borrowing. These liquid resources permitted multiple expansion of loans
and deposits, while deficit financing swelled note issue, and these
notes in turn flowed back into the banks' free reserves. Under the
new policy, the Bank was no longer crippled in its management of
the money supply, granting, as one always must in these matters,
that the success of the new rules of the game still depended in
great part upon the intentions of the players. Fortunately, for
Italy, their purposes were plainly honorable.

The immediate effect of the new reserve requirements was to
freeze some 110 billion of free reserves, cutting the latter to only
3.2 billion. As Table 5 reveals, at the end of September 1947, 14.7
per cent of the commercial banks' total deposits were now manda-
torily covered. Over the next eighteen months this ratio was steadily built up to over 24 per cent, closely approaching the 25 per cent

TABLE 5. Changes in reserves and deposits of commercial banks, before and after monetary stabilization, September 30, 1947 [a] (in billions of lire, month-end)

Year and month	Primary reserves			Total deposits [b]	Reserve ratios to deposits [c]		
	Total	Required	Free		Total	Required	Free
1946: December	145.8	2.2	143.6	567.9	25.7	0.4	25.3
1947: June	123.5	2.3	121.2	712.5	17.3	0.3	17.0
September	115.4	112.2	3.2	763.3	15.1	14.7	0.4
December	177.6	133.6	44.0	810.6	21.9	16.5	5.4
1948: March	211.7	170.2	41.5	896.6	23.6	19.0	4.6
June	276.5	208.4	68.1	1005.9	27.5	20.7	6.8
September	316.9	247.2	69.7	1108.7	28.6	22.3	6.3
December	299.7	279.6	20.1	1195.6	25.1	23.4	1.7
1949: March	337.5	308.2	29.3	1247.9	26.5	24.2	2.3
June	349.8	314.9	34.9	1320.6	26.5	23.8	2.7
September	366.9	341.6	25.3	1414.8	25.9	24.1	1.8
December	403.9	372.9	31.0	1532.8	26.3	24.3	2.0

[a] Prior to September 1947, "required" reserves refer to amounts deposited in tied accounts under limited observance of patrimonial rule—on this basis, the September figure would be 4.0 billion. For December 1946, figure for total reserves includes deposits of all banks at Bank of Italy; commercial banks not available separately.

[b] Includes savings accounts at commercial banks only. These deposits also are subject to reserve requirements, which were imposed only upon the commercial banks.

[c] Italian practice is to emphasize liquidity ratios, rather than free reserve ratios as here, including in liquidity vault cash and portfolio assets in government securities.

Source: Banca d'Italia, *Adunanza generale,* 1947–1949.

target fixed by the new policy. By the end of that time, deposits were fixed in a 4 : 1 relation to the required reserve base. Although the system was extended to the savings banks in 1958, the ratio remained fixed from early 1949 until January 1962.

It will also be noted from Table 5 that over the final quarter of 1947—the first one under credit control—the reserve base was permitted to rise by 62.2 billion lire (53.9 per cent), and, through this, free reserves could advance 40.8 billion. This was accomplished by some continued deficit financing at the Bank, by further advances to the banks, and by some return of notes that had been added to currency circulation.

What was being undertaken here was a conjoined effort to slow down the rate of expansion in bank loans and demand deposits without forcing a credit contraction and liquidation, without checking the recovery of production from its 1945 low, but also without allowing further inflation of the price level. There is no more difficult task for the art of monetary management, which always has the added handicap of being conducted within a much larger field of forces lying outside its direct influence.[17] Nonetheless, the task was accomplished with brilliant success.

One measure of this achievement is that prices fell sharply. The wholesale index began dropping at once, finally touching bottom in July 1948 17.1 per cent below its September 1947 high. The cost of living started down more slowly, reaching its trough also the following July, 13.7 per cent under its September peak. Behind the drop in prices was a decisive shift in sellers' expectations, brought on by a sharp tightening of credit in early October and the realization that the government was firm about its intentions. Once prices started to fall; they invoked a disgorging of inventories, which gathered force as the decline continued. Liquidation was helped along by many firms' need for added working capital to finance a 7.2 per cent general wage increase in October. Prices were also driven down by increased food imports—induced by capital repatriation under the franco-valuta program—and by sale on the home market of some goods intended for export, owing to a temporary sag in foreign sales occasioned by the improving external value of the lira.

As could be expected from credit restraint, interest rates advanced, and the stock market continued its decline from its April peak. Rates on commercial paper rose from 6–7 per cent to 7.5–8 per cent. By the end of the year, yields on prime industrial bonds ranged between 8 and 9 per cent, against 8–8.25 earlier. Five per cent governments, which had been yielding between 3 and 4 per cent, rose to 5.5 by November.[18]

Despite these familiar symptoms of deflation, private short-term credit, demand deposits, and note issue all continued to advance during the final quarter of 1947, although their pace was slower. Because of a change in the method of estimating the foreign investments of the banks, the true increase in their loans and advances to the domestic private sector cannot be established, although there is no doubt that some expansion occurred, probably at a reduced rate. Indeed, throughout 1948 and 1949, these investments continued to expand, meaning that in the aggregate there never was an actual credit contraction, although some speculative borrowers undoubtedly were squeezed.

Since the data for the components of money supply are available on a monthly basis, they afford more insight into the nature and effects of the new stabilization policy. Note issue plus circular checks increased sharply in each of the last three months of 1947. Net of vault cash, currency in circulation expanded 6.6 per cent a month, which compares with 4.4 per cent monthly in the preceding quarter. However, demand deposits show a quite different pattern, revealing the main thrust of credit control. In October they advanced only 0.28 per cent over September, while in November they actually fell 1.3 per cent, rising again in December by 4.1 per cent. Over the quarter, their average monthly increase was but 0.84 per cent. In sharp contrast, between June 1946 and September 1947, their average monthly gain was 7.6 per cent. Clearly, the inflationary expansion of deposit credit had been checked, and checked decisively, but not with an accompanying restraint of the entire money supply. In fact, despite credit restraint the money supply rose 12.7 per cent in the final 1947 quarter. Of this increase, 91.7 per cent was in currency in circulation. Nevertheless, prices fell over the first ten months of stabilization.

Credit restraint had broken the back of inventory speculation. As the decline in prices gathered speed, the public began building up its cash balances. In consequence, while the money supply continued to expand, money velocity declined. Accordingly, the price level could fall. Decisive to the success of stabilization policy was the reversal of expectations which its bold announcement and firm prosecution had brought about.

To illustrate the effect on cash balances, in 1938 currency plus demand deposits were 28.5 per cent of GNP at current prices. In 1947, this proportion was 24.1 per cent, or slightly under half the level in 1945. After stabilization, it rose to 26.7 per cent in 1948. Since the price level showed a moderate rise in the latter part of the year, the wholesale index for the year as a whole was 5.5 per cent above 1947. However, the bulk of the increase in money supply was absorbed through increased output and larger cash balances.

The success of stabilization was not attributable primarily to the mere mechanics of putting the brakes on private credit formation. This was but an overt aspect of a much more subtle undertaking, one that represented a remarkably adroit exercise in fiscal and monetary management. Table 6 sets out some main effects of the shifts in policy occurring in 1947.

The unavoidable rise in the cash deficit of the government presented a major threat to stabilization. If, as during the war, it were covered by note issue at the Bank of Italy, it might well have had the same explosive effects. The danger was surmounted by shifting this financing away from the Bank, which reduced its contribution by 42.1 billion lire in 1948, although the deficit itself was rising by 220.7 billion. To cover this increased requirement, the other banks expanded their financing by 243.4 billion lire, while the public enlarged its contribution by 56.2 billion. Of the banks' increased share, 76.3 billion entered their own portfolios instead of becoming primary reserves, which thereby curbed the expansion of the reserve base.[19]

Financing of the private sector reflected the same caution, as Table 6 shows. Here both the central bank and the other banks decreased their contributions, although total liquid resources supplied advanced by 159.0 billion.[20] This reduction was more than made up by increased recourse to the capital market for medium and long-term credit, and from the proceeds of a very substantially increased inflow of foreign funds, mainly on export account, whose recorded gain was 147.4 billion.

TABLE 6. Changes in liquid resources of government and private sectors, 1947 and 1948 (in billions of lire, for calendar years)

Item	1947	1948	Net change
Cash deficit of government	375.4	596.1	+220.7
Sources of financing:			
Bank of Italy [a]	118.7	76.6	−42.1
Other banks	102.5	345.9	+243.4
Public	48.1	104.3	+56.2
Foreign sector [b]	106.1	69.3	−36.8
Total	375.4	596.1	+220.7
Cash "deficit" of private sector	538.9	697.9	+159.0
Sources of financing:			
Bank of Italy	51.0	19.6	−31.4
Other banks [c]	383.5	366.3	−17.2
Public [d]	75.4	120.1	+44.7
Foreign sector [e]	29.0	191.9	+162.9
Total	538.9	697.9	+159.0

[a] Advances to treasury plus treasury current account.
[b] Value of imports entering under foreign aid programs.
[c] Loans and advances.
[d] Reflects purchase by public of securities issued by special credit institutes to finance private firms.
[e] Lira proceeds from earnings of foreign exchange and from import sales under foreign aid programs.
Source: Compiled from data presented in Banca d'Italia, Adunanza generale, 1948, pp. 190–191.

1372683

Credit control, production, and unemployment. Beginning in 1948, the program for monetary stabilization began to encounter severe criticism at home and abroad. Usually the critics acknowledged that the policy had succeeded in ending inflation. However, they contended variously, that it made interest rates too high, that it was deflationary, that it denied industry fully warranted credits, that it caused high unemployment and excess capacity, and that it obstructed both recovery and redress of the country's critical problems of regional imbalance. Some of those criticisms reflected the special pleadings of certain interest groups on the management and union sides. Others emerged from important official sources abroad.

For example, the American authorities responsible for the European Recovery Program (ERP) expressed impatience with what they considered the government's excessive concern about renewed inflation, and its consequent failure to use the rapidly accumulating counterpart funds to finance a long-term plan of public investment for development and housing, which could have employed these resources. In a document prepared in 1948 and published in February 1949, the ERP representatives declared:

The full utilization of Italy's industrial plant depends essentially on aggressive action by the Italian Government, in particular the launching of a coordinated public investment program. Under political conditions in Italy, and in the world, business confidence is weak, and private investment cannot be counted on to expand industrial plants rapidly or to build even the minimum of low-rent housing. Hence the need for wholehearted Government action in this direction. Such action has been impeded by an exaggerated lack of confidence in some official Italian circles that any new inflationary pressures generated by such a program can be controlled. While this fear is understandable in the light of past experience, industrial output is no longer limited, as in 1947, by shortages of imported fuel and materials and can be expected to expand quickly to meet any increase in purchasing power.[21]

Thus the question of long-term development entered the agenda of issues for economic policy, quickly gaining a place of priority that it has held ever since.

A year later, the United Nations Secretariat for the Economic Commission for Europe (ECE) voiced similar views.

In the summer of 1947, the Italian authorities adopted a restrictive policy, both in banking and public finance, which successfully checked the inflation with which they were then confronted, but only by turning it into a deflation. In the following years until well into 1949, the situation remained one of insufficient demand, and in the first nine months of 1949 wholesale prices fell by 14 per cent.

Recognizing that Italy faced some difficult structural problems, the UN officials expressed the opinion that West Germany and Italy, both of whom then suffered from severe unemployment, could resolve their problems only by vigorous expansion and a high rate of investment. Instead these nations had made things worse by deflationary policies. True, these authorities conceded, problems for the balance of payments and of price stability might follow a more rapid rate of expansion. Contrasting favorably the cases of the

United Kingdom and Scandinavia, they suggested the following possibility:

It may therefore prove that these two countries [Italy and West Germany], which paradoxically have been among the most insistent in attempting to abolish internal and external controls, have thrown away, by ending rationing and relaxing import controls, two of the weapons which experience suggests are necessary in dealing with structural problems of this nature.[22]

It is of some interest that Italy achieved stable prices in 1948 without direct controls, and at that very time was setting out on a fourteen-year boom that yielded one of the highest growth rates in the world—without price controls, without difficulties in the balance of payments, and with remarkably little inflation—an achievement that stands in sharp contrast to the records attained in the United Kingdom and Scandinavia, where conditions were in general a good deal better. Indeed, even in 1948 and 1949, when these criticisms were formuated and when the rate of increase in the Italian money supply was much more restricted than in later years, real GNP advanced 5.8 and 7.5 per cent—surely creditable figures for any country.

Of independent importance, while the ERP and ECE studies of 1949–1950 both properly acknowledged Italy's structural problems and the need for a high rate of capital formation for resolving them, neither recognized the role of rent control in holding down housing construction, or of legal restraints upon free internal migration as an obstacle to lasting improvement of economic conditions in the south, or of the wage policy of the industrial unions as a major impediment to higher employment in the north. Instead, the emphasis was entirely upon monetary expansion and effective demand.

Some of the criticisms turn on matters of fact: whether there was a deflation of either money or credit; whether stabilization policy depressed production and caused severe unemployment. Supplemented by references to monthly data, Table 7 provides most of the evidence required to evaluate these issues.

It is crystal clear that the supply of money was at no time contracted; and that while the formation of demand deposits was briefly slowed, these, too, continued to rise. The main change for money supply was one of reduced speed of increase. Between September 1946 and September 1947, it advanced 3.9 per cent

TABLE 7. Monetary movements before and after stabilization, September 30, 1947 ᵃ (in billions of lire, month-end)

Year and month	Actual figures				Quarterly changes			
	Investments of banks ᵇ	Money supply ᶜ			Investments of banks	Money supply		
		Demand deposits	Note issue	Total		Demand deposits	Note issue	Total
1947: June	616.5	471.0	624.7	1095.7	119.8	81.4	56.4	137.8
September	706.9	505.6	707.4	1213.0	90.4	34.6	82.7	117.3
December	783.3 ᵇ	518.4	848.5	1366.9	—ᵇ	12.8	141.1	153.9
1948: March	808.5	565.7	873.3	1439.0	25.2	47.3	24.8	72.1
June	848.0	651.5	892.9	1544.4	39.5	85.8	19.6	105.4
September	978.5	707.8	947.9	1655.7	130.5	56.3	55.0	111.3
December	1127.1	765.8	1033.4	1799.2	148.6	58.0	85.5	143.5
1949: March	1160.5	840.5	973.2	1813.7	33.4	74.7	−60.2	14.5
June	1214.9	900.5	964.8	1865.3	54.4	60.0	−8.4	51.6
September	1336.5	968.2	1021.5	1989.7	121.6	67.7	56.7	124.4
December	1469.4	1067.6	1091.0	2158.6	132.9	99.4	69.5	168.9

ᵃ None of these series is corrected for seasonal variation.

ᵇ Involves banks' short-term loans and investments, mainly to business firms. With December 1947, this series was revised to segregate more accurately the foreign assets of the banks (*conti valutari*) from their domestic investments. On the old basis, the figure for December 1947 was 723.2 billion; as revised, it was 783.3 billion. Because of this revision, the net change for December 1947 is uncertain, and is not shown.

ᶜ Demand deposits include those of the banks and of the postal checking system. Note issue includes those of Bank of Italy, and circular checks, net of vault cash at the banks; and excludes state coins and notes (less than 10 billion). For 1948–1949, figures for circular checks interpolated from values for each December. For December 1947, the Bank figure for this series was 133.0 billion, while *Bolletino mensile di statistica* reported 111.5 billion. The former was used. Beginning with December 1948, deductions for vault cash reflect new series of the Bank.

Source: Investments of banks; note issue (except circular checks prior to December 1947); and demand deposits (except postal checking accounts prior to 1948), from Banca d'Italia, *Adunanza generale*, 1947–1950. Circular checks and postal accounts for earlier dates from Istituto centrale di statistica, *Bolletino mensile di statistica*, 1947–1949.

monthly. For the same period in 1947–1948 it rose 3.0 per cent monthly. From September 1948 until the end of 1949, the monthly rate of increase was 2.0 per cent. As for demand deposits, in the year before stabilization the monthly gain was 4.9 per cent. During the year immediately following, it fell to 3.3 per cent. From September 1948 through December 1949, the monthly advance was 1.0 per cent.

Granted that credit control cut down on speculative lending and drove up interest rates—both unavoidable phenomena in breaking an inflation by classical techniques—it cannot be sustained that stabilization deflated the means of payment. Such was never its intent. In truth, for 1948 the cash deficit and private sector borrowing together exceeded the volume of funds collected from the public by 174.9 billion of new money—clearly an increase of liquidity. It should also be recalled that with the onset of credit control special provisions were made to help the sulphur and engineering products industries, and to provide certain assistance to the south, in a selective effort to meet problems in these fields.

What about production? According to Table 8, industrial output reached a peak in October 1947, then fell by 15.2 per cent through January 1948, while agricultural output held steady. These figures are seasonally uncorrected, and there is no doubt that the decline was enlarged by a seasonal drop.[23] Beginning with February 1948, industrial production rose steadily through July. By October, it was 3.8 per cent over a year earlier, while agricultural output was up 11.2 per cent. For the full year of 1948, industrial production rose 6.9 per cent, and in 1949 it advanced 6.2 per cent more.

Regarding production, then, a brief deflation did occur. Neglecting seasonal decline, it lasted four months. From February 1948, a strong upturn in industrial production began that continued through mid-summer, slackening in speed for the rest of the year. For 1948 and 1949 as a whole, industrial production and real gross product together recorded substantial increases. Beyond doubt, therefore, stabilization did not bring about a lasting decrease in output. Nor did it give rise to stagnation. Thus the issue boils down to rates of increase: whether the policy held down the expansion of output below feasible noninflationary levels. The position of ERP and ECE was that it did, that it restrained growth so much that a substantial margin of unused capacity and manpower had emerged by late 1948—a margin that more aggressive monetary expansion could and should have absorbed, without tangible risk of renewed inflation.[24]

TABLE 8. Movements in production, prices, and unemployment before and after stabilization, September 30, 1947 [a]

Year and month	Index of industrial production	Index of wholesale prices	Index of cost of living	Registered unemployment [b]
	(1938=100)			(millions)
1947: June	103	5329	4655	1995
September	100	6202	5331	1870
December	91	5526	4929	1779
1948: March	96	5318	4919	2253
June	99	5142	4835	2284
September	110	5769	4910	2117
December	105	5697	4917	——
1949: March	103	5557	4980	2134
June	111	5215	4990	1816
September	111	4910	4886	1723
December	112	4747	4753	2055

[a] Uncorrected for seasonal variation.
[b] These figures cover total registered unemployment, of which roughly 20 per cent includes already employed workers seeking other jobs, pensioners, and housewives.
Source: Indexes for production and prices, from Adunanza generale, 1950, pp. 136–137. Registered unemployment: (1947–1948), from Economic Co-operation Administration, European Recovery Program, Italy Country Study (Washington: Economic Cooperation Administration, February, 1949), p. 61; (1949), from Confindustria, Annuario di statistiche del lavoro, supplemento 1950 (Rome: Failli, 1951), p. 47.

To assert that stabilization did create a substantial margin of idle resources, usable without inflation, is to assume that the balance of payments could have withstood the risks of a more expansionary policy, and to attribute the undoubtedly heavy volume of registered unemployment at the time to a supposed deficiency of effective demand. The first step is to look at the behavior of unemployment itself.

Although the data for registered unemployment do not correspond closely with movements in production, it may be granted that the brief recession added modestly to the number out of work. Comparisons for March in 1947 and 1948 suggest an increase of 75,000. But before too much is made of this fact it should be recalled that there were 2.18 million registered unemployed in March 1947, when inflation was in full swing, as against 2.25 million a year later. Clearly, the country had a very severe unemployment problem at the time—with and without inflation. But it cannot be blamed on stabilization. In fact, in March 1949, the number stood at 2.12 million—below the level of two years before.

Thus the only way in which this formidable burden of unemployment can be blamed on stabilization policy is to contend that relatively tight money confined the expansion of output to a rate well below a safe noninflationary ceiling. Again the issue is whether there actually was an enforced deficiency of aggregate demand in 1948–1949.

The theory of demand deficiency was designed for the depression phase of the standard Anglo-American business cycle, where it fits very well. In such conditions, complementary resources—fixed capital, raw materials, and manpower—are all idle to some extent. Any method of expanding total demand for output will then translate itself into higher production and lower unemployment, without raising prices for a considerable time. All this Keynes pointed out in addressing himself to circumstances prevailing in the western industrial world in 1936. He also contended that eventually bottlenecks would emerge as expansion approached full employment; that since the marginal physical productivity of labor would be gradually falling, marginal costs of production and hence prices generally would begin to rise. Recall, too, that in its rigorous formulation Keynes' theory presumes a closed economy, so that balance of payments effects could be ruled out.[25]

The Italian case in 1948–1949 does not fit this model, and that was what the stabilization controversy was all about. The first discrepancy is that Italy is a nation extremely dependent upon foreign trade—as much so as the United Kingdom. Two thirds of its imports consist of food, fuel and raw materials, paid for traditionally by exports, emigrants' remittances, and tourists' expenditures, aided at that time by U.S. grants in aid. If in 1948–1949, output were to be increased at an even faster rate, money demand for output would have had to be expanded still more rapidly. Imports would have then promptly gone up, to provide the needed complementary raw materials and fuel, and to supply the increase in consumers' demand.[26] The shortage of internally available complementary goods was the heart of the production problem, as the proponents of stabilization well knew.[27] In other words, the working reserve of foreign exchange—then largely in inconvertible sterling—was still too small to cover the risk to the balance of payments implicit in a policy of the Keynesian type.

Another restraint upon faster expansion of output was the result of the restricted domestic supply of fixed capital. It was easy to claim that there were ample reserves of idle plant capacity, but little evidence was ever brought forward to support it. Granted that in some cases this margin did exist, for the whole system it could not have been large. Furthermore, the possibility of substantial absorption of the some two million unemployed at the time depended upon the marginal productivity of these additional workers. For two decades, labor supply had been excessive relative to capital stock. Emigration had been blocked since the early thirties, while Fascist policy had encouraged a higher birth rate. Autarchy and war had caused considerable misdirection of investment, and, beyond this, capital losses during the conflict had been severe. In contrast, after liberation the labor force was inflated further by demobilized troops, return of colonists, refugees, and a growing influx of young people. Given the restricted stock of fixed capital relative to manpower, any significant increase of employment in 1948–1949 could have been achieved only with a rapidly falling marginal physical productivity of labor—meaning steeply rising marginal cost curves and prices. Capital was just too scarce, while labor was far from a perfect substitute.

To have increased employment substantially was inseparable from a reduction in real wages. But this could not be done by cutting money wages—they were already low by western standards, and such a move was politically inconceivable. Nor could it be done by inflating the price level: wages were closely tied to the cost of living (the *scala mobile*), and the Italian workers had no illusions whatever about the value of money. Indeed, the unions were pressing at the time for higher real wages—not lower—as they have continued to do ever since. Furthermore, the Italian monetary managers were adamantly opposed to renewed inflation, and inflation was implicit in attempting to reduce real wages by the indirect route.

The anti-inflationists in the government knew well that rising exports were the key to rising imports, that more inflation would cut into exports and quickly erode the exchange reserve, causing unemployment to mount once more. They fully understood that increased real saving could not be forced by renewed inflation, because the middle- and upper-income classes were the main source of savings, while the wage escalator simply would have redistributed income to the wage earners, whose propensity to save was less. Finally, the anti-inflationists correctly reasoned that a reprise for voluntary saving depended upon a stable lira, and was imperative to rapid capital formation. Only by this route could the imbalance between capital and manpower be reduced. Beyond this, redress of this balance was the sole means to absorb the country's idle labor, given the rising level of real wages the trade unions were in a position to enforce on behalf of their employed members.

As the proponents of stabilization viewed matters, a stable value for the lira was not an end in itself but a key to everything else: freer trade, convertibility, higher exports, larger imports, freedom from dependence upon foreign aid, more saving, more investment, more output, and more employment. History was to prove them right, in diagnosis and in prescription. They were not confronted with a business depression in the conventional sense, but with a very complex structural problem, for which their old-fashioned thinking was quite appropriate. Regarding it, a distinguished committee of independent experts, reporting to the council of ministers of the Organization for European Economic Co-operation on June 18, 1952, had this to say:

We think it is no accident that, in all relatively free economies, the absence of monetary control in the post-war world has tended to be accompanied by inflation and external disequilibrium, and that, where monetary policy has been used with sufficient vigor and where perverse fiscal influences have not operated against it, it has never failed to fulfil its purpose.[28]

CHAPTER III. THE LONG BOOM, 1948–1961: OUTPUT, PRICES, AND INCOME

The immediate purpose of monetary reconstruction in 1947 was to stabilize the price level. However, the authorities in charge of economic affairs had a much broader set of objectives in mind, for which stable prices were but a mediating factor.

Strengthened by the bitterness of the Fascist experience, the leaders of the new regime were intellectually opposed to both economic nationalism and direct state planning. The word *leaders*, referring particularly to De Gasperi and Einaudi, must be emphasized, for while the cabinet was united against fascism, it was not at one regarding nationalization of industry, or direct state control of production and investment. Nor was it wholly united in its enthusiasm for its declared monetary and fiscal program. This was hardly surprising. Besides the necessity for ruling by coalition, the Christian Democratic Party itself was at the time and has remained a "rainbow" affair—an unstable mixture of leftist planners often of corporativist persuasion, moderate reformers and welfarists, economic liberals, and big business conservatives. Compromise was imperative in 1947–1948 and still is mandatory today. In consequence, it would be futile to look for a completely consistent line of government policy in all matters affecting the economy.

Nevertheless, the leaders who emerged with the reconstruction of the De Gasperi ministry at the end of May 1947 had a point of view, one that gave thrust and direction to the agenda that derived from it. Their clear preference was for the restoration of a market economy, firmly linked to the West, in which production and development would be guided primarily by the price mechanism. In their outlook, the price system and competition were adequate for accomplishing the main tasks of recovery, expansion, and internal balance—aided by the state and undertaken within a context of progressively freer international trade—provided that both inflation and deflation could be held in check.[1] As of 1947–1948, therefore, the government placed relatively little emphasis upon any need for an over-all development plan. Given a favorable environment of policy, private initiative was believed to be sufficient.

To critics on the left, all this was hardly more than a program on behalf of big business monopoly and the rest of the status quo. But this view was both narrow and doctrinaire. Emphatically, the De Gasperi government was not aiming at a laissez-faire regime, granting that for tactical reasons it tolerated rather than attacked certain monopolistic positions, probably because it chose recovery over reform, believing that as markets opened up with expansion the problem of big-firm dominance would gradually yield.

In truth, even if competition were well short of perfect, in many situations, the government favored the discipline and incentives that competition provides, although they were to be exerted within a much larger framework of positive state policy. Accordingly, it strongly supported the revival of independent unionism and collective bargaining; introduced a variety of social security measures calling for large increases in welfare benefits; obtained the passage of diverse statutes of assistance to the south; and preserved intact the IRI complex of industrial enterprises involving state participation and financing. In 1949, it initiated an extensive program for public housing, drawing for the first time upon the substantial accumulation of counterpart funds acquired through United States aid programs. Then in 1950 it introduced the ten-year *Cassa* scheme.

Thus the policy that began to emerge after 1947 involved the building up of a mixed capitalistic economy, in which private enterprise, competition, and the market mechanism were to play major parts, but with the state by no means in a passive role. In basic respects this approach was well to the left of the American New Deal, and it incorporated some principles similar to those followed by conterminous labor governments in the United Kingdom and Scandinavia. But it also differed from these regimes in one respect or another, and in this divergence it acquired more than a superficial similarity to the system emerging in Western Germany after monetary reform and the end of price control. In short, Italian policy was typified by a continuing belief that competition and private enterprise had a large and permanent place in the scheme of things; by firm adherence to monetary orthodoxy;

and by an old-fashioned devotion to the doctrines of free international trade and currency convertibility. The approach thus was both radical and conservative—radical because the problems of reconstruction and internal development were acute and extremely difficult and required extensive intervention by the state; and conservative because of a parallel need to gain price stability if saving, investment, and the exchange reserve were to perform their essential functions in helping to resolve these problems.

Viewed as a whole, the course charted in 1947 committed Italy to the ambient of the West, both politically and economically. To make this orientation stick, the government hoped that its policies would produce a rapid and continuing economic advance that would gradually win the bulk of the peasants and industrial workers to its side. Particularly did it wish to draw the latter away from their classic posture of noncooperation with bourgeois regimes—an evolution that was essential if Italy ever were to develop a stable political system. Thus, for reasons of practical politics as well as ideology, both the Communist and Socialist parties, who were out of the government and yet who then commanded a third of the votes, easily assumed the role of intractable opponents, able to exploit their hostility in a number of directions at once.

Monetary stabilization accordingly was but a part of a fundamental ideological choice and commitment, which gained strong endorsement at the polls in the crucial election of 1948. In turn, this choice was clearly in the nature of a gamble: that the policies it implied would eventually pay off in broadly distributed prosperity, and that this consummation would provide the requisite basis for an enduring system of western democracy. Given the low state of the economy in 1948, the rising clamor for immediate improvement, and the large number of disaffected voters, the odds favoring success were not impressive, although the stakes were enormous. Even more, lasting economic advance offered no assurance that whole-hearted commitment to parliamentary democracy and mixed capitalism would necessarily follow.

To gauge the outcome of what may be called on behalf of its proponents the De Gasperi–Einaudi experiment, one should examine the growth of output, the stability of that growth, the behavior of prices, the evolution of foreign trade and the foreign balance, and progress toward resolution of the problem of internal economic imbalance. For such purposes, the year 1948 is the logical starting point. It was the first full year of effective monetary control, and the first in which a stable price level was achieved postwar. Hence it is a natural base from which to measure the subsequent course of economic affairs.

THE GROWTH OF OUTPUT AND ITS STABILITY

The growth of output. The year 1948 ushered in the longest period of sustained economic expansion in modern Italian history, with comparatively stable prices prevailing throughout. Through 1961, increases were recorded in every single year for both real gross national product and industrial production. Of matching importance, very high rates of expansion were also achieved. Underlying this record was a remarkable improvement in labor productivity, which easily overcame the restraint implicit in an extremely low rate of increase in total population (0.616 per cent per year on linear trend). Table 9 depicts these accomplishments.

What these figures show above all else is that between 1948 and 1961 real gross domestic product jumped 119.6 per cent in total, and 102.5 per cent per resident, while the output of industry soared by 214.5 per cent—a record that would be difficult to equal, let alone exceed, anywhere else in the world.[2] In the same period, real gross investment climbed 222.4 per cent, while from 1950 the real value of exports of goods and services advanced by 291.6 per cent. By contrast, real consumption rose only 89.4 per cent over 1948—still adequate to yield a cumulative increase of 74.7 per cent per head, because of the very slow growth in population during these years.

To express these gains in compound annual rates without assigning undue weights to the end-points of the series, the annual observations were fitted to exponential trend lines by the conventional method of least-squares regression, using time itself as the independent variable. So calculated, total real product grew 5.86 per cent a year, and per resident, 5.23 per cent; while industrial output expanded at an impressive 8.81 per cent. Among the components of gross national product, the trend rates of annual increase were 4.71

per cent for real consumption, 9.02 per cent for real investment, and an almost incredible 13.54 per cent (1950–1961) for real exports.[3]

TABLE 9. Movements in population and production, 1948–1961 [a]

Year	Population [b] Resident (thousands)	Present	Real GNP Total (billion lire)	Per resident (thous. lire)	Industrial Production (1953 = 100)
1948	46,542	46,177	8,497	182.6	63.5
1949	46,899	46,437	9,175	195.6	67.9
1950	47,262	46,768	9,815	207.7	77.6
1951	47,516	47,159	10,511	221.2	88.5
1952	47,774	47,411	10,719	224.4	91.0
1953	48,091	47,655	11,480	238.7	100.0
1954	48,434	47,940	12,027	248.3	109.1
1955	48,730	48,186	12,860	263.9	118.9
1956	48,974	48,372	13,413	273.9	128.2
1957	49,214	48,593	14,280	290.2	138.1
1958	49,530	48,877	14,882	300.5	142.4
1959	49,901	49,227	16,088	322.4	157.9
1960	50,232	49,502	17,258	343.6	182.3
1961	50,464	49,801	18,663	369.8	199.7

[a] Except for 1951 and 1961, which were census years, figures for population are official estimates. Figures for real GNP are based upon prices of 1954, and refer to domestic GNP, defined here as gross available product adjusted for exports minus imports. Since this series does not go back before 1950, figures for 1948 and 1949 were obtained by splicing to an earlier official series based upon prices of 1938. The splicing procedure presumes that proportionate changes in the earlier series were applicable for carrying back the later one. The official index of industrial production was revised on a 1953 base; earlier years were obtained by splicing to the older index (1938 base).
[b] The difference here arises mainly because a large number of workers are temporarily out of the country each year for employment abroad.
Source: Population and real GNP from Repubblica italiana, Ministero del bilancio e Ministero del tesoro, Relazione generale sulla situazione economica del paese, 1961 (hereafter Relazione generale), II, pp. 348–349; index of industrial production, various issues.

The underlying upward trend in real GNP was so strong that fluctuations in this series were of very small importance. Although real consumption—total and per head—performed very well by international standards, the outstanding gains were in investment and exports, whose extremely rapid advance was the immediate reason for Italy's astounding fourteen-year postwar boom—an upsurge in activity that was still continuing at the end of 1962.

It will be recalled that the broader purposes of monetary stabilization in 1947 were to speed up capital formation, to avoid deflation, and to strengthen the country's position on the world market. The record shows that all these goals have been accomplished in most impressive fashion—to a degree probably well in excess of the most optimistic expectations.

The stability of growth since 1948. Since no decreases were registered in either real GNP or industrial production in any year of the entire period, the only sense in which one may speak of a "business cycle" is relative to variations in annual increases, although the whole series could be interpreted as constituting part of the upward phase of a Kondratieff long-wave.

There are two main ways by which fluctuations in annual rates of increase can be measured to isolate deviant years. One is simply to examine the annual changes themselves in the major series— presented in Table 10. The other is to compare the actual annual magnitudes with corresponding estimated trend values, shown in Table 11.

Inspection of the figures in Table 10 suggests that 1952 and 1958 were the two poorest years in the period. Regarding 1952, which was disturbed by the Korean War, the rates of gross investment and of exportation fell, while inventories suffered a net contraction. Gross product rose only 1.97 per cent, and industrial output 2.8 per cent. In comparison, 1958 was somewhat better: GNP advanced 4.2 per cent, industrial production rose 3.1 per cent, and no absolute declines occurred in the rates of investment and exportation or in the level of inventories. By contrast, 1951, 1955, 1957, and 1959–1961 were all exceptionally good years. Indeed, the last three were outstanding, suggesting that the rate of expansion was gathering even more force as the period drew to a close. Nonetheless, the really surprising thing is that even in the "worst" years increases were attained in both gross output and in industrial production. Evidently the forces at work behind the expansionary trend were so strong that they could easily thrust aside any potentially deflationary processes.

Table 11 presents a second method for sorting out the high and low years, by showing the amounts by which the actual yearly observations exceeded or fell short of the estimated trend values. Given the very high determination coefficients for both exponential trends, the divergences are inevitably small. For total GNP, 1952 and 1956–1958 fell significantly below trend, while 1951 and 1961

TABLE 10. Annual changes in leading economic series, 1948–1961 [a]

| | Annual totals | | | Annual changes | | | | | |
| | Consumption | Investment | Exports | GNP | Ind. prod. | Consumption | Investment | Exports | Inventories |
Year	(billion lire, deflated)				(index points)	(billion lire, deflated)			(billion)
1948	7,248	1,523	—					—	−36
1949	7,729	1,628	—	678	4.4	481	105	—	69
1950	8,096	1,862	1,017	640	9.7	367	234	—	123
1951	8,508	2,102	1,135	996	10.9	412	240	118	223
1952	8,930	2,085	1,100	208	2.5	422	−17	−35	−10
1953	9,494	2,295	1,328	761	9.0	564	210	228	30
1954	9,783	2,489	1,433	547	9.1	289	194	105	35
1955	10,142	2,895	1,637	833	9.8	359	406	204	190
1956	10,565	3,030	1,876	553	9.3	423	135	239	138
1957	11,000	3,277	2,313	867	9.9	435	247	437	84
1958	11,403	3,336	2,428	602	4.3	403	59	115	95
1959	12,027	3,726	2,846	1,206	15.5	624	390	418	97
1960	12,867	4,441	3,387	1,170	24.4	840	715	541	305
1961	13,729	4,910	3,983	1,405	17.4	862	469	596	300

[a] Annual data for GNP and industrial production appear in Table 9. Excepting inventories, figures for 1948 and 1949 derived by splicing new to old series. No data available for real exports before 1950. Inventories are in current prices.

Source: (1948–1949) Original data from Istituto centrale di statistica, *Indagine statistica sullo sviluppo del reddito nazionale dell'Italia dal 1861 al 1956* (hereafter *Indagine statistica*) (Rome: Failli, 1957), p. 271; (1950–1961) *Relazione generale*, 1961, II, p. 348 (GNP computed); and prior issues for industrial production. Inventories from *Indagine statistica*, 1948–1956, and (1957–1961) from *Relazione generale*, various issues.

TABLE 11. Differences between observed and estimated trend values, Real GNP and Index of Industrial Production, 1948–1961 [a]

Year	Absolute		Relative [b]	
	GNP (billions)	Ind. prod. (points)	GNP (per cent)	Ind. prod.
1948	−118	−1.4	−1.37	−2.16
1949	55	−2.7	0.60	−3.82
1950	161	0.8	1.66	1.04
1951	291	4.9	2.85	5.86
1952	−100	0.1	−0.93	0.11
1953	27	1.1	0.24	1.11
1954	−97	1.5	−0.80	1.39
1955	26	1.8	0.21	1.54
1956	−173	0.8	−1.27	0.63
1957	−103	−0.6	−0.72	−0.43
1958	−344	−8.5	−2.26	−5.63
1959	−30	−6.3	−0.19	−3.84
1960	195	3.7	1.14	2.07
1961	601	5.4	3.33	2.78

[a] Absolute differences calculated as actual less estimated values: positive values indicate "good" years relative to trend. For estimating equations, see Note 3 for this chapter.

[b] Calculated as absolute difference relative to estimated trend value for year, expressed as percentage.

Source: Data presented in Table 9.

were well above. Also, 1948 fell behind, the first year of relatively tight money, while the middle years also were behind. On the basis of industrial production alone, 1949, 1958, and 1959 were laggard years, while 1952 was almost exactly on trend. By contrast, 1951 and 1961 ran well ahead. Viewed as a whole, the highly aggregative data encompassed by those two annual series exhibit no sign of either a major or a minor cycle. At best, they reveal only small alterations in the pace of continuous long-term expansion.

However, if we go from annual to monthly data, switch to a broader array of less inclusive time series, and introduce adjustments to remove seasonal variation, then something akin to a short-cycle of 3.8 months' average duration can be detected for the Italian economy since 1945. Under the leadership of Professor Ferdinando di Fenizio and Dr. Gastone Miconi, the National Institute for the Study of Business Fluctuations (Istituto nazionale per lo studio della congiuntura—ISCO) has recently made such an investigation, modeling its efforts mainly upon the work of the National Bureau of Economic Research in the United States.[4] According to these studies, Table 12 shows that the swings in Italian business activity can be dated (Miconi's figures and data in parentheses where divergent from di Fenizio's).

TABLE 12. Dating of ISCO cycles

Cycle	Turning points			Duration (months)
	Initial trough	Peak	Terminal trough	
1. Monetary	May 1945	September 1947	March 1948 (June 1948)	34 (37)
2. Marshall	March 1948 (June 1948)	July 1949 (December 1949)	March 1950 (August 1950)	24 (26)
3. Korean	March 1950 (August 1950)	April 1951	June 1952	27 (22)
4. 1st European	June 1952	June 1955 (September 1955)	February 1956 (June 1956)	44 (48)
5. 2nd European	February 1956 (June 1956)	September 1957	August 1958	30 (26)

Source: Note 4 in this chapter.

To call the down-swings in these short cycles "recessions" is to over-emphasize them, given the strong underlying upward trends at work. Indeed, the discrepancies in dating suggest both the difficulty of detecting these movements and the large element of qualitative judgment implicit in the attempt. Nonetheless, the scheme indicates that during 1948–1961 "contractions" occurred during 1949–1950, 1951–1952, 1955–1956, and 1957–1958. These may be compared with the annual data for GNP and industrial production, which together give emphasis to 1952, 1956, and 1958.

Probably the most important findings of the ISCO studies are that the Italian economy is "open and vulnerable" to shocks from abroad, and that during the postwar period the system has been more responsive to underlying upward trends than to cyclical disturbances.[5] Certainly the annual data fully confirm the latter conclusion. However, this does not mean that Italy is now permanently immune to the business cycle. She has experienced them in the earlier past, and there is no a priori reason to believe that the present boom in exports and in capital formation will persist from now until the end of time.

ASPECTS OF THE BOOM

Savings and investment. The speed and steadiness of the rate of capital formation is a major influence in shaping the pattern of over-all growth in any economy. This is particularly true for countries such as Italy, where until very recently there has existed a large surplus of labor, such that the supply of manpower could exert no significant restraint upon the pace of aggregate expansion.

Table 13 provides some interesting clues regarding the behavior of capital formation during 1948–1961. Over the whole period, the annual rate of investment in plant and equipment more than tripled, while domestic GNP (current prices) advanced 196 per cent. Relative to GNP, these investments ran between 13 and 16 per cent throughout, edging up to the latter figure in the last few years. Of particular significance because of their high leverage upon labor productivity, their relative share of GNP in Italy at 16 per cent is about twice as large as it was in the United States during 1956–1961.

As Table 14 shows, the relationships between annual changes in capital outlays on plant and equipment, housing, and public works are of much interest. Spending on plant and equipment reflects the decentralized decisions of a large number of separate firms, guided by profit expectations. In consequence, annual changes in this component fluctuated very widely. Among the earlier years, they recorded large gains in 1951 and 1956–1957, while in 1960–1961 they soared by unprecedented amounts. In 1952–1953 and in 1958, they behaved badly, helping to account for the relatively poor gains in GNP in 1952 and 1958 in particular.

By contrast, and mainly because they are largely determined by government without regard to profits prospects, expenditures on public investment showed consistent increases and were much steadier. During 1949–1952, they rose strongly—initially under the influence of Minister Amintore Fanfani's newly introduced housing program, financed by release of counterpart funds by the American ECA mission; and later as public works were expanded with the

TABLE 13. Allocation of domestic Gross National Product, 1948–1961 (in billions of current lire)

Year	Consumption			Investment						Gross national product
	Private	Public [a]	Total	Housing	Public works	Plant and equipment	Changes in inventories	Net foreign [b]	Total	
1948	5,351	584	5,935	129	188	1,061	−36	−209	1,133	7,068
1949	5,736	622	6,358	169	178	1,030	69	−170	1,276	7,634
1950	6,231	631	6,862	230	175	1,122	123	−70	1,580	8,442
1951	7,089	737	7,826	304	213	1,343	223	−158	1,925	9,751
1952	7,704	864	8,568	386	285	1,430	−10	−409	1,682	10,250
1953	8,393	832	9,225	466	352	1,436	30	−340	1,944	11,169
1954	8,713	923	9,636	579	348	1,527	35	−245	2,244	11,880
1955	9,278	1,010	10,288	715	361	1,674	190	−233	2,707	12,995
1956	9,953	1,096	11,049	790	333	1,869	138	−248	2,882	13,931
1957	10,040	1,507	11,547	924	287	2,173	84	−187	3,281	14,828
1958	10,449	1,704	12,153	998	337	2,146	95	186	3,762	15,915
1959	10,886	1,840	12,726	1,064	340	2,326	97	355	4,182	16,908
1960	12,235	2,091	14,326	1,101	449	2,891	305	6	4,752	19,078
1961	13,194	2,288	15,482	1,192	485	3,381	300	135	5,493	20,975

[a] Primarily current services provided by government to the public.

[b] Exports minus imports. Includes services.

Source: Compiled from data in (1948–1956) Indagine statistica, pp. 261, 265, and 269; (1957–1961) from Relazione generale, various issues.

introduction of the southern development plan after mid-1950. Over the whole period, these outlays have risen relative to national product, absorbing about 8 per cent by the end, against 4.5 per cent at the start.

TABLE 14. Annual changes in plant and equipment expenditure and in public investment, 1948–1961 [a] (in billions of current lire)

Year	Annual change		Year	Annual change	
	Plant and equipment	Public investment		Plant and equipment	Public investment
1948	162	42	1955	147	149
1949	−31	30	1956	195	47
1950	92	58	1957	304	88
1951	221	112	1958	−27	124
1952	87	154	1959	180	69
1953	6	147	1960	565	146
1954	91	109	1961	490	127

[a] Public investment is sum of housing plus public works outlays. Part of housing is private, but figures are not separately available. Investment by government in state-controlled enterprises included in plant and equipment.
Source: Data in Table 13.

In part, swings in these annual increases have reflected discretionary decisions of the government, using variations in public investment as a stabilizing offset to swings in private outlays on inventories, plant and equipment—for example, in 1952 and 1958. Beyond these contracyclical efforts, the government sought deliberately as part of its Vanoni "plan"—announced in early 1955—to shift the weight of capital formation toward productivity-increasing outlays by industry. Thus expenditures on plant and equipment, which accounted for 62.2 per cent of plant and equipment and public investment together in 1954, rose to almost 67 per cent by 1961. At the same time, however, the introduction of the long-term *Cassa* program in 1950 imparted a strong upward trend to public investment, superimposing still another structural factor upon capital formation during these years.

In designing his stabilization program in 1947, Luigi Einaudi stressed most strongly its potential contribution to a reprise for saving, and the importance of saving to any real solution to the country's pressing problems of poverty and of incomplete and unbalanced industrialization. Although the comparative stability of prices that was subsequently achieved is not the only factor responsible for the amazing upsurge of production and investment that followed, there can be no doubt about the revival of saving itself, nor about its vital contribution to growth and development. Table 15 summarizes the essential facts.

TABLE 15. Gross saving in relation to Gross National Product, 1948–1961 [a] (per cent)

Year	Savings rate	Year	Savings rate
1948	16.0	1955	20.8
1949	16.5	1956	20.7
1950	18.7	1957	22.8
1951	19.7	1958	23.6
1952	16.4	1959	24.7
1953	17.4	1960	24.9
1954	18.9	1961	26.2

[a] Gross saving measured by gross investment.
Source: Data in Table 11.

Between 1948 and 1961, the proportion of gross product committed to investment jumped by nearly two thirds, bringing Italy to the very top rank among the high-savings countries of the world. Early in 1955, when the Vanoni program was officially presented to the OEEC, its projections included transition to a 25 per cent savings rate by 1964, although doubts were voiced that this was attainable without totalitarian forcing. In fact, this level was achieved in 1961—four years ahead of schedule, and within the ambient of a free economy. Back of it were the following forces: the recovery of private saving once inflation had yielded to stable prices; large-scale internal reinvestment of profits by large enterprises; a substantial rise in government investment; and a steady improvement in the relationship between exports and imports. Also significant, the demand for savings kept rising throughout, aided alike by the urge to modernize and develop industry, by the hunger of consumers for durable goods, and by the stabilizing influence of a large and steadily expanding program of public investment. Undoubtedly, the advent of the Common Market in 1958 also strengthened the export side.

Thus we can describe Italy's impressive postwar expansion as a

capital formation and export boom. Except for 1952, gross investment rose throughout the period. It first began to show its strength
in 1950–1951. After 1952 it continued to advance strongly except
for the comparatively weak years of 1956 and 1958. By the end of
the period it had attained incredible heights. In the early stages,
the main push came from plant and equipment, inventories, and
public investment. After 1952, exports began to show strength relative to imports, by 1958 turning net foreign investment positive.
After 1958, plant and equipment, inventories, net foreign investment, and public investment all joined in thrusting investment
strongly upward. Thus the boom in production and income during
these fourteen years was the direct consequence of an almost unbe-
lievable opening up of new uses for savings, by private firms and
government together.

TABLE 16. Movements in prices, 1948–1961 [a]

Year	Implicit GNP deflator (1948=100)	Wholesale (1948=100)	Cost of living (1948=100)	Exports (1953=100)	Imports (1953=100)
1948	100.0	100.0	100.0	——	——
1949	99.8	95.0	101.4	——	——
1950	103.2	90.0	100.2	——	——
1951	111.1	102.5	109.9	——	——
1952	114.7	96.8	114.7	——	——
1953	116.8	96.4	116.7	100.0	100.0
1954	118.4	95.6	120.0	97.1	95.9
1955	121.3	96.4	123.3	94.1	97.3
1956	125.5	98.1	129.5	91.9	100.4
1957	126.8	99.1	132.0	95.1	105.7
1958	130.0	97.3	138.2	90.6	93.0
1959	128.8	94.4	137.6	83.3	86.5
1960	131.1	95.3	141.3	86.6	85.4
1961	133.3	95.5	145.4	84.0	82.8

[a] Implicit GNP deflator extracted from official current and real GNP data.
Wholesale price index based upon splicing 1938 to 1953 index, and converting
derived series to 1948 base. Cost-of-living index converted from 1938 to 1948
base. Export and import price series not available before 1953.
Source: Implicit GNP deflator from Relazione generale, 1961, II, pp. 347–
348; exports and imports, I, p. 165; wholesale prices and cost of living,
Relazione generale, various issues.

Prices. As Table 16 indicates, the behavior of prices after 1948
presents a mixed story. Judged by wholesale and export prices, the
stabilization policies initiated in late 1947 have proved a smashing

success. Gauged by the more inclusive GNP deflator index, that success becomes somewhat less impressive. Measured by the cost of living, which comes closest to indicating the effects of price changes upon consumers' welfare, the best that can be said is that the speed of advance has been kept within tolerable bounds.

Between 1948 and 1961, the GNP deflator rose by 33.3 per cent. Converted to an exponential trend by linear regression, the annual rate of advance was 2.3 per cent, with some unevenness although the rise itself was unbroken.[6] This index embraces the largest array of components within the price structure, hence supports the verdict that from 1950 the Italian economy experienced a slowly but steadily rising price level—well within the limits of safety for the foreign balance, but persistently rising nevertheless. However, compared with the trend rates of its industrial neighbors and of the United States, Italy's 2.3 per cent rate stands up as remarkably good. Here, then, is a case of an economy that could achieve a very high and very well-sustained rate of over-all growth for many years, with comparatively moderate inflation at most.

Consider next the index of wholesale prices. It shows a net decline of 4.5 per cent between 1948 and 1961. Because it is a sensitive barometer of price changes, this index deserves detailed attention. At the start of the period, it recorded a declining movement that set in in late 1947 and continued through the first half of 1950, reflecting the impact of comparatively tight money upon speculative demands. With the onset of the Korean War at the end of June in the latter year, it rose strongly through March 1951, impelled upward by renewed speculation and later by an upsurge in prices of imports that continued into July.[7] After 1951, it moved irregularly downward, attaining a net decline of 6.8 per cent by 1961 relative to 1951.

A more detailed breakdown of this index—initiated from 1953—reveals declines in the following major components (through 1961): agricultural raw materials (−12.7 per cent); processed foods (−3.4 per cent); fuels and lubricants (−6.2 per cent); and chemicals (−11.2 per cent). By contrast, increases were recorded for agricultural food products (2.9 per cent); meats (9.6 per cent); timber (15.4 per cent); and building materials (4.7 per cent). Processed agricultural products other than foods and metal products showed no significant change. Over-all, the wholesale index declined one per cent during 1953–1961.[8]

Attention should also be called to export prices, which are rather closely allied to the wholesale group. As Table 16 shows, after 1953 the export price index registered declines in all years but two, winding up 16 per cent below their initial level.[9] Particularly noteworthy, these prices fell quite markedly after 1958, when the Common Market was formed, undoubtedly influenced by the broadened ambit of competition within the continent which these new trading arrangements began to bring about. Finally, this favorable behavior of export prices did much by itself to bring about the substantial enlargement of Italy's foreign markets during recent years.

Turn now to the cost-of-living index. During 1948–1950, when stabilization policy first came into effect, this index held steady. In the next three years it rose rapidly, influenced by the Korean War inflation, and by an initial but incomplete unblocking of rents, which had continued under tight control since 1938. After 1954, the index rose rather steadily except for a negligible drop in 1959. For the period as a whole, the trend rate of increase in the cost of living was 3.13 per cent yearly—nearly one-third more than for the GNP deflator, and sharply in contrast with wholesale prices, which recorded a modest net decline over the same years.[10]

Looking at the main components of this index, they show the following net increases for 1961 relative to 1948 (in per cent): [11]

Foods	58.1
Clothing	11.0
Light and heat	55.5
Rent	1711.5
Various	56.3

Rents, of course, stand out—reflecting the elimination of controls that had held this component far below its equilibrium level for many years.[12] Partial unblocking also occurred in utility rates, particularly in 1951, although some regulation continues in effect.

A new index of consumers' prices, compiled from 1953, throws further light on changes in the cost of living. It reveals substantial advances (through 1961) in the following components: rents (122.3 per cent); other services (46.0 per cent); transportation and communications (35.3 per cent); foods, beverages, and tobacco (13.8 per cent). Small declines occurred for private vehicles (−4.7 per cent), electricity and gas (−0.2 per cent). In the same period, the over-all index of consumers' prices advanced 17.8 per cent, compared with 24.6 per cent for the cost of living—which is based upon 1938 and is now obsolete—and 14.1 per cent for the GNP deflator.[13]

This survey of price behavior after 1948 reveals something of a paradox. The cost of living rose 3.1 per cent yearly on trend, and the GNP deflator 2.3 per cent. In contrast, both wholesale and export prices showed net declines. How may we account for the "price scissors" these opposing movements figuratively describe?

In one respect, the explanation is that the various indexes measure different components of the whole price system. But this is not very illuminating because it does not tell us why these separate components moved in diverse fashion.

A large part of the real answer probably lies in movements in wages and labor productivity. Both the wholesale and export price indexes are heavily weighted by industrial products that are priced at stages earlier than sale to final buyers. As is shown in the next section, very large and continuing gains in gross labor productivity were achieved in manufacturing industry throughout the period. These were only partly absorbed (about one half) by parallel increases in labor costs. To a quite moderate extent, the net savings so realized were passed on in lower prices, and this effect shows up in a very modest decline in wholesale prices (virtually none after 1953), and a somewhat larger one for the prices of exports. Perhaps, too, manufacturers may have experienced a slight worsening of their terms of trade with suppliers of raw materials. However, in the main these net savings became earnings of capital that were largely reinvested internally, perpetuating the productivity-generating process.

At the same time, organized labor in industry was able to win substantial annual increases in wage rates and supplements, through a combination of collective bargaining and state regulation. Given the nature of the wage-determining system, these yearly advances have served as patterns for comparable increases sought and won by unions in the nonmanufacturing sectors as well.

But in those sectors, offsetting gains in labor productivity have generally been much lower, while wage pressure has been comparable. In turn, this divergence helps to explain the basic discrepancy in the behavior of the various price indexes. An additional factor is the feed-back effect of the cost-of-living escalator for wages, which is of national application. Any significant rise in the cost of living for whatever reason becomes automatically translated into higher wage costs, and these in turn work back into prices in all sectors in which offsetting increases in productivity are small.

Another factor in the explanation is that the rapid rise of personal incomes during the boom has sharply increased the demand for services and for foods, both of which originate from sectors in which supply is comparatively inelastic, because economies of large-scale production are not available. Here productivity gains are much more difficult to achieve, and because such activities tend to be highly labor-intensive, rising wage costs become more readily translated into higher prices. Finally, both the cost-of-living index and that for consumers' prices were lifted to some extent by the decontrol of rents and utility rates, and by support-price programs for certain agricultural products.

Labor productivity. Although the underlying data are far from satisfactory, they are adequate to suggest strongly that substantial gains in the productivity of manual workers were realized in the advanced sector of industry during the postwar years.

To arrive at this finding, changes in the input of manual-worker man-hours by industry group were compared with changes in output for these groups, for 1953 and 1960.[14] The separate output data for the seven groups were then combined according to their relative weights in the over-all index of official production.[15] This weighted index was then related to the total input of manual man-hours, to yield an over-all group index of output per manual-worker man-hours.

The seven groups considered comprise the bulk of the technically advanced firms in Italian industry. The results show that for 1960 compared with 1953, the input of manual hours rose from 2.94 billion to 3.23 billion (9.7 per cent), while the weighted index of output jumped to 191.5 (1953 = 100). In consequence, output per manual-worker hour advanced to 174.5 (1953 = 100), or at the extremely high compound annual rate of 8.3 per cent. Since gross hourly wage costs for manual labor were advancing at a compound annual rate of 4.6 per cent, gross profit margins were undoubtedly widening, and probably net margins as well.[16] In short, productivity gains from production workers were more than adequate to absorb higher costs of manual labor. However, as indicated earlier, since wholesale prices of manufactures remained virtually unchanged between 1953 and 1960, it follows that the net savings on the cost of production labor—part of which were carried down to final profits were not being shared with the rest of the economy —an outcome that has occasioned increased official concern in recent years.

The data for the seven groups separately are shown in Table 17. They indicate some altogether fantastic gains in the productivity of production workers, particularly in the extractive and metallurgical industries, although the advances were substantial enough throughout. Despite the shakiness of the precise results, there can be no doubt that here will be found the secret of the stability of the wholesale price index, and the solution to the puzzle of rapidly rising industrial output despite persistent mass unemployment throughout the fifties.[17]

TABLE 17. Comparative changes in manual hours worked, output, and output per manual hour for selected industry groups, 1953 and 1960 (1953 = 100)

Industry group	Hours worked	Output	Output per hour
Extractive	63.2	179.9	284.6
Textiles	93.3	126.7	135.8
Primary metals [a]	108.3	227.8	210.3
Metal products [b]	124.9	187.0	149.7
Building materials	113.2	206.8	182.7
Rubber	99.9	172.8	172.9
Chemicals	122.5	242.4	197.9

[a] Includes iron and steel, nonferrous metals.

[b] Includes resmelting, nonelectrical machines, electrical machines, and transportation equipment.

Source: See Notes 14 and 15 for Chapter III.

The growth of output in an economy is the consequence of three separable factors: increased productivity per man-hour; increased input of man-hours; and a redistribution of man-hour inputs from less productive to more productive uses, as among and within sectors of the system. Considering this group of seven leading industries, what were the comparative contributions of these three factors in effecting an increase in the joint output of the group? [18]

To answer this question at least in a preliminary way, given the frailties of the data, the comparative net products and inputs of man-hours of the industries can be related for 1953 and 1960. The independent effects of each of the three factors can then be measured, with the other two held constant.

For example, the gain in group net product assignable to higher man-hour productivity alone can be found by holding constant the (group) total input of man-hours and its interindustry distribution at 1953 levels. Multiplying the 1953 inputs by industry by the 1960 average net product per hour by industry will then yield the change in industry net product attributable to productivity change alone.[19] By adding these hypothetical industry figures, the over-all group increase via higher productivity alone will then be found. Next, to determine the separate effect of redistribution of man-hours within the group—the employment weight-shift—both productivity and total man-hour input for the group are held at 1953 levels; but the 1953 input total is redistributed among the industries according to its 1960 proportions. Multiplying industry net products per man-hour (1953) by hourly inputs adjusted for this weight-shift, and adding the industry totals, then reveals the change in group net product attributable to redistribution only. Finally, to isolate the pure effect of increased input of man-hours alone, industry productivity per hour is held at the 1953 level; the 1953 distribution proportions are retained, but applied to the group input for 1960, to obtain industry-by-industry adjusted inputs. The last are then multiplied by the 1953 industry productivity figures, yielding the change in group net product assignable to change in group hourly input alone.

This procedure for partialling out the separate effects of the three factors shows that the joint increase in group net product assignable to all of them together was 1,368 billion lire, 1960 compared with 1953.[20] Of this gain, 83.5 per cent derived from increased productivity; 12.9 per cent arose from larger input of man-hours; and only 3.6 per cent was assignable to redistribution of man-hour inputs by industry.

All this is another way of saying that the enormous growth of output within this technically advanced sector—at a compound annual rate of 9.7 per cent during 1953–1960—was achieved by extreme emphasis upon labor-saving methods (through new investment and plant reorganization).[21] Since the estimated compound annual rate of increase in manual-worker output per man-hour stood at 8.3 per cent, the sector did comparatively little to enlarge the number of its employees and so to relieve massive unemployment. It was investing in output-increasing—not employment-creating—methods. A similar pattern was developing in agriculture as well, which enlarged its output while actually decreasing its labor force substantially.

The relevant figures are far from adequate, but they are sufficient to indicate what was happening to employment in the economy during the boom. Between 1951 and 1961, the total labor force was growing by about 150,000 a year, net of workers temporarily employed abroad. Registered unemployment (formerly employed plus new entrants seeking first jobs) fell by 343,000 persons from the level of November 1951, and the total drop occurred after 1959. Total employment rose by roughly 1.9 million. Since doors to jobs in the advanced sector were almost completely closed until 1960, while agriculture was contracting throughout the period, it follows that emerging employment opportunities were concentrated in trade and services, government, artisan industry, and small-scale manufacturing, and the labor force was redistributing itself accordingly. In general, these are sectors of low productivity and low returns to labor, where the rate of advance in productivity is comparatively slow. The reasons for this particular pattern of change in employment are examined more fully in Chapter XIV.

THE EFFECTS OF INTERVENTION IN THE SOUTH UPON INTERREGIONAL IMBALANCE

The evolution of the policy of intervention. By the end of the Second World War, political conditions were ripe for a serious attack on economic problems endemic to the south since unification. The basic tasks were threefold: modernization of agriculture, development of self-sustaining industries, and encouragement of internal migration to the north.

The approach taken was piecemeal and pragmatic, rather than one of central planning, and as such was quite in keeping with the basic tenets of the De Gasperi–Einaudi experiment. Accordingly, the underlying theory heavily stressed the creation of external economies by the state, in hopes that this would release the energies requisite to material progress. In the words of an American expert, Hollis Chenery, "Few countries having active development policies place such heavy reliance on the market mechanism to bring about the changes in the economic structure that are needed to promote growth." [22] Only very recently has the emphasis begun to shift toward direct state investment in commodity production as an added device intended to bring about self-sustaining expansion.

Prior to the formation of the Cassa per il Mezzogiorno in August 1950, as a special government agency, intervention was limited to encouraging investment by private industry. The incentives provided included more liberal credit terms, tariff exemption for imports of machinery and raw materials, lower rates of business taxation, and reduced railway freight rates. On the credit side, the southern banks were offered treasury guarantees of 70 per cent against loss on industrial loans carrying a ten-year term at 4 per cent.[23] Through these measures, southern industry gained a differential advantage over its counterpart in the rest of the country, although this merely reduced the former's real handicap.

On August 10, 1950, parliament enacted the *Cassa* legislation.[24] The date is significant because by that time economic recovery had proceeded far enough to permit practical action in the development field, action that international agencies had been prodding the Italians to undertake since 1948, perhaps prematurely and not always on well-considered grounds.

The declared purpose of the *Cassa* statute was a large-scale, coordinated, and "extraordinary" program of intervention. Its initial scope embraced land reform and reclamation, and provision of infrastructure (social overhead capital) preliminary to industrialization, to permit local industries to emerge or to develop—as part of a general plan to be executed by this agency. The *Cassa* was to follow these priorities: agriculture, transport and communications, aqueducts and sewerage, and tourist facilities. Nothing was then stipulated regarding direct development of commodity production. Geographically, the *Cassa's* activities were designated to include the seven regions of the south and the islands, together with certain depressed provinces in the regions of Lazio, Marche, and Tuscany. The initial appropriation, to be spent during 1951–1960, was one trillion lire ($1.6 billion). In 1952 this figure was increased to 1.28 trillion lire. In 1957 it was raised again, to 2.053 trillion, and the life of the agency was extended to 1966. Then in 1959 the appropriation was enlarged to 2.078 trillion lire ($3.325 billion).[25]

The next step in the evolution of policy came with the Vanoni Plan, submitted to the OEEC in early 1955, which, although a national framework scheme, incorporated the activities of the *Cassa*.[26] However, the latter retained its administrative autonomy. This plan, while still officially on the books, has never become operative, although some of its ruling objectives for 1964 have already been attained through the sheer force and magnitude of the boom. Nonetheless, the scheme ought to be made part of the record because it exemplifies once again the policy of fostering development mainly through market forces.

As projected for 1955–1964, the plan had three controlling objectives, deemed attainable if its econometric projections regarding tax, import, and savings propensities, and income growth were fulfilled. In fact these projections were not borne out, but some of the main goals were realized anyway. One was the creation of four million new jobs, to absorb the exodus from agriculture and those displaced by new industrial technology, and to reduce the number of unemployed to five per cent of the labor force. A second was to eliminate the deficit in the current foreign account, through an increase of 60 per cent in exports and not over 43 per cent for imports, relative to 1954. And the third goal is of particular relevance to the present context: to reduce the imbalance between north and south, specifically by bringing per capita incomes in the latter region to an interim level of 75 per cent of the northern one by the end of the plan's term of life.

For its effectuation, the scheme was predicted upon certain assumptions. One was that labor productivity would rise at least 3 per cent per annum; and another that wage policy would be one of restraint, to permit a stable price level. It was also presupposed that gross saving and investment would shift upward over the decade from 19 to 25 per cent of GNP, and that GNP would rise at an annual rate of 5 per cent. Investment in "propulsive sectors" (building, public utilities, public works) was to be the main mechanism for promoting and sustaining the desired growth rate. As for reduction of the north-south disequilibrium, the plan relied upon a growth rate of per capita income in the south that would be higher than in the north, which was to be the intended "multiplier effect" of investing the larger proportion of propulsive investments in that region. Of the south's quota, the *Cassa* was to be the main channel of investment, supplemented—as matters developed—by increased "ordinary" expenditures of the regular branches of government.

As the *Cassa's* total long-term spending plan expanded during 1950–1959, the pattern of expenditure shifted. Initially, the entire sum was to be allocated as follows: agriculture, 77 per cent; adueducts and sewerage, 11 per cent; transport and communications, 9 per cent; and tourism, 3 per cent. By 1959, those proportions have become 55.3, 15.0, 12.6, and 2.7 per cent respectively of the enlarged cumulative appropriation. Moreover, some new categories were added: industry, 11.8 per cent; education and vocational training, 2.2 per cent; artisan trades, 0.2 per cent; and fisheries, 0.2 per cent. Within these years, changes also occurred in the functional nature of these expenditures. In 1950, 89 per cent of the total was applied to infrastructure—roads, railways, ferries, aqueducts, sewerage, water storage and irrigation, land reform, and tourist facilities—while 11 per cent was assigned to subsidies to aid private initiative—all for improvements to farm lands. By 1959, outlays for infrastructure were to absorb 75.4 per cent of the total, while subsidies and other incentives now accounted for 22.4 per cent, and special expenditures for education (2.2 per cent) had been added.[27]

The last step before looking at some results of intervention is to examine the actual expenditures on behalf of the south.

The first fact that strikes the eye is the very high rate of support supplied to the south by the rest of the economy. In 1960, net regional income produced was 3533 billion lire, which was supplemented by 899 billion of net transfers from external sources—a support rate of 25.4 per cent provided by the rest of the country, and indicative of the burden levied by the southern program.[28]

Over the ten fiscal years from 1950–1951 through 1959–1960, the Italian government spent 3756.3 billion lire ($6.01 billion) on the south. Of this large sum, the *Cassa* accounted for 1496.8 billion, or 39.8 per cent, which was allocated to its "extraordinary" program. The remainder—60.2 per cent—derived from the "ordinary" activities of government, of which the share devoted to the south averaged 39.6 per cent of all such expenditures, lining up very closely with its share of the total population. Table 18 shows the course of both main categories of public spending for the south over the whole period.

TABLE 18. Government spending on the south, by main categories, 1950–1951, 1959–1960 (in millions of lire)

Fiscal year	Cassa	Ordinary	Total
1950–1951	4,000	174,958	178,958
1951–1952	50,300	164,495	214,795
1952–1953	116,900	212,828	329,728
1953–1954	157,100	203,971	361,071
1954–1955	181,700	192,383	374,083
1955–1956	197,400	220,686	418,086
1956–1957	173,800	202,371	376,171
1957–1958	154,500	277,674	432,174
1958–1959	221,400	253,272	474,672
1959–1960	239,700	356,860	596,560
Total	1,496,800	2,259,498	3,756,298

Source: La relazione al parlamento del presidente del comitato dei ministri per il Mezzogiorno (1961), as republished in Mondo economico, supp., XVI:20 (May 20, 1961), pp. XIX, XX.

It will be noted from these figures that the Cassa outlays did not reach a significant level until 1952–1953, and that they approximately doubled between this date and the last fiscal year in the series. Because of the routine character of the ordinary outlays, these began at a high level, although they more than doubled over the whole period. Noteworthy also, these expenditures maintained a quite stable proportion of the national total, about equal to the south's share of total population. Although the complaint has been voiced by partisans of the south that the government was substituting Cassa for routine spending, hence failing to allot the region its "fair share," these figures afford no support for the claim.

What about the south's share of gross domestic investment? In 1955 (prices of 1954), it accounted for 741.9 billion lire of a national total of 2895 billion, or 25.6 per cent. By 1960, these outlays in the south had risen to 1078.9 billion, or by 45.4 per cent. But because real investment in the rest of the country advanced 56.1 per cent over its 1955 level of 2153.1 billion, the south's share in 1960 actually fell to 24.3 per cent.[29]

Since the region had 37.8 per cent of total resident population in 1955 and 38.2 per cent in 1960, clearly it was lagging behind in attracting those additions to physical capital that play so prominent a role in effecting modernization of production techniques. Indeed, this fact lends strong support to the contention that private industry was reluctant to commit long-term outlays in the region. In turn, this finding has led to two far more controversial proposals for southern development policy: that industrialization of the south should be deliberately accelerated at the expense of the north, and that the only way to do this is for the state to set up government-operated plants, shifting away from the earlier emphasis upon investments in infrastructure to provide external economies for spurring indigenous growth through private initiative. An initial move in this direction was taken in 1957, under a new law requiring state firms in the IRI-ENI group to commit 60 per cent of their investments in new plants, and 40 per cent of all their investments, within the region.[30]

Some results. The simplest and most telling measure of the effects of these programs is to compare movements in total and per capita income in the south with those for the rest of Italy. These figures will not measure relative resource availabilities because they are net of fiscal transfers in favor of the south. Hence they emphasize the comparative ability of the south to produce income. The data appear in Table 19.

During 1951–1960, the income of the south at market prices rose 80.4 per cent, as against 98.7 per cent in the rest of the country. Per head of resident population, income in the south advanced 66 per cent, as against 89.1 per cent elsewhere. Expressed as exponential rates derived by linear regression, total income in the south increased 7.0 per cent yearly, and 6.0 per cent head. In the rest of Italy, the comparative figures are 7.9 and 7.4 per cent.[31] Although annual data were not available for the northern triangle alone, undoubtedly its rates were even higher than for the rest of the country as a whole, since the latter includes the less productive regions of central and northeast Italy.

TABLE 19. Comparative movements in total and per capita income, south and rest of Italy, 1951–1960 ᵃ (in current lire)

	Total income		Per capita income	
	south	rest	south	rest
Year	(billion lire)		(thousand lire)	
1951	1,958	6,878	110.9	230.1
1952	2,016	7,287	113.2	243.1
1953	2,356	7,837	131.0	260.3
1954	2,459	8,389	135.1	277.4
1955	2,593	9,278	141.0	305.9
1956	2,827	9,952	152.2	327.3
1957	3,077	10,651	164.3	349.4
1958	3,221	11,497	170.9	374.6
1959	3,347	12,430	175.6	403.1
1960	3,533	13,664	184.1	435.1

ᵃ Regional income consists of the sum of the net products of all sectors, including government, less an unspecified adjustment to private net product, less net income from external sources (negative for the south), plus indirect taxes. This conforms to the Italian definition of national income at market prices. Income for the rest of the country was obtained by deducting the southern totals from those for national income as a whole.

Source: Income and resident population for the south from *La relazione al parlamento del presidente del comitato dei ministri per il Mezzogiorno*, 1961, p. XV; national income and total resident population from *Relazione generale*, 1961, II, pp. 347, 349.

Clearly the hoped-for reduction of the south's income gap had not been attained by 1960. On the contrary, it widened further, from 48.2 per cent of the level in the rest of the nation in 1951 to 42.3 per cent in 1960. This single fact does not mean that intervention has been a failure, since southern per capita income did rise substantially in absolute terms, and the gap might have grown even larger without these policies. Moreover, it can be argued that the full effects of the program have not yet been felt. In this respect, there are preliminary indications that during 1961-1962 income per head in the south has suddenly begun to grow at a faster rate relative to the rest of Italy. In any case, the widening of the gap during 1951–1960 despite government outlays exceeding $6 billion accounts for the recent outbreak of caustic attacks on the program—from those who would expand it further, coupling it to over-all central planning and state control of commodity production; and those who would rely more heavily upon increased emigration to the north, concentrate efforts in agriculture and food-processing in the south, and reject attempts at full-scale industrialization as lacking economic justification.[32]

Additional evidence indicates that changes in the structure of economic activity in the south between 1951 and 1960 have indeed occurred, but not yet sufficiently to alter the traditional character of the region. Between the two dates, the share of agriculture in unadjusted total private net product of the south fell from 45.3 to 31.7 per cent, while that of industry rose slightly—from 28.3 to 32.0 per cent. However, in the rest of the country, agriculture's share fell from 24.9 to 16.6 per cent, while that of industry rose from 48.9 to 50.6 per cent.[33] Thus, although the dependence of the south upon agriculture was declining at the same time that the net product of this sector was increasing 22.6 per cent (current prices), farming continued to occupy a much more dominant place than in the rest of the economy, while industry remained in a reverse position. However, the net output of southern industry did increase by 97.8 per cent.

The disappointing widening of the relative income disadvantage of the south after 1951 was fully matched by the quite unimpressive growth of industrial employment in the region—all the more so when it is recalled that expansion of industry has been a major objective of policy since the first stage of intervention, beginning in 1947.

Comparison of the Census of Industry and Trade (ISTAT) for October 1961 with that for 1951 permits firm inferences regarding changes in interregional patterns of industrial employment.[34] It shows conclusively that the north increased even further its long prevailing dominance in industry, both absolutely and relatively. In 1951 it accounted for 67.3 per cent of all persons attached to extractive industry, manufacturing, construction, and public utilities, which together had 4,241,901 persons in the country as a whole. During the ensuing decade, industrial employment in the nation increased by 1,380,619 persons, or by 32.5 per cent. Three quarters of this increase, or 1,025,518 persons, found industrial employment in the north, which gained 35.9 per cent, enlarging its relative position to 69.0 per cent of all industrial employment by 1961.

During the same years, industrial employment in the south expanded by only 117,556 persons, increasing by only 16.0 per cent, or at less than one-half the relative rate of the north. Worse yet, the relative share of the south in total industrial employment actually fell—from 17.3 per cent (733,709 persons) in 1951 to 15.1 per cent (851,265 persons) in 1961, despite ten years of unprecedented boom and a very costly program of public investment in the region. Bear in mind, too, that its 15.1 per cent share of industrial employment compares with its 38 per cent portion of total population, indicating the south's very weak position as a center for industry.

For manufacturing alone, the story was essentially the same. Over the decade, the north increased its employment in this category by 740,601 persons, and the south by only 64,969 persons. In relative terms, the north expanded by 30.1 per cent, and the south by only 11.7 per cent. In 1951, the north claimed 2,463,725 persons in manufacturing—70.4 per cent of the total, while the south had only 552,930, or 15.8 per cent. Because the north accounted for three quarters of the absolute national increase, by 1961 it had raised its share to 71.3 per cent (3,204,326 persons). By contrast, the share of the south fell to 13.7 per cent, or 617,899 persons. Also worth noting, in 1961 the south had only 3.40 persons attached per local manufacturing establishment, as against 10.32 persons in the north—crude but persuasive evidence regarding the predominance of small-scale operations in the region.[35]

In view of the evidence regarding interregional comparisons of changes in employment and per capita income, one may conclude that intervention at a rapidly increasing pace from 1947 through 1961 yielded quite disappointing results. To be sure, the welfare of the inhabitants of the south increased with the improvement of its absolute position, but in relative terms they fell even further behind, exhibiting in minuscule the experience of the have-not countries in the world as a whole. Through 1961, at least, the ambitious attempt to bend the forces of the market toward modernization and above all toward development of the industrial sector did little more than initiate an economic transformation that has yet to enter the decisive stage.

Probably the simplest explanation is still the best: the south has yet to become a hospitable environment for industrial activity. Its markets are too small, its location is too remote, and its labor supply of too low quality to attract efficient and self-expanding plants.

Belated recognition of the very real difficulty of recasting the economic structure of the south doubtless accounts for the recent shift of emphasis from closing the income gap to the more modest goals of promoting self-sustaining regional growth, and of concentrating upon selected geographic "poles of development" where introduction of industrial complexes such as in steel and petrochemicals (Bari, Gela) supposedly will effect the desired breakthrough into the modern industrial age.

Perhaps they will. However, it seems more likely that economic transformation will receive its greatest impetus from the modernization of agriculture, particularly by reduction of the man-land ratio, a process that has great promise now that southerners at last are legally free to migrate north. In any case, intervention so far has failed to achieve most of its original declared purposes.

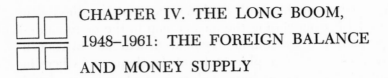

CHAPTER IV. THE LONG BOOM, 1948–1961: THE FOREIGN BALANCE AND MONEY SUPPLY

The current and capital accounts. A central objective of the De Gasperi-Einaudi program was to put the current balance of payments in order, which was essential to stabilizing the external value of the lira, to making it convertible, and to liberalizing Italy's foreign trade. Without detracting in any way from the astonishing rise in production, the most brilliant accomplishment of postwar policy is recorded in the changed status of Italy's international economic standing after 1947. The over-all data are presented in Table 20.

During the highly inflationary year of 1947, the deficit on goods and services account reached the dangerous level of $773.2 million, while the deficit in commodity trade alone stood at $634.7 million. The situation was temporarily saved by $416.6 millon of inflowing unilateral transfers (of which $351.7 million was official United States aid), plus $356.6 million inflow of private and official credits. At this point in the nation's fortunes, its credit abroad was approaching exhaustion, its gold reserve was close to the vanishing point, and its prospects for continued foreign aid were uncertain.

Nonetheless, over the next three years the deficits in both the commodity and goods and services accounts were sharply reduced, and, despite a decline in official grants in aid, the current account was converted to a substantial surplus.[1] Underlying this impressive recovery lay an 84.6 per cent jump (1950 compared with 1947) in export earnings from commodity trade (as against only a 4.3 per cent rise in commodity imports), a revival of tourism, and a substantial advance in emigrants' remittances.[2] Beyond any doubt, currency stabilization played a major role in these events.

During 1951–1952, the position of the current account again worsened, reflecting Italy's vulnerability to swings in the world

TABLE 20. Movements in principal components of balance of international payments, 1947–1961 ª (in millions of U.S. dollars)

Year	Current account				Capital account	
	Net balance on commodity trade	Net balance on goods and services	Net official and private transfers	Net balance on current account	Net balance on capital account	Errors and omissions
1947	−634.7	−773.2	416.6	−356.6	343.1	13.5
1948	−323.5	−344.1	417.0	72.9	−69.7	−3.2
1949	−245.8	−253.1	407.3	154.2	−184.3	30.1
1950	−120.6	−83.7	306.3	222.6	−39.0	−183.6
1951	−286.9	−280.5	322.6	42.1	−70.2	28.1
1952	−735.5	−638.5	298.6	−339.9	310.8	29.1
1953	−713.2	−459.5	268.9	−190.6	176.9	13.7
1954	−649.7	−240.3	166.4	−73.9	96.3	−22.4
1955	−672.1	−209.6	135.4	−74.2	95.4	−21.2
1956	−731.8	−271.3	176.6	−94.7	137.0	−42.3
1957	−766.1	−169.4	202.8	33.4	−39.8	6.4
1958	628.2	297.6	266.6	564.2	−601.2	37.0
1959	−133.0	560.1	194.9	755.0	−555.7	−199.3
1960	−633.8	98.5	218.5	317.0	−90.8	−226.2
1961	−555.9	236.4	272.1	508.5	−45.3	−463.2

ª Commodity trade is f.o.b. Net goods and services includes nonmonetary gold; freight and insurance; tourism; investment income; receipts from infrastructure and offshore purchases, supply of foreign troops; payments for infrastructure; workers' earnings abroad. Net official and private transfers include: (private) emigrants' remittances, grants in kind distributed by ENDSI; (public) credits and debits under intergovernmental aid programs and international agencies, reparations, and contributions to Somaliland. For capital account, negative sign denotes net increase in assets (claims) or decrease in liabilities of Italy relative to rest of the world. Includes inflows of monetary gold. Positive sign denotes net decrease in assets or increase in liabilities relative to rest of the world, including outflows of monetary gold. Errors and omissions refer mainly to unrecorded private short-term capital movements.

Source: International Monetary Fund (IMF), Balance of Payments Yearbook (1947–1952), vol. 5; (1953), vol. 6; (1954), vol. 7; (1955–1956), vol. 12; (1957–1961), vol. 14.

economy, in this case invoked by the Korean War, which drove up import prices relative to those for exports, and seriously weakened the market for Italian exports.

However, the year 1952 proved to be a turning point. Thereafter, the deficit on goods and services account shrank steadily, turning positive after 1957, although (except for 1958–1959) the import surplus in commodity trade remained very large. Earnings of Italian workers abroad and income from tourism were the main reasons. At the same time, the current account also recorded remarkable improvement, returning net earnings in every year after 1956, despite the disappearance of net official foreign transfer contributions to Italy after 1954. Here the principal factor was a large rise in emigrants' remittances. Table 21 shows the role of these various components in the over-all improvement of the balance on current account.

Going back to Table 20, attention should be called now to the behavior of the capital account. Unfortunately, intervening changes in the IMF's grouping of the subaccounts in this category preclude a detailed analysis for the years before 1957. However, a general interpretation is still possible.

In the full sense, the capital account is analogous to the balance sheet of an enterprise, in that it is a comparative statement of the assets and liabilities of a country relative to the rest of the world, as they are affected by the foreign transactions of its private citizens and firms, its banks, and its own government in relation with others and with international agencies such as UN, IMF, OECD, and IBRD. As such, the true capital account embodies a stock concept, in that it records the country's foreign assets and liabilities as of a given date. By contrast, the current account portrays the comparative flows of international receipts (credits) and payments (debits) during the year. If it shows a deficit (debit balance), then, assuming no errors and omissions, the change in capital account for the year must show a credit balance, meaning that foreign assets must have decreased and/or foreign liabilities must have increased, since the current deficit has to be financed in one way or the other, or both.[3]

Owing to rapid inflation during most of the year, Italy in 1947 had a net deficit of $356.6 million on current account, meaning that its receipts from abroad from sale of exports, provision of services, receipt of transfers, and the like fell short of its payments to the world on such accounts. In consequence, her international transactions during that year effected a net increase in her external liabilities (credits extended by foreign governments, banks, and private firms), plus a net decrease in her claims against the world (holdings of foreign currency, bank deposits, securities, and so forth). Together, these changes totalled $343.1 million, to which must be added algebraically $13.5 million for errors and omissions reflecting unrecorded capital transactions.[4]

TABLE 21. Movements in some principal components of the balance of payments on current account, 1952–1961 [a] (in millions of U.S. dollars)

	Goods and services account		Unilateral transfers	
Year	Earnings of Italian workers abroad	Net earnings from tourism	Net official transfers	Net private transfers
1952	——	75.0	166.2	132.4
1953	——	130.7	102.1	166.8
1954	——	138.1	55.2	111.2
1955	45.0	190.1	−14.5	149.9
1956	79.3	215.2	−14.4	191.0
1957	116.1	322.7	−35.9	238.7
1958	136.6	411.3	−9.2	275.8
1959	146.1	448.1	−26.8	221.7
1960	171.7	548.1	−36.8	255.3
1961	214.8	647.4	−48.4	315.6

[a] For detailed explanatory notes regarding the transfer accounts, see the note to Table 20. Private transfers are mainly emigrants' remittances.
Source: (Workers' earnings), IMF, Balance of Payments Yearbook, vols. 12 and 14; (tourism), vols. 5, 6, 7, 12, and 14; (transfers), vols. 5, 6, 7, 12, and 14.

So interpreted, the capital account shown in the table is not a complete statement of Italy's foreign assets and liabilities, but a record of annual net changes in the balance between them. Without pressing the enterprise analogy too far, these annual net figures indicate changes in the "net worth" of Italy vis-à-vis the world. On this basis, a minus sign does not denote a "loss" or adverse result for the year. Quite the contrary. As a net debit balance it means an increase in "net worth," that is, a net improvement of the nation's international position deriving from algebraic combination of changes in its external assets and liabilities together.[5]

Turning now to the net capital account itself, the inflation of 1947 generated a large deficit on current account, forcing Italy to liquidate scarce foreign assets and to increase her external debt. Over the next four years, stabilization policy and European recovery together enabled her to reverse the process—a substantial net excess developed in receipts on current account, which built up foreign assets while reducing foreign liabilities. One indication of this dramatic improvement is that during 1948–1951 Italy acquired a net inflow of monetary gold of $263.2 million. During 1952–1956, her position as a creditor and debtor abroad worsened once more, reflecting the reappearance of a net excess of international payments over receipts on current account. This was financed by drawing down foreign assets and expanding external debt. (No monetary gold was exported.) As the reverse side of the medal, it shows up in a return to positive (credit) balances in the net capital account, and in the latter as combined with unrecorded transactions.

During 1957–1961, a strong improvement in the current account effected a corresponding gain on the capital side. Thus the capital account shows a net debit balance in each of these figures. Behind these summary figures lay some interesting developments. First, the inflow of long-term capital (mostly private) from abroad began to become a torrent, jumping from $106.4 million net in 1957 to $511.5 million in 1961 as the confidence of outside investors grew. For the five years together, net investment from abroad aggregated $1378.4 million.

Second, holdings of monetary gold, foreign currencies, and other international balances swelled by $2853.4 million net.[6] Despite the increase in foreign obligations implied by the substantial rise in net credits for foreign investment within Italy, it was easily exceeded by the rise in the country's foreign monetary assets. The lira could now stand on its own feet, without the aid of the crutches that are the manifest signs of an overvalued exchange rate—propping operations on the exchange market, emergency foreign credits, rationing of foreign currency, import restrictions, and the like.

These, not deficits or surpluses in the various foreign accounts, are the stigmata of basic disequilibrium in a nation's balance of payments, reflecting as they do pressure on the exchanges against the external value of its currency. Between 1957–1961, if not earlier, the disequilibrium has been of opposite sign. The international demand for the lira at the official rate steadily exceeded supply. The gap was covered by a rise in Italy's net liquid foreign assets—so much so that these were fed into a rapid expansion of the money supply, one that by 1962 was clearly inflationary.

The astronomical dimensions of this strengthening in the international standing of the lira are well illustrated by the astonishing increase in the foreign monetary assets of the Bank of Italy since the end of December 1947. At that time, the Bank's publicly acknowledged holdings of gold and foreign currencies stood at 15.112 billion lire—the equivalent of roughly $26 million at the exchange rate then in effect. On December 31, 1961, these holdings had soared almost by light-years, to 2.873 trillion lire—$4.597 billion at the current rate of exchange.[7] This figure does not include all foreign monetary assets of Italy, nor is it net of her external monetary liabilities. But it does reveal in capsule form the vast improvement wrought in her international economic position by the fourteen-year boom.

The increasing external dependence of the economy. It would be easy to be carried away by the optimistic implications of this increase in international liquidity. As Professor di Fenizio says, the Italian economy is "open and vulnerable" to shocks from the outside world. Indeed it is—more so than most countries, as the following evidence will show.

Consider, first, the importance of sales abroad as a component in the total demand for gross national product, hence as a factor directly influencing the level of domestic output and employment. External demand is measured by total credits earned on goods and services account. In 1961, Italy acquired 81.1 per cent of these credits from exports of goods and services as such, 12.1 per cent from tourism, and 3.4 per cent via the wages of Italian workers temporarily employed abroad.[8] In total, earnings on all categories were 18.5 per cent of total demand for GNP. This compares with 25.5 per cent assignable to claims of home investment on GNP. Obviously, then, foreign demand for total product is strategically important for current and continued growth.

Probing a bit further, 31.9 per cent of total commodity exports ($4108.3 million in 1961) went to the other five of the six members of the Common Market; while all western Europe, its associated areas, and these five together accounted for 60 per cent. The United States and Canada took 10.5 per cent, and Latin America 7.3 per cent. Clearly, the demand for Italian commodity exports depends very heavily upon western Europe, where it is almost evenly divided between the Common Market countries and the rest of the nations of that region. Thus the continued prosperity of Italy is bound closely to the economic destinies of this latter group of powers.

TABLE 22. Italian commodity exports and imports by main category, 1961 ª (in millions of lire)

Category	Exports	Imports
Food and live animals	321,524	451,096
Beverages and tobacco	37,262	13,961
Crude materials, inedible, except fuels	95,098	12,193
Mineral fuels, lubricants, and related	137,949	415,339
Animal and vegetable oils and fats	5,269	82,583
Total, raw materials	238,316	1,310,115
Chemicals	164,303	214,583
Manufactured goods classed by material	577,611	479,597
Machinery and transport equipment	652,274	395,641
Miscellaneous manufactured articles	281,555	78,269
Total, manufactures	1,675,743	1,168,040
Commodities and transactions, n.e.s.	8,198	2,926
Grand total	2,281,192	2,946,189

ª Refers to special exports, f.o.b., and special imports, c.i.f. Manufactured goods classed by material includes rubber products, textiles, iron and steel, and nonferrous metals. Miscellaneous manufactured articles include clothing, footwear, scientific instruments, printed matter, and jewelry.

Source: United Nations, Department of Economic and Social Affairs, Yearbook of International Trade Statistics, 1961 (United Nations: New York, 1961), pp. 354–359.

The structure of Italian commodity exports, shown in Table 22, is also worth noting. This trade is dominated by exports of manufactures, which by themselves yielded a surplus of $812 million, helping to offset a deficit of $1922 million occasioned by import surpluses of food and raw materials. Within manufactures, nonelectric machinery (302,113 million lire), textiles (276,585 million), transport equipment (271,646 million), chemicals (164, 303 million), iron and steel (124,603 million), and clothing (101, 802 million) held the dominant positions. Of the total exports of commodities, 73.5 per cent were manufactures, 14.1 per cent food, and 10.4 per cent raw materials.

Between 1951 and 1961, total commodity exports (special trade, f.o.b.) rose 124.1 per cent (current prices), while manufactures raised their relative share from 69.7 to 73.5 per cent. Within manufacturing, the largest increases in export sales over 1951 were achieved by iron and steel (623.4 per cent), transport equipment (441.1 per cent), clothing (405.3 per cent), nonelectric machines (200.9 per cent), and chemicals (195.2 per cent). Textiles—traditionally a leading export—dropped 16.4 per cent.[9]

A second way to look at a nation's dependence upon external trade is to relate its imports (debits) on goods and services account to its GNP. Here the prime concern is the comparative importance of foreign supplies for total output, recognizing that the latter depends upon the availability of both domestic and foreign resources, and that recourse to external resources derives mainly from the fact that there is a comparative advantage in drawing upon them as against reliance upon domestic substitutes.

In this respect, total debits on Italy's goods and services account in 1961 ($6.0 billion) represented 17.9 per cent of domestic GNP. Of this total, 94.7 per cent was expended on imports of goods and services proper, while the small remainder arose from tourist outlays by Italians abroad, income returned by Italy on foreign-owned investments, and payments for services provided by other governments.

On the side of commodity imports alone ($4.7 billion in 1961), 30.9 per cent came from the Common Market group, while western Europe as a whole supplied 52.2 per cent. Of this region's share, the former group accounted for just under 60 per cent, from which Italy was a net importer.[10]

The structure of Italian commodity imports in 1961, shown in Table 22, plainly reflects the country's comparatively poor endowment of natural resources. As a world trader, Italy makes her way, and has for many years, as a processor and fabricator of imported raw materials, as a supplier of labor, and as a provider of tourist attractions. Of her total merchandise imports in 1961, 44.5 per cent consisted of raw materials, and food 15.3 per cent. However, there had been a considerable improvement over 1951, when raw materials accounted for 58.0 per cent, and food 17.9 per cent.

For 1961, the leading commodity imports within both groups were crude and partly refined petroleum (316,617 million lire), textile fibers and waste (272,677 million), and cereals and preparations (199,263 million).[11]

How important was the Common Market to the expansion of Italian commodity trade? Taking the year the organization was formed—1958—as a base, Italy's total merchandise exports rose 62.5 per cent, and her total imports 62.4 per cent. In the same period, her exports to the rest of the Six jumped 115.9 per cent, and her imports from them 108.1 per cent. Looked at in another way, these imports accounted for 21.3 per cent of the 1958 total, and 27.2 per cent of that for 1961, while exports to the Common Market in 1958 were 23.6 per cent of the total, as against 31.4 per cent in 1961. Beyond question, the Common Market group was substantially increasing its share of this branch of Italian trade, in both directions. Whether these shifts can be attributed to the special arrangements devised by the Six is a more subtle question that cannot be explored here. However, it can be said that, comparing 1950 with 1958, when total imports and exports were rising 123.9 and 115.8 per cent respectively, imports and exports involving the Common Market group alone were advancing 173.8 and 124.7 per cent respectively. Apparently the shift in Italian merchandise trade toward the rest of the Six since 1958 at least partly reflects trends of longer duration than any called forth by the Common Market itself.[12]

Considering the two types of external dependence noted earlier —exports of goods and services as a component of GNP demand, and imports in both forms as a partial source of GNP supply—has either undergone significant change since 1948?

In both respects, the answers must be strongly affirmative, as Table 23 shows. Over the fourteen years of the long boom, Italy's internal demand for labor and other resources used for production has become more sensitive than ever to business conditions in western Europe, the United States, and Canada. Thus between 1948 and 1961 foreign demand for Italian GNP jumped from 10.4 to 18.4 per cent. Particularly significant, as expansion picked up speed during 1960–1961, external claims on GNP rose very strongly, undoubtedly stimulating the rate of advance itself.

This strong upward trend in the relative importance of foreign demand should not be viewed as an adverse development, granting that it does mean that Italy must sink or swim along with her major trading partners. It is simple but dramatic proof of her increasing international competitiveness, and a direct reflection of the many benefits to be had from her enlarging participation in the world division of labor. Without this boom in exports, the rate of advance in real GNP would have been much lower.

TABLE 23. Imports and exports of goods and services in relation to domestic GNP, 1948–1961 [a] (in billion lire, current)

Year	GNP	Exports of goods and services	Imports of goods and services	Relative to GNP	
				Exports	Imports
1948	7,068	737	946	10.4%	13.4%
1949	7,634	805	975	10.5	12.8
1950	8,540	963	1,033	11.3	12.1
1951	9,853	1,279	1,437	13.0	14.6
1952	10,367	1,160	1,569	11.2	15.1
1953	11,308	1,337	1,677	11.8	14.8
1954	12,027	1,433	1,678	11.9	14.0
1955	13,163	1,620	1,853	12.3	14.1
1956	14,190	1,923	2,173	13.6	15.3
1957	15,266	2,373	2,560	15.5	16.8
1958	16,318	2,467	2,338	15.1	14.3
1959	17,477	2,755	2,451	15.8	14.0
1960	19,078	3,357	3,351	17.6	17.6
1961	21,083	3,871	3,760	18.4	17.8

[a] The official Italian trade figures have been used here for comparability with GNP data. They include: goods and services, wages earned by Italians abroad, investment returns, and tourism.

The GNP data do not accord with those in Table 13, because they were computed from global series, while those in Table 13 were built up from detailed figures on consumption and investment. At the time this study went to press, the revised detailed figures were not available.

Source: (1948–1949) Indagine statistica, pp. 261, 265, and 269; (1950–1961) Relazione generale, 1963, II, p. 381.

The story on the import side is essentially the same. Imports of goods and services accounted for 18.4 per cent of GNP in 1961, rising from 13.2 per cent in 1948. Again the increase in external dependence has been spectacular for the very buoyant years of 1960–1961.

And here, too, the change is favorable. A country cannot have the full benefits to be derived from the principle of comparative advantage if it is unwilling to increase its dependence upon the rest of the world. Enlarged reliance upon imports of food and raw materials simply means that these goods can be had from abroad more cheaply than from domestic production. In turn, this permits greater concentration of scarce real resources upon activities and lines of output from which returns are larger than if they were applied to turn out substitutes for these imports. In consequence of an increasing propensity to import, Italy's real gross output has been able to climb much faster than would have been at all possible if she had resorted after 1947 to an attempt to return to the delusions of autarchy of the Mussolini period.

The Einaudi program of 1947 to make the lira freely convertible and to open up international trade—under a parallel regimen of stable prices—was a case of building better than even its projector knew. It worked, and worked brilliantly. Undoubtedly it could do so because of the very strength of the resurgence of western Europe itself. Put a little differently, the Italian policy toward currency and international trade meshed perfectly with the emergence of a mass market and a much better integrated division of labor on the continent—a development from which all partners together have drawn enormous benefits. By deliberately keeping their sights on these objectives for some fourteen years, the Italians followed the soundest possible course for their developing economy. One can hope only that they, and their fellow peoples, will have the wisdom and the forbearance to continue in this fruitful direction, a course that unfortunately is by no means assured.

MONETARY AND FISCAL OPERATIONS

The money supply. Except for the brief period of 1951–1952, Italy followed an easy money policy throughout the long boom. This was a deliberate choice, made possible by the rapid and sustained improvement of the foreign exchange reserve which began immediately upon stabilization in late 1947—a consequence that was both foreseen and intended.

At that time, the authorities reasoned that since a return to autarchy was out of the question and therefore the economy would continue to be heavily dependent upon foreign trade, the first order of business was to rebuild the exchange reserve, so that a cushion could be had against shocks coming from abroad. On the one hand, they wanted Italy to share in the undeniable benefits of an increased international division of labor. On the other, they were fully aware that added vulnerability to external disturbances was the necessary price of those benefits.

If a temporary drop in export demand were to occur, measures could be taken to protect domestic demand and employment, without having to reduce badly needed imports—provided that the exchange reserve had a comfortable margin. Alternatively, if import prices were to rise, the reserve ought to be sufficient to finance this increase, so that reduction in import volume and home production could be checked. Barring protracted disturbances from abroad, then, the monetary managers would not be hampered by an inadequate supply of foreign currency and gold. In consequence, their policy could be shaped to serve several collateral purposes at the same time. It would be possible to keep the external value of the lira stable, to advance toward full convertibility, and to dismantle the whole long-standing apparatus of obstructions to free international trade. On the domestic side, the authorities then would be able to provide the necessary increases in credit required to finance a continued rapid expansion in output, to modernize and rebuild industry, and to carry out the various programs of public investment and development that began to emerge during 1949–1950.

Unquestionably, the decision in 1947 to put the rebuilding of the exchange reserve first was sound, and as matters worked out, it was a success even by 1950. In consequence, the field of maneuver for monetary and fiscal management began to widen even by 1948–1949, attaining comfortable dimensions by 1952. Following the British devaluation in September 1949, the lira was pegged at 625 to the dollar, a rate that has been maintained ever since. During 1950–1951, a series of measures were adopted to reduce import controls and duties. Also, the southern development program began to get underway in 1951. Finally, it proved possible to ride out the Korean War without a significant decline in production. Thereafter buoyant expansion continued through 1961, while the exchange reserve built up rapidly.

The monetary side of this lengthy upsurge after 1947 is summarized in Table 24. Over the whole period, the stock of money in circulation swelled by the astronomical magnitude of 6.86 trillion lire, or by 363.3 per cent. Expressed as an exponential trend derived by simple linear regression, the annual rate of advance was 11.6 per cent—a surprisingly high figure in view of the quite moderate rate of increase in the price level (2.2 per cent yearly for the implicit GNP deflator).[13]

TABLE 24. Changes in money supply, its composition, and its relationship to current GNP, 1948–1961 [a] (in billions of lire)

Year	Money supply		Ratios	
	Total	Changes in total	Money to GNP	Deposits to total money
1948	1888	442	26.4%	40.6%
1949	2262	374	29.3	47.2
1950	2511	249	29.4	47.4
1951	2943	432	29.9	50.4
1952	3416	473	32.9	53.9
1953	3834	418	33.9	56.6
1954	4138	304	34.4	57.6
1955	4604	466	35.0	58.8
1956	5038	434	35.5	59.0
1957	5342	304	35.0	59.6
1958	5911	569	36.6	60.6
1959	6641	730	38.0	61.8
1960	7518	877	39.4	63.4
1961	8748	1230	41.7	63.4

[a] Figures are for December 31 of each year. Money supply includes state coins and notes, Bank of Italy notes, AMG lire (retired in 1950), circular checks, current deposits in banks and postal savings system. After 1950, figures are net of vault cash in Bank of Italy. Vault cash of other banks included throughout.

Source: (1948–1949) Banca d'Italia, Adunanza generale, 1949 (Rome: Tipografia Banca d'Italia, 1950); circular checks for 1950–1953 from Banco di Roma, Review of the Economic Conditions in Italy, various issues; (1950–1961) all data other than circular checks for 1950–1953 from Relazione generale, various issues.

There were three reasons for the ability of the system to absorb this vast increase in money in circulation without exploding into open inflation. One was the sheer productive potential of the economy. Another was the rapid and remarkable steady growth of real output, which, reflecting that potential, rose on trend by 5.9 per cent annually. And the third was the desire of the public to build up its cash balance, indicated by the sharp advance in the ratio of the stock of money relative to current GNP—which jumped from 26.4 per cent in 1948 to 41.7 per cent in 1961. This increase in the primary liquidity of the public suggests an early and lasting confidence in the stability of prices.

The rise in the demand for money for purposes of liquidity as distinguished from transactions thus weakened any causal connection between changes in total money and in the level of prices, and between changes in total money and in real or current gross product. As pointed out earlier, the rise in the price level largely reflected "administered" price- and wage-making, decontrol or relaxation of rents and utility rates, support operations for grains, the combined squeeze exerted by statutory and negotiated increases in labor costs with their extension into sectors of low productivity gain, and the failure of prices of manufactures to fall despite declining unit costs.[14] In short, market imperfections operating on supply, rather than demand-pull, were the main factor in the slow rise actually registered by the price level in these years, with money playing at most a permissive role. If demand-pull had been at work, one would expect the rise to have been much more pervasive throughout the whole system of prices; to observe steadily increasing difficulties with the foreign balance and the exchange reserve; and to find at least the beginnings of a flight from money into goods. None of these things happened, although the economy was quite open, lacking in extensive direct controls, and free to respond to monetary excesses. It follows that the relationship between the rapidly increasing stock of money and the price level— while not to be denied in toto, especially for the longer run—was quite tenuous during these years.

However, Italy cannot count upon so fortunate a conjuncture forever. Indeed, the 3 per cent advance in wholesale prices during 1962 alone suggests that its end may already be at hand. After all, behind all this lay the desire of the public to build up its cash balances and a very rapid increase in real output. Experience suggests that the relationship between money supply and current GNP at stable prices has a normal level enforced by the habits and customs of the people. At some point this ratio will reach a ceiling that will require a slowing down of monetary expansion if prices are to be held at their given level. Further, if the 5.9 per cent rate of annual increase in real output cannot be maintained—which is likely as surplus labor is taken up and the gains from technical modernization begin to fall off—then this offset will also shrink, and the speed of increase in money supply will have to be checked even more.

What about the relationship of increases in the money supply to increases in real GNP? Undoubtedly the comparative ease with which the stock of money could be and was expanded accommodated the rapid growth of output. As such, certainly money was a permissive factor, but its increase was more passive than active (in the sense that it did not derive from a systematic effort to enlarge credit but from a willingness of the authorities to give comparatively free rein to the powerful nonmonetary forces of expansion then at work). In other words, the underlying facts of the boom suggest that the increase of money in circulation was far more the effect of real growth than its cause.

The primary stimuli for that growth were export demand, a very rapid expansion of private investment, and the group of government programs for internal development. Together these forces swelled personal incomes, making possible a substantial rise in consumption. In turn this enlarged the home market, contributing its own stimulus to investment. In short, the opportunities were vigorously exploited. Easy credit made this possible, but money itself did not bring the boom into being.

Three principal factors account for the enormous increase of money in circulation during these years. One was a long series of cash deficits in the national budget, covered in considerable part by sale of bonds to the banks, and by short-term credits provided by these institutions and the Bank of Italy together. Between the end of 1948 and the end of 1961, they increased their credits to the government (excluding purchase of long-dated issues) from 1353 billion lire to 2765 billion, or by 104.3 per cent.[15] These advances, provided mostly by the other banks, were fed directly into the money supply as government expenditures.

Second, there was a rapid expansion in short-term credits provided to private industry. Between the end of 1948 and of 1961, all banks together swelled these credits from 1128 billion lire to 8027 billion—a jump of 611.6 per cent. Obviously they were a major force in building up the money supply, made possible by the rapid growth in the reserve base.[16]

Finally, the rate of growth of money in circulation drew much of its impetus from the rapid expansion of the exchange reserve, reflecting the vast improvement in the foreign balance wrought mainly by soaring export demand. Between the end of 1948 and the end of 1961, the net position of all banks together on foreign account jumped from 174 billion lire to 2476 billion, a rise of over fourteenfold.[17] Much of the rapid inflow of foreign currency derived from private international transactions, and these acquisitions were converted to lire, adding greatly to money in circulation and to the primary reserves of the banks.

The monetary policy during these fourteen years was essentially one of permitting liberal expansion of credits to give the forces of expansion a full opportunity to exert themselves.[18] What guided the authorities was not the quantity of money or the speed of its increase as such, but a broader array of economic barometers. Among the decisive ones were the price level, the exchange reserve, employment and unemployment, and extensive needs for modernization and development in both the public and private sectors of the economy. Except for prices, employment, and unemployment, these indicators all gave an impressive account of themselves, as we have seen. Because of special factors quite insensitive to monetary management, the comparatively slow rise in manufacturing employment and the collateral persistence of heavy unemployment until the early sixties had to be put to one side in shaping such policy, apart from the over-all strategy of giving the boom its head and hoping for beneficial effects on the labor market.

Even if the behavior of prices did fall short of perfect stability, those in charge of monetary affairs recognized that a policy of tight money offered little chance of improvement in this respect, because the main source of the trouble lay not in a general excess of demand, but in a cluster of market imperfections—mainly of political origin although partly reflecting market power. In the nature of the case, these noncompetitive prices and wages had neither close nor direct dependence upon the level of aggregate demand. Beyond this, the larger costs of pursuing greater price stability by clamping down upon total demand were considered to be simply too great—slower growth of real output, even higher unemployment, and above all further delay in modernizing industry and in renovating the backward regions.

The instruments of monetary policy. Of the major instruments, the authorities have relied primarily upon three: a required ratio of reserves to deposits, specific devices to prevent "excesses," and informal influence exerted through close contacts with the banking community—"moral suasion" in American parlance.

From its inception in late 1947, reserve policy kept to the rule of 25 per cent coverage until January 13, 1962, when the ratio was cut to 22.5 per cent to enlarge the lending potential of the banks and so help the boom to keep going.[19] In January 1953, eligible government paper for reserve deposit was restricted to short-dated treasury bills. In 1958, the system of required reserves was extended to savings and pawn banks.

By continuous adherence to the 25 per cent rule until early 1962, the central bank could gear the lending potential of the commercial banks to the scale of their total reserves. This link was close throughout because of the voracious demand for credits. In consequence, the supply of money and credit depended mainly upon changes in the reserve position of the banks. In turn, the principal factor making for expansion in these reserves was the rapid accumulation of foreign funds—first through Marshall aid, and then from surpluses acquired on current balance of payments account. Here the government's monopoly of foreign currency through the exchange office (UIC) proved decisive for monetary expansion. In the mechanics of the process, the Bank of Italy bought inflowing foreign funds for the account of the UIC by advancing counterpart lire. Thus as the banks turned over incoming foreign currency, the counterpart lire were credited to their reserves. In short, operations on the foreign exchange market, rather than on the market for government securities, became the main source for expansion of the money supply.

Regarding the prevention of "excesses," the Bank was armed with certain powers in 1947, part of which were to be employed in cooperation with the Inter-Ministerial Committee on Credit and Saving (CICR). It had to approve all large grants of private credit by the banks, and to pass on new capital issues. It also was to regulate use of the rediscounting privilege by the banks, and to control advances of foreign currency by the UIC. Beyond exercise of these formal powers, the Bank has maintained close informal relations with the financial community to shape its policies.[20]

What then can be said about the two classic devices of central banking: control of the bank rate and open-market operations? So far as the former is concerned, it has cut a small figure throughout the boom. As for the latter, their role was both subtle and important, diverging sharply however from more familiar practices of having the central bank deal directly in government issues as a means of influencing the banks' free reserves and lending potential.[21]

The comparatively small importance of the bank rate devolves from the limited amount of rediscounting, except for the wheat bills emerging from price-supporting activities. With stabilization in 1947, the rate was advanced to 5½ per cent. In April 1949, it was cut to 4½, and in April 1950, to 4 per cent. It was then maintained unchanged until June 1958, when it was reduced to 3½ per cent. These reductions all coincided with slackening in the rate of expansion in private sector demand, and were taken presumably to encourage bank lending, although the cut in 1958 may have been intended also to check the inflow of foreign short-term funds since the balance on current account was already large in that year. Indeed, the very existence of this surplus has handicapped use of increases in the bank rate as a means of restraining excessive credit formation, for these would draw in short-term foreign balances, adding to the size of the already expanding reserve base.[22]

Open-market operations by the Bank are very interesting for two reasons. As noted earlier, because of the growing surplus on current foreign account, these operations have embraced the exchange market, where Bank purchases for lire have been the main reason for growth of the banks' reserves. In this respect, Italy has been in the comfortable position of being able to exploit disequilibrium in her balance of payments to expand money and credit to accommodate the boom.

The link between fiscal and monetary policy. Of greater importance for the present context, operations on the financial markets as a whole have provided the main link between monetary and fiscal policy, both in financing the deficit and in management of the national debt. To comprehend this side of the matter fully requires brief review of relations among the Bank, the treasury, the other banks, and the public.

Passing over for now long-term funding activities, the deficit can be financed from three major sources, each of them involving increase of floating debt: direct advances by the Bank to the treasury, sale of treasury bills to the banks, or their sale to the public. Because these bills carry maturities of one year or less, they are quasi-money, hence highly liquid assets for their owners. Obviously, therefore, the volume of treasury notes is of critical importance to the liquidity of both the banks and the public, and therefore to monetary stability. This fact becomes all the more significant when it is recalled that the banks can use these bills as cover for meeting their reserve requirements.

Here the composition and location of the banks' liquid assets become directly relevant. Recall that they must carry their obligatory reserve as a deposit either of cash or of securities with the Bank of Italy or the treasury. However, they may also hold other cash in their own vaults and other treasury bills in their portfolios. Deducting a safety margin from this cash to cover net drains from customers' deposits, vault cash and portfolio bills are free liquid assets with as much potential for credit formation as if they were free reserves already on deposit, since they can readily be transferred to the reserve account.

Assume now that the banks are fully loaned up, hence have no free reserves, and that they hold treasury bills (or free cash). By depositing the bills (or cash) in their reserves, they can create free reserves and then engage in multiple expansion of loans and deposits. In fact, in this way they could even buy additional new bills to replenish their portfolios, presuming that these are on offer, while retaining the older ones as a reserve deposit. On the contrary, if their cash and portfolio position were too tight, the banks could not create free reserves in this manner.

But there is another way by which multiple expansion conceivably could go on, still assuming that the banks are fully loaned up, with the added proviso that the cash proportion of their total reserves can be varied at their own option. In this case, the banks alter the mix of these reserves, by switching from cash to bills while leaving the total unchanged. Here the treasury offers a tap issue of new bills (monthly quotas were not then in effect); the

banks subscribe for them using cash in their reserve, putting up
the bills in replacement. The treasury then spends the cash, of
which the public will retain roughly 40 per cent in such form (currency added to circulation), while depositing 60 per cent with the
banks in checking and savings accounts. In result the banks will
have a rise in their deposit liabilities equivalent to 60 per cent of
the original government expenditure, from which they will deduct
up to one sixth for vault cash to protect their safety margin, credit-
ing the remainder (about 50 per cent of the original amount) to
their total reserves by depositing the balance of the cash so acquired. Of this added reserve deposit, one quarter will be tied as
cover for increased customers' deposits, leaving 75 per cent as
added net free reserves, although at the start the banks had no free
reserves at all.

Thus out of every 100 lire raised by the government from the
banks under these circumstances, 37.5 lire will end up as additional free reserves, or perhaps 40 lire if the marginal propensity of
the public to hold cash and of the banks to set aside for their safety
margins are slightly lower. Then, as the last step, the banks can resort to multiple expansion of loans and deposits, using this addition
to their free reserves. On the 25 per cent requirement, the amount
of this derivative expansion would approach fourfold, but would
fall short of this because of the need for additional vault cash to
protect against drain by the public. Counting up all the separate
contributions to the money supply we have 40 lire retained in cash
by the public out of the original injection by the government; 28
lire deposited by the public in current deposit accounts (at the end
of 1961 these deposits were 46.6 per cent of total deposits, meaning
that the public would put 32 lire in savings accounts); 10 lire
added to vault cash by the banks; and up to 150 lire of added cash
and current deposits provided to the public through multiple lending against the addition to the banks' free reserves. Thus the
original bill issue for 100 lire adds 228 lire to the money supply,
which means an expansion rate of approximately two and one-
quarterfold.

We have now considered two situations in which the banks can
create free reserves at their own initiative although fully loaned up
beforehand: by transfer of portfolio bills or surplus vault cash to
their reserves, and by raising the ratio of bills to cash in their re-

quired reserves. However, the main route for building free reserves has been a variant of the transfer process, made possible by expansion of vault cash and portfolios deriving from Bank of Italy purchases of inflowing foreign funds for UIC account. In turn, the growth of these reserves has permitted the banks to subscribe for additional treasury bills and to increase short-term lending to the private sector. Both channels have led to multiple expansion of checking deposits and total money in circulation, consequent upon the simple process of writing up deposits against the additions to net free reserves.

Given the fractional reserve system, it makes all the difference in the world whether the treasury sells its short-term notes to the banks or to the public. The former route will increase the money supply in multiple amount, while the latter does not increase it at all. It follows, then, that merely shifting deficit financing away from direct advances by the central bank, by selling bills to the banks instead, will not restrain the growth of liquidity of both the banks and the public, although the effects will be greater if the banks already have excess reserves at hand. During 1948–1961, three facts became decisive: free reserves were kept available by the running surplus returned by the balance of payments; the demands of the private sector for short-term credit grew rapidly and with fair steadiness; and the government ran a long series of deficits. In consequence, the money supply could expand rapidly, quickly absorbing additions to free reserves as required cover against increasing deposits.

To appreciate the significance of the process, consider that on December 31, 1947, the total money supply (cash plus current deposits) stood at 1446 billion lire, while total required reserves (against all deposits but not against coins and paper currency) came to 178 billion. Fourteen years later the money supply had swelled by 7302 billion, and total required reserves by 2103 billion. Thus the leverage exerted upon money in circulation by this increase of reserves involved a factor of 3.47. In interpreting this figure, it must be borne in mind that required reserves in 1947 did not include the savings banks, which came into the system in 1958, while the total for 1961 includes them. Furthermore, both in 1947 and in 1961 the requirement applied to savings deposits as well, although in 1947 these deposits so covered involved only those of the commercial banks. Finally, the reserve ratio imposed on the savings institutions was about 4 per cent, as against 25 per cent for the commercial banks.

What about the swing value of increased reserves available for cover against deposits only? Using the net change in total tied reserves between the two dates, and relating it to the advance in total current and savings deposits of all banks, yields a leverage factor of 5.18, while for commercial banks alone it is 4.28. The figure for all banks is made higher mainly by the difference in reserve ratios of the two categories of institutions. That for commercial banks alone exceeds the theoretical 4 : 1 ratio primarily because in the last years of the period the effective required rate was allowed to slip a couple of points below 25 per cent.[23] Absorption and release of cash by the public also influenced swing values throughout, although the trend clearly favored the substitution of checking deposits for coins and bank notes, as Table 24 clearly indicates. Undoubtedly this shift was strongly aided by the multiple expansion of short-term credit in these years.

Fiscal impacts upon money supply. The rapid emergence of long-run government development programs after 1949, together with increasing pressure for larger outlays on current account, had their inevitable consequence in a recurring series of annual deficits that could be varied within limits, but not eliminated. As a comparatively independent factor, the necessity for continuous deficit financing greatly complicated the task of the monetary authorities. The wonder is that the job was performed as well as it was, granted that, as with everything else, it was helped strongly by rapid growth and a favorable disequilibrium in the balance of payments.

The basic problem was to confine the rate of increase in the means of payment to one that was compatible with a maximum rate of growth in total output at reasonably stable prices. Deficit financing either through Bank of Italy advances or through sale of treasury bills to the banks had to be held within safe limits to forestall their explosive impacts upon the money supply. Accordingly, in its fiscal aspect the task of monetary management was complex and required several collateral lines of action.

One was to meet without difficulty the net cash requirements of the treasury, which were large, and which were the responsibility of the central bank as fiscal agent of the government. The second was to hold down on Bank advances to the treasury, to avoid recurrence of the inflationary process of World War II. The third was to hold within safe bounds the unavoidable rise in the treasury's floating debt—principally in short-dated bills—and to divert the sale of these bills to private investors instead of the banks, to prevent giving added thrust to the process of multiple expansion of loans and deposits except at those times when the private sector showed signs of flagging in its rate of expansion. And the fourth was to provide for periodic refinancing of part of this floating debt by converting it to long-dated issues, since these were ineligible after 1953 for reserve cover, and at the same time were an indirect means for controlling the total supply of bills. Respacing of the time structure of maturities in the public debt was inherently a delicate operation because it had to be timed to soak up excessive liquidity of the public. Otherwise it would have imposed undesired stringency upon the capital market, both for private industry and for the growing flotation requirements of the special-credit government institutes, which latter provided much of the financing for public investment schemes.

Referring to Table 25, it will be noticed that total internal debt rose by 4170 billion lire between June 30, 1948, and the same date for 1961—an increase of 241.0 per cent. On the earlier date, funded (long-term) debt accounted for 27.7 per cent of the total, rising to 39.9 per cent by 1961. Thus it did prove possible to lengthen the maturity of the debt over these years, which was accomplished chiefly by regular issues of nine-year bonds (*buoni del tesoro novennali*), which were timed to absorb excess liquidity of the public arising in the early months of each year or in consequence of large bulges in the inflow of foreign funds. Also worth noting, in relation to current GNP, total debt represented 24.1 per cent in 1948, advancing to 28.1 per cent by 1961. Although in this loose sense the "burden" of the public debt increased, it failed entirely to produce those unhappy effects so often claimed for it in popular discussion in the United States. No drastic inflation followed, while the moderate rise in prices that did occur bears no traceable connection to the growth of debt. Nor did productive capacity and available real output decline. On the contrary, they increased sharply, partly because of the continuing net contribu-

TABLE 25. Movements in composition of internal debt, fiscal years of 1947–1948 through 1960–1961 [a] (in billions of lire, as of June 30)

Fiscal year	Debt outstanding			Annual changes in debt			
	Floating debt	Funded debt	Total debt	Total debt	Funded debt	Floating debt [b]	
						Treasury bills	B.I. advances
1947–48	1251.0	479.3	1730.3	408.9	−9.4	310.7	107.5
1948–49	1693.2	453.6	2146.8	416.5	−25.7	445.1	−2.9
1949–50	1837.1	648.5	2485.6	338.8	194.9	124.8	19.1
1950–51	2058.0	752.8	2810.8	325.2	104.3	240.0	−19.1
1951–52	2212.6	896.7	3109.3	298.5	143.9	154.6	0.0
1952–53	2355.9	1115.7	3471.6	362.3	219.0	164.3	−21.0
1953–54	2593.4	1312.6	3906.0	434.4	196.9	148.5	89.0
1954–55	2649.9	1607.4	4257.3	351.3	294.8	24.6	31.9
1955–56	2771.2	1803.8	4575.0	317.7	196.4	179.3	−58.0
1956–57	2917.9	1917.9	4835.8	260.8	114.1	66.8	79.9
1957–58	3204.7	1889.0	5093.7	257.9	−28.9	220.0	66.8
1958–59	3455.7	1891.9	5347.6	253.9	2.9	453.8	−202.8
1959–60	3473.7	2340.2	5813.9	466.3	448.3	−83.9	101.9
1960–61	3548.3	2352.2	5900.5	86.6	12.0	n.a.	n.a.

[a] Figures for funded debt (debiti patrimoniali) include perpetual bonds (consolidati) and redeemable issues (redimibili), and a negligible amount of paper currency. The floating debt (debito fluttuante) consists of treasury bills (buoni del tesoro ordinari); various types of advances of the Bank of Italy (conto anticipazioni temporanee, conto anticipazione straordinarie garantite da speciali buoni del tesoro ordinarie); special advances for the occupation forces; an open drawing account for the treasury for the account of the local governments; cash borrowing; and advances supplied by certain other banking institutions.

[b] "Treasury bills" refers to those outside of Bank of Italy. Here it was assumed that all short-term debt except advances by the Bank of Italy took the form of treasury bills.

Source: (1946–1947—1959–1960) Annuario statistico italiano, issues for 1952, p. 409; 1956, p. 396; 1960, p. 344; (1960–1961) Relazione generale, 1962, I, p. 159.

tion of government (roughly the deficit) to total demand. Thus at no time were the Italian authorities bemused by the idea of budgetary balance as the one true fiscal objective. Instead they guided themselves by the overriding need for rapid growth, modernization and development, stable prices, and a healthy reserve of foreign exchange. So long as these goals could be realized, continuing deficits could be managed without undue difficulties, and in fact could contribute something of their own to the realization of these purposes. Indeed, the very buoyancy of total demand and of real growth in output undoubtedly made management of the debt and the control of inflation far easier than otherwise.

Returning to Table 25 and coupling it to year-end figures of the Bank of Italy for 1961, while funded debt increased 2060.8 billion over June 30, 1948, floating debt expanded 2545.1 billion. Despite this heavy dependence upon temporary financing, over these years the treasury was able to hold down upon recourse to the Bank of Italy, effecting significant reductions in 1950–1951, 1952–1953, 1955–1956, and 1958–1961. In fact, between the end of June 1948 and December 31, 1961, it decreased its indebtedness on this account by 208.6 billion lire. Over the same period, the stock of treasury bills outside the Bank of Italy rose from 777.6 billion to 3,531.3 billion, a jump of 354.1 per cent. In these years, when total debt was rising 4605.8 billion lire, the volume of bills expanded 2753.8 billion, and funded debt 2060.8 billion, while advances by the Bank shrank 208.6 billion.

As of December 31, 1961, then, floating debt accounted for 60 per cent of the total, while 40 percent was funded, compared with a 72 and 28 per cent ratio in 1948—probative evidence of at least moderate success both in lengthening maturities and in restraining treasury dependence upon short-term financing.[24]

There is good reason for concluding this review of fiscal-monetary operations after stabilization by reference to events between the end of 1958 and the end of 1961. This was the period in which very large surpluses began to be returned on current foreign account, and when real output began expanding at rates even above the very high trend established for 1948–1961 as a whole. It was also a period of substantial deficits and of extraordinarily rapid monetary expansion. Viewed through interest rates and availability of short-term credit, it was a time of quite easy money.

Foreign Balance and Money Supply | 99

Finally, these years are most informative regarding the short-term financing and debt-funding activities of the government.

TABLE 26. An over-all view of fiscal-monetary operations, 1958–1961 (in billions of lire)

Item	December 1958	December 1961	Net change Amount	Net change Per cent
Required reserves, commercial banks:				
Cash	770.0	768.4	−1.6	−0.2
Treasury bills	611.0	1351.3	740.3	121.2
Total	1381.0	2119.7	738.5	53.5
Short-term credit to govt:				
Bank of Italy	859.9	264.8	−595.1	−69.2
All other banks	991.8	1031.3	39.5	4.0
Public	1914.2	2500.0	585.8	30.6
Total	3765.9	3796.1	30.2	0.8
Funded debt of government:				
Banks	574.1	730.5	156.4	27.2
Public [a]	1353.8	1809.6	455.8	33.7
Total	1927.9	2540.1	612.2	31.7
Money supply [b]				
Currency	2003.9	2744.6	740.7	37.0
Demand deposits	3698.6	5790.6	2092.0	56.6
Total	5702.5	8535.2	2832.7	49.7

[a] Includes holdings of Central Post Office Savings Fund.
[b] Because of differences in definition and in treatment of vault cash, these figures diverge slightly from those presented in Table 24.
Source: All data from *Abridged Version of the Report for the Year 1961*, pp. 53 and 62.

Table 26 presents the relevant data. Money in circulation was soaring by almost 50 per cent, of which three quarters of the absolute increase was concentrated in demand deposits—indicating the vigor with which the process of multiple credit expansion was being conducted at the time. Look next at the changing reserve position of the commercial banks. The cash portion of these required reserves stayed virtually unchanged, while the volume of treasury bills jumped 740.3 billion lire. In consequence, the share of the latter in the reserve mix advanced from 44.2 per cent at the end of 1958 to 63.7 per cent three years later. Thus the entire net expansion in required reserves was met by the banks through increased investment in bills, acquired with the cash proceeds of inflowing foreign exchange and through direct expansion of deposit credit for government account.

Note in this connection that the 2836.8 billion rise in money in circulation was associated with a 738.5 billion advance in required reserves, implying a leverage factor of 3.8. This value is somewhat above that for 1948–1961 as a whole.

Consider now the financing of the government. Total short-term borrowing (new bill issues and advances) rose less than 1 per cent, while funded debt increased 612.2 billion. Here the mix of debt maturities was shifted strongly to long-dated issues, made possible by the high degree of public liquidity prevailing throughout. Over two thirds of these long issues were placed outside the banks. As for the latter's share, it accounted for about 23 per cent of all bank lending to the government on both dates.

The changing composition of short-term credit to the government is also of high importance. During the period, the treasury sharply reduced its indebtedness to the Bank of Italy—replacing 595.1 billion of such credits with 585.8 billion in additional borrowing from the banks. Viewed from the latter's side, the banks were substituting bills for cash to cover their increasing reserve requirements, and at the same time were adding bills to their portfolios—both of which were powerful mechanisms for actual and potential monetary expansion, as we have already seen. Here it should be noted that at the end of 1961 all banks together held roughly 1,100 billion lire of treasury bills in their portfolios, available for deposit as additional reserve cover if needed.

Concluding remarks on monetary policy. During 1949-1961, Italy's monetary managers undoubtedly had their task made easier by the rapid growth of total demand, the very favorable response of over-all physical supply, the impressive rise of receipts from abroad, and the desire of the public to build up its cash balances. Within this fortunate context, the main problems were to see that the supply of money and credit did get out of hand, and to provide safely for the treasury's ever-growing need for credits.

In these circumstances, management of the money supply rested upon four main devices: purchases of foreign exchange for building the reserve base; quantitative control of money and credit by imposition of a fixed fractional reserve ratio; variations in the placement and time structure of the public debt; and an array of formal and informal measures for keeping the lending practices of the banks sound. As part of this apparatus of control, the authorities have regularly employed open-market selling of new long issues of government bonds for the allied purposes of slowing the growth of floating debt and of absorbing temporary excesses in the liquidity of the public. However, here we encounter a certain asymmetry of practice: there has been no resort to open-market purchasing of government issues to expand reserves, and in consequence the central bank lacks a portfolio of bonds that could be sold to absorb cash from the public and the banks. There were three reasons for this curious situation. One was that parallel operations on the market for foreign exchange were at all times a readily available and efficient substitute for open-market purchasing—one that had to be employed anyway given both the commitment to peg the external value of the lira and a growing disequilibrium in the balance of payments. Of themselves, these exchange operations proved quite adequate for expanding the reserve base. In addition, the strong demands of government and industry for additional short-term credits needed no added stimulus. Moreover, the combined possibilities of direct Bank advances to the treasury and sale of additional bills to the banks were at all times a second alternative to open-market purchasing, rendering the latter superfluous under the circumstances.

This review of the Italian monetary experience raises a pertinent question: How well would these instruments of control work with an outbreak of inflation? [25]

It should already be evident that certain primary variables could well exert a perverse influence, obstructing efforts to reduce excess total demand. First, the political situation might dictate continued deficit financing. If the deficit were covered largely by the banking system, this would feed reserves and lending potential, despite the aim of credit restraint. Second, as long as the balance of payments remains positive, the danger exists that those acquiring foreign exchange would convert to lire, which also would build up the reserve base and credit formation. Third, if the discount rate and other interest rates were raised, this might attract short-term balances from abroad. This, too, could work in the wrong direction so far as reserves and lending are concerned.

Fourth, if the payments position were negative, the banks could still elude this deflationary influence so long as they were permitted to borrow abroad. Fifth, the banks also could enlarge their reserves by depositing their extensive portfolios of short-dated treasury bills. Sixth, there is an explosive potential in the public's extensive accumulation of cash balances, which for years have outrun the growth in total output. And finally, any attempt at price stabilization must confront the constant threat of serious wage inflation, because the wage level is now largely "administered" by controls that are insensitive to monetary measures, and that contain a built-in inflationary bias.

For all these reasons, monetary policy would encounter great difficulty in coping with inflation. Indeed, to work successfully it must have supporting measures on the side of government spending and financing, and of wages. Failing this cooperation, the monetary authority would face the unhappy choice of either bringing about an inflationary depression or of surrendering to the forces of inflation, with all the adverse consequences implied.

Within their own ambit, the Italian monetary managers are not without the means to attack inflation. There is, however, great subtlety needed in the timing and framing of the measures to be employed.

One weapon of great power would be a rise in the reserve ratio. Another depends upon advent of a payments deficit: an order to the banks to cease short-term borrowing abroad. Coupled to this, the payments deficit would force conversion of lire into foreign currencies supplied by the UIC—a process that would reduce customer deposits and banking reserves. Beyond these measures, the Bank of Italy could employ its considerable moral force within the banking community to slow down lending and to divert the sale of treasury bills to the capital market.

It must be realized that monetary policy in Italy is necessarily tied to the government's long-term program for over-all development and transformation of the south. In consequence, monetary restraint to check inflation has to be guided with extreme care. If the situation permits, the objective would be to slow the rate of increase in money and credit to noninflationary limits, without actually forcing contraction and recession. For this reason, increasing the reserve ratio becomes a weapon of last resort, because it carries the risk of deflation—a risk to be accepted only if all other measures fail. To have much effect, the advance in the rate must be adequate to offset induced transfers of cash and bills from the banks to their reserves. But the context is likely to differ from that of 1947, when the problem was to float the new reserve requirements at a level that would absorb almost all the banks' free reserves, without forcing deflation. Here the banks most likely would already be loaned up, and a sharp advance in the ratio would produce a credit squeeze possibly of panic proportions. Probably the safest course would be to raise the ratio in a series of steps, as a deliberate probing operation in search of monetary equilibrium. Similar caution is indicated for efforts to shift the weight and time structure of treasury financing to noninflationary sources. Together these considerations suggest that monetary strategy would have to be one of braking an inflation to a halt, rather than smashing it at one blow.

Obviously continued deficit financing would constitute a major threat to any program of monetary stabilization. The sale of treasury bills to the banks would have to be stopped. But then what? Substitution of direct advances from the Bank of Italy offers no escape, for it would still feed reserves. Clearly the most desirable action is the one most likely to be shunned by all politicians: a determined attempt at fiscal restraint, raising taxes and cutting spending to turn the deficit into a surplus. Failing this, the treasury would have to be compelled to get its credits from the public, as far as possible by sale of long issues. Probably this would raise interest rates. Even so, it would be preferable to subsidizing the treasury by forcing inflation upon the whole community. But it also carries with it the latent danger of recession.

By contrast with inflation, monetary policy has a somewhat easier task in coping with a fall of effective demand. The reserve ratio can be cut, and greater resort can be had to short-term financing by the central bank and the other lending institutions. If necessary, the deficit can be enlarged by some combination of tax reductions and acceleration of public investment programs. If the balance of payments remained positive, it would feed reserves and credit-creating potential. If it were to become negative, the exchange reserve, augmented if necessary by foreign credits, would be ample for pegging operations, while the lira proceeds so obtained could be employed for deficit financing. Admittedly, these devices provide no guarantee against recession. But they do offer assurance that it could be kept brief and mild, providing that if the deflation is of international scope, Italy's trading partners undertake their own countermeasures with adequate vigor. Over the longer run, the range of investment opportunities certainly should be broad enough to insure continued expansion, although the rate of advance will probably be somewhat lower than it was during 1948–1961.

PART TWO: THE LABOR MARKET

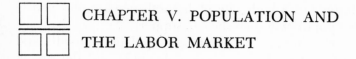 CHAPTER V. POPULATION AND
THE LABOR MARKET

For many decades before the onset of the long boom of 1948–1961, the trend rates of growth in output and employment in Italy were very modest. As early as 1900, the problem of chronic unemployment began to command attention. It continued to be manifest under Mussolini, and indeed was a primary consideration underlying the 1926 decision for restraint of internal migration, which grew steadily tighter, continuing until 1961. Because these restrictions tied people to the land, their effect was to conceal the real state of affairs—a growing lack of employment opportunities in agriculture. There was another side to the coin: these restraints also reflected the slow rate of job expansion in the nonagricultural sector, particularly in industry. After World War II, massive unemployment plagued the country long after the onset of the great boom. Only after 1959 did it start to diminish, yielding finally in 1961–1962 to talk of a growing labor shortage.

Because heavy unemployment was almost continuous for some sixty years, it was natural to blame it on population growth, and to look to emigration as the one way out. However, the demographic data for 1901–1961 show annual rates of increase that were consistently less than 1 per cent.[1] This was generally overlooked, and the main emphasis was on population growth—in short, on the supply side of the labor market rather than that of demand.

Even during the earlier years of the rapid postwar expansion in output, when registered unemployment ranged around two million, alleged population "pressure" was commonly cited as the main difficulty. Thus ECA's *Italy Country Study* (Washington: ECA, 1949) urged increased emigration "to help relieve the pressure of population on the Italian economy."[2] Addressing an international Congress on Population at Rome in September, 1954, Professor Rinaldo De Benedettini asserted flatly that Italy should have ten million less people, and that birth control was the only solution to the demographic problem.[3] And in a book published in 1955 for the Royal Institute for Economic Affairs, Muriel Grindrod contended that Italy "has a high rate of natural increase and consequently a larger population than she can support." [4]

What, then, are the facts concerning population growth and labor supply, and their relation to unemployment and the rise of per capita income?

QUANTITATIVE MOVEMENTS

Population growth. Between 1861 and 1961, both the number of legal residents (resident population) and the number actually present in the territory (population present) approximately doubled.[5] Although the absolute increase under both measures was large (24.5 and 24.2 million respectively), the compound annual rate of increase was very small—only 0.66 per cent for both categories.

TABLE 27. Movements in the Italian population, 1861–1961 [a] (in thousands)

| Year | Population within modern boundaries | | Net changes by decades | | | |
| | | | Actual | | Relative | |
	Resident	Present	Resident	Present	Resident	Present
1861	26,128	25,756	——	——	—%	—%
1871	27,899	27,578	1,771	1,822	6.7	7.1
1881	29,791	29,278	1,892	1,700	6.8	6.2
1891	31,819	31,421	2,028	2,143	6.8	7.3
1901	33,976	33,513	2,157	2,092	6.8	6.7
1911	36,996	35,905	3,020	2,392	8.9	7.1
1921	37,876	37,452	880	1,547	2.4	4.3
1931	41,220	40,814	3,344	3,362	8.8	9.0
1941	44,458	44,357	3,238	3,543	7.8	8.7
1951	47,540	47,224	3,082	2,867	6.9	6.5
1961	50,681	49,983	3,141	2,759	6.6	5.8

[a] Figures apply to boundaries established in 1947. "Resident population" refers to legal residents as listed at the local registry offices. "Population present" refers to those present in the national territory on the date indicated. The difference reflects the number abroad on temporary emigration. For 1861, 1871, and 1881, the figures for population present reflect direct census enumeration; but for 1861 and 1871 the figures for number of residents were estimated. For all other years except 1941 both series are estimated year-end values projected from censuses taken earlier in the same year. There was no census in 1941: the estimate for that year was based on the census of 1936.

Source: (1861–1941) *Annuario statistico italiano,* 1955, p. 369; (1951–1961) *Relazione generale,* 1962, II, p. 363.

As Table 27 shows, the increment in number of residents by decades reached its peak during 1922–1931. Over the next two decades, it slowly declined, turning upward again in 1952–1961. In relative terms, the largest gains occurred in 1902–1911 and 1922–1931. Substantially the same profiles are depicted for population present. For both categories, the critical fact is the slow rate of relative increase over the entire century.

In the earlier part of the whole period, emigration was the decisive influence in holding down the rate of increase. More recently it has been the fall in the birth rate. For example, in the decade 1902–1911 the excess of live births over deaths amounted to 7,220,000. However, population present within the territorial limits of the time advanced by only 2,261,000, suggesting that 4,959,000 persons left the country in these years.[6] At that time, birth and death rates were comparatively high, averaging 32.6 and 21.5 persons per thousand population present yearly, and yielding an average annual rate of natural increase of 11.1 per thousand. If no emigration of any kind had occurred during the decade, the increase in population present would have implied a compound annual rate of 2.02 per cent. In fact emigration pulled it down to only 0.67 per cent. Undoubtedly this substantial exodus was encouraged by limited job opportunities and very low per capita earnings.

Now compare these data with those for half a century later. For 1952–1961, the excess of live births over deaths totalled only 4,105,000 persons. In this later decade population present rose by 2,759,000 persons, indicating that some 1,346,000 left the country. In 1952–1961, annual birth and death rates had fallen, respectively, to 18.1 and 9.6 per thousand, yielding a rate of natural increase of 8.5 per thousand. Despite a sharp drop in the decennial emigration rate—from nearly five million to 1.35 million—the fall in the birth rate proved strong enough to pull down the relative rate of population increase. If there had been no emigration in the later decade, the compound annual rate of advance still would have been only 0.84 per cent. Actually it was but 0.57 per cent.

Birth and death rates. The decline in the natural rate of increase of the Italian population reflects a long-term drop in the birth rate, whose effects have been considerably offset by an even sharper persistent decline in the death rate. As Table 28 shows, the birth rate has fallen from 38.0 per thousand in 1881–1885 to 18.2 per thousand during 1957–1961, a decline of 52.1 per cent; while the death rate dropped from 27.3 to 9.5 in the same period, down 65.2 per cent. In consequence, the natural rate of increase fell from 10.7 to 8.7, or 18.7 per cent.

As of 1961, the Italian birth rate (18.8 per thousand) was above those of Japan (16.8), the United Kingdom (17.8), and France (18.4), but below the Netherlands (21.2) and the United States (23.4).[7] Obviously, Italy has ceased to be a leading producer of new generations, despite her long-established reputation to the contrary. The inference is that the practice of birth control has become widespread, particularly in the urban areas, a conclusion that draws firm support from the persistence of the marriage rate at slightly over 7.0 per thousand (except during World Wars I and II and immediately after) for over half a century.

TABLE 28. Natural changes in the Italian population, 1881–1956 [a] (per thousand population present)

Period	Average birth rate	Average death rate	Average rate of natural increase
1881–1885	38.0	27.3	10.7
1901–1905	32.6	21.9	10.7
1931–1935	23.6	14.1	9.5
1947–1951	20.4	10.5	9.9
1952–1956	17.9	9.8	8.1
1957–1961	18.2	9.5	8.7

[a] Data refer to boundaries in effect at the time.

Source: (1881–1885), Guglielmo Tagliacarne, "Demographic and Social Development," Banco di Roma, Review of the Economic Conditions in Italy, special number, Ten Years of Italian Economy, 1947–1956 (Rome [n.d.]), pp. 24–25. (1901–1961) Calculated from following data: live births and deaths for 1901–1954 and population present for 1901–1951 from Annuario statistico italiano 1955, pp. 369, 379; live births and deaths for 1955–1961 from Relazione generale, 1956, p. 62; 1960, p. 70; 1962, II, p. 75. Population present for 1952–1961, II, p. 363.

The remarkable decline in the death rate suggests that long-term improvement in social and economic conditions has lengthened life expectancy generally, as was the case in northwest Europe during most of the nineteenth century. To some extent this is true. However, the main cause has been an enormous drop in infant mortality, while life expectancy has been increased only moderately for age classes of over fifty years. According to Tagliacarne, infant mortality in the first year of life averaged no less than 220 per thousand during 1872–1875 (263 in the southern region of Basilicata), as against 48.6 per thousand in 1955, a decline of almost 78 per cent.[8] Since infant mortality rates in Trieste and Tuscany in 1955 had already fallen to 28.1 and 33.0, there is reason to expect a further decline generally as sanitation and medical care are further improved. This is particularly true for south Italy, where even in 1955 the rate of infant mortality in the first year of life was as high as 61.1 per thousand. In consequence, a further modest decline in the over-all death rate is likely. Even now the Italian death rate compares well internationally—in 1961 it was 9.4 per thousand, as against 7.6 in the Netherlands, 9.3 in the United States, 7.4 in Japan, 12.0 in the United Kingdom, and 11.0 in France.[9]

While Italy can no longer be described as undergoing rapid population expansion, her 1961 rate of natural increase (9.4) put her ahead of France (7.4) and the United Kingdom (5.8), and equal to Japan. However, she was well behind the United States (14.1) and the Netherlands (13.6). Despite this rather modest rate, Italy may be expected to share first place in Western Europe with the United Kingdom by 1971 because she is adding people at a faster rate than either the United Kingdom or West Germany, which today have larger populations.

In 1960, Italy had a population density of 164 persons per square kilometer, as against 19 in the United States, 83 in France, 215 in the United Kingdom, 252 in Japan, and 342 in the Netherlands. Although these comparisons suggest that Italy already has a relatively high density, not much significance can be given to this fact. Both the United Kingdom and the Netherlands have considerably higher densities, and yet both have much higher per capita national incomes. Moreover, population density is a poor index of material well-being because it fails to reflect the influence of other decisive variables—relative proportions of arable land to total territory, differences in the quality of arable land, differences in capital stock, differences in productive technique and in social-economic organization, and differences in the professional quality of the labor force. Even within Italy itself the region of Basilicata has a relatively low density. Yet because the other variables are so adverse it is one of the poorest sections of the country. The comparative well-being of areas and of nations depends not upon population density alone but upon the quality of the entire productive complex.

Three major forces have shaped the demographic evolution of modern Italy: the birth rate, the death rate, and emigration. Between 1861 and 1914, when both rates were quite high although moving downward, the growth of population was checked both absolutely and relatively by large-scale emigration. With World War I, emigration fell off sharply, never to regain its former scope. During 1922–1931, the decline of the birth rate was inadequate to offset the combined opposing effects of a rapidly falling death rate and sharply curtailed emigration. Accordingly, the population growth rate reached its decennial peak for the hundred-year period. After World War II, the birth rate fell faster than the death rate. Helped by a modest recovery of emigration, it pulled down the rate of population increase to values approximating those of the later nineteenth century, when massive exodus was the main restraint.[10] For the next two decades, there is every reason to expect these low rates of increase to continue.

QUALITATIVE CHANGES

The changing age structure of the population. The age structure of any human population reflects the combined effects of secular movements in birth and death rates, immigration and emigration, and changes in national domain. Pervasive movements in age structure have economic importance for two reasons: through the influence of changes in the relative size of the population of working age (fifteen through sixty-four years for Italy), they directly affect the size of the labor force, and through this the necessary rate of expansion to keep unemployment within reasonable limits. Moreover, shifts in age structure govern the ratio of the dependent population to the number productively employed, and so have significance for the over-all standard of living.

Probably the most important fact about the changing age composition of the Italian population is that since 1871 the share representing the productive age group declined until 1901, when it reached 59.7 per cent, and then steadily rose to 65.4 per cent in 1951. Looked at in a different way, as shown by Table 29, the decennial rate of increase in total population reached its peak (9.5 per cent over 1911 in 1921), declining slowly until 1941 and sharply thereafter. By contrast, the decennial rate of increase in the population of working age dropped even more sharply between 1921 and 1941, but then turned upward between 1941 and 1951,

TABLE 29. Movements in the age structure of the population, 1871–1951 (in thousands)

| Year | Population of working age | | Total population [a] | | Ratio of in- crease of working to total population, adjacent dates |
	Net change, adjacent dates	Per cent change, adjacent dates	Net change, adjacent dates	Per cent change, adjacent dates	
1871	——	——	——	——	——
1901	2650	——	5674	——	46.7
1911	1198	6.2	2196	6.8	54.5
1921	3317	16.1	3303	9.5	100.4
1931	2040	8.5	3203	8.4	63.7
1941 [b]	2079	8.0	3809	8.5	54.6
1951	2840	10.0	2173	4.8	130.7

[a] Population present within territorial limits of the time.

[b] Total for year-end; other totals are for date of census. Increase of population of working age estimated by straight-line interpolation of change between 1936 and 1951.

Source: (1871), from Francesco Coppola d'Anna, "Le forze di lavoro e il loro impiego in Italia," in La disoccupazione in Italia, vol. IV, part 2 (Rome: Camera dei deputati, 1953); (1901–1931), Annuario statistico italiano, 1955, p. 376; (1951), Annuario statistico italiano, 1956, p. 23.

when the rate of increase in total population was falling steeply. This late surge in the size of the working population reflects the high birth rates of the twenties, the repatriation policy of the thirties, the sharp decline of emigration during the war years, and the return of many refugees from the former colonies after the war. Undoubtedly, this discordant growth in the population of working age exerted acute pressure on the postwar labor market, accentuating the unemployment problem. However, it should not be allowed to obscure the longer-run tendency for the rate of increase in the population of working age to decline as the effects of the present slowing down in the rate of increase in total population become manifested in future years.

The effects of emigration upon the relative rates of increase in the two population categories are worth noting. Traditionally, emigration from Italy has been concentrated among unmarried males of working age and so has had disproportionate impact upon the population of working age and upon the labor force. Between 1871 and 1911 the emigration movement was at its height, unimpeded either by war or by drastic restrictive legislation. During this forty-year period the total population rose by 7.87 million or 29.4 per cent, while the population of working age increased 3.85 million or only 23.1 per cent. For each increase of two persons in the whole population, approximately only one was of working age. Now consider 1911–1951, when two major wars, restrictive legislation abroad, and Mussolini's repatriation policy all came into play. Total population rose by 12.49 million or 36.0 per cent, while the population of working age expanded by 10.28 million, or no less than 49.9 per cent. Even more impressive, almost seven out of every eight persons added to the population were of working age.

Despite this continuing tendency for the population of working age to increase relative to total population (65.4 per cent in 1951 against 59.7 per cent in 1901), there is no doubt that the aging of the Italian population has already set in, a conclusion that draws ample support from the figures in Table 30. Between 1931 and 1951 the proportion of the working age group belonging in the upper age bracket (forty through sixty-four years) increased markedly. The share of those between zero and fourteen years has fallen steadily since 1901 relative to total population, while those sixty-five years and over have increased relatively throughout the half-century. Moreover, the ratio of those over sixty years of age to those under twenty (Sauvy's index of aging), which stood at 21 per cent in 1871,[11] reveals a rapid and unbroken rise after 1901, soaring to 35.1 per cent by 1951. With the prospects of a continuing low birth rate in future years and lengthening of life expectancy for the elderly, Italy faces an aging population in which a larger and larger proportion of the total will belong to the dependent over-age group. Stated differently, the ratio of producers to nonpurchasers will increase even further.

What, then, is the outlook for the age structure as a whole? The estimates developed by Bourgeois-Pichat, Somogyi, De Meo, and ISTAT all agree on three major points:

(1) The population of working age will continue to increase as a relative share of the total population, reaching a maximum sometime between 1966 (67.2 per cent—ISTAT) and 1981 (68.1 per cent—De Meo), depending upon the particular projection.[12] Allowing for the continuance of net emigration, it is safe to conclude that by 1970 the aging process and declining birth rates will finally overtake the tendency for the productive age group to increase its relative share, which will stabilize at about 67 per cent. ISTAT predicts an annual growth rate of 194,200 for this group for 1956–1966, with a decline to 110,000 for 1967–1971, after allow-

TABLE 30. Indexes of the aging of the Italian population, 1901–1951 (per cent)

	Population of working age		Total population [a]		
Year	Relative to total population [a]	Those in 40–64 year age group	Those between 0–14 years	Those 65 years and over	Those over 60 years relative to those under 20
1901	59.7	38.8	34.1	6.2	22.1
1911	59.3	38.2	33.8	6.5	23.5
1921	61.7	37.0	31.0	6.7	25.4
1931	62.9	36.4	29.7	7.3	27.3
1951	65.4	41.2	26.3	8.3	35.1

[a] Owing to discrepancies between the reported totals for population present within the territorial limits of the time and totals recorded for the age and sex distributions, the latter were used.

Source: (1901–1941), Annuario statistico italiano, 1955; (1951), 1956.

ance for net migration. These figures compare with 284,000 per year during 1941–1951 and so suggest considerable reduction in pressure on the labor market starting as early as 1956. On the same basis, only 75.6 per cent of the annual increase in total population from 1956 to 1966 would belong to the working-age group, and only 47.6 per cent between 1967 and 1971, which compares with 130.7 per cent for 1941–1951.[13]

(2) The zero through fourteen years age group will continue to decline as a percentage of the total population. Bearing in mind that this group has been in relative decline ever since 1901, dropping to 26.3 per cent by 1951, it is not surprising that Bourgeois-Pichat and De Meo predict it will descend to 20.3 per cent by

1980–1981. De Meo, in fact, projects the decline to 18.9 per cent by 2001. Whatever the estimate, all of them foresee a decline in the proportion of children in the decades to come.

(3) The nonproductive age group (sixty-five years and over) will continue to increase its relative share of the population, maintaining a trend that raised it from 6.2 per cent in 1901 to 8.3 per cent in 1951. By 1970–1971, ISTAT foresees a rise to 10.7 per cent, Bourgeois-Pichat, 10.4 per cent, Somogyi, 10.5 per cent, and De Meo, 9.5 per cent. By 1980, Bourgeois-Pichat predicts this group's share at 12.5 per cent, while De Meo projects it at 11.6 per cent for 1981 and foresees a further rise to 13.8 per cent by 2001.

All assessments of current trends look for a continuing weight-shift toward the higher age levels of the Italian population over the next several decades. In the recent past, population pressure has shown itself in the relative growth of the productive age group, enhancing labor supply and creating a critical problem of generating economic expansion adequate to increase labor demand sufficiently to absorb the seemingly endless growth in the flow of new recruits to the labor markets. That problem has now passed into history. Instead of confronting chronic labor surpluses, Italy may well face increasing labor scarcity as time goes on, providing, of course, that the very high postwar rate of economic expansion will continue. If so, the implications could be very favorable for real wages and for the share of labor in the national income. Against these, however, a new kind of population problem would emerge: the rise, absolutely and relatively, of the nonproductive over-age group, considered as an increasing body of dependents exerting their economic claims upon the producing population.[14]

Emigration. For over half a century, the Italians have shown one of the highest "propensities to emigrate" in the world, while changes in the flow of Italian emigration have profoundly influenced both the growth and the age structure of the Italian population. On these points the experts are agreed, although their estimates regarding emigration in the past show great divergencies and a rather consistent tendency to overstate the facts, usually from a failure to take returning emigrants into account.[15] Moreover, there is a kind of devil's logic about the official statistics: the various components are each based on a consistent plan, but overall comparability is elusive and usually unattainable. Neither on a gross nor a net basis can the official emigration data be reconciled with net changes in population present or resident, either for the territory of the time or for that of today. The gross natural increases for any period since 1901 (excess of births over deaths), less gross or net emigration, simply do not coincide with recorded increases in population, however defined, in the same period.[16] In consequence, the only safe procedure is to examine the official statistics of emigration on their own terms and to avoid any comparisons with over-all population data.

TABLE 31. Gross and net emigration from Italy, for selected periods, 1901–1955 (in thousands)

Period	Gross emigration	Repatriates	Net emigration	Average annual net emigration
1901–1913	8,147	2,132 [a]	6,015	463
1914–1920	1,707	619 [a]	1,088	155
1921–1930	2,595	1,373	1,222	122
1931–1938	658	437	221	27
1939–1945 [b]	469	499	−30	—
1946–1950	1,126	379	747	149
1951–1955	1,365	539	826	165
Total, 1901–1955	16,067	5,978	10,089	

[a] No figures available for repatriates returning from European and Mediterranean Basin countries for 1901–1920. Figures here refer to overseas countries only.

[b] No data published for 1943–1945. Figures here refer to 1939–1942.

Source: (1901–1951), Annuario statistico italiano, 1955, p. 390–391; (1952–1955), 1956, p. 49.

The figures are presented in summary form in Table 31. They show that between 1901 and 1955 some 16.07 million Italians left the country; 5.98 million returned, partly reflecting seasonal migrations mainly to France and Switzerland, which suggests a net permanent exodus of 10.09 million over the whole period.[17] So far as trends are concerned, the most obvious one is the marked decline in the annual rate of net emigration after 1913, which reached negligible proportions during 1931–1938. Equally significant, however, is the recovery of net emigration that set in after World War II, which by 1951–1955 reached the highest rate achieved since 1913. Here it should be noted that the high rates achieved before World War I reflected the individual efforts of the emigrants themselves. After World War II, the outflow was aided by a series of international agreements and by the work of several official and private organizations. Nonetheless, as the able review of Italian emigration prepared by a study group headed by Giovanni Malagodi points out, emigration overseas remains primarily an independent movement by the emigrants, while organized emigration is mainly confined to intra-European movements largely of a seasonal type.

Great interest attaches itself to the impacts of net emigration upon the population of working age, because of their obvious connection with relief of pressure upon the supply side of the labor market. For the period before World War II, all that can safely be said on the basis of the available figures is that considerable relief was afforded until after 1914, and that during the interwar period it declined to insignificant levels.

What about the years after World War II? For 1946–1955, net emigration totaled 1.57 million. Using the data for 1952 only, the Malagodi group estimated that 70 per cent of the total net outflow consisted of males, and 30 per cent females. They also estimated that 95 per cent of the males were of working age, and 70 per cent of the females.[18] If these figures are applied to the realized annual average for net emigration during 1951–1955 (165,000), the flow would consist of 115,000 men and 50,000 women, of which 109,000 men and 35,000 women, or a total of 144,000, would be of working age. Now, on the basis of an assumed 75,000 rate of net emigration per year, ISTAT projected an annual average rate of increase of 194,200 in the population of working age during 1956–1966.[19] Applying the Malagodi ratio (87.3 per cent) for the net number of emigrants of working age relative to total net emigration, it follows that 65,475 persons in the 75,000 net exodus projected by ISTAT were of working age. Therefore the gross total, before net emigration, for average annual increase in the population of working age (ISTAT) becomes 259,675. If from this gross there is now deducted 144,000 (net emigration of working age on the basis of total net emigration at 165,000 per year instead of 75,000), then the population of working age would increase by only 115,675 persons per year during 1956–1966. In effect, therefore, continued net emigration at the 1951–1955 rate cuts the potential annual increase in the population of working age from 259,675 before allowance for net emigration to 115,675 after such allowance, a drop of 55.4 per cent.

If, further, the Malagodi assumption is adopted that 100 per cent of the males and 50 per cent of the females of working age would participate actively in the labor force, then the 1951–1955 figures for net emigration imply withdrawal of 126,400 persons yearly from the labor force, bringing down the implied annual increase for 1956–1966 in the labor force from 194,750 persons to only 68,350. On these assumptions, mere maintenance of the 1951–1956 average rate of net emigration would afford very great relief to the labor market in years to come.

Here, however, a word of caution must be entered. Maintenance of the rate of net emigration depends, among other things, upon the continued economic expansion of Western Europe and the United States. A prolonged and widespread recession would probably cut the emigration rate sharply. In addition, during 1961–1965 the flow of youngsters of fifteen years of age entering the labor market will turn out to be perhaps 10 per cent higher than before, because of the high birth rates of 1946–1950.[20] Putting these imponderables together, it is safer to conclude that, even allowing for net emigration, the domestic labor force will continue to increase by between 100,000 and 120,000 per year during 1956–1966.

Relief for the labor market when unemployment is chronically heavy, as it was in Italy until the sixties, is the most obvious effect of emigration. To the extent that it draws upon the unemployed, it involves no loss in current national product; indeed, there is a saving in relief expenditures. It can also be pointed out that emigration has long been helpful to Italy's international accounts. Earnings of Italian workers temporarily abroad together with emigrants' remittances totalled $195 million in 1955, and $530.4 million in 1961.[21]

Against these benefits must be set off the economic loss in the form of accumulated investment in human capital—education, technical training, and maintenance until productive age. The Malagodi group calculated this capital loss at $1.04 billion for each 160,000 emigrants. Granted that if these persons were wholly unemployed their "capital value" would have no economic significance other than as waste, the fact is that many of them are potentially productive citizens, as their subsequent experience usually shows. Thus there is a loss in potential economic product to Italy if means could be found to employ them.

Moreover, emigration in recent years has become increasingly selective. Opportunities to emigrate have become more and more concentrated upon younger males in the productive age group—those with skills and high productive capacity. Thus it tends to cut deeply into the most productive core of the labor force, removing many who are already employed and so lowering the average quality of the remainder. As the current population tendencies operate to make labor relatively scarce in the decades to come, the steady loss of this human capital will be felt more and more. Thus it has been pointed out for many years that the process has seriously debilitated the recovery of the long-stagnant southern Italian economy.[22]

Therefore, emigration obviously is no longer the cure-all for Italian difficulties. In the immediate context of the heavy unemployment of the first postwar decade, emigration provided a temporary, but by no means costless, palliative for an overburdened labor market. With the emerging labor scarcity of the sixties, the value of the emigrants to the Italian economy is likely to outweigh any benefits to be had from their departure from the scene.

Regional population changes. South Italy and the islands of Sicily and Sardinia constitute the great reservoir for population increases in the country as a whole, in the sense that for decades the rate of natural increase there has run far ahead of that for north and central Italy. If it were not for long-continuing emigration from the south both northward and abroad, this region long since would have acquired more than half the total population of the country. Put differently, if the birth and death rates of north Italy were representative of the whole nation, Italy's natural rate of increase would now be one of the lowest in the world, ranking with France and the United Kingdom. By contrast, if the southern rates were typical, Italy would rank among the rapidly growing industrial nations of the globe, such as the Netherlands, the United States, Japan, and Soviet Russia.

To demonstrate these sharp differences, Table 32 presents a comparison between the south and the islands taken together, and northern and central Italy, for 1955. In that year, the south accounted for 18.5 million people, or 37.6 per cent of the total resident population. At the same time, however, the south contributed almost exactly one half of the total births and just short of two thirds of the total increase in the whole population. The rate of increase in the southern population was slightly over three times as great as that in the northern and central sections. Here, then, is the geographical source of Italian population pressure.

TABLE 32. Interregional comparison of natural population movements, 1955 [a] (in thousands)

Region	Resident population, Dec. 31, 1955	Net excess of births over deaths	Rate per thousand of resident population		
			Births	Deaths	Natural rate of increase
Northern and central Italy	30,696	147,531	14.3	9.5	4.8
Southern Italy and the islands	18,493	275,082	23.2	8.4	14.8
Italy as a whole	49,190	422,613	17.7	9.1	8.6

[a] Northern and central Italy include the regions of Piedmont and Valle d'Aosta, Lombardy, Trentino-Alto Adige, Veneto, Trieste, Liguria, Emilia-Romagna, Tuscany, Umbria, Marche, and Lazio. The south includes the Abruzzi and Molise, Campania, Puglia, Basilicata, Calabria, Sicily, and Sardinia.

Source: Compiled from data in Annuario statistico italiano, 1956, pp. 22, 43–44.

Considered in greater detail, southern birth rates ranged between 17.8 per thousand (Abruzzi and Molise) and 25.1 (Calabria), as against 9.3 (Trieste) and 18.6 (Lazio) in the north and center. Southern death rates were closer together—from 7.5 per thousand in Calabria to 8.7 in Sicily and the Basilicata. In the north and center, death rates extended from 7.9 in Lazio to 11.7 in Piedmont. Natural rates of increase in the south ranked from 9.5 per thousand in the Abruzzi to 17.6 in Calabria, compared with −1.7 (Trieste) to 10.7 (Lazio) for the north and center. Here it is worth noting that two regions of the north—Piedmont and Liguria—together with the zone of Trieste, actually had deficits in the balance of births against deaths.

Despite the fact that north and central Italy are far more industrialized than the south and the islands, the latter section has long had a bigger share of its total population concentrated in large cities. In 1901 the nine largest metropolitan areas of the south accounted for 47.2 per cent of total population present, as against 49.4 per cent in 1951. For north and central Italy, the comparable figures were 31.1 and 37.4 per cent.[23] Undoubtedly, the persistently greater metropolitan concentration in the south reflects the long-standing inability of agriculture there to absorb more persons in productive employment. According to the census of 1951, 40.5 per cent of the resident population in the south and islands was located in districts with 10,000 inhabitants or less, as against 44.5 per cent for the north and center. Notwithstanding the paradox of greater urbanization in the south, where nonagricultural activities are far less developed, the nine largest cities in north and central Italy grew by 70.8 per cent between 1901 and 1951, as against only 46.8 per cent in the south. This reflects on the one side the rapid industrial expansion of centers such as Milan, Venice and Genoa, and of Rome as a political and cultural center, and on the other the negative impacts of net emigration upon the large metropolitan areas of the south. So far as the country as a whole is concerned, there is evident a well-advanced process of urbanization. Between 1901 and 1951, the eighteen largest cities increased 57.3 per cent in population, while the rest of the nation gained only 30.6 per cent. However, even in 1951 these centers accounted for only 41.9 per cent of the total population present, as against 37.1 per cent in 1901. Italy cannot yet be considered a metropolitan society, although the continued decline of agriculture, which today provides less employment than in 1921, points clearly in that direction.

Although the evidence is plain that the south and the islands are still a fecund source of added population, surprisingly enough their share of the total population has remained approximately constant for eighty-five years, amounting to 36.8 per cent in 1871 and 38.2 per cent in 1960, with very little variation between these dates. The explanation lies in emigration—northward and abroad. According to the Parliamentary Inquiry into Unemployment, the average annual natural rate of increase of the southern population for 1936–1951 was 13.2 per thousand, while the rate of net emigration was 4.2 per thousand.[24]

Less well known, however, is the continuing parallel flow of southerners to the north and central parts of the country. Its dimensions are difficult to establish, but as Tagliacarne points out from the census of 1951, the north and center had acquired 970,907 residents who had been born in the south or in the islands, while in turn the latter sections could claim only 218,809 persons originating from northern and central Italy.[25] Thus the north was the net beneficiary by a ratio of almost 4.5:1, although the south and the islands had but slightly more than a third of the population. In other words, net migration northward has helped to hold the southern share of the population constant, despite its propensity to increase three times as fast and despite severe statutory restraints against internal migration until early 1961.[26]

It is easy to exaggerate the negative aspects of this internal migration—the flight from poverty and the pressure on northern labor markets. In economic terms, however, the process is desirable, because it moves workers from centers of low or negligible productivity to those where output and earnings are higher, thereby adding to national income. Labor supply is thus being adapted to the distribution of capital, which remains highly concentrated in the north. However, there are offsetting private and social costs involved in this population transfer, along with political issues surrounding the geographic distribution of new capital investments. In addition, it should be noted that the outflow to the north makes the northern population more balanced in age structure, also relieving the now developing labor shortage in that region.

Recognizing the far higher rate of natural increase in the south, what does the future hold for the territorial distribution of the Italian population? This question is of vital importance because it links up directly with efforts to expand the Italian economy, particularly with the geographical distribution of new investment.

Working from alternative assumptions regarding birth and death rates, G. De Meo estimated on the basis of natural rates of increase alone, assuming no emigration, that by 2001 southern Italy (including the Islands) would be able to claim slightly more than half the total Italian population. Assuming the very conservative net emigration rate of 60,000 persons per year, De Meo predicts a rise in the southern share by 2001 to 44.6 or 47.6 per cent, depending upon the given combination of fertility and mortality rates.[27] If Italy can be said to suffer from population pressure, clearly it originates in the south, and not in the north. Obviously, too, this projected rise in the south's share of the total population would represent a major demographic change.

Professor De Meo's forecasts were prepared in the early fifties, at a time when the restraints against internal migration were strongly enforced and there was little prospect of their repeal. With their revocation in early 1961, the whole outlook has changed, and along with it the character of the development problem. At the start of the fifties, the ruling questions were how to find productive employment and to raise the lower standard of living of the more rapidly growing southern population, in a context of massive unemployment throughout the country. Granted, the problems of employment and income are still serious for the south, although substantial gains have been made since 1950. But now we find partisans of the south voicing concern at the loss of population, and no longer wringing their hands at the prospect of its relentless continued growth. With this triumph of regional loyalties over earlier fears about demographic pressure, the issues of economic development have become focused much more sharply upon the geographic distribution of investment—in short, on the question of policies to build up the capital stock and the industry of the south relative to the north.

Viewing matters as they stood in 1952, De Meo could join with many other experts in concluding that "unless the South can benefit in future years from a flow of capital and outlets for emigration much greater than at present, much of the great financial undertakings by the state and by private enterprise will only prevent a worsening of the present condition of depression." [28] Since that time, much investment has been made in the region, while emigration north and abroad has absorbed 150,000 persons each year. In result, per capita southern incomes have gone up substantially, and the regional labor force has begun shifting out of agriculture. Although the south has by no means attained economic parity with the rest of the nation, the prospects for this consummation are no longer as hopeless as they appeared a decade ago.

One final point: the question of population density. The population tendencies observed for the south might suggest enormous concentrations of people there, compared to the rest of the country. This is largely incorrect. There is great variance among the southern regions. Campania (which includes Naples) had a resident population of 336 persons per square kilometer of total area in 1955, which even exceeds that of the Netherlands (320 per square kilometer in 1952), one of the most densely settled countries of the world. However, Campania is the exception. At the other extreme are Sardinia and the Basilicata, with densities of only 57 and 65 persons per square kilometer, among the lowest in Italy. Population density for the south and the islands together is 150 persons per square kilometer of territory and 157 per square kilometer of agricultural and forest land. For north and central Italy, the comparative figures are higher—172 and 192 persons per square kilometer.[29]

The inadequacy of population density as a measure of material well-being has already been mentioned. The fact that the average density of population in the south is below that of the rest of the country should not obscure other decisive differences that have heightened the economic adversity of this part of Italy—weaker social incentives, relatively poor agricultural land, relatively low capital stock per head, and constricted development of the nonagricultural sector of the economy. Against these harsh obstacles, low density counts for little, while the relatively high rate of population increase exerts extreme economic pressure. Continuing and substantial emigration is the inevitable result. In short, high densities of population are entirely compatible with high per capita incomes, given either a highly productive agriculture or a well-developed nonagricultural economy possessed of sufficient comparative advantages to yield fruitful returns from specialization and foreign trade. The real problem of the south is that for a century it has been pitifully lacking in either alternative.

DOES ITALY HAVE A POPULATION PROBLEM?

The review of the evidence points to four basic facts about the demographic position of Italy today. First, the decennial rate of population increase is falling sharply. Second, the rate of increase in the share of the total population of working age is gradually slowing down. Third, net emigration is substantially reducing the rate of increase in the labor force. And fourth, the remaining population problem centers in the south. For the country as a whole, there is no basis for the view that it now suffers from extreme population pressure.

Neither the birth rate nor the natural rate of increase supplies ground for this contention. At the same time, the notion that Italy is overpopulated and has more people than she can support cannot be adequately sustained by appeal to the persistent mass unemployment of the fifties, or by reference to international comparisons that merely show that Italian per capita incomes and levels of consumption are low relative to northwest Europe and the United States. Finally, comparative indexes of population density, even with due regard to their limitations, do not prove the case for overpopulation.

It would be absurd to say that if the Italian population were cut by a third or a half that the people would be better off. It would be equally absurd to hold that per capita output and consumption are now at a maximum and therefore must fall with further increases in population. Judgments of this kind rest upon a too-exclusive preoccupation with the ratio of population to land, coupled with the mistaken notion that the existing productive complex is static, hence incapable of further increases in economic efficiency. The history of northwest Europe, and even of Italy itself, decisively refutes these claims, showing that total population, population density, the labor force, and per capita real incomes can all rise together. This association is not accidental, for it rests upon continuous improvement of the entire social-economic organization. What reason is there to suppose that this process of improvement must now come to an end?

If the concept of overpopulation is to have any useful meaning, it must be defined in a relative rather than an absolute sense. Once this is done, however, the arbitrary nature of the idea becomes obvious, while its utility for the interpretation of the population question becomes dubious. One could say that Italy is now "overpopulated" if the given state of its production technology, the quantity and quality of its capital stock, the quantity and quality of its land and labor supply, and its existing system of production and distribution together fail to yield now some arbitrarily chosen minimum standard of consumption, or some equally arbitrary minimum level of unemployment. This would simply be a way of saying that the Italian economy fails to produce or to perform at certain designated levels of aspiration. On the same basis, any nation in the world could be considered overpopulated, provided the standard were set high enough. Standards of this type can be highly useful as guides for the formulation of economic policy. They can also be highly misleading when employed for the interpretation of population phenomena. And when used for international comparisons, they involve the serious error of overlooking vital differences in underlying economic conditions.[30]

The Italian economy suffers from certain deep-seated structural difficulties centering in the relationship between agriculture and the nonagricultural sectors, and in the quality and geographical distribution of the labor force. In addition, the labor market of the postwar years suffered from extreme but transitory pressure from the side of supply. This cluster of difficult problems justifies the conclusion that postwar Italy did experience severe population pressure. But these difficulties should not be allowed to obscure the fact of substantial and sustained economic expansion, or to suggest the presence of absolute overpopulation. For decades the Italian economy has proved itself capable of improvement—in technique, in capital formation, in increase of employment, and in output per worker. Capital formation has proved able to outrun population growth. Higher employment and higher per capita real incomes have been the result. There is no evident reason why this process of improvement should not persist for the visible future. If so, Italy does not face an insurmountable population problem. Indeed, so far as numbers are concerned, a declining rate of increase has already set in.

What then is the Italian population problem? Basically, it is that the demand for labor until the sixties failed to increase rapidly enough to absorb an adequate proportion of the expanding labor supply, despite a rapid and well-sustained rise in output. This is a way of saying that the real difficulty was economic, rather than demographic. The demographic factor entered through a temporarily large increase in the postwar labor force, which obscured the eventually favorable implications of a comparatively modest and still declining natural rate of increase in total population. Still, the main problem lay in the demand for labor, rather than in permanently severe population pressure as such.[31] Allied to it is the continuing difficulty of maldistribution of the population between south and north.

The problem of inadequate labor demand must be mentioned

here for the valuable light it throws on the whole population question. Italian agriculture has been releasing workers from productive employment, rather than absorbing them, for the past forty years. This process is desirable in itself since it reflects the technical improvement of the agricultural sphere. At the same time, the nonagricultural sector has continued to expand, again indicating technical advance. However, it did not adequately absorb the rapidly increased labor force of the immediate postwar years. In the south particularly, the nonagricultural sector has hardly been able to enlarge at all; coupled to statutory restrictions, this bottled up the available labor supply in agricultural work of low productivity. Given the much higher natural rate of increase in the south, population pressure has been acute there for generations.

During the first postwar decade and a half, no real inroads were made into mass unemployment, notwithstanding rapid economic expansion. There is good reason to believe that this disappointing performance can largely be attributed to transient influences—a temporarily swollen influx of job-seekers, large supplies of redundant labor forcibly kept on the payrolls, extension of hours rather than of numbers as output increased, and predominance of unskilled and inexperienced young people among the unemployed. So far as these problems are concerned, vigorous economic expansion has now taken the country over the hump, although the southern question remains.

The absolute shrinkage of employment in agriculture need not be a disaster and gives every promise of being a benefit, provided that capital formation is adequate to permit the nonagricultural economy to expand its demand for labor at a sufficient rate. In this way the industrial countries of northwest Europe were able to develop total production and foreign trade, and so to raise per capita real incomes. Italy lags well behind, but a similar process is under way there too. Given the now declining pressure of population increase, it can safely be concluded that the basic problems are no longer demographic, but instead are economic. Since the Italian economy has proved itself capable of sustained improvement, the specter of overpopulation can be laid to rest at last.

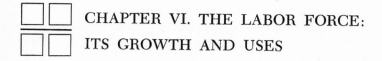

CHAPTER VI. THE LABOR FORCE:
ITS GROWTH AND USES

Italy today is in the select category of nations with the slowest rates of population growth below 1 per cent yearly. Accordingly, the pressure of population upon labor supply has ceased to be a major problem. Today the central demographic issue is the encouragement of emigration to the north.

Nevertheless, even into the earlier postwar years population growth continued to pose difficulties. At least since the turn of the century, the core of the trouble was demand for labor. Another difficulty came from the sluggish transformation from a predominantly peasant and handicraft society to a modern and well-balanced industrial one; and, of course, there was the growing disparity between north and south. Together with the much higher rate of natural population increase in the south, this failure of economic fusion between the two halves of the nation projected growing issues concerning internal migration, along with many other questions.

By the sixties, labor demand had finally caught up with supply in the aggregative sense. What remains is the problem of completing the transformation to modern industrialism. This task is inseparable from the renovation of the south. Moreover, it poses profound issues of both a political and an economic character regarding the pattern of economic development and its mechanism, and the extent of the internal redistribution of the population.

QUANTITATIVE AND QUALITATIVE CHARACTERISTICS

The evolution of the labor force since 1871.[1] When modern Italy became a nation in 1871, its economy was dominated by agriculture and surrounded by small artisan and mercantile enterprises of a family type. Agriculture comprised a complicated mixture of peasant holdings, sharecropping, large feudal estates, and some casual field labor. Outside agriculture, family enterprise was prolific, while industry in the modern sense was very restricted.

The ensuing decades have recorded the emergence of corporate enterprise, the large-scale firm, and the large industrial plant. They have also witnessed the development of much capitalistic agriculture, including many peasant holdings that are primarily market-oriented. However, these changes have by no means displaced the older productive system. Nor have they effected in Italy the degree of transformation that has been accomplished by Germany, whose evolution to a modern industrial and commercial economy began at about the same time. In Italy, agriculture retains much of its immemorial structure and organization, while family enterprise continues to have great importance in manufacturing, trade and services.[2]

In consequence Italy can be described as having a decidedly mixed economy, sharply differentiated from northwest Europe so far as the emergence of a massive system of capitalistic enterprise and of wage labor are concerned. The number of wage and salary employees remains relatively low even today, while self-employment has stayed high. Family enterprises in and outside agriculture, although not invariably inefficient, continue to provide a spongy productive structure that absorbs much of the working population, often in jobs of very low productivity, yielding low per capita incomes.

This peculiar combination of pre-capitalistic and capitalistic enterprises is plainly evident in the history of the Italian labor force. It is central to an adequate interpretation of the problems of unemployment and poverty. At the same time, the transformation of the pre-capitalistic segments of the Italian economic structure, not merely in the depressed south but throughout the country, constitutes the decisive factor in all efforts to deal effectively with these problems. Emphatically, the way of escape does not lie in the direction of make-work programs and unemployment relief as such, even if these expedients have temporary utility. Rather, it is to be found only in a major structural transformation of the economic system itself.

For the ninety years from 1871 to 1961, the available manpower data indicate conclusively that it has been extremely difficult to absorb the expanding labor force in productive employment.[3]

Table 33 presents the evidence in summary form. The first fact that immediately strikes the eye is the great lag in the growth of the active population relative to potential labor supply. Between 1871 and 1961 population present rose by 86.1 per cent, while the population of working age increased even more rapidly—by 96.6 per cent. In sharp contrast, the active population expanded by only 44.5 per cent.

TABLE 33. Comparative changes in population present, population of working age, and active population, 1871–1961 (1871=100)

| Year | Participation rate | | Population present [b] | Population of working age (15–64 years) | Active population [c] |
	Total population (per cent)	Population of working age [a] (per cent)			
1871	53.2	85.2	100.0	100.0	100.0
1881	53.2	84.9	106.2	104.4	106.2
1901	48.9	82.1	121.2	115.8	111.5
1911	47.1	79.7	129.4	122.9	114.7
1921	47.7	75.8	141.5	142.8	126.7
1931	44.4	70.7	153.6	154.9	128.6
1936	43.8	70.7	160.1	158.9	131.8
1951	41.7	63.7	175.9	184.4	137.8
1961 [d]	41.3	62.7	186.1	196.6	144.5

[a] Since the active population includes employed young people of ten to fourteen years and some persons of sixty-five years and over, the participation rates for the population of working age (fifteen through sixty-four years) are somewhat overstated.

[b] Applies to territory of the time census was taken.

[c] Includes those then employed, and then known to be unemployed who were formerly employed; excludes unemployed seeking first job and those temporarily employed abroad.

[d] Figure for population present is an official estimate for the year end, based upon the census count of October 15, 1961. Figure for population of working age obtained by applying the official estimate of the age structure of the resident population at the end of 1959 (65.9 per cent in fifteen to sixty-four years bracket) to population present at the end of 1961. Figure for active population estimated from official sample for November 10, 1961, deducting 304,000 persons seeking their first jobs to preserve comparability of this series.

Source: (1871–1951), Francesco Coppola d'Anna, La disoccupazione in Italia, vol. IV, part 2 (Rome: Camera dei deputi), pp. 32, 34; (1961) Relazione generale, 1961, I, p. 79; 1962, II, p. 363; and Annuario statistico italiano, 1960, p. 19.

Apart from small interim variations, population present and the population of working age kept pace with each other until 1931, after which time the working age group drew ahead, rising by 26.9 per cent as against only 21.1 per cent for population as a whole between 1931 and 1961. This relatively greater growth in the population of working age during 1931–1961 reflects the effects of temporary influences already mentioned: greatly reduced net emigration, inflated birth rates, and the influx of postwar refugees. More important, however, the active population increased by only 12.4 per cent during this time—dramatic proof of the increasing gravity of the employment problem on the one hand, and of the inadequate growth of the Italian economy on the other. Thus while the working age group was expanding by about 232,000 persons per year, the number who became active in the labor market fell far behind, advancing by only 76,000 annually.

The comparative behavior of participation rates (participation in the labor market), for both total population and population of working age, reveals more about the lack of job opportunities. Between 1871 and 1961, the ratio of active population to population present fell from 53.2 to 41.3 per cent, while the corresponding ratio for the population of working age dropped from 85.2 to 62.7 per cent. On a relative basis, the former rate fell by slightly more than a fifth and the latter by one quarter.

It is, of course, well known that rising levels of per capita income bring about declining participation rates. Wives and young people are less required to augment family incomes. Opportunities for higher education increase, extending the age of entry into productive work, while the age of retirement becomes reduced. Even in Italy these changes have been under way, and to this extent falling participation rates indicate rising economic welfare. However, this development must not be overrated. Per capita income in Italy is still low relative to the richer countries. Between 1871 and 1951, real per capita national income (prices of 1938) rose 86.8 per cent, or at the very low compound rate of 0.78 per cent a year.[4] Along with persistent heavy unemployment and underemployment until the end of the fifties, these facts suggest a radically different view of the sharp decline in participation rates—that the main explanation lay in lack of opportunities for jobs. Once more we are thrust back to the slow expansion of the Italian economy.

This question can be probed more deeply by examination of the growth of the active population by economic sectors, as indicated in Tables 34 and 35. What stands out at once is the absolute decline in the active population in agriculture, which in 1951 accounted for 8.08 million persons, or 15 per cent less than in 1901, and 20.4 per cent below the peak year of 1921. By contrast, as Table 35 shows, the nonagricultural sphere as a whole absorbed 80 per cent more people in 1951 than half a century before. Within this sector, however, by far the largest relative increases occurred in civil service jobs (up 115 per cent) and in the service category of trade, finance and insurance (up 97.7 per cent). Falling rather well behind, industry as a whole increased by slightly over two thirds.[5]

TABLE 34. Relative growth of the active population by economic sector, 1901–1951 [a] (1901=100)

Year	Agriculture, forestry, hunting and fishing	Industry [b]	Transportation and Communication	Trade, finance and insurance	Government [c]
1901	100.0	100.0	100.0	100.0	100.0
1911	96.4	116.8	135.3	101.0	103.5
1921	106.8	116.1	190.8	115.4	148.6
1931	98.4	131.6	185.3	141.1	165.9
1936	95.3	139.6	171.9	166.2	181.5
1951	85.0	168.6	180.8	197.7	215.0

[a] The active population includes employed minors of ten years and over, all other employed persons, and those known unemployed who had been formerly employed (including minors). The count is based upon the territorial limits prevailing at the time of the census. The data from the census of 1961 had not been published at the time this study went to press.
[b] Covers extractive industry, manufacturing, building construction, and electrical utilities. Includes enterprises operated or technically controlled by the Government.
[c] Public administration.
Source: Annuario statistico italiano, 1955, p. 377.

Between 1901 and 1951, the population of working age—the main source of the labor supply—increased 11.47 million.[6] During the same period, the active population attached to agriculture fell 1.42 million, while the nonagricultural sector expanded by 5.18 million. Because agriculture had already passed the saturation point and in fact was releasing people rather than absorbing them, the over-all growth of the active population was limited to only

3.76 million for the whole period. As a result, the labor market as a whole could absorb only one third of the net increase in the population of working age during this half-century, while the participation rate of the group as a whole dropped by one fifth.

The decline of agriculture as a source for employment is a familiar fact in many countries undergoing industrialization and so causes no surprise. On the side of absolute numbers, the shrinkage reflects technological improvements that have simultaneously reduced labor requirements and increased over-all farm output. Given, too, the limited extent and often mediocre quality of its land resources, Italian agriculture as a whole has been unable to

TABLE 35. Comparative changes in the agricultural and nonagricultural distribution of the active population, 1901–1951

Year	Nonagricultural sector		Share of total active population		
	Including industry	Excluding industry	Agriculture	Industry	Non-agricultural
	(1901=100)			(per cent)	
1901	100.0	100.0	59.8	23.8	40.2
1911	112.4	106.9	56.1	26.9	43.9
1921	123.7	134.8	56.2	24.3	43.8
1931	140.5	153.5	51.0	27.2	49.0
1936	152.3	170.6	48.2	28.1	51.8
1951	181.1	199.1	41.1	32.5	58.9

Source: Annuario statistico italiano, 1955, p. 377.

absorb more people in productive labor. At the same time, the nonagricultural sector has proved able to expand. Together, these influences account for the absolute and relative decline of agriculture as a user of manpower. Since 1951, all the evidence suggests that this decline has continued, probably at an accelerated pace.[7]

As a last bit of evidence regarding the slow growth of employment in Italy, the more recent experience of 1936–1951 must be considered. As with the preceding analysis, the active population —rather than employment as such—must be used, because adequate over-all employment data are not available. Granting that the active population figures include the known unemployed who had been formerly employed, and that the volume of such unemployment fluctuates over time, nonetheless they will serve as a rough measure of long-term changes in job opportunities.

During 1936–1951, the population of working age increased on the average by 283,800 persons per year. Each year 73,100 became attached to industry, and 49,600 became identified with other non-agricultural activities—for a total average annual increase of 122,700 persons. In the same period, agriculture released 65,600 persons annually, which reduced the net over-all expansion rate to only 57,100 persons. Not all these necessarily found permanent jobs. In consequence, only one fifth of the average annual increase in the population of working age became absorbed in the active population—a participation rate of only 20.1 per cent for the net increase in the potential labor supply. If the number of the formerly employed who were unemployed could be deducted, the net expansion and incremental participation rates would have been even smaller, for this type of unemployment certainly increased between the two census dates.[8] Even passing over this, merely to have maintained the 70 per cent participation rate existing in 1936 for the working-age group would have required an annual rise in the active population by 128,800, or one and one-quarter times more than was actually achieved. Once again the facts indicate that a chronic and serious lag in the expansion of job opportunities had been developing in the Italian economy. With the continuing decrease of employment in agriculture after 1921, the burden of expansion lay entirely with the nonagricultural sector, particularly in industry. After World War II, industrial output began to increase very rapidly. But until the sixties, employment expansion continued to grow much more slowly. Between 1951 and 1961, industrial output rose at a compound annual rate of 8.4 per cent while industrial employment expanded only 3.8 per cent yearly.[9]

Before completing this review of the history of the Italian labor force some attention should be given to the changing status of female workers and to certain regional differences in the development of the active population.

During the five decades ending in 1951, the proportion of females in both the total population present and the population of working age exceeded that for males. Both ratios were higher in 1951 than in 1901, as Table 36 shows. By 1951, there were 1.24 million more females than males in the total population and 1.12 million more females than males in the working-age group. War and emigration were probably the principal reasons for this persistent imbalance.

Over this half-century period, the female shares of the active population as a whole and of the nonagricultural active population alone both declined from about one third in 1901 to one quarter in 1951. In addition, the over-all participation rate (females in the active population relative to females of working age) dropped sharply, from 52.3 per cent to only 30.6 per cent. At the same time the corresponding participation rate for males dropped from 112.9 per cent to 99.3 per cent. In absolute numbers the active female population was less in 1951 than in 1901, falling from 5.15 million to 4.89 million, while the active male population rose from 10.75 million to 14.77 million.

TABLE 36. Changes in proportion of females in population present, population of working age, and active population, 1901–1951 (per cent)

Year	Population present	Population of working age	Share of active population		Participation rate [a]
			Over-all	Nonagricultural	
1901	50.2	50.8	32.4	31.7	52.3
1911	50.9	51.9	31.3	29.9	47.9
1921	50.7	51.4	28.6	26.8	42.1
1931	51.1	51.9	27.7	26.1	37.8
1936	50.9	51.5	27.9	28.9	38.3
1951	51.3	51.8	24.9	25.2	30.6

[a] Total females in active population relative to female population of working age (fifteen to sixty-four years).
Source: Annuario statistico italiano, 1955, pp. 376–377.

A breakdown by economic sector reveals that the number of females active in agriculture dropped by more than a third between the two dates, while those active outside agriculture rose 44 per cent. Nonagricultural expansion failed to offset the withdrawal of females from agriculture, which helps to account for the over-all fall in the female participation rate.

It must, of course, be granted that a declining female participation rate is a normal sign of improved per capita real incomes. At the same time, however, it is by no means a complete explanation. Both the expulsion of women from agriculture and the fall in the nonagricultural female participation rate strongly reflect the increasing difficulty of obtaining employment, an obstacle common to both men and women. On an international comparison, both the female participation rate alone and the over-all rate—relative to the respective populations of working age—are low: in 1951 they were 30.6 and 63.7 per cent. The pressure in Italy is for earned income, not for leisure. Thus the basic reason for the restricted participation of women in the labor market has been lack of job opportunities, rather than increased per capita incomes over the years.

There remains the question of regional differences in the development of the active population. Fully comparable data are lacking on a regional basis, but reasonably satisfactory approximations can be had for the census years of 1871, 1936, and 1951.[10] In every instance the figures sharply emphasize the plight of the southern economy. Between 1871 and 1951 the number of persons attached to agriculture in north and central Italy fell by one fifth. Yet in the south and the islands, the active population in agriculture actually rose by one quarter. Lack of alternative opportunities was the reason. Over the entire eighty-year period the number attached to industry in the south rose by only 15.6 per cent, as against 136.2 per cent for the north. Taking the nonagricultural active population as a whole, the south expanded by only 18.6 per cent, while the north soared by 116.8 per cent, or roughly six times as fast. On an over-all basis, the active population of the north and center increased by one third, as against slightly more than one fifth in the south and the islands, even though the relative increases in total population were almost identical in the two sections of the country.

Participation rates tell the same story. Relative to total population, the active population in the north stood at 57.8 per cent in 1871 and fell to 43.6 per cent by 1951. By contrast, the south had a lower rate in 1871—53.1 per cent—and by 1951 suffered a decline to only 37.1 per cent. Over the same period, the female participation rate (active relative to total female population) fell sharply in both the north and the south. Again, however, the south was worse off—its rate in 1951 being only 16.2 per cent, compared with 22.7 per cent in the north. In part, the lower rate for females in the south reflects a strong cultural tradition there that favors confining women to the home. However, restricted economic opportunities undoubtedly have been the principal influence.

The behavior of the southern labor supply since 1871 shows a perverse expansion of agriculture, very limited growth in the nonagricultural sphere even relative to a restricted Italian standard, and a sharp decline in participation rates. The key to this paradoxical behavior is that southern Italy for years was a blocked economy, badly constricted by capital shortage, lack of skilled manpower, and lack of markets. Its nonagricultural activities could expand but little, while its agriculture was suffocated by excess population, tied to the soil for a quarter-century by restrictive legislation.

The labor force in 1961. No full-scale enumeration of the labor force has been published since 1951, although a new census was taken in 1961. During the intervening years, ISTAT undertook a series of field surveys, from which it prepared over-all estimates. Because these samples were gathered at shifting times during the different years and thus were affected by seasonal movements, and because they involve shifting definitions, they cannot be relied upon to reveal temporal movements in employment and unemployment.[11]

Nonetheless, the estimate for 1961, based upon four field surveys undertaken in that year, provides some useful insights regarding the present position of the Italian labor force. As of 1961, it involved 20.5 million persons, or 41 per cent of population present in that year.[12] Of this total, 19.8 million were employed, and 708,000 (3.4 per cent) were unemployed.[13]

According to the ISTAT survey (see Table 37), 72.2 per cent of the labor force and 72.3 per cent of the employed consisted of males. Males also constituted 68.9 per cent of the estimated unemployed. However, they made up only 59.3 per cent of those unemployed who were looking for their first job—indirect evidence of the greater difficulty women encounter in obtaining employment. This is also suggested by the much larger proportion of males (75.1 per cent) among the unemployed who had formerly been employed, and again by the very large number of women (77.7 per cent) in the ranks of occasional workers.

Rates for participation and for unemployment tell a similar story. Relative to their part of the total population, the male participation rate was 61.0 per cent, while the female was only 22.5 per cent—conforming well to tendencies evident during 1901–1951. Of the female labor force, 3.9 per cent were unemployed, as

against 3.3 per cent for males. Although the over-all unemployment rate—3.4 per cent—was low, its relatively modest value
could be misleading. Among those counted as employed are over 2.6
million assistants who normally work in family enterprises without
pay. Furthermore, there is a serious discrepancy between the sample value and registered unemployment—enough to suggest that
the former substantially understates the facts. Finally, the unemployment rate does not adequately reflect underemployment—for
example, those working at the time of the survey who cannot
expect to work throughout the year, and those employed at below
normal hours.

TABLE 37. Estimated labor force and total population, 1961 (in thousands)

Employment status	Males	Females	Total
Labor force	14,839	5,705	20,544
Employed	14,351	5,485	19,836
Unemployed	488	220	708
Formerly employed	325	108	433
Seeking first job	163	112	275
Inactive population	9,472	19,683	29,055
Occasional workers	196	682	878
Total population	24,311	25,388	49,699

Source: Relazione generale, 1962, II, p. 80.

Further insight into the current state of the labor force can be
had by examination of the distribution of those employed, according to sex, economic sector, and occupational status. This information, presented in Table 38, reveals much about the peculiar structure of the Italian economy.

Probably the outstanding fact indicated by Table 38 is the relatively small number of dependent employees in the employed
population—only 50 per cent of the total. This group consists of
wage workers in the sense of manual employees under the direction of others. Sixty per cent of them are concentrated in industry,
with only a sixth belonging to agriculture. Among those in agricul-

ture, a significant portion are field hands on annual contracts, which means that paid day laborers in farming constitute a very small proportion of the employee category.

Another important fact suggested by Table 38 concerns the peculiar category of assistants. In a sense this group too consists of employees, but not in the strict sense of wage labor. Rather, it is made up of family members. Three quarters of them are in agriculture, with an additional 16.9 per cent in trade and services. It cannot be said that they are economically unproductive, for they perform essential work in the family enterprise. But since the custom in Italy is to treat family income as a global return to the head of the household, from which maintenance of all members is provided, the assistants are not strictly wage labor, even though they are "employees."

The number engaged in this primitive category accounted for 12.9 per cent of estimated total employment in 1961, while one quarter of all employed females were in this group. Care must be exercised in relating the assistants to the employment problem, for it would be easy to conclude that in its entirety it simply represents a form of concealed unemployment, an improvised and private program of make-work. Obviously peasants, artisans and small retailers are not generally so stupid or so indifferent to making an income that they would tolerate the use of labor yielding a zero or negative marginal product. The problem is more subtle than this. On the one side, it is often not possible to employ these assistants at normal full time, either on a daily or on an annual basis. On the other, the aggregate demand for labor in the Italian economy has persistently been too feeble to provide alternative opportunities, particularly for young people in this group. Thus they remain at home and share the work of the family enterprise —work that otherwise often could be rearranged and concentrated among fewer hands, affording fuller employment to this remaining group.

The ISTAT survey shows that the two categories of self-employed and assistants absorbed over one third of the total employed population, accounting for 15.9 per cent of all industrial employment and 29.1 per cent of that involved in "other" activities (trade, finance, services, and government). Obviously, Italy has not yet become an employee society, although the future points in

TABLE 38. Estimated distribution of employed by occupational status, economic sector, and sex, 1961 [a] (per cent)

Occupational status	Distribution within sector			Distribution of over-all total	Distribution of over-all occupational totals			Distribution of occupational total by sex	
	Agriculture	Industry	Other		Agriculture	Industry	Other	Males	Females
Self-employed	36.6	13.5	22.1	22.9	46.6	23.2	30.2	25.7	15.6
Dependent employees	28.9	76.5	36.1	50.0	16.9	60.5	22.6	52.5	43.4
Assistants	33.6	2.4	7.0	12.9	75.7	7.4	16.9	8.4	24.8
Entrepreneurs, executives, professionals and clerks	0.9	7.6	34.8	14.2	1.7	21.3	77.0	13.4	16.2

[a] "Other" refers to trade, finance, insurance, and other services. "Assistants" refers principally to unpaid family labor on farms and in artisan and mercantile enterprises.

Source: Relazione generale, 1962, II, p. 86.

that direction. It must be conceded that there is a continuing place, even in a modern economy, for the small self-employed farmer, artisan and tradesman. However, the survival of these ancient forms of employment at such relatively high levels even today is a clear sign that the economic transformation of Italy has by no means been completed. Both self-employment and family labor increased during 1951–1961, making the improvement in over-all employment somewhat more apparent than real.

MOVEMENTS IN THE STRUCTURE OF EMPLOYMENT

By sector since 1901. Although they have the disadvantage of including those unemployed who had formerly held jobs, the census statistics for the active population can be used to indicate gross changes in employment by main economic sectors. These data are presented in Tables 39 and 40.

TABLE 39. Changes in distribution of the active population by main economic sectors, 1901–1951 (in thousands)

Year	Agriculture, forestry, and fishing	Industry	Transport and communication	Trade, finance and insurance	Government	Total
1901	9,510	3,788	402	1,599	605	15,904
1911	9,171	4,401	544	1,615	626	16,357
1921	10,158	4,397	767	1,846	899	18,067
1931	9,356	4,984	746	2,251	1,044	18,341
1936	9,066	5,290	691	2,657	1,098	18,802
1951	8,082	6,387	727	3,162	1,301	19,659

Source: Annuario statistico italiano, 1955, p. 377.

The statistics suggest that over the half-century from 1901 to 1951 employment probably did not rise by much more than a third, while the potential labor supply soared by almost 85 per cent. More important, as Table 39 shows, there was a marked slowing down in the rate of expansion of employment as a whole. In the first two decades from 1901 to 1921, the active population increased by 13.6 per cent, while, in the period from 1931 to 1951, when the pressure of increasing labor supply was even greater, employment expansion proceeded only half as fast as before—6.4

per cent. In this latter period, industry and the service group (trade, finance and insurance) both markedly increased their rates of expansion, while government slowed down. Transportation and communication, and agriculture recorded decreases.

TABLE 40. Relative rates of change in active population by main economic sectors, 1901–1951 (per cent)

Sector	1901–1921	1931–1951	1921–1951
Total active population	13.6	6.4	8.8
Government	48.6	29.5	44.7
Trade, finance and insurance	15.4	40.1	71.3
Transportation and communication	90.8	−2.4	−5.3
Industry	16.1	28.1	45.2
Agriculture, forestry, fishing	6.8	−13.7	−20.5

Source: Table 39.

As Table 41 shows, important changes occurred in the inter-sector distribution of the active population. Both industry and the trade-finance-insurance group substantially increased their relative importance, while agriculture declined sharply. Yet even in 1951 farming was still the leading sector of employment, although it was displaced by industry in the decade following.

TABLE 41. Changes in the distribution of the active population by sector, 1901 and 1951 (per cent)

Sector, by rank order	Relative weight, 1901	Relative weight, 1951
Government	3.8	6.6
Trade, finance and insurance	10.0	16.1
Transportation and communication	2.5	3.7
Industry	23.8	32.5
Agriculture, forestry, fishing	59.8	41.1

Source: Table 39.

Within the industrial sector after 1911. Given the rapidly in-creasing importance of industrial employment throughout the first half of the twentieth century, it is interesting to attempt to isolate the growth nodes of employment among the different industries, and to see how they were distributed between "advanced" and "traditional" categories.[14] This can be done approximately by comparing the census data for 1911 with those for 1951. These figures do not embrace the total number attached to all industry on the two dates: for 1911, they cover just under one half, while for 1951 the proportion is about two thirds. Nonetheless, the coverage should be quite complete for the advanced group, meaning that most of the undistributed remainder falls within the category of traditional, small-scale activities. The figures are presented in Table 42.

Generally speaking, the advanced group includes the industries most likely to employ large-scale plants, modern techniques, machine power, and wage labor. Because family and artisan enterprises are much less prominent here, the employment data are much less weighted by self-employment and family assistants. Also, the group contains most of the larger firms, whose labor policies are more likely to be governed by union agreements and statutory regulations. By contrast, the traditional category largely presents the reverse of all these characteristics.

Looking first at the industries showing the largest increases, they turn out to be metal products and repair services (+639,000), constructure (+410,000), clothing and furnishings (+180,000), textiles (+156,000), chemicals and related (+149,000), and foods and related (+102,000). Together these industries accounted for 85 per cent of the indicated over-all increase in industrial employment.

Of the 1,914,000 total increase for the advanced and traditional groups together, 57.6 per cent appears assignable to the former category. Undoubtedly this figure is an overstatement, for in the 1951 census miscellaneous machine repair shops were lumped together with primary producers of metal products, although repair services typically belong to the traditional group. Unfortunately, their comparative shares in the totals for 1911 and 1951 are not known, and the appropriate redistribution cannot be made.

Despite this handicap, it can be asserted safely that the traditional group as a whole was of about equal numerical importance in contributing to the increase of industrial employment over these four decades. In short, no tendency is evident for such employment to concentrate within the technically more progressive branches of industry. This indicates the relatively slow pace of industrialization down to 1951.

However, this view of the matter tends to understate the degree

TABLE 42. Changes in employment within the industrial sector, 1911 and 1951 [a] (in thousands)

Industry group	1911	1951	Absolute change	Relative change
Advanced group:	1332	2435	1103	82.8%
Extractive	105	119	14	13.3
Manufacturing	1227	2316	1089	88.7
Primary metals	142	145	3	2.1
Metal products & repair services [b]	258	897	639	247.7
Building materials	182	207	25	13.7
Chemicals and related [c]	51	200	149	292.1
Textiles	495	651	156	31.5
Leather and skins	21	39	18	85.7
Paper	33	63	30	90.9
Printing and publishing	39	74	35	89.7
Rubber	6	40	34	566.7
Traditional group:	840	1651	811	96.5
Foods and related [d]	258	360	102	39.5
Clothing and furnishings	231	411	180	77.9
Wood and furniture	210	294	84	40.0
Construction	122	532	410	236.0
Miscellaneous manufactures	19	54	35	184.2
Total, all manufactures	2067	3967	1900	91.9
Grand total (Advanced and traditional)	2172	4086	1914	88.1

[a] The following groups in Lutz's array for 1951 were excluded here for lack of data for 1911: electricity (67,100), photo-phono-cinematographic (11,100), water (11,800), and gas (14,100). Figures apply to 1951.

[b] Metal products in 1951 was a mixed census category, including on the one side production of transportation equipment and office machines, and on the other thousands of tiny firms engaged in miscellaneous repair services. Lutz's partial separation could not be observed because of lack of data for 1911.

[c] Includes chemicals proper, hydrocarbon derivatives, and cellulose-artificial and synthetic fibers. Lack of comparability precluded separation for 1911.

[d] Includes food processing, beverages, and tobacco manufacture. Lack of comparability for 1911 precluded separation of tobacco.

Source: 1911 census data from Francesco Coppola d'Anna, "Lo sviluppo della popolazione addetta ad attività non agricole nell' ultimo cinquantennio," vol. IV, part 3, La disoccupazione in Italia (Rome: Camera dei deputati, 1953), pp. 60, 64–65; 1951 census data from Vera C. Lutz, "Some Characteristics of Italian Economic Development," Banca nazionale del lavoro, Quarterly Review, no. 39 (December 1953).

of technological change that actually took place, for it rests upon absolute quantities of employment in 1911 and 1951, and absolute changes between the two dates. For this reason new industries and subgroups, necessarily having very small weights at the most in the 1911 totals, ordinarily could not be expected to figure significantly in the absolute growth of employment. Yet on a relative basis, they stand out prominently: for example, rubber and chemicals; within chemicals the subgroups of hydrocarbon derivatives and cellulose and synthetic fibers; and within extractive industry the fuels group. Also within the advanced sector, metal products also showed great relative growth, reflecting rapid expansion in subgroups such as automobiles, transportation equipment, and office machines.

Employment within the advanced industrial sector, 1948–1961. The very strong upsurge in industrial output during the years of the great boom drew its greatest contribution from the advanced sector of industry. At the same time, we know that unemployment remained severe until the sixties, suggesting that this sector failed to expand employment in proportion either to its annual rate of increase in output, or to its two third's weight in the index of industrial production.[15]

The reasons for this failure are examined in Chapter XIV. Here we shall be concerned with structural changes in employment among the industries comprising the technically advanced sector. For such purpose, the manual-worker figures collected by the Ministry of Labor and Social Welfare (ML) are the best ones available, granting that they have their limitations.[16] In Table 43, these data are presented for certain years, selected to permit comparison with other sources and to indicate the over-all changes occurring during the boom period.

The main structural changes between 1948 and 1961 were the very large expansion of the metal products group, and the substantial contraction of textiles. Behind the upsurge in metal products were three forces: rapidly increasing sales of automotive vehicles, reflecting the rise of personal incomes with the boom; impressive growth in the demand for machinery and equipment, responding to the high rate of capital formation; and the very rapid growth of exports. The contrasting sharp decline in textile employment centered in cotton and woolen goods. These lines of production had

TABLE 43. Changes in employment of manual workers within the advanced sector of industry for selected years, 1948–1961 [a] (in thousands)

Industry group and industry	1948	1950	1951	1961	Net changes Numbers 1948–1961	Net changes Numbers 1951–1961	Net changes Per cent 1948–1961	Net changes Per cent 1951–1961
Extractive	67.6	57.1	59.5	37.3	−30.3	−22.2	−44.8	−37.3
Manufacturing:								
Textiles	552.9	525.3	527.9	433.6	−119.3	−94.3	−21.6	−17.9
Primary metals	108.1	98.8	101.2	116.2	8.1	15.0	7.5	14.8
Metal products	531.9	525.3	525.7	751.3	219.4	225.6	41.2	42.9
Building materials	99.9	103.4	108.2	144.6	44.7	36.4	44.7	33.6
Chemicals	111.1	108.6	110.7	150.0	38.9	39.3	35.0	35.5
Rubber	34.3	33.0	32.1	33.2	−1.1	1.1	−3.2	3.4
Total	1438.0	1394.4	1405.8	1628.9	190.7	223.1	13.3	15.9
Grand total	1505.8	1451.5	1465.3	1666.2	160.4	200.9	10.6	13.7

[a] Within the manufacturing industries shown, the following components are included: primary metals (iron and steel, nonferrous); metal products (resmelting, nonelectric machines, electrical machines and equipment, transportation equipment). As of 1956, the ML Sample embraced 18,500 establishments, employing 1.75 million manual workers, about 55 per cent of the total for all industry. For September 1961, the ML count totalled 2.07 million for all industry, which was 45.0 per cent of the census enumeration for November, 1961.

Source: Rassegna di statistiche del lavoro, various issues.

dominated Italian industry from the beginning of industrialization, both in number of workers and in size of value added to total industrial product. Since the war, Italian textiles have suffered from extremely keen foreign competition, finally to become displaced from their traditional position of leadership.

For 1951–1961, the average yearly rate of increase in employment within the inner sector was only 20,000 workers, on the ML tally. However, this figure is quite deceptive, because the total number of manual employees in the sector in 1959 was identical with that for 1951—1,465,000. Thus the entire net gain over the full decade was achieved in 1960 (+99,200) and 1961 (+101,300). The statistical explanation is simple. During 1951–1959, the large gains attained by metal products, supplemented by much more modest ones in chemicals and processing of nonmetallic minerals (building materials) were being cancelled out by the sharp decline in textiles, augmented by a smaller one in extractive industry.

With 1959, the situation changed in several respects. The already high rate of advance in industrial production began to accelerate even further, and this was translated into a jump of 130,000 manual employees in metal products over the next two years. Substantial gains also occurred in chemicals, and in the metallurgical group (iron and steel, nonferrous metals). At the same time, employment in textiles finally turned upward, adding 25,000 manual workers by 1961.

Comparison of September 1961 with September 1962 permits the record to be extended into the period when serious inflation finally reappeared. Over these twelve months, employment within the advanced sector expanded by 79,000—a substantial gain viewed against the whole boom period, but well short of the annual average for 1959–1961 (100,000). Over two thirds of the 1961–1962 increase was concentrated in metal products, although all other industries except extractive also recorded gains.

It was during the 1959–1962 period that all measures of overt unemployment at last began to show substantial decreases. No doubt the expansion of manual jobs within the advanced sector contributed significantly to this highly important change in the labor market.

However, from a lengthier perspective this new development does not describe the behavior of employment within the advanced sector over the entire post-1947 boom, when output was steadily and very rapidly expanding, while indicated manual-worker employment was lagging far behind. Consider Table 44. Except for textiles, the increases in output have been literally enormous. Yet in every case, indicated increases in manual-worker employment have been very modest in comparison. For the earlier years of 1948–1953, the same contrasting relationship prevailed.

TABLE 44. Comparative changes in output and in employment of manual workers, advanced sector of industry, 1953–1961 [a] (1953=100)

Industry group and industry	Output	Employment
Extractive	194	61
Manufacturing	202	114
Textiles	126	88
Primary metals	248	117
Metal products	213	139
Building materials	224	124
Chemicals	275	130
Rubber	191	106

[a] The year 1953 was used because it is the base date for the current indexes of output. The employment categories match the output ones quite well as a rule, because they are defined according to the UN code.

Source: Output except for building materials and rubber from Organisation for European Co-operation and Development, Statistical Bulletins, General Statistics; building materials and rubber, Relazione generale, 1961; employment, from Rassegna di statistiche del lavoro, various issues.

How may we account for this curious disparity within the inner sector? For the earlier years after 1947 there was a good deal of unneeded labor on the payrolls of these industries. For political reasons, it could not be laid off. This excess labor capacity made it possible to increase output without increasing employment, a situation that lasted even into the early fifties. Furthermore, employers in the sector found it more economical to lengthen hours than to add new workers, because of lump-sum charges imposed under the quite heavy social security levies. Also, they preferred not to add new men because of the difficulty of making later layoffs.

However, these were transitory factors. By all odds, the dominant influences involved economies of scale, plant reorganization, and technological change. Increased economies of scale were inherent in the enormous expansion of production continuously going on. Plant reorganization partly was affected by the same process. In addition, along with technical improvements, it resulted from the extremely high rate of industrial investment prevailing throughout these years, most of which was internally financed. The main gains here were not derived from simple quantitative expansion of the stock of capital. Rather, they flowed from the embodiment of new technology in this new capital, which largely differed qualitatively from that composing the base to which it was added. And in view of the great discrepancy between the growth of output and of employment, the conclusion is evident that most of this new capital was highly labor-saving.

By 1959, two changes began to assert themselves. On the one side, output of the sector began to increase at a still faster rate. On the other, the huge annual gains in gross labor productivity began to shrink at last. The great reserve of exploitable technology available after the war had largely been worked down. The catch-up phase was about over. Accordingly, the gap between the rates of increase in output and in employment finally began to narrow.

An objection may be that the gap itself is imaginary, arising because the ML figures greatly understate the real increase of employment within the sector. The burden of proof for sustaining this contention lies with those who make it. The assignment is not easy, because of the lack of adequate data for the advanced sector. SVIMEZ made an estimate for 1950–1957 suggesting that total employment in the manufacturing part of the sector (not manual workers alone) rose about 36,000 yearly, or about 3.7 times the rate indicated by the ML series.[17] Assuming without deciding that this relationship is a correct adjustment to the ML series for 1953–1961, it turns out that by 1961 (1953 = 100) "true" employment was 137. Over the same years, output in the manufacturing segment of the sector rose to 202 by 1961. Even with these figures, therefore, employment was clearly lagging well behind output. Hence the original contention remains unshaken.

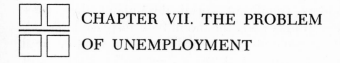

CHAPTER VII. THE PROBLEM
OF UNEMPLOYMENT

A seeming contradiction is posed by the persistence of massive unemployment during almost the whole of the unbroken fourteen-year boom that followed monetary stabilization in 1947. The explanation for this apparent paradox lies in the acceptance of certain preconceptions about the phenomenon itself. In Anglo-American thinking, severe unemployment is associated with the depression phase of the business cycle. Since 1947, Italy has experienced nothing resembling a major cyclical downturn. Over-all growth has been both rapid and steady. Nonetheless, throughout the first fifteen years following defeat in the Second World War, the nation was plagued by heavy unemployment.

Gauged by the number of registered unemployed, the peak was not reached until as late as 1954. Contraction did not even begin until 1957, after a decade of impressive expansion in production. Not until 1959 did the number of registered unemployed begin to shrink in significant degree. More than this, the other dimensions of the problem have continued to pose difficulties until even today —an excessive number of casual and short-time jobs, excessive amounts of unpaid family labor, employment of many persons in jobs well below their levels of skill and ability, and lack of opportunities for a great many young people.

The key strategic factor in the postwar unemployment problem lay in inadequate expansion of total labor demand, rather than in a high trend rate of increase in labor supply. In short, the problem was economic, not demographic, while at the same time it was long-term rather than cyclical in nature. Probed more deeply, the evidence shows that the growth of labor demand did not center in the rapidly growing advanced sector of industry, but instead favored those parts of the nonagricultural economy where small proprietorships, family labor, low-wage jobs, and traditional activities all are prominent, and those in which government employment without regard to profits prevails. At the same time, a sustained contraction of agricultural employment has been in course since the twenties, gaining significant speed throughout the fifties. Despite statutory restraints upon the mobility of displaced agricultural workers, considerable illegal internal migration went on until repeal of this legislation early in 1961, adding to the pressures of supply upon urban labor markets. Moreover, that pressure was augmented further by a widespread desire to approach a modern "Western" plane of living—by those hoping to transfer to better-paying jobs, and by housewives and young people deciding to enter the labor market for the first time.

Accordingly, an adequate interpretation of the unemployment problem must set out from a distinction between long-run forces affecting labor demand and a transitory cluster of influences projected by the war and its termination. Furthermore, unemployment should be viewed not simply as too many people completely without work, but as one dimension of a much larger problem— the failure of the economy to provide enough full-time jobs of a satisfying kind, yielding rates or remuneration somewhere close to the new-found aspirations of the Italian people. In other words, the structural character of labor demand, as much as its total size and aggregate rate of expansion, are at stake.

THE HISTORY OF THE UNEMPLOYMENT QUESTION IN ITALY

Structural vs. *cyclical explanations.* The persistence of massive unemployment throughout 1945–1959 gave credence to the idea that "structural" rather than cyclical forces were at work. Although the advocates of this view shared the belief that unemployment was a largely intractable, long-term phenomenon, not amenable to conventional, contracyclical fiscal and monetary policies of the postwar type, they were anything but agreed on the strategic factors that made the problem "structural."

Some blamed overpopulation or population increase, along with the restriction of emigration after 1930 (the *demographic* view of the problem). Relying on postwar theories of growth, others contended that a rigidity in the technical ratios of labor-to-capital inputs limited the rate of expansion in employment to the rate of capital formation. Since capital formation was held to be too low relative to the rate of increase in the labor force, unemployment was inevitable (the *technological* version). Still others pointed to the level and rate of increase in real wages in the unionized sectors of the nonagricultural economy, particularly in advanced industry (the *market imperfections* theory). Finally, there were those who attributed the trouble to a maladaptation of the structure of labor supply to that of demand—in skills, experience, training, and locational distribution (the *unbalanced labor markets* explanation).

Given this plethora of opinions, the only real measure of agreement lay in the use of "structural" in preference to "cyclical," and in the common conviction that unemployment was chronic.

The problem and its interpretation before 1945. The structural view of unemployment is relatively new, displacing the cyclical explanation that came into prominence in Italy around the turn of the century, and continued to be popular well into the Fascist period.

At the time of unification, there was great optimism.[1] Italy was predominantly agricultural, and, without a large-scale market for daily wage labor, any fluctuations were felt in agricultural prices and incomes, rather than in extensive labor displacement. As Luzzatto observes regarding the agricultural depression after 1883, prices declined by about one third and many holdings were foreclosed. Yet there was probably not much unemployment.[2] However, this was the beginning of the great wave of emigration, which certainly could be considered evidence of disguised unemployment. Indeed, by the nineties considerable professional interest in the economic importance of emigration began to emerge.

The nineties also witnessed the rise of modern Italian industry and the first appearance of the problem of unemployment. Once more emigration proved vital. In the over-all depression of 1887–1894 the rate of emigration nearly doubled.

By the close of the century, professional observers began taking note of certain developments that greatly influenced the unemployment question. One was the formation of an urban-industrial labor market, shown in the parallel rise of the great cities, the industries of the north, and foreign trade. The other was the beginning of the marked economic divergence between the north and south. In the north, industrial expansion and rising incomes were already apparent. In the south, stagnation, poverty, and lack of alternatives began to be apparent (for which very heavy emigration was the only avenue of relief).

Although Italy in 1900–1914 did not possess the kind and extent of industrialization already achieved in England, the United States, or even in Germany, her markets for wage labor were now well enough advanced to make them vulnerable to economic fluctuations. The foreign situation, particularly that in Great Britain was studied for its pertinence to Italy. In keeping with the convention of the time, Italian works dealing with unemployment stressed the cyclical view. Unemployment was considered a natural phenomenon in a competitive society, and natural forces supplied their own corrective and eventually would establish a new equilibrium.[3]

World War I temporarily curtailed interest in the unemployment question. It did not revive until the world crisis of 1921–1922. Beginning in 1919, a system of government labor exchanges was set up, providing statistics of registered unemployment that extend to September 1935, after which publication was suspended by the Fascist regime. Although these data cannot be considered particularly accurate, their movements indicate the changing dimensions of the problem for most of the interwar period. They are presented in Table 45.

The figures indicate that the demobilization crisis of 1919 was passed satisfactorily only to be followed in 1921–1922 by a heavy rise in unemployment. Using the active population as a rough substitute for nonexistent labor force data, the peak 1921 level of unemployment (512,260 persons) represented only 3 per cent.[4] However, bearing in mind that unemployment was heavily concentrated in the industrial sector, which accounted for only 4,397,000 persons in an active population of 18 million, it can be concluded that the actual burden was far higher.[5]

Unemployment declined again after 1922, and comparative prosperity prevailed until 1927. At the end of that year, the lira was stabilized at an overvalued rate, and a severe deflation got under way, soon to be accelerated by the world depression. Unemployment began an almost unbroken rise until 1933, exceeding one million in 1932 and 1933. Again using the active population as a substitute for the labor force, the census of 1931 indicates a peak over-all unemployment rate of over 5 per cent, approaching 20 per cent for the industrial sector alone.[6] After 1933 unemployment subsided somewhat, although Italy continued to be in the throes of the world depression in 1935, when publication of unemployment statistics ceased.

TABLE 45. Movements in registered unemployment, 1919–1935

Year	Number	Year	Number
1919 [a]	325,354	1928	324,422
1920 [a]	179,294	1929	300,787
1921 [a]	381,202	1930	425,438
1922	407,364	1931	734,454
1923	246,396	1932	1,006,442
1924	164,853	1933	1,018,953
1925	110,298	1934	963,677
1926	113,901	1935 [b]	765,815
1927	278,484		

[a] Midpoint between annual maxima and minima.
[b] Average per first nine months only.
Source: Confederazione generale dell'industria italiana, Annuario di statistiche del lavoro, 1949 (Rome, 1950).

From his extensive survey of the professional literature of the interwar period, Caffè concludes that opinion still favored the cyclical explanation. However, as unemployment became acute after 1929, emphasis began to shift away from the natural cycle toward stress on institutional rigidities enforced by industrial and trade union monopoly, political fixing of wages on the basis of income aspirations instead of demand and supply, and obstacles to the mobility of the factors of production.[7] Concern with the predicament of agriculture and the general plight of the south began to be expressed, leading to sporadic government efforts toward relief. At the same time, the dominant tone of professional opinion continued to be hostile to political intervention, expressing fear of dangerous inflationary consequences.

As for official policy, its main responses to growing unemployment were two. Beginning in 1926, it clamped down on the internal migration of workers, steadily tightening these controls between 1928 and 1939. Then with the mid-thirties it turned to colonial conquest and a large-scale armament program.

Italy's defeat in the Second World War was accompanied by a literally disastrous crystallization of adverse economic forces—a collapse in the demand for labor, a great rise in the total number seeking work, widespread threat of starvation, and drastic declines in agricultural and industrial production. The economic position of the south was now at its lowest ebb in half a century. Yet it was within this highly unpromising environment that free government had to assume the difficult tasks not only of economic reconstruction but of economic transformation. Challenged by massive unemployment and soon to come under constitutional mandate (1948) to enforce the right of every citizen to work at adequate wages, no government ever faced greater obstacles.[8] In these difficult circumstances, it is small wonder that professional opinion began to speak of "chronic structural unemployment," and to look toward government intervention in place of more conventional reliance either upon the "natural forces of recovery" or more tepid as well as timid anticyclical devices.[9]

POSTWAR UNEMPLOYMENT

Aggregate and structural movements. The only over-all source of continuous unemployment data is the monthly statistics gathered by the local registry offices of the Ministry of Labor and Social Welfare. After 1928, virtually all workers except independent professionals have had to be hired through the official labor exchanges, a system that still continues in force. The registration data thus derive from operation of the system. Table 46 presents the figures for total registered unemployment in the form of annual averages for 1946–1962.

Whether the ML registration statistics depict with reasonable accuracy the scale of overt unemployment throughout the postwar years, they do interpret the scope and nature of the phenomenon.

First, they indicate that total registered unemployment passed through four waves. During 1946–1948, with rapid inflation in the first two years, unemployment rose. This advance continued after price stabilization. In 1949–1950, while price stability continued, unemployment fell. Between 1951 and 1956, it rose once more, reaching its postwar peak in 1954, and remaining on this plateau through 1956. Yet by 1951 total output had already overtaken its prewar high, and it continued to advance rapidly. During 1957–1962, unemployment was in unbroken decline, although this drop did not attain significant speed until 1959–1962.

Second, the volume of overt unemployment was extremely heavy right through 1959, not falling below 10 per cent of the labor force. Indeed, the unemployment rate for industrial workers alone was well in excess of this figure. Here it will be recalled that for the boom period of 1948–1961 the trend rates of growth for real gross output and for industrial production were 5.9 and 8.8 per cent per year respectively, with little variation. Yet this rapid expansion failed to cut into registered unemployment until after 1956, and not substantially until after 1959. By 1962, however, the unemployment rate was down to 6.4 per cent of the labor force, at the lowest level in the whole postwar period.

TABLE 46. Movements in registered unemployment, 1946–1962 [a]

Year	Number (thousands)	Index (1948=100)	Year	Number (thousands)	Year (1948=100)
1946	1655	77.3	1955	2161	100.9
1947	2025	94.5	1956	2171	101.3
1948	2142	100.0	1957	1970	92.0
1949	1941	90.6	1958	1955	91.3
1950	1860	86.8	1959	1874	87.5
1951	1938	90.5	1960	1746	81.5
1952	2073	96.8	1961	1608	75.0
1953	2151	100.4	1962	1311	61.2
1954	2197	102.6			

[a] Includes (1) those who had lost a job just prior to registration; (2) those under twenty-one years of age and those demobilized from military service, seeking a first job; (3) housewives seeking a first job; (4) pensioners seeking employment; and, (5) those currently employed seeking another job.
Source: Rassegna di statistiche del lavoro, various issues.

Although we cannot accept the ML statistics without question, they do strongly suggest that mass unemployment persisted in the midst of sustained rapid growth for over a decade. Certainly this strange conjuncture does not suggest a cyclical explanation. In fact, this is the main reason for the emphasis upon structural factors in the literature about the unemployment problem.

Comparative evidence on unemployment. The ML statistics

have been criticized many times over the years—by those who believe they overstate the problem, and by those who believe the opposite.[10]

Review of the procedures followed by the ML local offices reveals five major weaknesses leading to understatement of the phenomenon of unemployment. First, those enrolled in government schools for vocational training or retraining are not counted, although they are referred through the registry offices. Second, in certain agricultural districts the local office is too remote to be fully effective as a labor exchange, and so does not register all of the unemployed. Third, certain categories of workers do not register when unemployed, but instead rely upon personal contacts to get jobs. These include skilled manual and white-collar groups. Fourth, at the end of each month the ML offices cancel out all those who fail to renew their registrations (required each month). These include many who are literally unemployed, but who consider their prospects to be so hopeless that renewal would be futile. Finally, there is some evidence that a substantial secondary labor force exists in Italy, consisting of those who would only actively enter the labor market when job opportunities are rapidly expanding. Although this group partially merges with the fourth, it does not wholly coincide, because not all its members are in need. The Vigorelli experiment with full employment in fourteen localities in 1949 indicated that there may be a fairly large number of these "latent unemployed."

The other side of the coin involves administrative procedures that work to inflate the figures. First, the statistics include some "hundreds of thousands" (Curatolo) of workers in casual jobs—field hands, building laborers, and unskilled industrial workers—the so-called *turnanti* who work for a set number of days per month, then, rotate into unemployment to make way for others. They are required to register only once, without renewal, and if they do not happen to be working on the last day of the month, they are counted as unemployed. Second, there are those seasonal workers who are members of agricultural cooperatives or are crop-sharers, and whose work does not permit a full-time year. They may register and be counted during off-seasons, although they are not available for continuous full-time jobs. Their number is unknown, but Curatolo says it is "considerable."

Third, the data include a "substantial" (Curatolo) number of persons who are not really seeking work, but who must maintain their registrations in order to continue to receive various welfare benefits—family allowances, military or civilian benefits for disabilities incurred in war, unemployment compensation paid to certain classes of pensioners, and local assistance programs for the poor. Fourth, the statistics fail to exclude registrants who are partially or totally disabled for physiological or psychological reasons that make them economically unemployable. Finally, there is a small amount of double-counting involving seamen, who may register through their own special exchanges and again through the ML offices.

The evidence at hand permits no possibility of determining on net balance whether the data overstate or understate the true amount of overt unemployment. However, the judgment is current that they err on the side of excess.

Skepticism about their validity led to an official decision in 1952 to have the Central Institute of Statistics (ISTAT) undertake sample field surveys for preparation of over-all estimates—as part of the large scale Parliamentary Inquiry into Unemployment (Commissione parlamentare di inchiesta sulla disoccupazione in Italia) conducted in that year. Excepting 1953, ISTAT has continued to make these studies for each subsequent year, varying definitions and criteria in certain respects, and shifting to quarterly samples after 1958. However, it has maintained a division of the unemployed into two categories: the formerly employed, and those seeking a first job (termed the "inemployed" or *inoccupati*). Without at this point comparing the definitions of the two ISTAT categories with their ML counterparts (Classes I and II), we can place the two sets of results side-by-side for matching months before 1959, and as annual averages thereafter. They appear in Table 47.

Both series indicate that for the two categories together the volume of overt unemployment grew worse between 1952 and 1956, if we neglect the impacts of seasonal variations influencing the results through shifts in the months selected for the surveys.[11] After 1956, both series show unbroken declines through 1962. However, the gap between the two totals begins to widen enormously after the same date, reaching 700,000 persons both in 1960 and 1961. This huge discrepancy is the reason why some observers

TABLE 47. Comparison of ISTAT and ML statistics of unemployment, 1952–1962 [a] (in thousands)

Year	Formerly employed		Seeking first job		Total		Difference
	ISTAT	ML	ISTAT	ML	ISTAT	ML	
1952 (September)	814	1034	679	501	1493	1535	42
1954 (May)	872	1272	797	662	1669	1934	265
1955 (May)	880	1266	611	604	1491	1870	379
1956 (April)	1170	1381	697	644	1867	2025	158
1957 (May)	1054	1295	608	535	1662	1830	168
1958 (October)	845	1151	495	501	1340	1652	312
1959 (average)	757	1194	371	495	1128	1689	561
1960 (average)	557	1094	289	452	846	1546	700
1961 (average)	433	997	275	410	708	1407	699
1962 (average)	344	855	267	308	611	1163	552

[a] Where the ISTAT estimate is based on a field sample for a given day in a given month, the ML figures for that month are used. Where ISTAT has constructed annual averages from more than one survey in a given year, the ML annual average is used. Seasonal influences make it unwise to use these series as indicators of actual movements between years.

Source: (ISTAT), Annuario statistico italiano, 1957, p. 352; 1959, p. 314; 1960, p. 318; Relazione generale, 1962, II, p. 80; (ML), Rassegna di statistiche del lavoro, various issues.

could conclude that Italy had finally reached full employment by 1960, at the same time that others could contend that even by 1962 this target was well short of attainment. Thus, for the latter years, the unemployment rate implied by the ISTAT figures was but 3.0 per cent of a labor force estimated to be 20.5 million, while the ML data suggest a rate of 5.7 per cent.[12]

Comparison of the two series for both categories separately reveals that the main difference centers in the formerly employed. Thus for 1962 the ML figure for this group exceeds that of ISTAT by 511,000, while for those seeking a first job the ML excess is only 41,000 persons. However, these discrepancies tell us nothing about the comparative reliability of the two sets of figures. In the end, no final judgment is possible with the data at hand, although comparison of the respective criteria will permit a more informed choice to be made.

The ISTAT estimates derive from a stratified random sample, collected in two stages, from about 75,000 nuclear families. The characteristics enumerated for the sample population apply to the specific day and week of the survey. These data then permit an estimated division of the population as a whole as follows: (1) the labor force, which includes (a) the employed, (b) the formerly employed unemployed, and (c) those unemployed seeking a first job; (2) those not in the labor force (a) minors up to fourteen years if not regularly employed, (b) those of working age but without an occupation (females in nuclear families, students, draftees, pensioners, the well-to-do, and the idle), and (c) persons engaging in "occasional work" (attività lavorative occasionali).

This last category accounts for much of the discrepancy between the ISTAT and ML series, since its members are excluded from the unemployed in the ISTAT data, but would in good part be so counted in the ML statistics. As defined by ISTAT, the group involves those persons who performed some work during the survey week but who on other grounds are considered to be outside the labor force. The majority are women. If they did no productive work during the survey week, they are considered to be "engaged in household activities" rather than as unemployed. In fact they constitute a secondary labor force that preferably should be distributed between the employed and the unemployed according to cut-off limits for working time, and thus be included in the labor force.

Furthermore, the number of these occasional workers has been large throughout the years, averaging between 1.8 and 1.9 million in the estimates for 1952–1957, and dropping steadily thereafter to reach 579,000 in 1962, of which 77 per cent were women. The very fact that this later sharp decline in their numbers closely matches the fall in unemployment under both the ML and ISTAT measures shows that occasional or part-time work is very sensitive to over-all conditions of employment. Clearly, the inclusion of the group within the labor force is justified.

As of 1960, when the total was 961,000, 17.8 per cent were pensioners and 5.3 per cent students. As of the survey week in that year, 34.6 per cent of the whole group had worked less than 15 hours, and 46.6 per cent below 25 hours. Beyond question the category includes numerous part-time workers that on conventional definitions would be counted as employed or unemployed.

Next, consider the unemployed. Under the ISTAT criteria, these include all persons over fourteen who had lost a previous job either in self-employment or as dependent workers, or who were seeking a first job in either employment status. This lumping together of the two statuses departs from international practice and from that of the ML, both of which count dependent employees only. Beyond this, ISTAT's procedure is to accept the respondent's declaration that he is "seeking" work, and not to evaluate his fitness to perform work.

Regarding the formerly employed, the survey for April 4, 1960, showed that 69.5 per cent of a total of 505,000 were employees on layoff or who had been dismissed for cause (plant closure or other), while 19,000 were persons who had abandoned self-employment, and 135,000 involved those who had lost employment for "other" reasons (mostly as unpaid family assistants). As for those seeking a first job, these include returnees from military service, but little is known regarding the composition of the group as a whole.

The ISTAT definition of the employed is also important, because it affects the number who on other definitions might qualify as unemployed. The reason is that the following categories are defined as "employed" even if their members are not working in the survey week: those on holidays or vacation, on strike, on temporary layoff for "other" causes, or barred from work by sickness, disability, or bad weather. Of incidental interest, ISTAT counts among the employed citizens working abroad (429,000 in 1960), those in military careers (250,000), and regularly employed minors within ages ten to fourteen (100,000).[13]

Turning, now, to the ML procedures for comparison, the first major difference is that registration is confined exclusively to those persons wishing work as dependent labor (*lavoratori subordinati*) —roughly, "employees" but excluding unpaid family assistants. This definition eliminates those seeking self-employment (the so-called *autonome*), those in independent professional practice, or executives and officials. On the same basis, crop-sharers and members of agricultural cooperatives usually cannot qualify. Also excluded are occupations having special labor exchanges: seafaring, dock work, domestic servants, and the entertainment industry.

Until February 1961, those eligible to register had to do so at the office in the locality of their regular residence, and to deposit their labor books (*libretti di lavoro*) at the time, both as safeguards against multiple registrations as well as devices to prevent internal migration. Today it is possible to register at a more distant office, but duplication is still unlikely.[14] Normally, registration must be renewed each month.

The ML offices segregate the registrants into five alternative classes that are supposed to be mutually exclusive, but in fact are not strictly so. Classes I and II are of particular interest, because in principle they conform to the ISTAT distinction between the formerly employed and those seeking a first job.

Class I includes those who had lost jobs just before their initial registration. However, no test of fitness for work is made. Hence this group includes some who are unqualified either by extreme youth or age, or lack of suitable experience or training. Some effort is made to correct this by arbitrarily assigning all the formerly employed below twenty-one years of age to Class II, covering those seeking a first job. As a result, Class II partially overlaps Class I. Furthermore, Class II includes all returnees from military draft, regardless of age. Beyond this, Class II is made more ambiguous by inclusion of unemployed female apprentices below the age of twenty-one, while other women below this age who are seeking work are assigned instead to Class III, creating an overlap between these classes. Class III itself is a rather amorphous category intended to include females seeking an initial job who otherwise are assumed to be engaged in household duties as members of nuclear families (*casalinghe*). However, any woman over twenty-one who has formerly been employed in productive work will be assigned not to Class III but to Class I.

Class IV covers pensioners seeking work, and Class V persons desiring new jobs who are already employed full or part time. The former is inflated somewhat by those who are not seeking work, but who must maintain active registration to receive welfare benefits. Class V is somewhat inconsistent in that it includes some who are currently self-employed—a status excluded from all other categories. Also, in the earlier years Class V included persons with very low earnings, usually for lack of full-time employment. More recently, those whose earnings fall below a designated level are considered to be unemployed and assigned to Class I if currently engaged as dependent workers, or to II if they are self-employed.

Putting the ISTAT and ML data back-to-back, we can make the following points. First, ISTAT's exclusion of occasional workers from the labor force—either as employed or as unemployed—is the major factor accounting for its much lower figures for unemployment. If the sample evidence for April 20, 1960 can be relied upon, then at least one third of these workers could be considered unemployed, because they worked less than fifteen hours during the survey week. For earlier years, when the labor market was far more slack, this proportion was probably considerably higher. Granting that some workers on short time prefer such jobs and would reject opportunities for longer hours, there is good economic reason for considering most of them to be involuntarily unemployed. To deny this is to imply that the categories of unemployment and employment are not really mutually exclusive, that the real phenomenon is more complex, including underemployment and work below true capacity. There is a good case for such a multidimensional view, but this is a separate issue. Here we are concerned with definitions already in use.

Second, even if the occasional group were redistributed on some criterion—weekly hours or earnings level—between the employed and the unemployed, this would not fully overcome the divergence between the two series. The unknown remainder still would be too large. It could be explained in two principal ways: as deriving from sampling errors and systematic bias toward understatement on the ISTAT side, and from factors leading to overstatement on that of the ML.

Third, the procedures of both organizations fail to include adequate tests either for job fitness or for sincerity of applicants' intent. This factor inflates both series to an unknown extent but tells nothing about the size of the discrepancy between them. However, we may venture a guess that the impact is relatively greater for the ML statistics, particularly in Class I.

Fourth, ISTAT's inclusion of those seeking self-employment operates to narrow the differences between the two series. Moreover, exclusion of certain trades and occupations from ML coverage lowers these totals to some extent.

As a result, our conclusion is far from satisfactory: that the truth regarding overt unemployment lies in between the two sets of figures. A priori, there is compelling reason to place it closer to the ML totals for Classes I and II together. Despite the ML's exclusion of certain industries and occupations, the very extensiveness of the system of local registration gives it a far better chance than a small sampling, no matter how rationally and carefully its underlying procedures are designed.

More than this, for the employment categories covered by the ML—which certainly cover the great bulk of the Italian economy —placement of the unemployed through the registry offices is required by law, backed up by severe sanctions upon both worker and employer. This was clearly the case after 1939 under fascism, and save for a brief interregnum after 1945, under the new regime that followed. In 1949, these controls were tightened even further. Even with abandonment of statutory restraints against internal migration early in 1961, the state has retained its monopoly over the placement of the vast majority of all dependent workers.[15]

In consequence, most of the overt unemployed turn up as registrants at the local offices. To the extent that some do not, this works to depress, rather than inflate, the ML figures. Other factors —suitability, seriousness of declared intent—work in the opposite direction. On balance while we are probably safe in holding that the ML statistics involve some net overstatement, inherently they are a better measure of unemployment than are the ISTAT estimates.

The significance of the whole issue now may be seen at once, both as a question of fact and as a guide for economic policy. If we accept the ISTAT estimate for unemployment as well as its figure for the labor force, then, in 1960, when employment and unemployment were estimated at 19,969,000 and 846,000 persons respectively, the implied rate of overt unemployment was only 4.1 per cent; indeed, only 2.7 per cent if we count only the 557,000 formerly employed, as ISTAT does. Although the underlying definitions diverge sharply from United States practice, a pure rate of only 4.1 per cent itself would constitute virtual full employment on the current American standard.

Now if we make certain adjustments, we obtain a radically different result. First, accept the ISTAT figure for the employed, *faute de mieux*. Next, consider also as employed the 65.6 per cent of the occasional workers working 15 hours or more during the survey week of April 20, 1960, and apply this proportion to the 909,000 average number in such status in 1960. Add this number—596,000 —to ISTAT's total for the employed, to get an adjusted figure of 20,565,000. Deduct 429,000 working abroad, whom ISTAT includes among the employed, and the adjusted figure becomes 20,136,000. Now add the ML figure for average unemployment in 1960 for Classes I and II only—1,546,000—and the adjusted figure for the labor force becomes 21,682,000. Accordingly, the unemployment rate becomes 7.1 per cent—three quarters larger than that implied by the bare ISTAT figures, and clearly far short of full employment on anyone's definition. In fact, even if all of the 909,-000 occasional workers were counted as employed, the rate of unemployment remains very high—7.0 per cent.

Next, consider the President's Commission (United States) approach. It accepts, with one minor exception, the ISTAT figure for unemployment in 1960—846,000. However, the commission adjusts ISTAT's employment estimate to make it conform more in principle with American definitions. It deducts 100,000 regularly employed children of ages ten to fourteen, 250,000 career personnel in the armed services, and 429,000 Italians working abroad— for a total of 779,000. It then adds back all 909,000 occasional workers, adding net 130,000 to get a figure of 20,099,000 for employment. The commission then deducts 50,000 for workers on layoff or awaiting report on assured jobs, adding the same number to the unemployed, which figure now becomes 896,000. Putting the adjusted totals for the employed and the unemployed together, the commission estimates the labor force at 20,945,000. In result, it obtains an unemployment rate of 4.3 per cent, one that conforms reasonably well to United States concepts. The commission then concludes that, prevalent opinion to the contrary, the Italian rate in 1960 "was actually somewhat lower [than that of the United States] when measured by United States methods and definitions." [16]

In truth, the matter is a good deal more than one of definitions. Basically, it turns on the evidence to be used. We have already given our reasons for believing that the ML figures for Classes I and II lie closer to the true magnitude for overt unemployment than do the ISTAT estimates. Accordingly, it follows that in 1960 a rate close to 7 per cent actually prevailed, even on United States standards, rather than ISTAT's implied rate of 4.1 per cent, or the commission's 4.3 per cent. If so, Italy was far from full employment in that year on either Italian or American standards and definitions. For the same reason, overt unemployment was relatively worse in Italy than it was in the United States at the time.

The changing structure of registered unemployment. The composition of registered unemployment can be examined in three major ways: according to the five classifications earlier considered; relative to its distributions by economic sector; and in respect to its interregional allocation.

Looking, first, at the five classifications, the basic data for selected years appear in Table 48. From this evidence, it is obvious that Classes I and II dominated the totals throughout, starting at 86.8 per cent and ending at 88.7 per cent. Within the two groups taken separately from the remainder, Class I showed no over-all relative change, accounting for 73.7 per cent of the separate total in 1950, and 73.5 per cent in 1962. However, between 1950 and 1955 Class II gained relatively, moving up from 22.8 to 28.2 per cent, and reflecting an influx of young people into the labor market.

Going back to the over-all totals, the proportion of women held

TABLE 48. Changes in the distribution of the registered unemployed among the five major classifications, selected years, 1950–1962 [a] (in thousands; 1950 = 100)

Year	Class I		Class II		Class III		Class IV		Class V		Total	
	Number	Index	Number	Index	Number	Index	Number	Index	Number	Index	Number	Index
1950	1190	100.0	425	100.0	156	100.0	32	100.0	58	100.0	1861	100.0
1955	1303	109.5	610	143.5	138	88.5	60	187.5	50	86.2	2161	116.1
1958	1236	103.9	523	123.1	84	53.9	60	187.5	52	89.7	1955	105.0
1961	997	83.8	410	96.5	58	37.2	94	293.8	50	86.2	1609	86.5
1962	855	71.9	308	72.5	41	26.3	67	209.4	40	69.0	1311	70.4

[a] Figures are annual averages.
Source: Rassegna di statistiche del lavoro, various issues.

almost constant at one third. By contrast, the proportion of women within Class I alone rose substantially throughout—from about one quarter at the start to just under one third at the end. However, little change occurred in their relative share of Class II. Note also the sharp absolute decline of Class III, composed entirely of females. This shift offset their rising share of Class I, and so held constant their share of the over-all total. As for Classes IV and V, the important facts do not concern distribution by sex, but their small proportion of the totals throughout, the absolute rise in the number of pensioners seeking work, and the absolute decline in the already employed who were seeking new jobs.

Besides the fivefold classification by status, the Ministry of Labor also attempts to identify and group the unemployed according to economic sector. Unfortunately, its procedure here is not clear-cut, partly because of statutory constraints and partly because of inherent difficulties. "Industry" is a recognizable sector of production and employment, while "common labor" is purely an occupational category that cuts across all sectors. Yet both are classifications in this scheme. Common labor has to be treated separately because it involves unskilled workers, many of whom have never had a job, and all of whom could compete for this kind of work.

Moreover, the distribution includes all five status classes, which means that it merges those who have lost former jobs in some sector with those who are merely hoping to be assigned one in a given sector. Obviously, there is a world of difference between displacement and hope for future work. The classification is further confused by assigning some of the unemployed to gross intersector categories—common or clerical labor.

Notwithstanding these serious limitations, the breakdown of registered unemployment yields some interesting insights into the phenomenon itself. The data are summarized for selected years in Table 49. It shows that agriculture has held fairly steady at one fifth, while declining sharply in absolute numbers. Industry's formal share has behaved much more irregularly, declining relatively and absolutely through 1961 and then turning upward again.

Particularly noteworthy is the fact that common labor has dropped sharply and consistently, while the number entering the labor market from work or vocational training projects has swung

TABLE 49. Distribution of total registered unemployed by economic sector, selected years, 1953–1962 ª (in thousands)

Sector or category	1953		1957		1961		1962	
	Number	Share	Number	Share	Number	Share	Number	Share
Agriculture, forestry, hunting and fishing	492	22.5%	441	22.4%	270	16.8%	277	21.1%
Industry	942	43.2	872	44.3	560	34.8	626	47.8
Transportation and communications	19	0.9	19	1.0	19	1.2	19	1.5
Trade	51	2.3	53	2.7	58	3.6	54	4.1
Finance and insurance	28	1.3	20	0.9	17	1.1	22	1.7
Clerical labor	41	1.9	35	1.8	40	2.5	35	2.7
Common labor	440	20.2	296	15.0	204	12.7	159	12.1
Various services and activities	168	7.7	153	7.8	52	3.2	92	7.0
Released from work projects or training programs			80	4.1	388	24.1	26	2.0
Total	2181	100.0	1969	100.0	1608	100.0	1310	100.0

ª These classifications were adopted in the fall of 1952, except for "released from work projects or training programs," which was added in 1957. Figures cover Classes I–V inclusive, and are monthly averages for each year.
Source: Rassegna di statistiche del lavoro, various issues.

wildly. Perhaps the enormous decline in this latter category between 1961 and 1962 accounts for the absolute rise for industry in the same years. As for the other sectors and categories, their overall impact has been slight throughout.

Probably the most interesting observations are that unemployment in agriculture was able to decline 215,000 between 1953 and 1962, and that industry has dominated the totals throughout. This shrinkage in agriculture is all the more remarkable because of the very rapid rate of displacement and voluntary exodus occurring in this sector throughout the period. On the same count, the net decline of 150,000 for industry, and 281,000 for common labor (much of which involves industry), are equally significant, since the outflow from agriculture has built up the industrial labor supply. This suggests that, so far as straight numbers are concerned, industry as a whole has been able to absorb this influx from agriculture, and even to exceed it, particularly after 1957.

We turn now to the third main dimension of the structure of registered unemployment: its regional distribution, which appears in Table 50 for selected years between 1950 and 1962. A few preliminary comments are in order regarding this table.

The years 1954 and 1956 were included because the former involves the peak of registered unemployment for the whole period since 1945; while 1956 was the last year before the sustained downtrend in the totals finally set in. As for the geographic groupings, these correspond to official Italian practice, and reflect quite sharply diversities in the territorial distribution of economic activity. The north was—and remains—the overwhelmingly predominant center of industry, while the south was—and still is—primarily agricultural, with the center of Italy roughly midway between both extremes.

The figures in Table 50 show that in 1950—on the eve of the southern development program—36.7 per cent of the total unemployed were in the south, and just under one half were in the north. In that year, the south had an almost identical share (37.7 per cent) of estimated total population present in the country, as against 43.8 per cent for the north.[17] Between 1950 and 1954, the numbers of unemployed increased in all regions, but by far the greater part emerged in the south, whose share of the total jumped to 42.7 per cent.

TABLE 50. Comparative movements in the regional distribution of total registered unemployed, selected years, 1950–1962 [a] (in thousands)

Region	1950		1954		1956		1961		1962		Change, 1954–1962	
	Total	Share	Total	Share	Total	Share	Total	Share	Total	Share	Number	Relative
North Italy	915	49.2%	950	43.2%	889	41.0%	593	36.9%	460	35.1%	−490	−51.6%
Central Italy	258	13.9	309	14.1	305	14.0	225	14.0	194	14.8	−115	−37.2
South Italy	687	36.9	938	42.7	977	45.0	789	49.1	657	50.1	−281	−27.2
Islands only	186	10.0	243	12.3	268	12.3	214	13.3	177	13.5	−66	−27.2
All Italy	1860	100.0	2197	100.0	2171	100.0	1607	100.0	1311	100.0	−886	−40.3

[a] Includes Classes I–V.
Source: Rassegna di statistiche del lavoro, various issues.

Between 1954 and 1962, unemployment in the north fell by 50 per cent, ending up in the latter year as only 35.1 per cent of the national total, probably well under the northern share of the total population.[18] Over the same years, unemployment also declined in the south, but only by 30 per cent—reflecting that region's low participation in the burgeoning industrial boom. By 1962, half of the total unemployed were now in the south, well in excess of its estimated 36.8 per cent of total population at the time.[19] So far as central Italy is concerned, its number of unemployed also fell after 1954, and at a faster rate than the south's, while its relative share of the national total held steady at 14 per cent throughout—undoubtedly below its proportion of national population.

Viewed in summary fashion, these interregional comparisons illustrate in yet another way the familiar "ladder of economic disadvantage" within the Italian economy, one that consistently places the south on the bottom rungs, the center in the middle range, and the north on the top. Just as the south has not shared proportionately in the boom—measured by growth of total employment or of industrial employment alone, or in the absolute and relative advance of per capita income—it has accordingly suffered a slower rate of contraction in unemployment. Moreover, its burden now relative to the national total and to its share of the population has actually increased. Absolute improvement in its volume of unemployment indeed has occurred, but it was delayed in starting until after 1956, and since then has failed to keep pace with the rest of the country.

As described elsewhere, since 1950 a great amount of public expenditure has been devoted to the south, but the reduction of registered unemployment so far has been disappointingly slow, particularly relative to the north. One reason for this is undoubtedly that the pressure to find jobs, especially outside the badly paid and swarming agricultural sector, pushes up the figure for registered unemployment even when employment itself is expanding. Moreover, when public works are undertaken, they attract farm workers because the pay is better. But when projects are completed in given localities, these workers usually cannot return to agriculture because others have taken their places. Frequently, therefore, the project workers wind up among the registered unemployed. Beyond this, the southern problem is so vast and the place of industry in the southern economy so small that sheer growth of the labor force tends to outstrip any increases in nonagricultural employment.

Thus it is not surprising to find almost half the unemployment concentrated in a section of the country with only 37 per cent of the population, and to discover that the decline of unemployment in recent years has been relatively less in that same unfortunate section.

THE QUESTION OF UNDEREMPLOYMENT

Clarification of concepts. The observation has been made over and over again by specialists that persistent heavy unemployment has not comprised the whole of the postwar Italian problem by any means, that along with it has gone a great deal of "underemployment," together with "concealed unemployment" in various forms. However, these alternative forms of unemployment are often cited, frequently with figures, but without precision either as to meaning or method of estimation. Obviously, some clarification is in order.[20]

To be "employed" conventionally means to engage in economically productive work from which some form of money income is received, while to be "unemployed" is to be seeking such work without success. Right here trouble begins. Are we to include among the employed those working at below "normal" hours per day, week, or year; or those working at "normal" schedules but at below "normal" rates of remuneration; or those working at "normal" schedules and at "normal" rates of return, but at jobs below their level of professional training? As for the unemployed, what is to be assumed regarding expected money income, expected occupation, and expected sector and location of employment? Or regarding employability? These, of course, are questions of definition, but they are not merely academic, for they have everything to do with the scale of results yielded by any measures of employment and unemployment.

Strictly speaking, unemployment cannot practicably be divorced from the price of labor or from the type of work for which a person can qualify in the locality in which he offers his services. Practice in compiling such statistics decrees as a matter of convenience that the going wage or salary be used as a solution to the price problem, although this is admittedly arbitrary. Even this expedient causes difficulties where artisans and independent contractors, both of which are self-employed, are concerned, and these are very common in Italy. Here the problem is to define the going price of labor, hence to decide if such persons are unemployed if they seek other work to obtain better earnings.

Going further, however, the thorniest issues center in the mixed category of the partially employed. Here distinction should be made between persons working short time, persons working at jobs below their level of preparation, and persons working at normal schedules in jobs at low pay. In Italian industry and trade there are many persons who work below the standard forty-eight-hour week, while in agriculture there are many who work 150 days or less when the normal agricultural year is 270–280 days. Ignoring the possibility that even in a poor country there are some who deliberately choose part-time work, part of those on short time can certainly be considered to be partially involuntarily unemployed, and their lost time treated as equivalent man-years of unemployment on a par with full-scale unemployment. Unfortunately, the statistics of registered unemployment to some extent reflect part-time unemployment, but not completely. In any event, here is a form of underemployment that is reasonably clear-cut. Looked at from the side of demand, there may be good technical or economic reasons for short-time work—the planting and harvest cycles in agriculture, seasonal variations in production and trade, declining industries and firms. Nonetheless, from the standpoint of income aspirations, most underemployment in short-time work is a form of unemployment and should be so viewed.

Short-time underemployment shades off into a much vaguer category often termed "concealed unemployment" or sometimes "overemployment." These terms are used to refer both to short-time underemployment itself and to full-time work yielding very low money returns. Conventional examples would include self-employment in petty enterprises and services, family assistants (*coadiuvanti*) on peasant holdings and in small retail shops and artisan firms, unnecessary workers forcibly retained in agriculture by law and in industry by trade union pressure, and a large number of peasants and farm laborers struggling to gain a living from small and often scattered holdings.[21] No one would contend that all persons in these categories are "really" unemployed or that they add nothing to total production. However, it is contended that many of them are forced to remain in this kind of work because there is no other economic space for them to occupy in the highly constricted Italian system.

The difficulty with this amorphous category is that it includes two separate phenomena: persons who cannot work full time in these activities and whose productivity and earnings are low; and persons who do work full time and even overtime in the same activities, but who also may have low productivity and earnings. The former group is a genuine case of underemployment involving equivalent unemployment that is concealed by sharing total available work time. In contrast, the latter group is a much more subtle case. To some extent it, too, involves sharing, not of the work time but of the output, which is a way of saying that even the underemployment is concealed, hence that there is considerable equivalent unemployment also implicit here. But again, this group also includes many persons who not only work full time but who are fully occupied and working to capacity. These are not underemployed, nor under existing technical conditions of production are they a case of concealed unemployment. What aligns them with the others is simply low productivity and earnings.[22]

The basic reason why this whole group of employed people is generally considered to be a case of underemployment or of concealed unemployment is that if production here could be reorganized and coupled to innovations in the form of fresh capital, a great many persons would become redundant and be displaced. The same aggregate output, in other words, could be obtained with much less manpower; indeed, output could be even increased compatibly with considerable displacement of labor. But if the progressive industrial sector does not expand employment at the desired rate, the effect of such improvements and innovations, not to mention abolition of compulsory restraints against dismissals, would be mainly to add to the number of absolutely unemployed. In this respect, underemployment and concealed unemployment represent what Pierre Schneiter has termed "relative overpopulation." [23] That is, many workers are blocked off in these forms of employment because institutional restraints and capital scarcity have so far precluded technical improvements and innovations both in industry and in agriculture. If these changes could come about in the right way, workers could be drained off from these largely low-paying activities and could find more productive jobs at far better rates of return.

Unemployment as such means here those persons without work, who are capable of holding some kind of job and who are actively seeking employment at current rates of pay. In Italy most of them are involuntarily unemployed because they would be willing to work at any positive rate of pay (wage, salary, or other form of return), not merely at rates established by law, collective bargaining, employer policy, or local custom. As a practical matter, the official registration statistics do not ideally conform to this definition, mainly because they do not include all those actively seeking work, while they do include a small number who already hold other jobs.

Underemployment. This problem involves those who work less than standard daily, weekly, and/or annual hours, and who would be willing to work full time at their current hourly wages or rates of return. Conceptually this group suffers annual lost time in man-hours that can be expressed as equivalent absolute unemployment. To some extent, underemployment is reflected in the statistics for registered unemployment, for those either on full-time layoff or, as in agriculture, for those who are idle during certain periods of the years. However, the data do not include those working short days or weeks.

Concealed unemployment. This is a loose description for those working in low-paid jobs, either full time or part time. Obviously there is an overlap here with the underemployed, an ambiguity for which there is no evident statistical remedy. The chief utility of the concept is to point to persons who are working in those marginal zones of the Italian economy who are most vulnerable to the impacts of transformation and technological change. To call this "concealed" unemployment is really to say that continued employment in these economically exposed zones is only possible for the relatively near term, pending the development of adequate capital formation and the will to change, whereupon large-scale displacement will occur. "Latent" rather than "concealed" might be the better word, for this is the group that is the main target of future economic development. For a given moment in time and therefore in a static view, concealed unemployment does not stand in an additive relationship with underemployment and unemployment as such. However, in the dynamic sense, the weak competitive position of, and low returns yielded by, these activities make it essential to take them into account as part of any practical program to deal with key weaknesses in the Italian economy.

It should now be apparent that the common theme running through all discussions of the Italian problem is inevitably a normative one: the per capita incomes of the people are lower than their aspirations. What the absolutely unemployed, the underemployed, and the concealed unemployed share, although in different degrees, are low money incomes—relative to others and to their desired standard of living. This deficiency in money earnings in turn reflects inadequate aggregate demand for labor, an unsatisfactory structure of labor demand, and with minor exceptions, relatively low productivity of labor in most forms and most sectors of employment. Undoubtedly a central cause for the persistence of these phenomena is a lack of capital to execute the necessary transformation of agriculture and industry at a speed sufficient to bring rapid and dramatic improvement in the range, quantity, and quality of job opportunities. The economist may simply dismiss the problem as a case of failing to reconcile popular aspirations with what is objectively possible in the near term, and so reject all attempts to estimate the "real burden" of unemployment, or underemployment and concealed unemployment, as speculation.

Unquestionably, it is the duty of the economist to deal dispassionately with what is and what can be. Nonetheless, he is not debarred from taking popular aspirations into account, hence from helping to formulate policies that are well grounded in reality and yet aim in a practical way to effect needed changes. Accordingly, there is merit in an attempt to view the unemployment problem in wider perspective, as a necessary initial step in comprehending the real nature of the task implicit to even a partial attainment of the economic expectations of the Italian people today.

Evidence concerning underemployment. Relatively little is known about the quantitative dimensions either of underemployment or of concealed unemployment, because most of the figures that have been thrown out since the war appear to be little more than guesses, rather than estimates derived from application of explicitly formulated inquiries. For 1948, the Economic Cooperation Administration (United States) suggested there were 600,000 equivalent unemployment who were underemployed in agriculture, and 100,000 unneeded workers in industry.[24] In its survey for 1949, the United Nations declared that there were 2.2 million persons in concealed unemployment and a "surplus" of 250,000 unneeded workers in industry.[25] Writing in 1952, Orlando refers to a sample study of laborers and direct cultivators in agriculture which suggests that actual unemployment in agriculture was between 1.6 and 1.8 million, which compares with an average for registered unemployment of some 425,000 in that year.[26]

An attempt was made in the 1951–1952 agrarian year by the National Institute for Agrarian Economy (INEA) to estimate with some care the extent of underemployment in agriculture, as a contribution to the large-scale Parliamentary Inquiry into Unemployment.[27] The survey involved a sample drawn from zones dominated by share-cropping, peasant farming, and casual field labor. Daily supplies of available man-days of labor were set off against daily demands both for "ordinary" farm work as such and for "extraordinary" work in the form of special labor projects for road building, reforestation and flood control, and part-time employment in nonagricultural activities where the latter were available. Allowance was also made, on the demand side, for legislation requiring the employment of additional hands, which was also considered "extraordinary" labor. A "full-time" agricultural man-year was taken to be 270–280 days, according to local custom.

The results indicated an average idleness of 94 man-days per worker in agriculture per year, with regional values of 117 days in the south and the islands and 63 days in the north, or an aggregate of 640.7 million total man-days of estimated lost time. Given roughly 7.6 million persons active in agriculture at the time, it could be concluded either that they were all idle one third of the working year or that 2.5 million were "in surplus." However, the authors were careful to note that this "surplus"—or in Schneiter's terminology, "relative overpopulation"—could not be withdrawn wholly from agriculture without seriously reducing farm production, barring a major reorganization and extensive new investment.

In truth, therefore, the INEA estimate covers both underemployment and concealed unemployment. On the one side it indicates that on an annual basis effective unemployment greatly exceeded the 425,000 registered unemployed (1952). On the other, it underscores the magnitude of the labor displacement implied as the transformation of the farm economy proceeds.

When we go beyond agriculture, we find ourselves in largely uncharted territory. So far as manual wage workers in the advanced part of industry are concerned, the ML sample, which in 1957 covered 1.8 million workers or about 55 per cent of this group, indicates that underemployment was less serious. Indeed, it has probably been considerably reduced. Taking forty-eight hours as the standard Italian workweek, roughly 10 per cent were working less than forty hours in 1957, and another ten per cent at forty hours, as against 19.7 and 21.3 per cent respectively in 1948.[28] On an annual basis with 2001 to 2100 hours as a normal man-year, 36.3 per cent of these workers fell short of this standard in 1952, and 33.5 per cent in 1956—less indicative of a decline in short-time work than the weekly figures. However, almost all those below the norm were in the 1701–2000 hour bracket, which implies relatively little, equivalent, full-time unemployment.

It was pointed out earlier that the ML sample is far more representative of the better-situated, advanced segment of industry than for the industrial sector as a whole. For example, in 1961 it covered 2.15 million manual employees, while by contrast the average for that year derived from the ISTAT field samples involves a figure of 7.84 million. Of this very large difference of roughly 5.7 million persons, no doubt a substantial number takes in persons occupied in some status and capacity in many small firms, often of artisan type, where underemployment and concealed unemployment are far more likely to exist. Unfortunately, the data permit no quantitative precision regarding the dimensions of the problem.[29]

Outside of agriculture, the ISTAT estimate for 1961 suggests that within industry and other nonagricultural activities there were roughly 2.7 million self-employed, and 624,000 unpaid family assistants.[30] The total of 3.3 million persons for both categories affords some insight into the potential scope for underemployment and concealed unemployment in types of work outside the status of dependent employees. Clearly, these dimensions of the problem remain large, despite the rapid contraction of overt unemployment between 1959 and 1962.

A COMPARISON WITH WEST GERMANY, 1951–1961

Although there are sharp differences between the economies of West Germany and Italy, a comparison of the experience of the two countries can be highly illuminating for casting the peculiar contours of the postwar Italian unemployment problem in bold relief.

Germany began her rapid transition to a modern industrial society about three decades earlier in the nineteenth century than Italy, although national unification occurred at the same time, in both instances emerging from a background of separatism and local markets. Germany had better natural resources, a qualitatively better labor supply, and a remarkable record of advances in science and technology. Rates of capital formation and output growth have consistently exceeded those in Italy, undoubtedly accelerating the process of economic transformation. Finally, the spirit of capitalistic rationalism has long enjoyed a wider acceptance in Germany, while at the same time she has not been encumbered with a problem of regional stagnation and backwardness.

Nonetheless, considerable postwar parallelism can be found between the two nations. Both were defeated powers, and both had suffered severe losses in national capital from war damage. In 1951 the two countries had populations of almost identical size. West Germany had the advantage of a lower birth rate (15.8 *vs.* 18.4 per thousand), while almost identical death rates gave her a natural rate of increase of only 5.3 per thousand, as against 8.1 per thousand for Italy.[31] Offsetting Italy's disadvantage were two powerful influences: substantial net emigration from Italy, and an enormous influx of refugees into West Germany. As of October 29, 1946, some ten million persons had entered West Germany either from other areas or in flight from the Russian-occupied East Zone.[32] During the decade after 1951, net immigration into West Germany from all countries amounted to no less than 3.04 million persons, of which a significant proportion entered the labor force, adding greatly to the nation's employment problem.[33] By contrast, Italy lost at least half as many people through emigration. Finally, although West Germany still enjoyed a superior resource base and a somewhat greater surviving industrial potential after the war, she had to adjust to a far more serious disruption of her entire economic complex because of the twin impacts of a large-scale loss of national area and of the insidious effects of protracted occupation and control by the major powers. In particular, although it must be conceded that the two burdens greatly differ in nature, the enormous German handicap of east-west division at least in the early postwar years was comparable to the incubus that the south has long represented for Italy.

Examination of Table 51 will reveal the comparative experience for employment and unemployment in the two nations between 1951 and 1961, when both were undergoing unprecedented expansion in output. Unfortunately the comparison has to be limited to the start and finish of the period, because the Italian data are too poor to be relied upon for the inner years.

Clearly, agriculture was a far greater source for employment in Italy. However, it was contracting with great rapidity, seriously augmenting the burden of labor supply in the nonagricultural sector, a handicap of no significance whatever for West Germany. Next, consider nonagricultural employment. In Italy it increased by 3.8 million (35.8 per cent), while in West Germany it soared by 6.8 million, or 50 per cent. In fact, so great was the market for German output, particularly industrial, that the large influx of immigrants proved to be a labor reserve of immense importance, rather than the burden it seemed to be. In this connection, observe that in 1951 unemployment was 1.7 million in both countries, that by 1961 it had fallen to a negligible 100,000 in West Germany, or by 1.6 million, while in Italy it declined by only 300,000. Actually, by 1961 West Germany was in a state of over-full employment, and was depending heavily upon imported labor to keep her industries going.

The difference in the labor supply situations of the two countries over these years shows up clearly in the contrasting behavior of their labor force statistics. In 1951, Italy had the larger number, but over the decade it increased by only 1.7 million, or 8.5 per cent. Net emigration and lack of job opportunities greatly slowed its growth, despite a higher natural rate of population increase than in West Germany. In the latter country, the labor force soared

TABLE 51. Comparative movements in employment, unemployment and labor force, Italy and West Germany, 1951 and 1961 [a] (in millions)

| | Italy | | | | | West Germany | | | | |
| | Employment | | | | | Employment | | | | |
Year	Agriculture	Non-agricultural	Total	Registered unemployed	Labor force	Agriculture	Non-agricultural	Total	Registered unemployed	Labor force
1951	7.8	10.6	18.4	1.7	20.1	0.98	13.6	14.58	1.7	16.3
1961	6.0	14.4	20.4	1.4	21.8	0.58	20.4	20.98	0.1	21.1
Net change, 1951–1961	−1.8	3.8	2.0	−0.3	1.7	−0.4	6.8	6.4	−1.6	4.8

[a] The figures for West Germany were taken directly from official sources. For Italy, all figures except registered unemployment had to be estimated by adjusting original data. For 1951, the census figures for November for the active population had to be deflated to remove the formerly employed, who were included (those seeking first jobs were excluded from the original data). This was done by (1) finding the relative shares of agriculture and nonagricultural activities in the unadjusted active population; (2) applying these figures (42.2 and 57.8 per cent respectively to the 1,210,574 persons in Class I of registered unemployment); (3) deducting the corresponding proportions from the original totals for the agricultural and nonagricultural sectors. These estimates for sector employment were then combined with registered unemployment (Classes I and II) to get the labor force for November 1951, which was assumed to apply for the full year.

For 1961, it was found necessary to adjust the ISTAT sample estimate as follows. Of the 878,000 "occasional workers" whom ISTAT excluded from the labor force, it was assumed that one third could be dropped as wholly unemployed, on the basis that in 1960 roughly 34.6 per cent worked less than 15 hours during the survey week. Of the 585,000 remainder, who were considered to have been employed, two thirds were added to ISTAT's estimated nonagricultural employment (14.0 million), and one third to its total for agriculture (5.8 million)—on the premise that these proportions adequately corresponded to the actual sector distribution of employment in 1961. The ML figure for average registered unemployment (Classes I and II) was then added to adjusted total employment to obtain the labor force.

Source: Data for West Germany from Statistiches Jahrbuch für die Bundesrepublik Deutschland, issues for 1955, p. 119; 1962, pp. 149–150. For Italy, active population for 1951 from Annuario statistico italiano, 1956, p. 26; employment and occasional workers for 1961, from Relazione generale, 1962, II, pp. 80, 85; registered unemployment for November 1951 and average for year 1961, from Rassegna di statistiche del lavoro, IV:6 (November–December 1952), p. 670; XV:3 (May–June 1963), p. 266.

by 4.8 million, or 29.4 per cent.[34] Here the case was exactly the converse: very substantial net immigration, ample job openings, and a lower natural rate of population increase.

Common to both countries during the years in question was a very rapid rate of expansion in output. Taking the end-years alone, real gross product in Italy rose at a compound rate of 6.0 per cent a year. For West Germany, the rate was even higher—7.2 per cent yearly. For industrial output alone, Italy expanded at an annual rate of 8.5 per cent, somewhat above West Germany's 8.3 per cent.[35] However, when changes in output are compared with those for employment, the behavior of the two countries becomes quite discordant.

Over the full decade Italian real gross product jumped 79.0 per cent, while total employment increased only 10.8 per cent. In West Germany, gross output soared 101.7 per cent, while employment rose 43.9 per cent. For industrial output alone, using total nonagricultural employment as a measure of labor input in this sector, Italy expanded by 125.6 per cent, while employment advanced only 35.8 per cent. In West Germany, industrial production increased 121.5 per cent, and nonagricultural employment 50 per cent. Evidently output in Italy was considerably more responsive to increases in labor input than it was in West Germany. Obviously other factors besides the quantity of labor input will influence the volume of output, among them the quality of labor, scale effects, the quantity of capital, and technological innovations that are likely to find expression in changes in the quality of increments to capital stock. Granting that these factors were at work in both nations, it is still worthwhile to compare the gross effectiveness of labor inputs in both cases, by putting it on a common relative scale. Let us call the ratio of the percentage increase in output (O) to the percentage increase in employment (N), the elasticity of output with respect to changes in employment, e. Disregarding the error implicit with large percentage change, e may be expressed as

$$e = \frac{\Delta O}{O} \bigg/ \frac{\Delta N}{N}$$

For real gross output and total employment in Italy, $e = 7.3$; for West Germany $e = 2.3$. In short, in Italy a 1 per cent increase in employment yielded a 7.3 per cent increase in output, with the help of the other factors noted above; while in West Germany it produced only a 2.3 per cent increase in output. For industrial production alone, in Italy $e = 3.5$, as against $e = 2.4$ for West Germany.[36]

If we can trust the Italian figures for employment, and for the present purpose they are reasonably reliable, output in Italy was much more responsive to increases in employment than it was in West Germany. This is another way of saying that, given large increases in output in both countries over the period, Italy had a much worse record in both expanding employment and in reducing overt unemployment. Many factors enter into her discrepant behavior in this regard, but the suspicion dawns that among them must have been a highly labor-saving type of capital investment.[37]

WHY PERSISTENT MASS UNEMPLOYMENT, 1945–1959?

For the fifteen-year period following the end of World War II, the Italian economy exhibited a curious dualism in its behavior: rapid and unbroken growth of output conjoined to continuing heavy unemployment. One is led immediately to infer that here is an instance of the classical case of economic development with unlimited supplies of labor. But the main characteristic of that case is constant real wages, particularly in the expanding industrial sector. Yet, as we show in Chapter IX, real wages rose steadily and substantially, both within and outside that sector. Indeed, this fact provides an important clue to the explanation of the unemployment problem. Although some elements of the explanation require recourse to material presented in later chapters, it is nonetheless appropriate to deal with the question at this point.

There is strong reason to doubt that this persistence of mass unemployment can be accounted for by deficiency of over-all demand. In the first place, between 1948 and 1961 aggregate real demand rose at the very high linear rate of 5.9 per cent yearly, with almost no variation. Furthermore, stabilization in late 1947 brought about only a very brief pause in expansion, lasting less than half a year. The data show no significant deflationary swing, and none occurred in the ensuing fourteen years. Finally, the very high rate of investment achieved over the period, which also was very well sustained, indicates clearly the absence of any detectable excess plant capacity or oversavings gap of Keynesian type.

In view of these facts, then, the explanation of chronic unemployment is not to be found by appeal to deficiency of over-all demand. Rather, it is to be sought in a cluster of "structural" factors.

To say that unemployment is structural in cause is to mean more than that the unemployed are heterogeneous and can be classified according to various attributes—sex, age, skill, location, and so on. These descriptive characteristics are present at all times. The ruling idea is much more fundamental. It is that the labor market has failed to work efficiently by reason of obstructions that have prevented it from bringing labor supply and demand into adequate balance—so much so that the over-all rate of unemployment consistently runs well above an appropriate frictional minimum. But what were these obstructive forces?

The one most commonly cited is capital shortage coupled to fixed co-efficients of production, either for each product or for the system as a whole. This technological explanation is examined more fully in Chapter XIII, where reasons are given for rejecting it. In essence, the explanation says that if workers must be used in fixed ratio to quantity of available capital, and if the stock of capital is both fixed and inadequate, then part of the labor force must be left unemployed. And if capital stock increases at a slower rate than the labor force over the longer period, then the mass of unemployed must increase.

There is ample reason to reject this version of the structural theory. First, throughout the boom period in Italy capital stock grew much faster than the labor force. Despite this, the number of unemployed rose until 1955, and stayed high through the end of the decade. More than this, no evidence has ever been put forward to show that in fact labor-to-capital co-efficients actually are rigidly fixed, either for the whole economy or for all or part of the entire array of particular products. On the contrary, input-output studies for numerous industrial economies show quite the reverse: that product coefficients vary considerably through time. In addition, there is no reason to believe that the over-all production function for any industrial economy ever displays this assumed rigidity.

Accordingly, we must look elsewhere for an acceptable explanation of the peculiar Italian case.

The first factor was transitory: a temporary bulge in the labor force during the immediate postwar years, occurring at a time when accumulated plant destruction and shortages of raw materials precluded more rapid expansion of output and employment, despite a large amount of unfilled effective demand. Since labor is never a perfect substitute for capital, this enforced imbalance in labor supply and demand should occasion no surprise, granted that its occurrence does not depend upon any presupposition of strict complementarity between labor and capital. As for the bulge itself, its origin lay in demobilization of the armed forces, together with an influx of refugees and of returning colonists from the former empire.

The second factor—statutory restraint of the internal migration of labor—was far more fundamental, lasting until early 1961. By binding workers to their places of legal residence, it perpetuated disequilibrium in the labor market. This was a source of great damage to the south, which long had much higher birth rates and rates of natural population increase, and which at the same time suffered from partial closure of the traditional safety valve of overseas migration. The plight of the southern labor force, moreover, was made all the worse by the inability of its small industrial sector to expand at more than a negligible rate, and by an almost complete lack of employment opportunities in agriculture, where the man-land ratio had been too high for many years. Extremely high unemployment in the south was the lasting consequence of this unhappy cluster of forces. It did much to inflate the national totals over the whole period.

The third factor in the postwar unemployment problem was a continuing and substantial exodus of workers from agriculture, a movement that gathered speed in the fifties, and that contributed to the large pool of unemployed. On the one side, legal obstacles to internal migration prevented an adequate geographic redistribution of these workers toward nonagricultural employment. On the other, the advanced sector of industry absorbed new workers at a very slow rate during these years. In the main, this meant that workers released from agriculture had but three alternatives: emigration from Italy, jobs in the weaker parts of the nonagricultural sector, or unemployment.

This connects up with the final factor in the problem: wage-price behavior in the advanced sector of industry, which also was the most rapidly growing source of national output, as well as one of its most important in relative contribution to total product at all times. Wage- and price-making in this sector did much to bring about the slow rate of expansion in its employment. Here the restriction of internal migration served as an important reinforcing factor, in effect largely negating what appeared statistically to be unlimited supplies of available industrial labor. Because many of the unemployed were being kept out of the industrial labor market by these legal controls, much support was provided to the enforced rapid rise of real and money wages in industry, which were steadily being pushed up through collective bargaining and statutory intervention. At the same time, profits in the sector were growing, and were largely being reinvested internally in labor-saving equipment. This yielded a very rapid advance in output per man-hour, more than enough to finance the advance in money labor costs. But by reason of the quasi-monopolistic nature of much of the sector's product markets, the fall of unit labor costs was not passed on to the rest of the economy. Instead, it was retained as added profit.

Here, then, was a mutually reinforcing process that worked to the detriment of increased industrial employment: upward pressure on labor costs, probably encouraged further by rising profits; labor-saving investment, made possible by rising profits, and intensified by wage pressure; substantial derivative gains in labor productivity; and stability of the internal price level for industrial goods, permitted by the weakness of market competition, strengthened by wage pressure, and serving as an independent source of higher profits additional to those yielded by increasing market demand. In these circumstances, the growth of demand for industrial workers was slowed down.

Viewed as a whole, then, the fifteen-year problem of high unemployment was the joint consequence of a rapid transformation of agriculture, a highly capital-intensive development of industry, anti-competitive wage and price policies within industry, and legal barriers to labor mobility.

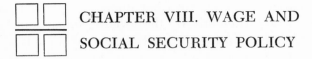# CHAPTER VIII. WAGE AND
SOCIAL SECURITY POLICY

Any wage system is the reflection both of the larger scheme of industrial relations and of the exigencies of its particular socio-economic environment. The modern Italian wage system is no exception. It emerged during the Fascist corporative regime when there were neither independent trade unions, nor effective collective bargaining. Nonetheless, fascism did provide for a peculiar kind of collective wage determination, with minimum occupational pay rates, certain supplements to base rates, and an apparatus of differentials based upon sex, geography, age, and industry.

With World War II, this system came under considerable modification, inspired mainly by a vain effort to reconcile a wage freeze with adjustments for inflation. By the end of the war, inflation burst all bonds. Peace brought back independent unionism and collective bargaining after two decades, but all opportunity to restore order to the wage system was blocked by the more urgent problem of general increases to offset inflation. Interestingly enough, the revival of collective bargaining did not end the Fascist tradition of centralism in the making of wage policy, a tradition that inflation actually continued to foster. Centralism, moreover, fitted well the Communist ideology of the central union confederation at the time, while also conforming to the preferences of the major employer groups.

According to Heraclitus, the essence of life is strife between opposites—in his system, love and hate. In essence, the post war history of Italian wage policy turns upon a ceaseless struggle over four pairs of extremes. The first is in the conflict between centralization and decentralization—between wage determination by peak bargaining associations on the one side, and by particular sectors, industries, enterprises and unions on the other. Closely connected is the choice between wage uniformity and wage diversity, which goes specifically to questions of geographic, intra-industry and interindustry differentials, interlacing with the issue of centralization of bargaining structure. Third, there is the struggle between equalization and differentiation of wages, focusing upon occupational differentials and provoked particularly by the leveling impacts of flat-rate cost-of-living bonuses during the postwar period. Finally, and in keeping with the history of wage labor everywhere, Italian wage-making involves a polarity between the principles of productivity and of need, between payment in proportion to productive contributions and the "right" to a living wage. In this case, the antinomy is not confined to wage-setting alone, but shows up with equal force in a now elaborate system of welfare benefits.

ITALIAN WAGE POLICY SINCE THE THIRTIES

A preliminary sketch of the current wage system. The wage and salary system in 1962 applied to some 10.2 million employees ("dependent workers" in Italian terminology) who made up a little over one half of the employed labor force. About 6.2 million of these employees worked in industry, which has been the leader throughout in the making of wage policy. Another 1.7 million were in agriculture, while the balance (about 2.3 million) worked in transportation, construction, trade, finance, and government.[1] Excluding government, where salaries are fixed by legislative enactment and ministerial decree, wages are mainly set by collective bargaining. Here, too, statutory controls are important, because the weakness of the Italian unions, together with a long-unresolved dilemma over the choice between the political and bargaining routes, has involved extensive resort to government intervention into wage determination.[2]

Collective bargaining is conducted on three levels in Italy. At the top are the peak associations. On the employer side these are separated according to main economic sector. On the union side there are now four general labor confederations. These are not split up by sector, although their strengths vary greatly in this respect. Within industry there is a second level, consisting of employer associations for each distinct product group. Counterpart union bodies also exist here and are in multiple, reflecting their respective confederation affiliations. Then at the lowest level is the single enterprise, where further negotiation occurs between the employer on the one side and the representatives of the respective national unions on the other. In the usual case, the four-way split among the union confederations leads to multiple representation of the workers at all three levels.

Since 1954, when for industry a major shift toward more decentralized bargaining occurred, bargaining at the peak association level has concentrated upon operation of the sliding scale (*scala mobile*) system for cost-of-living allowances (*indennità di contingenza*). However, it was at this level that the path-breaking agreement on pay consolidation (*conglobimento*) was consummated, on June 12, 1954.[3] This agreement assigned to the particular category associations at the second level the task of translating its general provisions into specific wage minima for their respective domains. Between 1945 and 1954, however, the decisive elements of wage determination—the sliding scale, adjustments for skill and other differentials, and the classification of employers by geographic zone and product group—had been negotiated at the peak level. So far as the lowest layer is concerned, that of the single firm, wage minima have largely continued to be handed down from above. However, these minima have mainly been determined by the weakest firms' ability to pay, which has meant that better situated enterprises have frequently conceded terms above scale, achieved through negotiation at the local level.

Today the wage of an industrial worker consists of the basic minimum (*paga base*); a supplement to cover increases in the cost of living since 1954; a variety of other supplements (*elementi accessori*) providing for holiday pay, the Christmas bonus or so-called "thirteenth month," paid vacations, piece-rate earnings, and various special premiums; and on top of the rest, if he qualifies, a family allowance (*assegno familiare*) that is paid to him from a state fund financed by employer contributions.[4] These three main elements by no means account for the total cost of each worker, because there are many other social welfare programs to which the employer is required to contribute, as well as private benefits he may provide on his own. Even so, this tripartite structure of wage and salary compensation is a miracle of simplicity compared to the system that developed between 1945 and 1954.

Between the thirties and 1945. Collective wage determination was also characteristic of the Fascist period, at least in the sense that the individual employer and employee both were bound by terms formulated for them by the syndicates. However, state control was supreme, and there was no genuine bargaining between autonomous and freely chosen representative bodies. Nonetheless, the regular accoutrements of collective wage fixation were retained and extended under fascism—minimum job rates and an apparatus of occupational, geographic, sex, age, and interindustry wage differentials. Also, as early as 1929, the national agreement for the engineering and metallurgical industries established a guarantee of minimum earnings under piece rates (*sistema di cottimi*). In December 1937 these principles were extended throughout industry in a peak-association contract.[5]

The onset of the great depression led to wage cuts in Italy, followed in 1933 and 1934 by reductions of the workweek in industry from forty-eight to forty hours. This cut in hours set the stage for one of the most important innovations ever made in the Italian wage system—the family allowances. Originally introduced in the wool industry at Biella in 1933, their purpose was to soften the impact of lower earnings through reduced hours upon workers with families. By means of an interconfederative (peak level) agreement dated October 11, 1934, they were extended over the rest of industry. Initially, the family allowances were financed by contributions from both employers and employees. In a decree law of August 21, 1936, the whole cost was shifted to the employer, and the system was extended to trade, finance, and insurance. In the following year, a second decree brought in agriculture and the rest of the economy.[6] It was inevitable that these allowances would eventually stray from the original purpose. Indeed, in June 1941, a second allowance was introduced into the social security system, by means of the earnings equalization fund (Cassa integrazione guadagni operai dell'industria) to supplement the earnings of workers whose hours had been cut below forty per week because of wartime production difficulties.[7] These payments continue today for eligible industrial workers along with the family allowances. However, the family allowances are available to all workers in the economy and no longer are connected with working hours.

A second wage supplement, one of the "accessory elements," also made its appearance in the thirties—the Christmas bonus. Originally granted to clerical workers, it spread rapidly over the manual group from 1938 onwards.[8] Today it remains an extra item of compensation.

Italy's entry into the war in June 1940 marked the beginning of the disruption of the Fascist wage system, a development that was to end in its complete destruction by early 1945. The first step was a decree law adopted June 19, 1940, which froze all wages. As inflation began to gain ground, a series of special supplements to preserve illusion of a stable wage level were adopted. The first was the attendance bonus (*indennità di presenza*), introduced by contract on April 21, 1943, first for clerical workers and then extended to the manual group. It was justified as special compensation to workers in zones exposed to hostilities.[9] In December 1943, after the Allied invasion had begun, the already crumbling Fascist regime abandoned the wage freeze and ordered a general wage increase of 30 per cent for base pay up to 2500 lire monthly, with a tapered increase of 15 per cent for sums above this amount. By this time the Mussolini Government had already yielded much of central and southern Italy to the Allied forces, which divided the country along what was known as the "Gothic Line." South of the Line the Allied occupation forces ordered general increases varying ultimately between 10 and 70 per cent, including the 30 per cent awarded by the retreating Salò Republic headed by Mussolini.

On September 26, 1944, the Salò Government added the "war bonus" (*indennità di guerra*) to the wage scale. This supplement applied to both clerical and manual workers, and was larger for heads of families. In January 1945, it was reduced, finally to disappear the following June, when liberation of Milan permitted negotiation of a new cost-of-living bonus through collective bargaining.[10]

The final gesture of the Salò Government in the field of wage policy was a decree on February 22, 1945, establishing still another supplement, the "bread allowance" (*indennità di caropane*), which was tied to a price index for cereals used in bread and *pasta*. This measure proved wholly abortive, since the pending withdrawal of the German forces from the north dissolved the authority of the Salò regime. As the Allied troops took over new territory, collective bargaining supplemented the Salò decrees, replacing the bread allowance by a new cost-of-living supplement that came into almost general effect at the very time the bread allowance was ordered. However, a new bread allowance appeared in the inflation of 1947.

From 1945 to the pay consolidation agreement of June, 1954. From early 1945 until the fall of 1947, Italy found herself in economic disorganization and severe inflation. In consequence it proved impossible to construct a stable wage structure. Wage policy was accordingly characterized by a series of expedients and dominated at all times by the overriding problem of adjusting the general level of earnings to the soaring cost of living. Naturally the main task of wage setting fell upon the peak associations. Although these bodies did succeed in formulating a system of principles by which wage minima were to be determined throughout industry, the minima themselves could not be made permanent, and the entire compensation system was complicated by the addition of further supplements. Furthermore, the rise in the cost-of-living allowance invoked during 1945–1947 by rapid inflation led to severe compression in skill differentials, which in turn was partly offset by other pay supplements introduced in 1949 and 1950.

Thus the nine-year period from 1945 to 1954 involved three main developments, of which inflation was the primary cause. First, preoccupation with the wage level made the peak national associations in the main wage-setting agencies. Second, a great deal of the bargaining in this period centered upon modifications in the sliding scale, by which the cost-of-living allowance was determined. Third, the sliding-scale system yielded flat-rate sums, differentiated only by sex and for minors. As a result, when the allowance rose with inflationary movements, the base minima rapidly lost significance, while skill differentials accordingly were drastically compressed. Thus from time to time the peak organizations were compelled to address themselves to problems of wage structure as well. Unfortunately, they were ill equipped to take local differences into account. Hence the emerging wage system was rigid and overcentralized, while the exigencies of the time precluded adequate development of a more flexible and realistic system of local bargaining.

The outset of 1945 saw the country divided by the Gothic Line, which brought about a dual wage policy and administration. During the first half of the year, the attendance bonus and the war allowance disappeared from the north. In the center and south the peak associations introduced a new cost-of-living allowance, in an agreement dated February 24. This bonus was extended to the north by agreements dated June 23 and July 8, 1945.[11] Thus the postwar sliding-scale system was initiated, and was applied as a bonus added to the base pay and determined for each province according to the relationship between the price index for the province and a larger group average. Of considerable interest because of its precedent-setting character, the northern system provided a flat sum for all categories of industrial workers, differentiated only for women and minors, who received smaller amounts, and for heads of families, who were awarded 20 lire extra daily plus 15 lire for each dependent in excess of the first and not exceeding three. The retention of this flat-sum general allowance was soon to make itself felt in marked compression (*appiattimento*) of skill differentials.

On December 6, 1945, a major peak agreement was executed for the north, which set down the main principles by which basic minimum wage and salary rates were to be fixed throughout industry. This contract was also a precedent, for it laid out the main dimensions of the wage structure. Except for elaboration the following year, the principles adopted in December 1945 were to control the determination of minimum rates and their differentials until the next major basic wage agreement of June 1954.

First, the 1945 contract divided the industrial sector into three distinct product groups, which permitted the minima of each specific industry to be differentiated roughly according to productivity or ability to pay. Second, this structure was crosscut by creation of three territorial zones, intended again to allow for variance in ability to pay and also to reflect an urban-rural distinction in living costs. Third, for purposes of setting minima in each firm and industry, all job classifications were to be bracketed in four basic pay grades for manual workers; four for clerical; and three for women. In this way a rough kind of job evaluation was applied to the grouping of particular jobs according to pay bracket. For the manual group, the brackets were, in descending order: specialized worker, qualified worker, specialized laborer, and common laborer (*operaio specializzato, operaio qualificato, manovale specializzato,* and *manovale comune*). Clerical jobs were grouped in four main categories (*categoria*) and female workers in three.

From the point of view of the enterprise, therefore, the *minimum* plant wage scale (overscale rates were of course allowed by agreement) depended first upon the product-group in which it was classified, and second upon its geographic zone. Then the applicable pay brackets were to be employed to determine the occupational rate structure and female differentials. In addition, the cost of living and other supplements also applied.

On May 23, 1946, the system was extended to central and southern Italy, while a special "third element" or supplement was granted for the north, to become part of the cost-of-living allowance, to effect equalization of total pay with the south, whose level had been temporarily higher. Then on October 27, 1946, the first national peak agreement for wages and salaries in industry was reached, known as the "wage truce and settlement" (*Sistemazione e tregua salariale*). Its purpose was threefold: to bring into being a national wage structure for industry, in balance with the cost of living; to check the rise in basic pay rates after award of general increases to cover the interim rise in the cost of living since the May agreement; and to introduce a modified and uniform sliding-scale system. Bear in mind that by July 1946 inflation had resumed after a brief period of stability following the end of the war.

The agreement awarded a 35 per cent general increase in all basic rates, applicable to the minima established in the December 1945 northern contract and the May 1946 contract for the center and south. Individual industries and plants were also permitted to negotiate additional local increases not to exceed 15 per cent.[12] Beyond these, basic rates were to be stabilized, with further increases in total pay to be tied to the cost of living.

Going to the determination of the industrial wage structure, the agreement provided, first, for five product-groups to which firms were to be assigned. Group A (metal products, rubber, chemicals, building, and others) was to be the base category. Group B (quarries, wines and liquors, part of the wood industry) was to have base rates 4.8 per cent less. In Group C (clothing, wood), the minima were to be 5.0 per cent below A, while in Group O (foods, building materials, printing, paper, electricity, gas, water, telephones, transportation) was to have minima higher than for A, but varied by industry. Group T (textiles) was set out for separate determination of minima.[13] Second, geographic differentials were provided through division of the national territory in four zones: Zone 1 (Milan, Turin, Genoa, Rome, and Naples) served as the base category, with basic pay 6 per cent lower in Zone 2, 11 per cent lower in Zone 3, and 14 per cent in Zone 4.[14]

On the occupational side, the pay brackets earlier described were retained for manual and clerical workers and for women, and a new category of "intermediate workers" (foremen and supervisors) was created parallel to the clerical structure. Female jobs were grouped in three brackets, equated to the lower three manual brackets, but at base rates 30 per cent below the males. Minor females (under eighteen) were limited to the lowest two brackets, with differentials varying between 40 and 60 per cent below the male rates. Rates for minor males were also scaled downward.[15]

So far as the sliding scale was concerned, the agreement set out the system that was to remain in force until 1951, building on principles already developed in the previous agreements of 1945–1946, while unifying the system on a national basis.

To reconcile the wage truce with adjustments to preserve real wages, the new sliding scale distinguished between the base pay (minimum job rates) and the cost-of-living allowance (a so-called "variable element" in total pay). A study commission formulated a four-person family budget and estimated the cost of its components in each provincial center for the base period, June 16—September 15, 1946.[16] By territorial averaging, the commission calculated the interim required allowance at 185 lire daily, relative to an average base wage of 240 lire, making total pay 425 lire daily. At the start, therefore, the allowance represented 43.5 per cent of average total pay. Accordingly, subsequent adjustments for price increases were to be calculated by multiplying the percentage change in the price index by a coefficient of 2.3.[17] For women, the coefficient was fixed at 2.0, while their allowance was set at 87 per cent of the standard for adult males.[18] For subsequent adjustments for all workers, price indexes were to be compiled in the provincial centers, and revisions in the allowance to be made every two months. For each revision, the cumulative percentage price change from the base period was to be multiplied (for males) by 2.3, with the percentage product to be applied to the original base period allowance of 185 lire. In this manner, subsequent changes in the allowance were tied to the original base allowance, so that a 1 : 1 relationship was preserved between the percentage change in the provincial price index cumulative from the base period and the percentage change in total pay from the same base period.

This procedure accomplished the dual objective of preserving technically the average real wage of the base period while maintaining separate and intact absolute base pay rates and the geographic and occupational structure of those minima. This was in keeping with the twin objectives of a wage truce and of maintenance of real wages. By stabilizing base rates, the agreement prevented subsequent price inflation from enlarging the employers' social security charges and piece-rate payments, which were customarily calculated as percentages of base pay. At the same time, however, this advantage was purchased at a price: continued rise in the cost-of-living allowance, which was distributed at a flat sum without regard to occupational or geographic differentials in base pay minima, and which had the joint effect of largely obliterating the importance of base pay while closing up the differentials in gross earnings—leveling and compressing them. This was the problem that was to dominate subsequent peak negotiations.[19]

The hoped-for stability to be provided by the October 1946 agreement was not to last long, for inflation continued at a rapid pace into 1947. On May 6, 1947, a new bread allowance (*caropane*) was introduced, adding a second supplement to the base wage. This allowance was tied to an index of cereal prices and was scaled according to heaviness of labor.[20] Then on May 30, a new peak agreement was reached for the industrial sector, renewing the previous wage truce but only after revision of basic pay scales. Of the existing cost-of-living allowance, 104 lire daily was converted to base pay. To offset intervening compression, manual skill differentials were revised, to restore the base rate ratios of October 1946, while the upper brackets of clerical base salaries were also increased.[21]

With the full application of the Einaudi program for monetary stabilization, which took effect September 30, 1947, inflation's back was broken, and the price level started downward, projecting the problem of a sliding scale in reverse. This possibility had been foreseen but not provided for in the October 1946 agreement.

Hence a new peak agreement was formulated on November 28, 1947 to deal with the question. Again the objective was to reconcile two conflicting purposes, this time to increase real wages while reducing the allowance and therefore total pay as prices fell. The solution adopted was to leave the allowance intact for the first 8 per cent drop in the provincial price indexes; to reduce it by 1.2 per cent for a drop in prices of between 8.1 and 12 per cent; and to reduce it by 4 per cent for a drop extending between 12.1 and 20 per cent. Thus for an aggregate decline in prices of 20 per cent, the allowance would drop only 5.2 per cent.[22]

With the end of the first postwar inflation, attention could finally be directed to other vital parts of the wage system, in particular to occupational and other differentials. The first attempt came with the peak industrial agreement of April 14, 1948, which revised base salaries for the clerical group. The base rate for the top category, which had been set at 118 per cent above the bottom in the agreement of May 30, 1947, was now fixed at a level 209 per cent higher. The intermediate groups were awarded tapered increases in descending scale. However, these changes did not resolve the compression problem, for gross earnings differentials were still kept relatively much closer together than the base rates.[23]

Gross earnings were also affected in 1948 by a new law, effective August 1, which revised the 1947 bread allowance. For normal jobs, this supplement was now fixed at 20 lire daily; for heavy labor, at 30 lire; for very heavy work, 40 lire; and for miners and woodcutters, 60 lire. Furthermore, the family allowance was raised, to extend the bread allowance to dependents.

Continued stability of the price level released the employers and the unions from preoccupation with the sliding scale, permitting them by 1949 to turn to the more constructive task of revising occupational differentials. By this time the problem of leveling had become critical, following a four-year period dominated by flat-rate general increases under the sliding-scale system. Its nature can be demonstrated in two ways: by comparison of changes in real wages for key occupational groups since 1938, and by comparison of the ratios of the upper groups to those at the lowest level, also since 1938. For 1948, ISTAT reported that the top brackets of government employees (Groups A and B) received real wages 42.2 per cent below 1938, while the top clerical bracket in industry

(Category 1) had real wages 31 per cent under 1938. In the manual group for industry, the top skill group (specialized worker) had the same real wages as in 1938, while common laborers were 35.5 per cent above their 1938 level, and women 59.1 per cent higher.[24]

Looking at compression in its other aspect, taking common labor in industry as 100, the drastic nature of the leveling process, particularly for skilled manual workers, can be seen in Table 52.

TABLE 52. Changes in wage and salary ratios in industry, 1938 and 1948 (common labor=100)

Occupational group	1938	1948
Clerical:		
1st category	293	199
2nd category	215	158
3rd category (A)	147	124
3rd category (B)	117	109
Manual:		
Specialized worker	153	109
Qualified worker	133	105
Specialized laborer	113	103
Common laborer	100	100
Women	50	83

Source: Cesare Vannutelli, "Cause ed effetti dell' appiattimento salariale," Rivista di politica economica, 3rd series, XXXIX:3 (May 1949), p. 560.

A comparison for various white-collar occupations in Rome, using the bottom category of government clerks (Grade XII) as 100, revealed for 1948 relative to 1938 that clerks of Grade VII had fallen from a 289 per cent differential to only 69 per cent, while the top clerical brackets in trade and finance respectively had fallen from 75 per cent to 9 per cent, and from 27 per cent to 5 per cent.

Viewed as a widespread phenomenon in the Italian economy at the time, the compression of skill differentials stemmed basically from inflation and a sliding-scale system that usually provided for flat-rate general increases. For government employees, tight budgets under the 1947 stabilization policy forced deterioration of salaries in the upper brackets, while the small increases that became possible were concentrated within the lower grades.

Throughout the economy in these early postwar years, restricted availability of consumers' goods made an overriding concern for the protection of minimum standards of living inevitable. Flat-rate uniform allowances, discriminating against the higher-paid occupations, were the natural remedy. Moreover, within the trade unions, which were then dominated by Communists, there was a strong current of equalitarian bias, favoring the lowest paid categories. In consequence, there occurred what Vannutelli terms a "proletarianization of the laboring bourgeoisie"—a marked deterioration in the living standards of the higher skilled groups.[25]

Opportunity for moderate redress of skill differentials came by mid-1949 in industry with the decline of the sliding-scale price indexes within the initial 8 per cent limit. By peak agreement on August 5, 1949, possible increases in the allowance were blocked at the June 1949 level, to provide time for working out a new sliding scale. Further, there was a sum set aside equivalent to the implied increase in the allowance upon a four-point rise in the price indexes, to be used jointly as an additional wage supplement and to augment the family allowances. As a supplement, it was employed to widen occupational differentials by discriminatory increases in total pay, and became known as the "first revaluation quota" (quota di rivalutazione). To avoid repercussions on the structure of basic pay rates, these sums were treated as still another allowance. The quotas were uniform geographically and throughout industry, although differentiated in favor of males and of adult workers. They were also differentiated by skill group: specialized workers received 56 lire daily; qualified workers 24 lire; and specialized laborers 12 lire. The clerical group was exempt from this supplement.[26]

The 1949 agreement was but one of a series of efforts, starting in 1947, to reconstitute an economically rational structure of occupational differentials. The peak national contract for industry of December 8, 1950 carried the process one step further. This agreement applied to both manual and clerical groups. It widened from four to eight points the "exemption zone." Within this zone a rise in the cost-of-living index was not to yield an increase in allowance, but was to provide an increase in the differential earnings of skilled workers. For the manual groups, this second adjustment quota was again treated as a supplement, while for the clerical it was incorporated in a new schedule of base salaries. The effect was a considerable improvement in differentials for the higher occupations. Clerks in the top category now received salaries 110 per cent over the bottom group, as compared with 82 per cent in 1948; while specialized workers had a 25 per cent differential over common labor, as against only 9 per cent in 1948. However, the contraction since 1938 was still by no means overcome, for, in that year, top category clerks had a 150 per cent differential, and specialized workers 53 per cent.

It was recognized in the 1949 agreement that the existing sliding-scale system was in need of revision. Accordingly, the allowance itself was blocked at the June–July 1949 level, and the first of the two differential readjustment quotas was created from the exemption range thereby established. The confederations also agreed at this time to undertake studies for substituting a national cost-of-living index for the provincial indexes upon which the allowance was then based.

Criticism of the existing *scala mobile* involved several issues. Flat-rate allowances inevitably led to relative compression of gross earnings, without regard to differences in skill, responsibility, or training. The provincial price indexes diverged in methodology, producing complaints about inequitable geographic differentials in the allowances. Finally, the family budget had been adopted at a time of economic difficulties, and was now regarded as rigid and obsolete.[27]

The brief interlude of price stability vanished abruptly with the outbreak of the Korean War at the end of June 1950. Because Italy is a heavy importer of foodstuffs and raw materials, she was acutely vulnerable to the rapid rise in world prices which set in. Once more, therefore, the sliding scale acquired overriding importance for wage policy.

On March 21, 1951, the peak negotiating bodies for industry agreed to a major revision in the system, this time with the express purpose of combining the technical preservation of real wages with the maintenance of occupational differentials according to the structure achieved with the 1950 quota agreement.

The first step was ISTAT's task of preparing a new family budget to serve as the basis upon which prices were to be collected and base-period expenditure weights obtained, which in turn would permit construction of a national cost-of-living index.[28]

Second, the new index was to reflect prices in sixteen regional capitals and to start from a base period of November–December 1950. In order to provide an immediate increase in the allowance, the base rate was considered as 98 instead of 100. The index itself was to be calculated for each two-month interval, with the allowance correspondingly changed for the fourth and fifth months following, which allowed one month for ISTAT to work up the data. Since the new family budget could not be available until the beginning of 1952, a temporary national index was to be used during 1951.[29]

Third, the allowance was to be geared to the index on a 1 : 1 basis—each one-point rise in the index (= 1 per cent) would lead to a one-point rise (1 per cent) in average contractual wages of the base period. However, the sum obtained would be added to the existing allowance, which at the start was differentiated by provinces at the June–July 1949 levels under the old system. Furthermore, the wage base chosen was not a national average but a dual one deriving from a division of the country into two main zones. The first included the north and the provinces of Naples and Rome, and the second the remainder of central and southern Italy. In Zone 1 average daily contractual wages at the time were 1000 lire, as against 800 lire in Zone 2. In consequence, a one-point rise in the index implied a 10 lire daily increase in the allowance for workers in Zone 1, and 8 lire in Zone 2.[30] Thus the new system provided for geographic differentiation of the allowance, probably on the basis of an urban-rural differentiation in living costs.

Fourth, increases in the allowance were to be weighted upward according to the four manual and four clerical occupational grades, to preserve the differentials established with the 1950 quota agreement. This arrangement also incorporated cross-differentials in the allowance, according to sex and age. In summary, the pivotal grade was common laborer, in which men in Zone 1 would receive 10 lire daily for each point-increase in the index, women 8.4 lire; and in Zone 2, 8 and 6.72 lire respectively. Table 53 presents the essence of these differentials.

Fifth, in accordance with a union request, the system also provided for setting aside increases in the allowance associated with certain intervals in the price index, these to be diverted to increases in the family allowance. In this way an element of uniformity in accordance with the doctrine of the living wage was combined with the two ruling objectives of preserving real wages and effective occupational differentials. This was done by a set-aside applicable to the following intervals in the index: (base period = 100) 105–106, 110–111, 115–116, and 120–121. For each point increase within these intervals, the family allowance would rise roughly by 10.79 lire daily per dependent.[31] Strictly speaking, these adjustments were not wages as such but a welfare supplement paid by the state out of employer contributions.[32] In fact they represented, as does the family allowance as a whole, what can be termed an arbitrary "sociological" differential in favor of married workers.

TABLE 53. Differentiation of industry cost-of-living allowance for each point-change in national price index, new sliding scale of 1951 [a] (in lire, daily)

	Zone 1		Zone 2	
Occupational grade	Men	Women	Men	Women
Clerical:				
1st category	23.94	23.94	19.15	19.15
2nd category	18.04	15.51	14.43	12.41
3rd category (A)	13.43	11.55	10.74	9.24
3rd category (B)	11.38	9.79	9.10	7.83
Foremen and superv.				
1st category	17.50	15.05	14.00	12.04
2nd category	13.30	11.44	10.64	9.15
Manual:				
Specialized worker	12.54	[b]	10.03	[b]
Qualified worker	11.26	9.46	9.01	7.57
Specialized laborer	10.66	8.95	8.53	7.16
Common laborer	10.00	8.40	8.00	6.72

[a] Age differentials not shown. For clerical and foreman groups, rates apply to those over twenty-one; for manual, those over twenty. For ages below these, the differentials are tapered downwards.

[b] Women are excluded from this skill bracket.

Source: "Il nuovo sistema di scala mobile dei salari nell'industria" (unsigned), Rassegna di statistiche del lavoro, no. 1 (May–June, 1951), p. 275.

Finally, the system incorporated a provision for decreases in the price index, by tapering the corresponding decreases forthcoming in the allowance. For the first four-point drop in the index, the allowance was to remain intact; between 4.1 and 11.0 points, the allowance was to drop 4 points; from 11.1 points and upward in the index, the allowance would decline in 1 : 1 relationship.

The new sliding scale went into effect for industry with the March 1951 agreement. On May 17, 1951, it was extended to the trade sector. In Vannutelli's judgment, the new system was a marked improvement: it removed union influence on the collection of price data; it reduced inequitable local differences in the allowance; and it continued built-in protection against leveling. Even more, it allowed the unions to transfer their interest from the conservation of purchasing power to the development of a wage policy having a more equitable structure and providing for genuine increases in real wages where possible. The very automatism of the system ended bargaining over what were technical questions, allowing the unions to turn their attention to the wage structure itself. As Vannutelli observes, the sliding scale can be neither unique nor adequate as a basis for union policy, a fact that quickly becomes evident when the price level stops rising and the allowance accordingly becomes stable.[33] The latter fact also means that the system did not create inflation, although its operation undoubtedly contributed to the rise in prices already in course. Whether the rise would have been greater if both sides had not been bound to the system is of course another question.

The pay consolidation agreement and after. As could be expected, the unions did turn their attention to wage questions.[34] Since the main issue was the consolidation of the several supplements with the base pay (which was achieved for the clerical group in industry in 1952 and for the manual group in 1954), we should consider the elements of the industrial compensation system as they stood on the eve of consolidation. Although there were differences in particulars, a similar structure of rates and earnings prevailed for employees in trade, transportation, and agriculture.[35]

Total Wage or Salary Compensation

1. Minimum base pay rate
   Structured by product-group, territorial zone, occupational group, sex, and age.
2. Regular allowances supplemental to base pay:
   a. Cost-of-living allowance
   b. Bread allowance (legislative)

   c. Readjustment quotas to restore skill differentials
   d. Other premiums:
      1) Clerical length-of-service bonus
      2) Piece-rate earnings bonus
      3) Overtime, night, and holiday work bonuses
3. Other supplements to base pay:
   a. Paid vacation
   b. Holiday pay (16 days) (legislative and contractual)
   c. Christmas bonus ("thirteenth month")
   d. Dismissal pay
   e. Other supplements:
      1) Lunch pay or cash in lieu
      2) Uniform, travel, and outside work allowances
4. Social security benefits: (legislative)
   a. Regular supplements to compensation:
      1) Family allowances (legislative and contractual)
      2) Earnings equalization (to workers on short-time)
   b. Contingent:
      1) Pensions
      2) Unemployment
      3) Occupational injuries and illnesses
      4) Sickness
      5) Tuberculosis
      6) Maternity
      7) INA-Casa program for workers' housing

There exists here a system of compensation as elaborate as in any of the other industrial nations. Naturally the question arises: what bearing did the pay consolidation agreements of 1953 and 1954 have upon this structure?

The issue of consolidation centered around inclusion of the cost-of-living and bread allowances in the base salaries of the clerical group and the inclusion of the two readjustment quotas for manual workers. For the clerks, the readjustment quota had already been incorporated in base pay in the earlier agreement. For both groups, therefore, consolidation involved the regular supplements (excluding family allowances). At the same time, however, inclusion of these sums in the pay base would have had direct impact upon the cost of the other supplements as well as upon social security charges, since most of these were calculated as percentages of base pay. In fact, the latter implied increases in total labor cost were the major reason for the employers' reluctance to embark upon a consolidation program.

A rash of demands for wage increases following the 1951 agreement on the new sliding scale brought the consolidation issue to a head in the spring of 1952. On June 14, the first peak agreement on consolidation was formulated. It provided, first, that the cost-of-living allowance was to be included with base salaries in calculating severance pay and length-of-service bonuses for the clerical group. Second, it granted both the clerical and manual groups an additional increase in the family allowances, beyond that provided in the 1951 agreement. Finally, it established a study commission to evaluate the industry-by-industry impacts of consolidation for both groups.[36]

This commission reported back to the parties in 1953 that the program would be impossible without substantial increases in labor costs. Discussions began in September, quickly revealing that there were formidable obstacles to eventual agreement: the unions wanted to add general increases to the increased benefits implied by consolidation per se; piece-rate percentages to be applied to base pay would have to be cut with enlargement of the base, but if set too low the low-paid groups would suffer, and, if set higher, the better paid would gain disproportionately; the bread allowance, if incorporated in the base, would now raise the cost of piece-rate quotas, the Christmas bonus, and severance-pay allowances; finally, to get greater geographic uniformity in base pay would be inseparable from higher wages all around.

Negotiations were stalled for a time, but in February 1954 the CISL offered to limit increased money benefits solely to those implicit in consolidation itself. Some progress was made until the Communist-led CGIL again began demanding increases. The employers refused, and the CGIL withdrew. However, the CISL and UIL continued to bargain, and, since Italian law does not accord exclusive representation rights to any union body, the parties eventually arrived at the first postwar peak agreement to be consummated without the CGIL. The employers then proposed to extend its benefits to workers belonging to bodies affiliated with the CGIL. The CGIL protested violently, demanding referenda that in the event of rejection would bind the employers to offer better proposals. The employers responded by offering to allow CGIL members to contract out and remain in status quo ante. This the CGIL refused, countering by permitting its members to receive the increases as a "downpayment." By this act the CGIL divorced itself from the agreement, placing itself in the uncomfortable position of being on the outside looking in. Accordingly, it could claim no credit for the benefits finally achieved.

Two peak agreements alternately emerged from these negotiations: that of June 12, 1954, pertaining to consolidation itself and to the rearrangement of the system of zones by which geographic differentials were determined; and that of July 28, 1954, which set up the new scale of base wage and salary minima for the peak interconfederation level. Following these, a series of separate industry contracts were then negotiated, using the peak agreements for minima only and as guides for administration of principles in each sector of industry. Eventually, too, the consolidation program was extended to other parts of the economy, outside industry.

First, the two peak agreements for industry provided that for clerks, foremen, and supervisors the salary base would now include the existing cost-of-living allowance and the daily 20 lire minimum bread allowance. For the manual group, the base wage would now include both these items and the two readjustment quotas (for skill differentials) of 1949 and 1950. Bread allowance differentials in excess of 20 lire daily (for heavy labor) would remain separate.[37]

Second, thirteen new geographic zones were established. Since the previous cost-of-living allowance had been differentiated according to province with the operation of the sliding scale until 1951, its incorporation in the basic pay was inseparable from provision of differentiated general increases to achieve greater geographic uniformity in base pay. These increases ranged between 1 and 8 per cent. In addition the sex differential against women was cut from 20 to 16 per cent. Finally, interindustry differentials were affected by rearranging industry groups in three main product-groups. Workers whose base minima exceeded those provided were granted "red circle" exemption rates that were to disappear with turnover of incumbents in the classification.[38]

Third, piece-rate quotas were adjusted to average 8 per cent of the new pay base, as against 20–24 per cent of the old one, which of course was lower. According to Vannutelli, this change added another 4–8 per cent to labor cost.

Last, the 1951 national siding scale was retained, with future allowances to be treated as supplements separate from the new pay base. Since the price index rose three points between July and September 1954, wages rose by an additional average 3 per cent for this reason.

As an upshot, pay consolidation was not fully achieved, since the differential bread allowance for heavy labor and the subsequent cost-of-living allowance both survived as supplements to base pay. This, of course, is to say nothing of the remaining fringe benefits which naturally had to remain separate. Nevertheless, the program did much to simplify the wage and salary structure, and, even more, to restore some meaning to the base wage itself, from the standpoints both of economics and of industrial relations.

Of even greater importance, the pay consolidation agreements were the first step toward decentralized and more flexible collective bargaining, since the task of applying the peak level minima and controlling standards in the segments of the industrial sector was turned over to individual industry associations. According to a government study, these local bodies for the first time gained full freedom of action, including the right to negotiate minimum rates above or below those in the peak agreements.[39] As these new "category agreements" began to emerge later in 1954, they provided for additional increases of 3 to 7 per cent over the minima established by the peak agreements.[40] In this way, wage relationships achieved a degree of stability that was to endure into 1957.

However, in that year the sliding-scale system was revised once more.[41] Three main criticisms of the 1957 arrangements brought this about. The trade unions objected to the four-month lag between a rise in the index and adjustment of the bonus; and to the undervaluation of the bonus increment for each point increase in the index. The value of each point had been based upon average 1951 wages, and base pay increased substantially in 1954. The employers disliked the one-way nature of the system: it produced wage increases with rising prices, but not pro rata decreases when they were falling. Less partisan experts found the system was not only too rigid downward, but too sensitive upward. Thus it quickly translated seasonal upswings in food prices into larger bonuses, and by its nature perpetuated those higher labor costs after each seasonal decline.

It was agreed on all sides to set up a study commission on the problem. This in turn led to a new peak agreement on January 15, 1957, which introduced the present system.

The first change was to shift to a quarterly basis, in which a rise in the price index in the preceding three months would lead to immediate increase in the bonus at the start of the following month. This required that the initial and closing dates of the quarter be placed within the appropriate months, to provide time for calculation. Second, some effort was made to achieve two-way symmetry, although any forthcoming reduction was not to take effect for an extra quarter. Third, the cost-of-living index was given a new base, May–June 1956, while the weights for the sixteen cities were revised. New pricing standards were adopted for fruits and vegetables, but rents were still to be based on houses under rent control.

Fourth, the bonus value of a point change in the index was raised 43 per cent for adult male common laborers in Territory A, and 53.75 per cent in Territory B, making the wage increments per point 14.3 and 12.3 lire daily. No changes were made in the structure of differentiated point values according to product group, occupational level, or age, but those for sex were narrowed slightly in favor of females. Also, every fifth point, starting with the first fifth, instead of the first sixth, was to be credited to the family allowance instead of the bonus, to keep the former closer in line with prices.

Apart from two exceptions, the interconfederation agreements of 1954 and 1957 set down the main principles of the wage system prevailing in industry today—principles that in important respects also apply to the other sectors of the economy as well. One modification occurred in 1958, when the unions succeeded in having parliament adopt a measure detaching government-controlled industrial firms from bargaining jointly with Confindustria, the private employer association in this sector. The technical case for separation was that the wage and industrial relations policies of Confindustria might clash with those of the government. Since these state firms are controlled by a special ministry, a conflict involving constitutional issues was possible. Initally, the declared intent of the statute was to avoid such issues, and the representative of the state firms continued to bargain jointly with those of Confindustria. However, the real purpose was to weaken the bargaining power of these enterprises, both by dividing the management side and by opening the way to political influence, which could be exerted directly through the ministry in charge.[42]

The second exception was extension of the sliding-scale system to government employees, starting in 1959. In consequence, the system included dependent employees in all the main sectors of the economy—industry, trade, finance and insurance, agriculture, and government.

Concluding observations. At the beginning of this chapter it was noted that the evolution of modern Italian wage policy reflects the opposing pulls of certain polarities and so may be interpreted as a series of compromises that have been shaped according to the relative contemporary strengths of the major pairs of alternatives confronting the employers and the trade unions at the time. Viewed in the large, in periods of inflation and of economic stress, the dominant questions have centered in the general wage level and aspirations for a minimum standard of living for all workers. At these times highly centralized bargaining, flat-rate general increases, and resort to the political route have proved dominant. By contrast, when inflationary pressure abated and a measure of economic recovery was achieved, those market forces that work toward differentiation of the wage structure have again come into their own. In turn they have fostered more decentralized bargaining, greater diversity in wage movements, more emphasis on productivity rather than need, and greater reliance on private bargaining in place of government intervention.

An interpretation of wage policy as the outcome of a dialectic of opposites is not to be viewed as a shadowy dance of metaphysical abstractions. Quite the contrary. Each of these pairings stands for visible and tangible alternatives for the role of wages in modern, industrial society, for ideas that have manifested themselves in the hard facts of negotiation and agreement, of lobbying and legislation, and of wage scales and statistics.

Between 1954 and 1960, decentralization, diversity, differentiation, and payment roughly in accord with economic productivity dominated the wage-making scene. In later 1961, inflation reappeared. Operation of the sliding scale quickly translated the rise in the cost of living into a rapid and broad advance in wages, augmented by large negotiated general increases inspired by the unions' renewed interest in the wage level. This inflationary process continued over the following three years. Thus it is safe to say that any return to questions of wage structure must await stabilization of the price level.

THE RECENT EVOLUTION OF THE SOCIAL WELFARE SYSTEM

Its origins. For many years Italy has had a complete system of income security, covering all of the major risks to interruptions or cessation of earnings from employment. Although the benefits provided by each of these social insurances have always been modest by international standards, total disbursements are very large and have been increasing more rapidly than national income. For example, provisional figures for 1962 show that contributions by employers and workers to welfare funds totaled 2412 billion lire, or 13.1 per cent of national income at factor cost. In 1955, 1154 billion was paid in, representing 11.4 per cent of factor income.[43] Thus the share of income diverted to social security has jumped nearly 15 per cent in just seven years, while the sum itself has soared by 109 per cent. The cost burden associated with these transfers is large and growing, hence cannot be overlooked in an analysis of the causes of continued massive unemployment throughout the fifties.

The great bulk of the benefits deriving from these contributions is financed by taxes levied upon employers and connected with earnings from employment. Accordingly, they should be considered in a discussion of compensation. In some instances the supplemental compensation provided by the benefits is current— for example, the family allowances. In others, it is deferred—old-age pensions. Last, it may be contingent—unemployment, accident, or tuberculosis insurance.

The purpose here is not to review the social security system in detail, either from the standpoint of the actuary or of the welfare worker, but rather to set out the main lines of its development and to relate both to the costs and the compensation of labor. In this way the system can be linked up with wages and salaries, to give an over-all picture.

Insurance against occupational accidents began in 1898, as did old-age pensions. Maternity insurance appeared in 1910, followed in 1919 by disability pensions and unemployment insurance. Between 1922 and 1929, tuberculosis insurance and protection against occupational diseases emerged. During 1934–1937, the family allowance system was introduced, while semiprivate sickness insurance plans started to appear. In 1941, subsidy for earnings reduced by short time was introduced to industry by means of the Earnings Equalization Fund. In 1943 an abortive attempt was made to consolidate and standardize the sickness insurance system.[44] Finally in April 1949, a marginal type of welfare program was established with the INA-Casa scheme, which has the dual purpose of increasing employment and providing workers' housing. This program is financed by mutual contributions from employers and workers.[45]

Postwar changes in the social security system. Four main developments have occurred in the system since the war. Inflation rapidly depreciated the funds for those programs financed by accumulated investments, making necessary a cumbersome system of pay-as-you-go supplements. Benefits were also increased, both to keep up with the soaring price level and to increase the real value of existing allowances, which were usually very low. This in turn required increased levies, mainly upon employers. Finally, coverage was extended for most forms of protection.[46]

Because the existing system was found to be badly in need of repair, a special study commission was created in 1947, to make a survey and recommend a plan of reorganization. In February 1948, this commission submitted its report. As against actual disbursements in 1947 of almost 300 billion lire, the report proposed a program that would initially have raised this sum to 960.6 billion lire, with an eventual increase to 1.5 trillion lire at stable prices. It is worth noting that the initial outlay would have represented 19.1 per cent of 1947 national income at factor cost, and the target sum just under 30 per cent. These impossibly large amounts flowed directly from the commission's underlying premise of the right to assistance and its parallel decision not to consider problems of financing.[47]

Since the commission's proposals far transcended the economic capacity of the country, they were not adopted. Instead, the program as a whole continued to be modified from year to year, as

it had been since 1945, by a series of pragmatic and largely discon-
nected measures. The main elements of these changes are summarized below for each of the principal forms of protection.

The sickness insurance program, which is compulsory, is administered mainly by INAM (Istituto nazionale per l'assicurazione
contro le malattie) and is fiananced entirely by employer contributions. These are charged against total wages. In 1950–1951 they
were increased from 5 per cent to 6.53 per cent. In 1950, coverage
was extended to women who were absent for pregnancy and child-
birth. Between 1952 and 1955, coverage was also extended to
domestics, family assistants, direct cultivators and artisans and
their families, disabled and retired workers, and apprentices. In
1958 and 1962, levies upon employers for these programs were increased further.

Insurance against occupational accidents and diseases, also compulsory, is managed by INAIL (Istituto nazionale per l'assicurazione contro gli infortuni sul lavoro). During 1945–1948, both the
funds and benefits were increased, but no increase in the rate of
employer contributions occurred through 1957. Levies are fixed
relative to the total wages weighted by a risk factor. Workers do not
contribute. In 1950–1952 a new schedule of benefits was adopted
for total and partial disabilities and for accidental death. In the
former year accident coverage was extended to agricultural workers, with temporarily lower benefits. In 1957 a new law brought
this group into the occupational diseases program as well. By 1962,
these protections accounted for one fifth of all contributions.

The main postwar changes have affected pensions for disability,
old age, and pensions paid to survivors. This system is administered mainly by INPA (Istituto nazionale della previdenza
sociale), supplemented by other agencies for special occupational
groups. The base charges are paid by employers, supplemented by
tripartite contributions (employer, employee, and state) to finance
a special fund (Fonde adequamento pensione) created in 1952 to
permit higher benefits to offset the increased cost of living and
leveling of payments under interim increases since 1945. In 1957
direct cultivators were brought into the system. In the following
year, a special levy was imposed upon employers, and pensions
were increased in 1962. In 1962, joint contributions to pension

funds totaled 904 billion lire, or 37.5 per cent of the over-all total contributions.

The next main type of social provision is tuberculosis insurance, also controlled by INPS. Contributions are paid solely by employers, on total earnings. Rates were increased in 1951 and 1952, while in 1956 benefits were raised to correspond with the family allowances. In 1954 coverage was extended to members of agricultural cooperatives, share-croppers, and their families.

INPS also manages unemployment insurance, which is financed wholly by employer contributions levied on total wages. Beginning in 1946, when benefits were raised to 200 lire daily plus 32 lire for each child, and in 1947 when a supplemental bread allowance of 104 lire monthly was added, the program has been expanded to become a form of assistance rather than a straight insurance plan. A special parallel allowance was created for ineligible workers in 1949, in addition to relief payments introduced in 1946. By 1952, an eligible unemployed worker with a wife, two children, and dependent parents received 549 lire daily. No payment is made for Sundays or for twelve other holidays, while the benefit period has a maximum of 180 days in a given year. A 1949 law extended coverage to agricultural field-hands and to clerical workers generally. Compensation rates were raised in 1958 and 1960.

Within the entire social security system, the family allowances are one of the dominant forms of disbursement, accounting for almost one quarter of all outlays in 1962. Over the postwar years benefits have been steadily increased, even beyond the amounts needed to preserve their real value. By 1962, the daily allowance for a married male worker with three children reached 708 lire daily for manual employees in industry, or 28.5 per cent of the average total wage for all skill levels. The system is compulsory for the covered parts of the economy and is managed by INPS. Contributions are paid entirely by the employer.

The earnings integration fund, as was noted earlier, exists to supplement the earnings of industrial workers scheduled below forty hours. The supplement is fixed at two thirds of normal total pay and runs to a maximum of six months. Costs of the fund are charged solely to employers and in 1952 ran at 1.5 per cent of a 900 lire daily wage maximum for each male worker. This program is limited to industry, with certain exemptions within that sector. While all covered employers must pay the charges, the benefits are limited to eligible workers. During the 1945–1946 economic crisis, this form of assistance was widely used for firms closed down for lack of raw materials or for war damages. In 1955 special provision was made for the depressed cotton industry, for firms temporarily suspended or on short time. With the decline of short-time work after 1959, this fund has lost importance.

This survey covers all the major public programs except the INA-Casa building fund, which is mutually contributory on a 3 : 1 basis for employers and employees.[48]

TABLE 54. Changes in total contributions to social security programs and to major types of protection, selected years, 1951–1962 [a] (in billions of lire)

Year	Pensions	Family allowances	Sickness and maternity	Unem- ployment	Total contri- butions
1951	147.7	173.4	129.0	18.3	558.0
1955	381.5	336.1	191.9	47.0	1113.6
1960	1005.8	462.8	391.7	93.5	2300.0
1962	904.0	584.0	501.4	111.3	2411.7
Change, 1962/1951	+512.2%	+236.7%	+288.7%	+509.5%	+332.3%
Share, 1962	37.5%	24.2%	20.8%	4.6%	100.0%

[a] These figures are only approximate, because of variations in reporting over the years by the many different public institutions involved. Contributions include those of employees and employers together, plus, for pensions, special appropriations of the central government. Figures apply to national and local government, and exclude private programs. Sickness funds include special levies to combat tuberculosis. For 1960 and 1962, unemployment contributions include those for the earnings integration fund, known now to be very small. Figures for total contributions cover all other programs besides those separately indicated.

Source: (1951 and 1955) Relazione generale, 1955, p. 256, and 1956, pp. 317–318; (1960 and 1962) Rassegna di statistiche del lavoro, nos. 5–6 (September–December 1962), p. 227, and no. 3 (May–June 1963), p. 228.

Using official figures and merging them according to the four main types of income protection, one can readily see how the rise in total contributions since 1951 has been brought about. The data appear in Table 54. Clearly, the pension system has been the principal factor and now dominates the total. Family allowances come next in relative importance, while sickness and maternity benefits are not far behind (and indeed have risen faster). Despite heavy levels of unemployment until 1960, contributions to unemployment insurance have been of small comparative importance, although charges levied have grown rapidly. In the main, therefore, the social security system has aided the employed workers.

In 1951, the four leading types of protection accounted for 83.9 per cent of total contributions, as against 87.1 per cent in 1962. Their increase has been the joint effect of higher rates of benefit and of extensions of coverage, but the comparative effects of these factors cannot be ascertained from the available data.

Further comment is desirable regarding family allowances. The original intent when introduced was to aid married workers whose incomes had been cut by reduced hours of work. Within a short time the family allowance became a new type of socialized income. In 1938 it represented 10.6 per cent of the average minimum, contractual daily wage for married manual workers in industry. A decade later it had risen to 21.5 per cent. By 1962 it accounted for 28.5 per cent of average base wages.[49]

Since the family allowance is a flat-rate supplement differentiated only by type and number of dependents, it has no relation to job content. Nor is it scaled to the amount of total earnings. Thus it is completely divorced from labor productivity and from interfirm differences either in profitability or in local labor supply. The allowance starts from and ends with the premise of family need. Since most workers are married, the allowance contributes significantly to a leveling of gross earnings, although at the same time it differentiates earnings according to marital status and size of family. Thus in 1962 the average contractual base pay of a specialized male worker (top skill bracket) was 24.1 per cent over common labor before inclusion of the family allowance. After inclusion this skill differential fell by almost one third, to only 16.8 per cent.

Because these allowances are a regular part of the gross wages of employed married workers, they stand on a different footing from the other social security benefits, all of which are paid only upon contingent loss of income from productive labor. The rationale of the family allowances is to promote family life by assuring a minimum level of income. The system is in vogue in many Catholic countries, while in Italy it is the natural outgrowth of an unusually powerful tradition of family loyalty, one that transcends religious considerations.

In the large, however, these allowances are not financed through the tax and transfer mechanism of the state. They are a cost levied against the gross product of the enterprise itself. Where, as in most of Italian industry, bilateral monopoly prevails in the labor market, the wage is economically indeterminate within limits, and the employer adjusts employment to the level of wages actually negotiated according to the relative strengths of the two sides. This poses the question: are the family allowances actually a *supplement* to wages or an *alternative* to higher basic rates and larger benefits in other forms?

Since the contractual wage level in each branch of Italian industry is set at the level of the least profitable (marginal) firms in the trade, we may conclude that for these firms the family allowances as well as the other private and social security benefits are obtained at the sacrifice of a higher basic wage scale. For the more prosperous intramarginal firms, higher scales frequently are paid. Because the limit to wage-paying ability is not reached, it is much more likely that the allowances are supplemental, rather than divisions from potentially higher base rates.

By its nature, the family allowance works against higher employment, because it is a daily lump sum payment. When an employer has a substantial increase in demand and wishes to schedule more production, it is cheaper for him to increase the hours of the existing force than to add new workers, because he can thereby spread the fixed cost of existing family allowances over more units of output. Charges for the earnings equalization fund, which are also fixed as a percentage of the maximum daily wage—a maximum now usually exceeded throughout industry—work in a similar way against higher employment and in favor of longer hours. Finally, union pressure against layoffs in slack periods has had the same distorting effect.

What were the underlying causes that have shaped the emergence and growth of this complex wage and social security system?

First, obviously, there was inflation. Between 1940 and 1947, it destroyed the existing level and structure of wages and wrecked the prewar social security system. On the one side, it compelled a series of general increases and wage supplements, at the same time requiring emergency increases in social security benefits, financed by special funds. On the other, it wiped out the functions of basic wage differentials, leveled the wage structure, and projected the problems of restoring meaningful wage differences and consolidating certain compensation with the basic wage. Granting that a rapidly rising cost of living inevitably leads to preoccupation with the general wage level and an associated equalitarian bias, nonetheless the parties continued to recognize the vital importance of wage structure, starting as early as 1946.

In part the reason was economic, and in part it arose from the equities implicit in collective bargaining. On the economic side, differences in gross earnings had to be developed simply to provide an adequate supply of skilled labor and to furnish such workers enough incentive to work effectively. Economically, it was also necessary to relate wage costs to the varying profitability of firms, industries, and sectors of the economy, because only by rational wage discrimination of this type could the volume of employment be kept from falling even lower.

Second, wage-making since the war has responded to the innate equities precipitated by unionism and collective bargaining. Even during the Fascist period, when collective bargaining was hampered, skill differentials, holiday pay, the Christmas bonus, and the family allowances were all negotiated for industry. After the war, a dual conflict emerged between the manual and white-collar groups on the one hand, and between those with low and high skill within both groups. In the end, skill differentials were successively increased. Furthermore, other fringe benefits were established or improved—payments for lost earnings on holidays or with dismissal, and premiums for work at unfavorable times or locations.

Third, the major benefits from the social security system have been a natural outgrowth of the rise of dependent wage-labor everywhere. Their common purpose is to furnish a measure of protection against risks that impair the worker's earning power. The underlying theory is that his earnings are too low to permit him to protect himself and that these hazards are part of the social overhead costs of modern industry, to be paid almost entirely by the enterprise itself along with normal business costs. The logic may not be unassailable as a matter of pure economics, but its force as a political fact cannot be questioned.

Finally, there is the doctrine of the living wage, or national minimum, or call it what you will. The notion itself may be vague, but it too is a political force to be reckoned with in modern life. In Italy it was strong enough to transform the family allowance from a special protection to a matter of right for working-class families in general. The same force has been a powerful influence in increasing and extending other social security benefits, and it also underlies the sliding scale for wages.

These, then, are the main reasons for the growth and increasing complexity of the Italian compensation system. It will be noted that the system has developed in two directions—one the route of collective bargaining, and the other that of political action and statutory enactments. Indeed, the sliding scale is a joint product of both, one that for the most part has allowed the unions and employers to concentrate upon matters of money wage structure and levels, leaving the protection of real wages to an automatic mechanism.

Resort to both the political and economic routes, along with the traditional centralization of Italian unionism, reflects an unresolved dilemma that goes way back. As a class movement devoted to socialism and equalitarianism, the Italian unions have always favored political action and centralization. However, as the post-was period unfolded, they gradually developed an interest in the structure of wages, as differentiated by factors of comparative productivity—a course that puts more emphasis upon collective bargaining. It remains to be seen whether, in time, as the nation becomes more fully industrialized, the balance will shift further toward bargaining, and if it does, toward bargaining at more decentralized levels.

CHAPTER IX. POSTWAR MOVEMENTS
IN WAGES

Until the sixties, the Italian economy was beset with massive general unemployment, although it was undergoing rapid growth in output. To what extent did the employee improve his material position? Did the tightening of the industrial labor market after 1959 alter the situation? Of what importance were collective bargaining and government intervention in effecting such improvements? How did the various employee groups fare relative to one another in this period? Could a wage-push be said to have been at work, and if so, what was its significance for unit labor costs, prices, and employment? Let us consider these questions.

WAGE MOVEMENTS BY MAIN SECTORS

Relative income shares, 1950–1962. As Table 55 shows, the employee group in the labor force has sharply increased its relative share in net national product at factor cost. In 1950, it absorbed just over one half of net product. By 1962, it had raised its proportion impressively—by 6.4 percentage points, or 12.6 per cent. Among the sectors contributing to employee income, industry expanded its quota by 243.9 per cent. Of the others, government wages and salaries rose 216.4 per cent; trade, transportation, services, finance and insurance, 208.9 per cent; and agriculture, forestry, and fishing only 62.9 per cent. In toto, employee income advanced 7119 billion lire, or 210.2 per cent, while rent, interest, profits, and entrepreneurial returns increased 4570 billion, or by 139.3 per cent.[1]

Several influences account for this upward shift, but the data do not permit them to be identified with quantitative precision. Foremost is the rapid industrialization of the country during these boom years, which increased the number of employees in the labor force faster than the other categories of employment. As a rough indication of this change, after adjustment to remove the formerly employed unemployed, the census of 1951 shows that 46.3 per cent of all employment consisted of manual workers only, while by 1961 the ISTAT field surveys suggest that this group accounted for one half of total employment.

TABLE 55. The share of employee income in net national product at factor cost, 1950–1962.[a]

Year	Net product at factor cost	Employee wages and salaries (billion lire)	Nonwage income	Employee share (per cent)
1950	6,666	3,386	3,280	50.8
1951	7,604	3,806	3,798	50.1
1952	7,945	4,190	3,755	52.7
1953	8,839	4,649	4,190	52.6
1954	9,292	5,042	4,250	54.3
1955	10,145	5,514	4,631	54.4
1956	10,774	6,018	4,756	55.9
1957	11,593	6,479	5,114	55.9
1958	12,381	6,986	5,395	56.4
1959	13,525	7,415	6,110	54.8
1960	14,833	8,178	6,655	55.1
1961	16,287	9,006	7,281	55.3
1962	18,355	10,505	7,850	57.2

[a] Net product includes net income from abroad, which is quite small. Employee wages and salaries include all supplements, payments in kind, executive salaries, and contributions to government social security programs. They exclude mixed capital-labor incomes received by artisans, crop-sharers, and family assistants. Nonwage income includes these latter forms, plus returns to property (rent, interest, and profit).

Source: Net product (1950–1955) from Statistiche indagine, p. 248; (1956–1958) Relazione generale, various issues; (1959–1962) Banca d'Italia, Assemblea generale ordinaria dei partecipanti, 1962, p. 33. Employee wages and salaries is an official series, published in Rassegna di statistiche del lavoro, no. 3 (May–June 1963), p. 226.

Even more important, industrialization has effected a substantial redistribution of the labor force, involving a large-scale exodus from agriculture and a strong expansion of the nonagricultural sectors. In 1951, manual workers in agriculture represented 27.4 per cent of the total for this group, while a decade later they accounted for only 16.9 per cent. In this structural shift, industry raised its share of these workers from 48.7 per cent in 1951 to 60.5 per cent in 1961.[2] Because wages have been relatively much lower in agriculture throughout the period, the comparative decline of employment in this sector and its correlative rise outside have brought about a rise in wage payments, an increase that would have occurred even if total employment and wage and salary rates had remained steady throughout the decade.

On a more speculative plane, there is the possibility that the political and bargaining effectiveness of the employee group, most of which is unionized, has enabled it to encroach upon property returns, and profits in particular. Evidence to be considered later indicates that in the industrial sector this incursion did not occur before the sixties, because until then the offset of rising labor productivity proved more than enough to absorb the advance in money wage costs. However, this need not have been so in the less efficient branches of the nonagricultural sector, which at all times were more vulnerable to wage pressure.

Finally, it should be recalled once more that throughout the boom period output and income rose rapidly and very steadily. At no time was there a downturn of the economic cycle to pull down profits disproportionally, and to invoke a relative rise in the employees' share. Instead, the rise in that share was associated with a very strong upward trend in total activity. Moreover, it occurred within a context of heavy general unemployment throughout the fifties.

Intersector movements in wages and salaries. Although continuous series for actual wages and salaries in the different sectors are not available, ISTAT does publish indexes of gross money and real wages on a 1938 base. Because the figures are incomplete for 1948, intersector comparisons must be tied to this prewar year.

These indexes are not measures of movements of total money earnings but instead are a fairly close approximation of changes in the over-all required pay of an average worker in the sector.[3] They are available both inclusive and exclusive of the family allowance, which permits us to weigh the importance of the latter in changes in over-all income. The underlying averages include all elements required by law and union contract—base pay, cost-of-living bonus, bread allowance, Christmas bonus, and other supplements peculiar to the occupation or sector. Thus these indexes can serve as an adequate measure of relative changes among the different sectors. By deflating them with the official cost-of-living index, they will indicate comparative changes in real wages and salaries as well. Table 56 presents the comparative data for 1938 and 1962.

Starting from 1938 and overlooking the sharp interim losses of the war and early postwar years, gains were recorded in real wages by 1962 for all sectors and for both the manual and clerical groups. However, there are some notable differences in these movements.

TABLE 56. Indexes of gross contractual money and real wages and salaries, inclusive and exclusive of family allowances, by main economic sectors, 1938–1962 [a]

	Excluding family allowance		Including family allowance [b]	
Sector	Money (1938=1)	Real (1938=100)	Money (1938=1)	Real (1938=100)
Manual:				
Agriculture	121.7	163.3	142.7	191.5
Industry	99.6	133.7	109.5	146.9
Transportation	88.5	118.8	109.0	146.3
Trade	41.8	123.1	108.9	146.1
Clerical:				
Industry	76.9	103.2	83.0	111.4
Trade	84.4	113.2	92.0	123.4
Government	85.9	115.2	87.2	117.1

[a] Includes base pay, various regular supplements (cost-of-living, bread, Christmas bonus) and special premiums peculiar to each group. Money wage indexes prepared by ISTAT. These were deflated by national cost-of-living index.

[b] For all categories except government, the family allowance has been arbitrarily added to male base rates. For manual workers, figures assume a wife and three children with allowance added to male base rate. For clerical, assumes wife and two children, with allowance added to total pay.

Source: Except for manual workers in industry excluding the family allowance, all money wage indexes from *Relazione generale*, 1962, II, p. 104. Figures for exception from *Rassegna di statistiche del lavoro*, no. 3 (May–June 1963), table VI.2, col. 3, p. 271; cost-of-living index, p. 278. Full account of coverage appears in *Annuario statistico italiano*, 1957, pp. 360–361.

First, manual workers have done far better than clerical workers in increases in real income since 1938. Basically the cause has been threefold: severe inflation, an accompanying initial concentration of trade union efforts upon protecting the position of the lowest paid groups, and budget restraints that held down the pay of government workers until major adjustments were made in 1951, 1955 and thereafter. Prior to the war, white-collar workers were distinctly better off in real terms. Until 1948, however, inflation actually reduced the real incomes of the clerical group, while keeping the manual group abreast or ahead of 1938 levels. Since 1948, however, the larger relative increases have gone to the white-collar workers, although their gains in real income relative to 1938 still lag behind. Second, there was considerable variance in the changes by sector. Within the manual group, excluding for the moment the family allowances, agriculture far outstripped the other sectors in both money and real wages. Partly the reason lies in the very low level of farm wages in 1938, but some influence was probably exerted by the growing postwar scarcity of agricultural workers in certain areas. Moreover, in all sectors these data are far more representative of those employees covered by union agreements than they are for unorganized employees, while they do not apply to unpaid family assistants at all. Unfortunately, the Italian statistics are inadequate for a more ambitious survey.

Third, in all cases except government, both money and real incomes were substantially increased over 1938 by addition of the family allowances. Again the manual groups were far in the lead in all sectors, although over-all the impacts of these allowances varied considerably.

As noted earlier, family allowances favor married men. There can be little doubt that to a considerable extent postwar increases in these payments have been obtained at the sacrifice of larger increases in base rates and other bonus items; now they are a substantial fraction of the basic wage. However, the wage data are not weighted to allow for their effect, which precludes an over-all assessment of movement in gross wages by sector or within sectors. The only remaining expedient is to show net changes with and without these allowances.

If we shift the base year to 1950 instead of 1938, a somewhat different pattern emerges, shown in Table 57. All groups now show gains in real wages, and the clerical workers no longer lag far behind the manual group. Excluding the family allowances, government clerical workers enjoyed by far the largest relative gains in money and real wages; and manual employees in trade fared the least. Including the allowance, the government group still ran well ahead, while next in order were manual workers in agriculture, clerical workers in industry, and manual workers in transportation.

The comparative strength shown by the clerical group in all three of the sectors in which they are represented is somewhat deceptive. In 1950 those workers had a much lower standard of living than in 1938, owing to severe inflation and a wage policy that discriminated in favor of the lower-paid manual group. Beginning in 1948, efforts were finally initiated to close the gap and to restore traditional differentials in favor of white-collar employees. None-

TABLE 57. Indexes of gross contractual money and real wages and salaries, inclusive and exclusive of family allowances, by main economic sectors, 1950–1962 [a] (1950=100)

	Excluding family allowance		Including family allowance	
	Money	Real	Money	Real
Manual:				
Agriculture	175.3	114.1	204.9	133.3
Industry	181.5	118.1	188.0	122.3
Transportation	185.4	120.6	190.5	123.9
Trade	170.3	110.8	176.8	115.0
Clerical:				
Industry	193.3	123.8	193.3	125.8
Trade	185.9	120.9	186.0	121.0
Government	232.1	151.0	229.7	149.4

[a] See notes to Table 56.

Source: (1950) *Rassegna di statistiche del lavoro*, no. 6 (November–December 1952), p. 673; (1962), no. 3 (May–June 1963), p. 270 (except manual in industry excluding family allowance, which was taken from Table VI.2, col. 3, p. 271). Deflation to real wages based upon official index of the cost of living.

theless, even as late as 1957 this group generally lagged behind the manual workers in comparative gains in real wages.[4] Only quite recently have the clerical employees really begun to share proportionately in the postwar expansion of the Italian economy.

What were the comparative trends in money and real wages by group and sector during 1950–1962? A reasonably good measure of such movements can be had by calculating compound rates of increase between the two end dates. All the indexes were rising consistently, and we are not concerned with the steadiness of these rates.

Excluding the family allowance, the annual rates of increase for the manual group ranged between 4.18 per cent in trade and 4.86 per cent in transportation. Including the allowance, the range extends between 4.48 per cent in trade and 5.67 per cent in agriculture. If the sector rates are weighted by proportions of manual employees recorded in the 1951 census, the average annual compound rate of advances in money wages for the manual group in all four sectors is 4.58 per cent excluding the allowance, and 5.17 per cent including it. These are the most inclusive measures obtainable for movements in money wages for blue-collar workers in the economy as a whole.

Looking now at the clerical group, money salaries excluding the allowance rose within a range of 4.88 per cent yearly in trade to 6.69 per cent in government. Including the allowance, the range extends from 4.89 per cent in trade to 6.61 per cent in government. Weighting the values for industry, trade, and government by their 1951 proportions of white-collar employment, the average annual rate of increase in salaries was 6.14 per cent without the allowance, and 6.09 per cent including it. Either way, the clerical group enjoyed a faster rate of increase than the manual.

Regarding real wages, the range for the rate of advance excluding the allowance extends for the manual group from 0.79 per cent yearly in trade to 1.45 per cent in transportation. Including the allowance, it runs from 1.08 per cent annually in trade to 2.23 per cent in agriculture. The weighted averages for the manual group as a whole are 1.19 per cent yearly without the allowance, and 1.75 per cent with it. For the clerical group, the range without the allowance reaches from 1.47 per cent in trade to 3.22 per cent in government. Including the allowance, it extends from 1.48 per cent yearly in trade to 3.14 per cent in government. The corresponding over-all weighted average rates of increase are 2.68 and 2.63 per cent yearly.[5]

Looked at as a whole, then, wage movements in real terms over the period favored the clerical group over the manual. Within the latter, married workers fared considerably better than single ones, owing to the influence of the family allowance. For both groups together, the highest rates of increase were to be found in government and agriculture. This fact can be misleading, because agricultural workers were the lowest paid group in the country in

1950, while government employees on that date still had not regained their real income level of 1938. Thus the speed of advance for both groups in a sense reflected redress of markedly unfavorable starting positions.

POSTWAR WAGES IN INDUSTRY

Interindustry movements in net and gross hourly earnings. In the previous chapter, distinction was made between the base pay rate and gross earnings, a difference that is quantitatively large for manual workers in industry because of the number and variety of wage supplements in the Italian system. If one's interest lies in the factors responsible for changes in earnings and in labor costs, it is essential to separate net from gross movements. If it is concerned with the rate of improvement in real incomes, then gross figures become relevant.

The only comprehensive industrial wage statistics are those compiled by the Ministry of Labor from its regular monthly sample, which also includes employment and hours worked. These data apply to manual workers only and are gathered from 43 separate branches of industry, of which 13 are fully enumerated and the rest only partially. The figures for net and gross average hourly wages are computed by dividing the net and gross wage bills in each branch by its total input of hours for the month. Thus they represent interestablishment weighted averages for all labor grades in the branch, although, beginning with 1961 in some cases, earnings by labor grade have also been computed.

In Table 58, net hourly wage data are shown for nine leading industries for 1948–1962. Excluding foods, all of them belong to what we have called the technically advanced sector of industry. In all cases, the average of the sample has been considered adequate enough by research experts at the Bank of Italy to justify their use for measurement of unit labor costs. This is not true for most of the remaining segments of the industrial sector. In consequence, it was decided to examine the same group, extending the series back to 1948, and constructing a weighted average for the group based upon 1948 industry proportions of total group employment as revealed in the same sample.

At this juncture, it is extremely important to understand what is measured by net hourly wages. They include the pure base rate; earnings on piece rates; bonuses for night shift, holiday work, and overtime; the cost-of-living and bread allowances; the adjustment quotas to restore skill differentials; attendance bonuses; and, where applicable, special allowances for housing and uniforms.[6] Thus the figures do not measure pure job rates as such, but include earning elements dependent upon production rates, which introduce a "drift" factor. However, the element of base pay is predominant, and, more than this, many of the supplements are closely tied to it and are customary enough to be considered properly part of the base rate. Accordingly, movements in average net wages are a reasonably good measure of changes in job rates, particularly because they exclude the family allowance, holiday and vacation pay, and the Christmas bonus.

The real trouble is of a different order: the basic "job rate" in Italy does not mean what it signifies for the theory of job evaluation. The reason is that the excluded elements also represent mandatory components for pay on the job independent of any influence of production rates upon earnings. Excepting the family allowance, these are usually calculated with reference to the basic job rate itself. Thus there is a good case for holding that gross hourly wages are really a better measure of the true job rate. However, even if this contention is accepted, the difference between net and gross still must be known if one is to account for movements in the total job rate itself.

The figures in Table 58 indicate that between 1948 and 1962 average net hourly pay in these nine industries rose between 106.0 per cent in building materials and 153.8 per cent in transportation equipment. The increase in the weighted average for the whole group was 122.2 per cent. Expressed as a linear logarithmic trend, the annual rate of increase in net hourly wages was 5.07 per cent, with very little variation among the years.[7]

In 1948, the average net hourly wage in primary metals was the highest in the group, while foods were lowest, with the ratio of the former to the latter standing at 1.56—a considerable wage advantage even granting the influence of differences in the distributions of workers by skill level. By 1962, transportation equipment —a rapidly expanding industry—had become the leader, while foods were still at the bottom. Now the ratio had become 1.59.

TABLE 58. Average net hourly wages of manual employees, excluding regular supplements, leading branches of industry, 1948–1962 [a] (in lire)

Year	All manufacturing	Foods	Textiles	Rubber	Chemicals	Building materials	Primary metals	Machines, nonelec.	Machines, elec.	Transp. equipment	Weighted average
1948	134.2	112.6	117.5	168.0	136.9	129.3	175.5	140.1	147.1	153.6	134.1
1949	140.9	115.5	119.9	169.7	142.6	131.8	185.0	147.3	152.7	162.3	139.0
1950	143.5	116.2	122.2	177.0	149.3	134.0	193.7	151.9	155.9	173.7	143.5
1951	157.5	128.2	133.1	198.2	165.2	145.3	213.8	166.5	172.3	189.8	157.3
1952	165.0	133.5	138.6	200.2	173.0	151.3	221.5	175.3	179.6	198.8	164.1
1953	168.9	138.4	142.0	206.5	179.0	155.2	223.0	177.2	182.8	205.7	167.8
1954	174.6	143.8	147.2	219.8	187.3	159.5	229.2	181.4	188.0	213.2	173.5
1955	185.3	155.9	153.8	247.1	200.0	169.2	243.5	187.9	195.9	227.0	182.9
1956	197.5	162.9	161.1	257.6	212.3	179.8	261.8	202.1	208.7	246.9	194.5
1957	206.6	170.2	168.1	269.6	222.9	185.9	274.6	211.4	215.9	259.8	203.4
1958	215.7	180.1	173.2	278.2	233.6	195.5	280.6	220.4	225.7	272.3	211.3
1959	220.7	183.3	176.5	291.6	241.0	198.8	288.3	226.7	230.0	286.4	217.2
1960	231.9	188.7	187.4	305.8	246.3	205.1	305.4	238.2	239.9	302.4	228.2
1961	248.2	203.9	198.2	318.7	268.7	222.9	324.8	253.3	257.0	321.5	243.2
1962 [b]	303.7	245.0	255.6	368.3	316.3	266.3	383.9	306.5	306.0	389.8	298.0

[a] These figures are official and are compiled by the Ministry of Labor from its running monthly sample. They exclude the following supplements: paid holidays and vacations, family allowance, Christmas bonus, and other unspecified "integrating" elements. Thus they come fairly close to a measure of base pay.

The weights used for the weighted average were those of 1948 proportions of each of these industries of total manual worker employment for the whole group, as indicated by the same ML sample. The latter embraces other industry groups and industries as well, but is too thin for reliable interpretation.

[b] November 1962.

Source: *Rassegna di statistiche del lavoro*, various issues.

More important, despite this shift in leadership, there was very little change in the rank order of industries between the two dates, shown by a coefficient of rank correlation of .8833, which is significant at 5 per cent. Thus it may be surmised that wage policy in these years was not directed at leveling out interindustry rate differentials.

TABLE 59. Comparative changes in average gross and average net hourly wages of manual workers in nine industries, 1952–1961 [a] (in lire)

Industry	Gross hourly wages			Net hourly wages		
	1952	1961	Index (1952 = 100)	1952	1961	Index (1952 = 100)
Foods	179.4	270.1	150.6	133.5	201.4	150.9
Textiles	179.8	257.8	143.4	138.6	198.2	143.0
Rubber	255.0	405.7	159.1	200.2	318.7	159.2
Chemicals	233.3	362.7	155.4	173.0	268.7	155.3
Building materials	202.6	305.7	150.9	151.3	222.9	147.3
Primary metals	295.0	440.8	149.4	221.5	321.0	144.9
Machines, nonelectric	226.9	330.9	145.8	175.3	253.0	144.3
Machines, electric	225.7	337.0	149.3	179.6	256.9	143.0
Transportation equipment	256.8	433.0	162.9	202.1	321.5	159.1
Weighted average	215.2	321.7	149.5	164.5	242.7	147.5

[a] *Rassegna di statistiche del lavoro* regularly publishes the net figures, but not the gross. Both are prepared by the Ministry of Labor, which publishes them in *Statistiche del lavoro*. Data for earlier years were not available. Since these figures are published only on a monthly basis, the annual averages had to be computed. For each industry, this was done by compiling annual totals for input of man-hours, net wages, and gross wages, dividing the last two by the first.

These averages will reflect statistical shifts in the distribution of workers between low and high wage establishments within the industry, and as among low and high wage occupations within the industry. There are no data for correcting for these influences. However, the average for the group eliminates the effect of interindustry shifts, because fixed base-year weights were used. To permit comparison with the weighted averages in Table 58, the same weights were employed: relative proportions of group employment of manual workers in 1948.

Source: Statistiche del lavoro, various issues.

The next step is to look at changes in average gross hourly wages. Because the data available were limited, comparison is confined to two years, 1952 and 1961. The figures are shown in Table 59, where gross and net hourly earnings are placed in contrast. Recall in this connection that the gross figures include paid holidays and vacations, the Christmas bonus, and the average value of the family allowance as spread over all hours worked.

In all industries but one, the relative increases for these industries were greater at the gross than at the net level, suggesting that the value of the additional supplements was increasing somewhat faster than the base wage as such. For the whole group, gross hourly wages rose 49.5 per cent, as against 47.5 per cent for net. Expressed as compound annual rates, gross wages for the group advanced 4.1 per cent yearly. This figure will serve as a satisfactory measure of the annual rate of increase in average money earnings in the advanced sector of Italian industry during this period. However, it is not an index of the rate of change in the average cost of a manual worker in the sector because it does not include social security changes paid by the employer, except for the family allowance, which is more in the nature of a wage payment.

At the gross level, the primary metals industry paid the highest wages both in 1952 and 1961, while the food group was lowest in the former year, and textiles in the latter. In ratio to the lowest industry, primary metals stood at 1.64 in 1952, and 1.71 in 1961. Thus there was little change in the relative wage advantage of the best paying industry over the worst, although the percentage gap itself continued to be substantial. Even more significant is the fact that there was virtually no change in the rank order of industries at the gross level between the two dates, for which the rank correlation coefficient was .97, which is significant at the 5 per cent level for the nine industries involved. For net wages for the same dates, the coefficient was .92, indicating slightly more shifting in rank order at that level.

Average money and real wages in manufacturing. At this point we should turn our attention from changes in the interindustry wage structure to over-all movements in average wages in manufacturing as a whole. For such a purpose, the only continuous series including the entire boom period from 1948 is one published by Confindustria. These figures are compiled from the data collected in the ML sample, converted to monthly rather than hourly averages. They exclude the family allowance, but include the elements entering into net wages of manual workers, together with the other regular supplements (paid holidays and vacations, Christmas bonus). As such, they measure gross money wage earnings in the strict sense, as an average per month in each year for a manual worker. These averages are compiled from annual weighted aggregates whose quantity components shift from year to year, and data are not available to permit removal of these weight-shift factors. In consequence, the inter-year movements in the monthly averages will reflect changes in the distribution of workers by labor grade, by industry, and as among low and high wage plants. In other words, they are not a pure statistical measure of changes in wage rates and supplements alone, although there is reason to believe that the effect of quantity shifts is minor.

The main deficiency is of another order, that of coverage. As noted earlier, the ML sample is heavily weighted by large firms in the advanced segments of manufacturing, hence is not adequately responsive to the numerous low-wage industries in which small-scale enterprises predominate. Because there is no way to remedy this defect, the figures should be interpreted as more typical of advanced industry than of manufacturing as a whole, although their scope is broader than that applicable to the data for average net and gross hourly wages previously cited.

These statistics show that average monthly earnings per manual worker in manufacturing rose from 24,855 lire in 1948 to 55,897 lire in 1962, an increase of 124.9 per cent. Between 1948 and 1954, when the pay consolidation agreement was made, they rose 41.9 per cent, or at a simple average rate of almost 7 per cent yearly. From 1954 through 1960, they advanced 42.0 per cent, again at 7 per cent yearly. In 1961, the market for industrial labor had finally begun to tighten. In addition, in January of that year a "pay equalization" agreement was achieved, providing for substantial increases. Nonetheless, during 1961–1962 the relative increase in wages over 1960 was only 11.6 per cent, or at a simple annual rate of 5.8 per cent.[8] However, this understates the strength of the up-thrusting prices at work, for the increase in 1962 alone was 10.5 per cent over 1961, while between the single months of November 1961 and 1962 the average soared by 20.5 per cent.[9]

To determine the trend rates of advance in monthly wages throughout the boom, the figures for 1948–1962 were converted to logarithmic values for simple linear regression analysis. In result, the trend rate of advance turns out to be 5.8 per cent yearly, with very little variance over the period.[10] This figure may be taken as the best available measure of the rate of advance in average wage earnings for manual workers in manufacturing, as reflected by the

234 The Labor Market

ML sample, for the period of the great boom. Bear in mind, however, that the underlying data are uncorrected for weight shifts and may well be biased upward by the undue influence accorded to the technically advanced sector, where wages at all times have been undoubtedly higher and where the largest gains in labor productivity unquestionably have been attained. The latter gains have left the big firms considerably more "space" for wage increases, and in consequence their base rates have consistently run well above the negotiated interconfederation industry and regional minima.[11]

It is less easy to establish the movement in real wages implied by this series because the choice of a price deflator is not easy to resolve. To obtain a matching series for the full period, one must use the national cost-of-living index, which is relatively obsolete because its base is 1938. One alternative is to substitute the implicit price deflator for real consumption, which is based upon prices of 1954. However, this index cannot be carried back of 1950. In addition, it includes public goods and services deriving from government, as well as many market items that are not part of the worker's budget. The better solution would be to use the new index of consumers' prices. However, it begins with 1953—too short a period for our purpose.[12]

Deflating average monthly wages by the cost-of-living index, it turns out that real wages rose 46.2 per cent between 1948–1962, or at a logarithmic trend rate of just under 2.6 per cent yearly.[13] Working from 1950 instead and using the implicit price deflator for total consumption, we obtain an indicated rise in real monthly earnings of 45.7 per cent through 1962, as against only 32.0 per cent using the cost-of-living index—a very substantial difference. As a result, for this period the mean annual geometric rates of increase turn out to be 2.9 per cent under the implicit price index, and only 2.2 per cent under the cost-of-living index.

Thus under either measure the rate of improvement in the real earnings of manufacturing workers turns out to be much less than that for money earnings. Probably the true compound annual rate lies closer to 2.9 per cent than to 2.6 per cent. For a country having the comparatively modest industrial circumstances of Italy, this is a very good performance, all the more so because it has been so steady for fifteen years, and because it so greatly exceeds the rate of improvement attained in the earlier decades of the modern period. Professor Vannutelli's real wage series for industry (prices of 1938) shows a cumulative rise of only 26.6 per cent for the entire period of 1901–1938—which implies a mean geometric rate of annual increase of but 0.62 per cent.[14] By contrast, under either method of deflation the annual rate for the postwar boom years is more than four times as great. Here again is reason to describe the record after 1947 as the Italian economic miracle, an achievement that is still not fully appreciated by the western world because the West German experience has commanded so much attention.

Despite this sharp upward break in the trend rate of advance in real wages after the Second World War, a puzzling element remains: it still lags well behind the 4.1 per cent compound annual rate of increase in per capita real consumption for 1950–1962 (price of 1954).[15] It would idle to do much speculating about the significance of this divergence, because much of it no doubt turns on statistical definitions and procedures. For example, even in 1948 real national product per head (prices of 1938), and by implication consumption per head, was still 7.8 per cent below 1938. By contrast, Vannutelli's series for real wages in 1948 shows them to be 25.9 per cent above their 1938 level. This marked difference in starting points for 1948 strongly affects the derived annual rates for the period thereafter. Furthermore, divergent impacts of inflation seem to be another factor of importance, which would show up in the contrasting behavior of the price-deflating indexes employed. Thus a comparison of per capita real consumption with real monthly earnings, both with 1950 = 100, reveals that the ratios of the former to the latter series widened sharply during 1952–1953 and 1961–1962. Finally, real consumption for 1950–1962 includes nonmarket goods, whose valuation and deflation may well introduce upward bias because of the great expansion of government activities during the boom years. Using current values, because deflated figures are not available, public consumption was 9.2 per cent of total consumption in 1950 and rose to 15.1 per cent by 1962.

For these reasons, then, it is prudent not to conclude that the discrepancy between per capita real consumption and real wages indicates that manufacturing labor failed to share fully in the fruits of the boom, or to regard the divergence as revealing a trend freighted with ominous implications for the future.

Factors in the rise of money wages in industry. Viewed in essence, the increase in money wages can be attributed to three main factors: the rise in basic job rates, larger earnings from piece rates and overtime, and enlarged payments for supplements to base rates. However, this view of the matter is too simple for two reasons. The mechanical effects of the operation of the wage system are quite complex in themselves. Beyond this, analysis of the mechanism says nothing directly about causation.

The first complication is that base rates throughout 1948–1962 have been augmented substantially by the cost-of-living allowances. More than this, the size of the allowances has risen over the years. One reason, and it is central, is that the controlling price index has advanced almost without interruption. Another is that the system itself by which the bonus is determined has been revised twice, in 1951 and 1957.

Ideally, we require an index of pure job rates for the period, against which the incidence of the allowance could be compared. Unfortunately, none exists. Accordingly, it is necessary to use fragmentary data to obtain some grasp of the importance of the sliding-scale system for the rise of money wages. On this expedient, the results are inevitably rough.

The initial postwar version of the system—introduced by inter-confederation agreement on October 27, 1946, set out from an average daily base wage for manual workers of 240 lire, to which 185 lire were added in redress for a higher cost of living. This enlarged base earnings by 77.1 per cent. The bonus accounted for 43.5 per cent of total daily pay, excluding earnings from piece rates, overtime, and all other supplements. By March 1951, the average bonus stood at 575 lire daily, increasing by 210.8 per cent over 1946. On March 21, 1951, the second version of the sliding-scale system was established. Between that month and September–October 1956, the new mechanism added an average of 220 lire daily in Zone 1 (the north plus Rome and Naples), following a cumulative rise of 26 points in the price index, of which 22 were applicable to the bonus and 4 to the family allowance. In fact, the actual bonus was differentiated by labor grade, sex, and age, as well as by territory.

On January 15, 1957, the system was again revised, using November 1956—January 1957 as a base. From the latter quarter through that of November 1962—January 1963, the price index rose 18 points, of which 16 were applied to the bonus and 2 to the family allowance. In result, another average 228.8 lire daily were added to base wages in Zone A (formerly Zone 1). Thus starting from a level of 185 lire daily in October 1946, the bonus had risen 838.8 lire on average by the end of 1962, an increase of 453.4 per cent. In consequence, by the end of 1962 the sliding scale had added roughly 1023.8 lire to the worker's base rate. In truth, daily wages in late 1962 were not actually being augmented by a bonus of this approximate size, because on occasion part of it has been converted to base rates, as happened in the pay consolidation agreement of 1954.

TABLE 60. Incidence of cost-of-living allowance upon estimated average interindustry contractual wage rates, for selected dates, 1951–1962 [a]

Date	Net contractual wages	Bonus	Total wages	Impact of bonus on net wages	Share of bonus in total wages
	(lire, eight-hour day)			(per cent)	
March 1951	382.0	575.0	957.0	150.5	60.1
Sept.–Oct. 1956	488.4	795.0	1283.4	162.8	61.9
Nov.–Jan. 1962–63	727.7	1023.8	1751.5	140.6	58.4
Net change:					
Actual	345.7	448.8	794.5		
Per cent	90.5	78.1	83.0		

[a] Net contractual wages equals total wages less bonus. Total wages refer to interindustry contractual minima, weighted in base year by occupational distribution and sex ratio. Average obtained applied to men and women.
Source: Rassegna di statistiche del lavoro, no. 4 (July–August 1952), p. 382; no. 2 (March–April 1957), p. 144; and no. 3 (May–June 1963), p. 280.

We now can comprehend in a rough way the changing relative importance of the bonus to net contractual wages. This requires use of the Confindustria series for average minimum contractual wages as estimated by that organization for a broad array of industries. This series refers to those minima fixed by interconfederation agreement, which have consistently been well below the actual job rates negotiated for particular industries and better situated firms. These estimates do not constitute a measure of pure base rates, because they include the cost-of-living and bread allowances, along with piece rate and overtime earnings. However, by deducting from these totals our estimates for the cumulative value of the bonus for certain dates, net figures can be obtained that are a quite close approximation of average base rates. The results appear in Table 60.

The heart of the matter is that the increase in the cost-of-living allowance accounted for 448.8 lire in the 794.5 lire rise of total contractual minimum pay over these years, or 56.5 per cent of it. Note also that it represented around 60 per cent of total pay throughout. Beyond doubt, the sliding scale was a factor of major importance to the slippage or drift of actual wages relative to theoretical job rates in these years.

But this is by no means the whole story, for several other influences have inserted themselves between the pure interindustry job rates negotiated by peak agreement and the actual take-home earnings achieved. One of these derives from the simple fact that the interindustry minima are but a floor upon which to build, because they are set low enough not to disturb employment in weak marginal enterprises. The extent of this gap for the whole period of 1948–1962 can be measured with fair accuracy by matching the Confindustria interindustry series for estimated minimum contractual wages with the ML series for average net hourly earnings. It will be recalled that, like the former, the latter includes the bonus together with piece-work and overtime earnings, but excludes all other supplements.[16] Table 61 presents the comparative behavior of the two series.

This evidence shows clearly that the contractual wage minima negotiated at levels below the peak interindustry agreements have run well ahead of the latter minima at all times. In fact, they have been widening rather consistently. In 1948, the lower level minima exceeded those for the peak agreements by 22 per cent on average. By 1962 the excess had become 37.8 per cent. widening in all years but three. By far the largest increases in spread occurred in 1961 and 1962, influenced no doubt by the tightening of the labor market that finally set in at this time.

Why, then, was the divergence so pronounced even as far back as 1948, and why did it widen by another eight percentage points through 1959, when the labor market was consistently so burdened with heavy unemployment? A systematic answer must be deferred until later, but it can be pointed out now that the explanation centers in the growing offset of increased productivity of labor. Its speed of increase probably exceeded 8 per cent yearly as a compound rate. This left plenty of space for wage increases, and accordingly the 5.8 per cent trend rate of advance in gross monthly wages could be absorbed with comparative ease by industry, without marked pressure upon unit costs of production. For the same reason, basic wage rates could rise at a similar rate. By contrast, the minima set by the over-all peak agreements have been geared consistently to the weakest firms in the various industry groups. In consequence, they have lagged well behind.

TABLE 61. Comparative movements in interindustry average minimum contractual wage rates and interindustry average net wages [a]

Year	Contractual wage rates (lire per hour)	Average net wages	Ratio	Relative changes in ratio	
				Index (1948 = 100)	Year to year (per cent)
1948	110.6	134.9	122.0	100.0	—
1949	112.3	139.8	124.5	102.0	2.0
1950	115.5	144.8	125.4	102.8	0.7
1951	126.3	159.0	125.9	103.2	0.4
1952	131.4	166.9	127.0	104.1	0.9
1953	135.0	171.1	126.7	103.9	−0.2
1954	140.0	177.1	126.5	103.7	−0.2
1955	146.7	187.4	127.7	104.7	0.9
1956	155.3	200.3	129.0	105.7	1.0
1957	162.3	209.4	129.0	105.7	0.0
1958	170.7	219.4	128.5	105.3	−0.4
1959	172.8	224.7	130.0	106.6	1.2
1960	180.9	235.7	130.3	106.8	0.2
1961	188.5	252.4	133.9	109.8	2.8
1962 [b]	208.9	287.8	137.8	113.0	2.9

[a] Contractual wage rates from Confindustria estimate. Average net wages from ML running sample. Both series include cost-of-living allowance and overtime and piece rate earnings, but exclude all other supplements. Confindustria series rests on fixed base weights. ML series involves floating quantity weights.
[b] First eleven months only.
Source: *Rassegna di statistiche del lavoro*, no. 3 (May–June 1963), p. 269.

We are now ready for the final question: what were the underlying mechanics of the process that produced rising money wages for manual workers in industry during the boom years? The answer lies in evaluating separately the main factors at work, which with the limited data at hand can be done by comparing net changes in lire per hour between March 1951 and November 1962.

Between these two dates, the ML figure for average net hourly earnings of manual workers in industry advanced from 151.0 lire to 307.8 lire, an increase of 156.8 lire. The problem is to identify and measure as best we can the separate contributions to this last sum deriving from the increases in sectorwide minimum base rates, in the average interfirm contractual minima as built up from the sector rates, and in the sliding-scale allowance. This can be done in approximative fashion by comparison of the Confindustria sectorwide figures with the ML data of average net wages on the two dates in question. Unfortunately, both sets of figures include the influence of added earnings from piece rates and overtime and holiday work, while the ML data will also reflect weight-shifts. Although both of these distorting elements can be presumed to be small, their effects cannot be removed, and so the results must be considered rough. Moreover, to obtain the net change in pure sectorwide base rates, the cumulative value of the bonus must be estimated and deducted from these figures. In addition, the net change in pure sectorwide rates must be deducted from the over-all change in average net wages, to isolate the increase in pure interfirm base rates net of the underlying advance in the sectorwide figure. Table 62 presents the results of these evaluations.

These figures indicate that almost three quarters of the total increase in average net wages flowed from the operation of the sliding scale and from the negotiation of above-sector minima at the establishment level. In short, the minimum rates set by peak agreement were a minor factor in the rise of industrial wages, keyed as they were to the wage-paying potential of the weakest firms. Put in slightly different fashion, sectorwide increases alone raised average net wages only 28.6 per cent over the eleven and a half year period. Additional settlements at the enterprise level brought the over-all advance in negotiated rates up to 66.7 per cent. Adding in the rise in the cost-of-living bonus brings the total increase up to 103.9 per cent.

Clearly, then, negotiations below the peak level were of major importance, despite the apparently high centralization and rigidity of the Italian bargaining system. But this inference must not be pressed too far, for it must be recalled that the sliding scale itself is a product of peak agreements. When it is combined with the advance in sectorwide rates, both will account for almost two thirds of the over-all increase. Nonetheless, enterprise bargaining has contributed significantly both to the rise of wages and to diversity of rates over the system.

TABLE 62. Estimated contributions of sectorwide and interfirm base rates and of sliding scale to rise in industrial wages, March 1951–November 1962 [a]

Contributing factor	Increase (lire per hour)	Share of total increase (per cent)
Sectorwide base rates	43.2	27.5
Interfirm base rates	57.5	36.7
Sliding scale	56.1	35.8
Total increase	156.8	100.0

[a] These estimates derive from the comparative behavior of the Confindustria series for minimum contractual wage rates (all industries and labor grades, for men and women) and the ML series for average net wages. The former series rests on fixed quantity weights, while the latter is uncorrected for weight-shifts. For details of procedure, see accompanying text.

Estimate for sliding scale is for Zone A (formerly Zone 1), which includes the most important industrial centers. It was obtained by computing the net increase in the allowance for March 1951 through November–December 1956, plus the cumulative increase between the latter date and November 1962, without adjustment for incorporation of part of the bonus in base rates.

Source: Rassegna di statistiche del lavoro, various issues.

Earlier in this analysis, distinction was drawn between average net and average gross hourly wages in the ML statistics. The joint effect of increases in the dual set of minimum rates plus the sliding scale has been to pull up average gross wages along with average net. The reason is simple: except for the family allowance, gross wages differ from net because they include paid holidays, paid vacations, and the Christmas bonus—all of which are computed from the basic daily rate plus the cost-of-living bonus, and hence move in proportion. Because the number of days covered by these benefits has shown little change over the period, this proportionate relationship has been maintained. However, the gross level also includes the family allowance, which has been increased at irregular intervals both by diversion of certain increases forthcoming under the sliding scale and by special provision. Moreover, the impact of this allowance upon the gross average will vary with the proportion of heads of families in the work force and with the average number of their dependents. Accordingly, the gross average loses some of its proportionality under the influence of these factors. Furthermore, it would not be meaningful to compare movements at the gross and net levels for the same dates, because the incidence of the added elements in some cases varies with the month —for example, the Christmas bonus is concentrated in the December average, and paid vacation in June and August. However, it is safe to say that on a yearly basis advances at the gross level were tied closely to increases in base rates and in the sliding scale.

Causal factors in the rise of industrial wages. We have considered the mechanics of wage-setting and wage-raising in Italian industry. The question now becomes one of causation. What influences have loomed most important in the rise of wages, and what magnitudes can be assigned to them? [17]

From what has already been established regarding the mechanics of wage determination, the hypothesis suggests itself that changes in the cost of living (P) should be a powerful factor in invoking movements in money wages (W) in the same direction, although the possibility of feedback effects from wages to prices cannot be overlooked. Allowance for the price factor will give recognition to the role of the sliding scale, and indirectly of peak association bargaining, as an institutional element in Italian wage making.

The second hypothesis is that the volume of unemployment (U) has also influenced wage movements.[18] Here the argument runs that tightness or looseness of the factor market should operate to encourage or to restrain wage movements, by directly affecting the scale of union demands, the intensity of employers' resistance, and the magnitude of settlements actually made. It is known that unemployment was very heavy during 1948–1959, and that it decreased rather sharply during 1960–1962. Thus it should have been a braking influence in the earlier years, and a propelling one in the later period.

There remains a third force that should have proved important for wage movements: the extent of the "wage space" available to the industrial firms. If small, it could be expected to sharpen the employers' resistance and to temper union demands; and, if large, to have the reverse effect. Wage space can be measured with the Italian data in two ways: by gross labor productivity per manual-worker man-hour (O/M), which in relation to wages would indicate unit (manual) labor cost; or by property returns per manual-worker man-hour (RP/M), which in a crude way expresses profitability per hour worked. Until 1962, labor productivity ran well ahead of money wages, and profitability per hour of labor input rose strongly and steadily, meaning that unit manual-labor cost was falling and that, since industrial prices were steady during 1953–1961, gross profit margins per unit of output were widening. Our reasoning is that wage space was increasing in these years, and that it should have exerted an upward influence both at the sectorwide and the enterprise levels of negotiated settlements. By implication, therefore, this hypothesis gives recognition to institutional forces in wage-setting, to productivity, and, by implication, to the strength of final demand in the product market. However, here, too, there exists the possibility of a feedback effect: wage pressure from the union side may well have accelerated employers' efforts to raise labor productivity.

We emerge, then, with the following general hypothesis: that wage changes in Italian industry since the war can be explained by changes in the cost of living, in the volume of unemployment, and in the productivity or profitability of the input of man-hours. The hypothesis can be put in general form as a problem for linear multiple regression as follows:

$$W = f\ (P,\ U,\ O/M) \qquad \text{or}$$
$$W = f\ (P,\ U,\ PR/M),$$

depending upon which measure of wage space is to be used. Because we are interested primarily in the degree of wage change associated with a given degree of change in each of the posited independent variables taken separately, with the others held constant, the basic data have been converted to logarithmic form, which will permit measurement of the regression coefficients as elasticities.[19]

Annual data are available for all the variables. Wages and unemployment can be carried back to 1948, and property returns to 1950. Output per man-hour can be calculated from 1948, but only by splicing the 1953 index of industrial production to the older one for 1938. Because of this limitation and of the swamping effect of the 1951–1952 Korean inflation, it was decided to restrict the analysis to 1953–1962. For wages, the ML series for average net hourly wages throughout industry was used. Unemployment was measured by the ML registration statistics for the unemployed in Classes I and II together. Output per man-hour was obtained by dividing the over-all index of industrial production (manufacturing, construction, public utilities, and extractive industry) by the ML series for annual input of manual worker man-hours, which does not include construction. Property returns were calculated by deducting annual wages and salaries for indutry from value added by that sector (inclusive of depreciation and without correction for duplications), and were divided by the ML series for man-hours to measure gross profitability per manual hour worked.[20]

The results of the regression analysis are as follows:

(1) $\log W = 0.633 + 1.029 \log P - 0.253 \log U + 0.152 \log O/M$,
    $\quad\quad\quad\;\; (0.245) \quad\quad\quad (0.053) \quad\quad\quad (0.085)$
    $$R^2 = 0.997,$$

or, alternatively,

(2) $\log W = 0.716 + 0.999 \log P - 0.287 \log U + 0.143 \log PR/M$,
    $\quad\quad\quad\;\; (0.245) \quad\quad\quad (0.053) \quad\quad\quad (0.085)$
    $$R^2 = 0.998.$$

Taking the first equation, it states that there is almost a one-to-one direct correspondence between changes in the cost of living and changes in wages. That is to say, if the other independent variables are held constant and the cost of living were to rise 5 per cent, wages will rise 5.15 per cent—which bears out statistically the close linkage imposed by the sliding scale. There is also a close inverse tie between changes in the level of employment and the level wages. If unemployment were to drop 5 per cent, then the indicated rise in wages would be 1.27 per cent, if the other factors remain unchanged. Finally, the variable for wage space, measured here by gross labor productivity per manual hour, has exerted a somewhat weaker influence: if it rises 5 per cent, with the other factors constant, this would invoke an advance of only 0.76 per cent in wages.

Regarding this equation, note that the standard errors for the first two independent variables are well within satisfactory limits. Unfortunately, this is not true for labor productivity, because of the high collinearity involved. However, as measured, the influence of this variable is so small that a change of its magnitude could not affect the over-all results significantly. Finally, the proportion (R^2) of the total variance in wages "explained" by this equation turns out to be extremely high, meaning that the addition of other explanatory variables would not improve the fit obtained.

In the second equation, the productivity variable has been replaced by gross returns to property per unit of manual labor, without significant effect for the over-all results. Here separate 5 per cent increases in cost of living or in wage space, or a 5 per cent decrease in level of unemployment, respectively would invoke the following changes in wages, when each variable is taken alone: cost of living, +5.0 per cent; unemployment, +1.44 per cent; and wage space, +0.72 per cent. The standard errors conform similarly to those in the first equation, and so the earlier remarks again apply. Also, R^2 is again very close to 1.0.

Strictly speaking, these equations measure closeness and direction of statistical association between wage changes and changes in any one of the independent variables. They do not establish an order of causation.[21]

In fact, wages need not be solely a dependent variable, and the others exclusively independent. Through feedback effects and in other ways, wage changes may invoke changes in the cost of living, unemployment, and wage space. Thus in a rigorous view, all these variables are interdependent elements in a system of simultaneous equations, despite the close fit obtained. However, it can be affirmed with confidence that this association with these variables has been very close during 1953–1962.

Was there a wage-push at work? Starting with 1948, five fundamental forces began to assert themselves in Italian industry. The first was a vigorous, but on the whole well-controlled, policy of monetary expansion, which did not start to get out of hand until 1961. The second was a powerful upsurge in industrial output, which was well sustained at a compound rate of over 8 per cent yearly. The third was a strong uptrend in wage rates and supplements, approaching 6 per cent yearly compounded, and gathering speed with the advent of the sixties. This upthrust in money wages produced a trend rate of increase in real wages of between 2.5 and 3.0 per cent yearly, depending upon the deflator used. The fourth pervasive factor was massive unemployment until the sixties, at which time it began to contract substantially. And the fifth influence was a persistent and extraordinarily rapid improvement in the gross productivity of manual workers, probably as high as 8 per cent yearly compounded in the advanced portions of industry. Undoubtedly this offset restrained any long-term tendency for the price of industrial goods to rise, and from 1953 until late 1961 they held steady, while export prices actually fell. But by the close of the period this was no longer true: the rate of advance in labor costs had finally overtaken that of productivity gains, and industrial prices started shooting upward.

TABLE 63. Unit labor costs and unit gross property returns in industry, 1953–1963 [a] (1953=100)

Year	Unit labor costs	Unit gross property returns
1953	100.0	100.0
1954	100.1	97.9
1955	101.5	99.5
1956	102.3	98.1
1957	101.6	99.9
1958	105.3	101.7
1959	100.4	102.0
1960	98.0	99.1
1961	98.6	98.7
1962	107.9	95.4
1963 [b]	122.6	91.6

[a] Gross property returns were calculated from value added in industry less gross wages and salaries in industry. Value added data cannot be corrected to remove duplications and depreciation, and include rents and interest. They exclude indirect business taxes. Index of industrial production was used as divisor for both series.

[b] Preliminary.

Source: See Note 20 in this chapter.

We can gain a rough idea of the over-all behavior of unit labor costs and of gross profit margins in industry by dividing, respectively, gross wages and salaries and gross property returns in that sector by the index of industrial production for 1953–1963. The results appear in Table 63.

Except for 1958, unit labor costs held quite steady until 1961, when they started upward. During 1962–1963, they broke all bounds, encroaching on gross profit margins. . . .[22] This was the period when the long boom gave way to inflation. At the same time, it was also the period when the rates of growth and of investment dropped below their preceding trends. In addition, it was the time when industrial labor shortages at last began to appear.

Given this context, it is easy to interpret the upswing of wages as the apparent consequence of demand-pull working against a growing real scarcity of labor. But is this the whole story, or has Italian industry been experiencing a noncompetitive wage-push from 1948 onwards?

If the wage level in the industrial sector of an economy were determined solely by full competition, then wages would respond only to the underlying conditions of labor supply and demand. And, so long as the supply of industrial labor is unlimited, the expansion of labor demand would not draw up the wage level. If, then, money and real wages in industry nonetheless do rise persistently in these circumstances, the explanation must lie in noncompetitive forces operating in the labor market—in short, a wage-push is at work.

Viewed in this way, a wage push can operate even if productivity gains are so large that unit labor costs are steadily falling. In other words, a wage-push is a separate phenomenon from a price-push, although it may lead to one. Rising unit labor costs may be the outcome of a wage-push, but they are neither a necessary nor a sufficient condition for the existence of the push itself. Indeed, they can originate solely from excessive labor demand, without any wage-push at all. But if money and real wages consistently advance in the industrial sector, even while unlimited supplies of surplus labor are always available, we can infer that a wage-push is present.

From 1948 through 1960, Italian industry was confronted at all times by an ample labor reserve, as the high figures for registered unemployment readily indicate. Nonetheless, the money wages of industrial labor steadily advanced at a trend rate of over 5 per cent yearly, while the upward trend in real wages was at least 2.5 per cent annually. For this lengthy period, then, there is clear evidence of a wage-push. After 1960, industrial wages began to rise even faster, so much so that they were severely encroaching on gross profit margins, thereby invoking a price-push as well.

Since in these latter years the industrial labor reserve began to dry up, we are justified in attributing part of the accelerated advance in wages to the belated emergence of inelastic labor supplies relative to the continued expansion of labor demands. But this is not the full explanation. For if noncompetitive forces could drive up real and money wages despite the earlier handicap of an unlimited labor reserve, they could do so with even greater vigor after this excess was finally absorbed. In short, in these years the wage-push gained even greater strength, aided as it now was by a more favorable relationship between labor demand and supply.

Consider, now, the forces responsible for this upthrust in industrial labor cost since 1948. They derive, first, from the system of multiple bargaining at the sector, industry, and enterprise levels through which minimum job rates were negotiated, and to which most of the wage settlements were automatically tied. Second, they were directly affected by the sliding-scale mechanism, which in its internal mechanics was biased upward. Third, labor costs were increased further by statutory mandates affecting social security charges levied upon the employers. And, finally, during the years before 1961, the restraining influence of the excess labor reserve was negated in considerable part by statutory restraints against internal labor migration. Together these diverse forms of intervention into the labor market fostered a wage-push throughout the period.

Its consequences were several. By bringing about a substantial overvaluation of industrial labor, it provided much added impetus to capital substitution, which had much to do with the rapid rise in labor productivity. By the same token, it slowed the expansion of industrial employment, despite the fast pace of advance in output. At the same time, the rise in labor cost helped to shore up industrial prices when they should have been falling—a predictable result of imperfect markets on both the labor and product sides. This enforced stability in the prices of industrial goods denied to the less well-developed sectors full opportunity to lower their own costs of production. More than this, the rise of industrial wages had spill-over effects, transmitted by extensions of patterns of increases to these weaker sectors, where the offset of rising labor productivity was usually smaller, and where prices accordingly were more vulnerable to upward cost pressure. Indeed, this very process was partly responsible for the steady rise in the prices of consumers' goods and services throughout the period, an advance that was then fed back into industrial wages through the cost-of-living escalator.

THE BROADER SIGNIFICANCE OF THE BIFURCATED WAGE SYSTEM

The organization of Italian workers in trade unions necessarily has been far from complete throughout the postwar years. Lying beyond the compass of the unions' market power were the unemployed, the family assistants in tiny retail and service establishments, the artisan shops, the peasantry, the self-employed, and the employees in many small enterprises even within industry itself. Among these diverse groups, incomes generally have been, and remain, much lower than those of the fully employed union worker in industry. Because union coverage is still far from complete, and, by reason of the wage policy prosecuted by these organizations, the country has long possessed a divided system of labor markets.

Two factors have enforced this separation. On the one side, until early 1961 statutory restraint of internal migration operated throughout the postwar years to tie the worker to his traditional vocation (if he had one) and to his community of origin. This helped to dam up the flood of southern labor to the northern industrial centers, although never entirely. On the other side, the policy of rapidly rising money wages has imposed a second barrier to transfers of occupation—by restricting the quantity of labor demanded by industry. In other words, to make high wages higher, the unions were willing to make low wages lower.

Although it is not the only factor operating to preserve a divided economy, this bifurcated system of wages and of labor markets has worked to retard the full modernization and industrialization of Italy. In this respect, its principal malign effects have been three. First, it has helped to perpetuate heavy unemployment, because most of the unemployed could not scale the high-wage barrier to new jobs. By 1962, wage inflation had even begun to threaten the solvency of the nation and the continuance of the boom itself, with grave implications for total employment. Second, the double wage system has provided the necessary shelter for the survival of many weak nonunion firms, beyond the reach either of collective bargaining or of enforcement of social security taxes. Markedly lower labor costs in turn have permitted the preservation of obsolete techniques. Third, even within the segment of industry under union organization the enforced attrition of regional differentials under successive peak agreements has added to the competitive handicaps of many southern firms, checking the expansion of opportunities for industrial employment in that overcrowded and impoverished region.

The double wage system has helped to delay the industrialization of Italy, although by no means has it been the only retarding influence. In the chapters to follow, we shall consider more fully the nature and causes of the peculiarly divided Italian economic system.

PART THREE: DIVERSITIES OF STRUCTURE

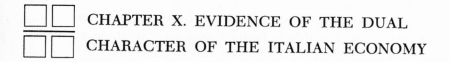

CHAPTER X. EVIDENCE OF THE DUAL CHARACTER OF THE ITALIAN ECONOMY

INTRODUCTION

With the current dissolution of the Europo-centric point of view, an awakening interest in far-distant peoples and places is emerging, quite in parallel with that inspired by the geographic explorations of the fifteenth and sixteenth centuries. A major aspect of this new internationalism involves what is loosely called "industrialization." Thus it is common today to distinguish the industrial societies from all others—"traditional," "transitional," "native," "subsistence," and even "pre-industrial." But what is it that makes a society industrial?

Among the hallmarks, of course, are the widespread use of machines and of scientifically based technologies. Other conventional characteristics are large-scale plants, the predominance of wage and salary employees within the labor force, and the preponderance of nonagricultural activities within the total economy. However, we must also include the fact that a large share of all economic activities is carried on by rationally organized enterprises, dedicated to economic efficiency, with a few exceptions. Equally decisive, whether public or private, these firms typically produce in volume, for large-scale markets, often broadly extended, even beyond the national domain.

For the purpose at hand, the important common quality of each of these industrial economies is their internal coherence. There exists substantial interdependence among specialized activities, among factors of production as well as products, and among the different geographic areas and regions. Generally, too, the peoples of these countries share an enthusiasm for technical and material progress and a faith in the benefits that industrialism bestows.

For the western industrial nations in particular, their coherence expresses itself tangibly in the interlocking of their many internal markets. Through the money and market mechanisms, made effective by modern communication and transportation, there has thus been brought into being an extremely complex division of labor. Obviously, too, there exists substantial freedom for resources and products to move within national boundaries. In these ways economic coherence has been achieved, strengthened by a unified cultural outlook, and strengthening that outlook in turn. The symbiosis of this coherence with the industrial way of life is what sets these economies apart from the traditional subsistence societies so common elsewhere in the world.

This is not to say that the industrial nations of the West are wholly free of elements of backwardness or of stagnation, or that pockets of absolute poverty no longer exist within their national borders. It is not even to say that differences of income for work of comparable skill and difficulty have disappeared. Quite the contrary. But within each of these societies substantial economic unification has been achieved.

Looked at in this way, Italy must be classed as a mixed case, largely western in character and outlook, but by no means free of the economic traits of the Orient and of the Middle East. And so it is a land of paradoxes, as we have remarked before.

Accordingly, the task of this chapter is first to look more closely at the notion of economic dualism, to see how the concept may usefully be applied to the Italian case. The next step will be to review the evidence affirming the twofold nature of the Italian economy. Then we shall evaluate the reasons for the failure, so far, of the emergence of a fully integrated economic structure. Finally, with this analysis in hand, we shall examine the economic consequences that dualism has imposed.

Conceptions of dualism. The problems and effects arising from the penetration of nonwestern cultures by western political and economic institutions have long been of interest to administrators and anthropologists alike. Thus the impacts of contact and of intrusion have usually been examined in a colonial context, although in their larger bearing they have also appeared even within the same country, whenever the industrial way of life has found a foothold in a traditional society.

Responding to lengthy experience in the Netherlands East Indies, the late Dutch economist, Julius H. Boeke, was led to define the ensuing clash between an indigenous and an imported social system as a "dual society." [1] In his interpretation, the heart of the matter is the invasion of a "noncapitalistic" or native economy by institutions and enterprises of a "capitalistic" type, which results in two distinct kinds of economic organization, two kinds of technique, two kinds of labor, and two sets of goals and incentives—in essence, two different ways of life within the same geographic territory.[2] Without accepting Boeke's questionable thesis that western economic theory is inapplicable to "noncapitalistic" societies, undoubtedly his conception of economic dualism has proved the starting point for a valuable line of analysis, having much broader application than to the Southeast Asian context for which he originally envisaged it.

Broadly viewed, then, economic dualism involves the coexistence within the same area, region, or nation of modern and traditional techniques of production and distribution, and modern and traditional ways of organizing economic activity, ways of earning, ways of living, and ways of thinking. Or, alternatively, dualism signifies a *markedly* incomplete transformation to modern industrialism, hence weak coherence of the internal economy, provided that "industrialism" is taken to mean more than merely large-scale plants or factory production.[3]

The stigmata of dualism may show up in a society in diverse ways. They may appear even within the same line of activity—the large printing house and the tiny artisan shop; or the large capitalistic wheat farm and the tiny peasant holding. Or, from a broader perspective, they may manifest themselves in the coexistence of two distinct and partially isolated sectors of the whole economy. On the one side, the highly developed sphere uses modern technology, relies upon rationally organized firms (often large-scale), depends upon wage and salary employees, and yields high incomes per earner. Here may be found industries with high capital-to-labor coefficients, turning out commodities such as chemicals, petroleum products, iron and steel, machinery and industrial equipment, automobiles and trucks, cement, pulp and paper, packaged foods, durable consumers' goods, transportation and utility services. However, it must be borne in mind that the range of industrial products and services will be much narrower in strictly underdeveloped areas. There industrial activity will usually be restricted to mining or petroleum production, plantation products, and rail or pipeline transportation, because the internal market will be too small and because comparative advantage will dictate more economical locations for manufacturing and distribution. In these "colonial" cases, dualism owes its origin to resource-oriented industrial activities imposed upon a predominantly traditional economy.

In the traditional segment of a dual economy will be found techniques of production that are old or even obsolete in the international sense, typified by use of little capital and by high ratios of labor to capital. Here the unit of enterprise will be very small or even tiny, depending heavily upon self-employment and unpaid family labor. Incomes per earner will be far lower on the average than those in the advanced sector, well beyond any differentials warranted by transfer costs from peasant agriculture or by higher urban costs of living. Indeed, the income gap may show up within the same urban center, for work of comparable skill and difficulty.[4] Here will be found the citadel of artisan handicrafts, petty shopkeeping, primitive services, and peasant agriculture.[5] Here exists a much lower level of labor compensation, made possible by the family enterprise, self-employment, and the absence both of union wage scales and of effective social security charges. Here the small-scale enterprise can survive, in activities such as furniture-making, shoes, apparel, bricks, ceramics, basket-making, repair service, retailing, personal services, and even local transportation in large part. In these cases, the market will usually be local and constricted, while machinery and large-scale organization will offer no decisive advantages.[6]

Although the double structure exemplified by the two sectors is often characteristic of the same given area, it may manifest itself most sharply in a geographic contrast. Thus in some cases it will appear in rural areas that are physically and economically isolated, for example, rural Quebec, the Tennessee and Kentucky hills, the Spanish-speaking settlements of the American southwest, or the interior communities of the Calabrian Sila. Alternatively, geographic separation may take even more extreme form—for instance, the now-famliar "north-south" dichotomy of which South Italy and the Islands are a leading example.[7]

To sum up, then, economic dualism can appear in three major ways, in each case revealing differences in technique, organization of the enterprise, and income per earner. First, it may show up within the same line of production or activity.[8] Second, it may reveal itself more broadly through two contrasting sectors of activity, having different wage levels and yields per earner, different forms of enterprise, recourse or nonrecourse to modern technology, and differences in products or services turned out. And, third, dualism may also find geographic expression, within given activities and in the two-sector sense, most strikingly in the concentration of modern industry and agriculture in one region (the "north"), and of traditional forms in the other (the "south"). Needless to say, Italy possesses all three variants, principally because it is a society in which the transition to a modern economy is still far from complete.

Recognition of the degree of transition makes it essential to introduce historical time into the classification of dual economies, for duality in structure will partly reflect the extent of time during which the process of industrialization has gone on, in addition to the obstacles that the process itself may have encountered. Indeed, the barriers themselves will depend partly upon the time elapsed. Industrialization requires capital formation, which depends importantly upon the rate and volume of internal saving. Here time is a critical variable, for it affects the expansion and current size of the capital stock, so shaping the range and extent of the transition itself as of any given date.

However, once the role of time is recognized, it is equally important to recall that there can be more than one pattern of industrialization. Only in very general terms is there a uniform or unilinear sequence to the emergence and subsequent spread of industrial activities. In each case, the particular pattern of change will reflect the local nature of the decisive variables: national policies affecting the speed and direction of industrialization and the geographic allocation of investment; the intensity of protective efforts on behalf of the backward sector; the available margin for economic expansion; the endowment and spatial distribution of natural resources; the rate of population growth; wage and price policies in the two sectors; the availability of technicians and of skilled labor; the possibility of large-scale domestic and foreign markets; the quality of the transport and communications network; the availability of housing and of community services; and, above all, the willingness of the population to accept the commitment to industrialization itself. Accordingly, the industrial economies, even those that are well unified, will in fact exhibit considerable diversity.

DUALISM IN THE ITALIAN ECONOMY

Some comparative data. Verification of the contention that Italy offers a strong case of economic dualism is not easy to accomplish with precision. The statistical data are simply not good enough. Nonetheless, the evidence is abundant enough to make a persuasive case in favor of the claim.

We can make a good start by a structural comparison of the economically active populations of Italy, France and Germany, as presented in Tables 64 and 65. For 1950–1954, the totals for the economically active populations of the three countries are quite close. The first fact that stands out is the high proportion of persons attached to agriculture in Italy at the time—42.2 per cent, as against 27.2 per cent for France and only 23.2 per cent for Germany. This marked concentration does not arise because Italy enjoys a highly productive agricultural economy, such as Denmark. Quite the contrary. Land resources are limited and generally quite poor. Arable soil per person attached to agriculture amounted to only 1.89 hectares, as against 4.08 hectares in France.[9] No, the high Italian concentration is not due to large per capita returns but to the restricted development of opportunities outside agriculture, as we have already pointed out. In consequence, much of Italian farming remains at the traditional subsistence level, having only limited trading relations with the outside economy. Here, then, is a clear sign of dualism.

In a gross way, dualism is also suggested by the comparative productivities of the economically active population of the three nations. Although the Italian group was only 2.1 per cent larger than the French one, the gross national product of France was between 60 and 75 per cent larger than the Italian in 1950, depending upon the measure used. The German group exceeded the Italian in numbers by 12.7 per cent, but German gross product ran ahead of the Italian by between 47 and 57 per cent.[10] Many factors lie back of Italy's much poorer position, but clearly one of the major reasons for the low output of her productive population is the markedly incomplete character of her industrial society.

Returning to Table 65, it will be noted that 23.5 per cent of the Italian group consisted of employers and self-employed persons, as

TABLE 64. Comparative distributions of the economically active population, Italy (1951), France (1954), and Germany FR (1950) [a]

Employment category and for economic sector	Italy [b]		France		Germany FR	
	Number	Per cent	Number	Per cent	Number	Per cent
Distribution of the economically active by sector:						
Agriculture, forestry, hunting and fishing	8,261,160	42.2	5,212,760	27.2	5,113,732	23.2
Nonagricultural activities	11,316,120	57.8	13,954,220	72.8	16,960,275	76.8
Manufacturing, mining and quarrying	4,720,195	24.1	5,348,540	27.9	7,506,671	34.0
Nonagricultural activities excluding manufacturing, mining and quarrying	6,595,925	33.7	8,605,680	44.9	9,453,604	42.8
Total	19,577,280	100.0	19,166,980	100.0	22,074,007	100.0
Distribution of the economically active by employment category, all sectors:						
Employers and workers on own account	4,605,257	23.5	4,104,300	21.4	3,258,315	14.8
Wage and salary employees	11,565,983	59.1	12,541,820	65.5	15,631,302	70.8
Unpaid family workers	3,406,040	17.4	2,520,860	13.1	3,184,390	14.4
Total	19,577,280	100.0	19,166,980	100.0	22,074,007	100.0

[a] The "economically active population" as defined here includes persons unemployed at the time of the census, but excludes students, women engaged solely in domestic duties, and persons who are retired, or living on private means, or wholly dependent upon others.

[b] The Italian figures exclude persons seeking their first jobs.

Source: International Labour Office, Year Book of Labour Statistics, 18th issue (Geneva, 1958), pp. 1–2, 44–45, and 48–49.

TABLE 65. Comparative distributions of the economically active population by employment category and sector, Italy, France, and Germany FR [a]

Distribution of the economically active by employment category and sector:	Italy [b]		France		Germany FR	
	Number	Per cent	Number	Per cent	Number	Per cent
Employers and workers on own account:						
Agriculture, forestry, hunting and fishing	2,572,042	55.8	1,946,200	47.4	1,252,395	38.4
Nonagricultural activities	2,033,215	44.2	2,158,100	52.6	2,005,920	61.6
Manufacturing, mining and quarrying	725,239	35.7	568,880	26.4	729,967	36.4
Total	4,605,257	100.0	4,104,300	100.0	3,258,315	100.0
Wage and salary employees:						
Agriculture, forestry, hunting and fishing	2,687,347	23.2	1,196,900	9.5	1,128,594	7.2
Nonagricultural activities	8,878,636	76.8	11,344,920	90.5	14,502,708	92.8
Manufacturing, mining and quarrying	3,861,783	43.5	4,669,660	41.2	6,631,952	45.7
Total	11,565,983	100.0	12,541,820	100.0	15,631,302	100.0
Unpaid family workers:						
Agriculture, forestry, hunting and fishing	3,001,771	88.1	2,069,660	82.1	2,732,743	85.8
Nonagricultural activities	404,269	11.9	451,200	17.9	451,647	14.2
Manufacturing, mining and quarrying	133,173	3.9	110,000	4.4	144,752	4.5
Total	3,406,040	100.0	2,520,860	100.0	3,184,390	100.0

[a] See note [a], Table 63.
[b] See note [b], Table 63.
Source: Same as Table 63.

against 21.4 per cent in France and only 14.8 per cent in Germany. Taken in relation to the comparative figures for gross product, it is apparent that the Italian data are inflated by large members of very small firms and tiny farms, and by persons who sustain themselves in menial activities dignified by the statistical euphemism of "services"—all of these providing additional signs of dualism.

Note also in Table 65 the very high concentration of employers and of the self-employed in Italian agriculture—55.8 per cent of this group, as against 47.4 per cent in France and only 38.4 per cent in Germany. Even more, Italy had the largest number of unpaid family workers—3.4 million, which compares with only 2.5 million in France and 3.2 million in Germany.

The heavy concentration of the Italian work force in agriculture is but a reflex of the restricted development of the nonagricultural sector. Thus the latter accounted for only 57.8 per cent of the total work force, while in France it claimed 72.8 per cent and in Germany over three quarters. Within manufacturing and extractive industry, there were to be found only 24.1 per cent of the Italian work force, as against 27.9 and 34.0 per cent in the other two countries. Taken together, manufacturing and extractive industry, construction, utilities, and transport and communications accounted for only 36.1 per cent of the Italian work force, compared with almost 41 per cent of the French and 48.1 per cent of the German. Finally, the remainder of the nonagricultural sector, consisting mainly of trade and services, claimed but 21.7 per cent of the Italian work force, as against 31.9 per cent of the French and 28.7 per cent of the German.

The lower level of industrialization in Italy is also strongly indicated by the relatively small proportion of wage and salary employees within the economically active population—59.1 per cent of the over-all total, compared to 65.5 per cent in France and 70.8 per cent in Germany, suggesting the strong persistence of family forms of enterprise and of primitive types of self-employment. The point may be driven home even more strongly by looking at the employee category outside agriculture. In Italy, nonagricultural activities accounted for 76.8 per cent of all employees, while in France and Germany the comparable figures were much larger—over 90 per cent.

Despite the obvious frailties of comparative international statis-

tics, the evidence is strong enough to point dramatically to the disabilities suffered by the Italian economy relative to two of its close
neighbors, disabilities that are collectively attributable to its failure, so far, to achieve a comparable transformation to modern
methods of organization and production. Next we shall examine in
greater detail the relevant facts for Italian industry and trade
themselves.

TABLE 66. Distribution of personnel according to type of enterprise and
average numbers for each type, census of November 5, 1951 [a]

Type of enterprise organization	Number of units	Number attached	Attached per unit
Sole proprietorships	1,359,584	3,068,866	2.2
Societies:	136,367	3,220,739	23.6
Corporations	12,732	1,937,489	152.2
Cooperatives	10,782	137,885	12.8
Limited partnerships	3,217	135,041	42.0
Other [b]	109,636	1,010,324	9.2
Public and other bodies [c]	8,076	491,487	60.8
Total, nonartisan enterprises	1,504,027	6,781,092	4.5
Artisan houses [d]	650,635	1,026,025	1.6
Total, all types	2,154,662	7,807,117	3.6

[a] Covers nonagricultural sector only, but does not embrace all economically
active persons in that sector.

[b] Includes mutually insured societies, those with limited responsibilities, and
others.

[c] Includes nationalized railways, monopolies, and banks; enterprises of local
governments; and private associations to conduct economic activities. Private
corporations having state participation are included under "corporations."

[d] "Artisan houses" are defined as those with a single manager-proprietor,
who does some manual work, with or without family assistants or outside personnel, with production on a nonserial basis, usually of craft or simple repair
services.

Source: Istituto centrale di statistica, III Censimento generale dell'industria
e del commercio, November 5, 1951, vol. XVII, "Dati generali riassuntivi"
(Rome: Failli, 1957), pp. 13–14.

The labor force in 1951. The first step is to examine the distribution of personnel attached to the various forms of enterprise within
the nonagricultural sector, as set out in Table 66. It will be noted
at once that the average enterprise in Italy in 1951 was very

small, having only 3.6 persons attached in all occupational categories. For typical artisan houses, the number was only 1.6 persons, and only 2.2 persons for sole proprietorships. In fact, almost two thirds of the total number attached to all forms of enterprise belonged to establishments whose average size was less than ten persons. Clearly, the small firm dominated the nonagricultural sector, excepting corporations, whose average number of personnel slightly exceeded 150, and public enterprises, where the average was 60.8 persons. The marked contrast between the corporate group and the sole proprietorships and artisan houses together is but another symptom of the dualism with which we are concerned, emphasizing the continued dominance of small family enterprises over large-scale organizations and professional management.

TABLE 67. Distribution of manual wage-earners according to major branches of nonagricultural activities and average numbers per firm in each branch, census of November 5, 1951 [a]

Branch of nonagricultural sector	Number of firms	Number of wage-earners	Number per firm
Extractive industry	6,196	97,949	15.8
Manufacturing	606,093	2,127,995	3.5
Construction	34,182	433,579	12.7
Electricity, gas and water	3,211	58,457	18.2
Transportation and comm.	61,872	320,056	5.2
Trade	698,249	181,356	0.3
Total [b]	1,504,027	3,296,382	2.2

[a] Includes all forms of enterprise except artisan houses.
[b] Includes, in addition to the categories above, finance and insurance, various activities and services, and sanitary services.

Source: III Censimento generale dell'industria e del commercio, November 5, 1951, vol. XVII, "Dati generali riassuntivi" (Rome: Failli, 1957), pp. 39–40, 213–217.

The next step is to look at the distribution of manual wage-earners within the major branches of nonagricultural activities, shown in Table 67. Again small size is indicated, and while these averages conceal the presence of some large-scale operations, size distributions confirm validity of these averages. In manufacturing, the average firm, excluding artisan houses, had only 3.5 manual employees. In trade, the figure was only 0.3, because the firms in this field are so largely family ventures.

Consider, next, the numbers of all categories of personnel attached to "local operating units" of the firms in the nonagricultural sector. These units exceed the number of firms because some enterprises have more than one plant or locus of activity. Table 68 shows both the relative importance of local units having ten or less persons attached and the average numbers attached per local unit in each major branch of the sector. The first fact that meets the eye is that 96.1 per cent of all local units had ten or less persons attached, and that these units embraced nearly half the 6.6 million persons in all categories of personnel. In manufacturing alone, almost a third of total personnel belonged to these tiny local units. Finally, for all local units together, only 4.1 persons were attached per unit. There can be no doubt that Italy is a land of small enterprise, much of it attributable to incomplete transformation of the economic system.

The remaining body of statistical evidence yielded by the 1951 census and pertinent to the general theme concerns the artisan houses. As Table 69 shows, as of 1951 over one million persons gained their livelihood from the traditional craft and service activities these houses provide. Eighty per cent of the artisan local operating units were strictly hand-operated, without mechanical or electrical power of any kind. Ninety-two per cent of these employed no hired labor at all, relying upon the artisan-proprietor himself, aided in some cases by family assistants. Eighty per cent of the units belonged to the manufacturing sector, where they were heavily concentrated in food processing, tailoring, shoemaking and shoe repairs, wood-working and furniture making, and various types of mechanical repair services—almost invariably supporting less than two persons on the average. Beyond manufacturing, artisan units were common in local pick-up and delivery, and in barber and beauty shops.[11]

It must be repeated that, whether artisan houses or sole proprietorships, not all small enterprises are less than optimal in economic size. Undoubtedly, there is a continuing place for small business, even in a well-advanced industrial society.[12] Increased size brings no economic advanges, and indeed may invoke disadvantages, in activities such as personal hygienic services, shoe repairing, retail specialty shops, restaurants, custom tailoring, and other custom trades specializing in skilled hand work. However,

TABLE 68. Distribution of personnel attached to local operating units of nonartisan firms outside agriculture, and average numbers attached per unit, by major branches, census of November 5, 1951 [a]

Branch	Up to 10 attached		All local units		Per cent of total with 10 or less units		Number per unit
	Number of units	Number attached	Number of units	Number attached	Units	Attached	
Extractive industry	6,149	18,329	7,742	116,197	79.4	15.8	15.4
Manufacturing	596,009	1,106,083	627,817	3,449,210	94.9	32.1	5.5
Construction	26,612	91,806	37,631	509,792	70.7	18.0	13.6
Electricity, gas and water	5,949	15,580	7,330	74,713	81.1	20.9	10.4
Transport. and comm.	71,074	146,361	75,596	520,214	94.0	28.1	6.9
Trade	739,418	1,426,752	747,893	1,574,315	98.9	90.6	2.1
Total [b]	1,555,112	3,019,497	1,617,586	6,597,429	96.1	45.8	4.1

[a] Excludes local units without personnel attached, artisan houses, and personnel attached to central administrations.
[b] Also includes finance and insurance, various activities and services, and sanitary services.
Source: III Censimento generale dell'industria e del commercio, November 5, 1951, vol. XVII, "Dati generali riassuntivi" (Rome: Failli, 1957), pp. 156–163.

TABLE 69. Distribution of personnel attached to artisan firms, by selected sectors of activity and occupational status, census of November 5, 1951

Branch	Artisans and family helpers	Hired labor	Apprentices	Total attached	Attached per unit
Manufacturing [a]	684,344	79,766	68,357	832,467	1.6
Foods and related	66,664	12,717	986	80,367	2.0
Clothing	253,145	19,586	30,911	303,642	1.4
Lumber and wood products	136,895	16,677	11,042	164,614	1.6
Metal products	143,246	17,144	17,350	177,740	1.6
Transport. and communications	62,406	—	164	62,570	1.3
Various activities & services	81,091	12,213	6,609	99,913	1.5
Total [b]	847,983	101,337	76,705	1,026,025	1.6

[a] Includes other industries besides those appearing immediately below.
[b] Includes other sectors besides those shown here.
Source: III Censimento generale dell'industria e del commercio, November 5, 1951, vol. XVI, "Artigianato" (Rome: Failli, 1957), pp. 265–266.

even here greater productivity would be possible with larger resort to mechanical and electrical power.

As measured by average numbers of personnel and by their large share of total personnel, very small-scale units dominated the Italian scene in 1951, even reaching startling proportions in manufacturing itself. As such, they extended into activities that in more industrialized countries would be conducted by firms with much larger numbers of hired wage workers. Examples would include retail stores, factory-made clothing and furniture, local cartage, food processing, and lumber milling, to name a few.

The general displacement of small firms from fields of this type in the more developed countries became possible with greater availability of low-cost capital, with improvements in technology, and with the growth of markets of large volume. For Italy today, the technology is at hand. Yet small family firms continue to dominate the entire economy, even where large ones are conceivable substitutes. The explanation lies in the high cost of capital, the low cost of "small-firm" labor because of its exclusion from trade-union agreements and from social security benefits (principally as working proprietors, artisan-owners, and family assistants), restricted markets in many local areas, and, in commerce, by licensure practices designed to protect those already in the trade. If there were no dual wage structure, no disadvantage in procuring capital relative to the already well-established larger firms, and no protective policy, most of the decisive advantages of small size would disappear, particularly where large and small units now coexist in the same field. Bigger firms would then emerge, with much greater resort to hired wage labor.[13] In this sense, then, the continuing preponderance of small units under preindustrial forms of ownership and organization serves as substantial added evidence of the dual nature of the Italian economy.

The agricultural side. Turning now to agriculture, three main types of data attest to dualism. One involves relative average incomes per person economically active in agriculture and in extractive and manufacturing industry. These figures can be obtained in rough form by dividing the net value products of each sector by the respective numbers economically active in 1951. For agriculture, net product per economically active person was 261,222 lire in 1951, as against 595,526 lire per person in extractive and manufacturing industry. Thus the latter sector yielded an income advantage of 2.28 to 1, or 228 per cent.[14] Bearing in mind that many persons attached to agriculture suffered an even greater income and productivity disadvantage than this, and even conceding that some income differential in favor of urban-industrial incomes will exist because of higher living costs, costs of movement, and lessened availability of incomes in kind, the average differential between the two sectors is far too large—so large as to be a pathological sign that a legal and economic blockage was in effect, walling off too many people in agriculture. As of 1951, that obstacle did exist, in statutory restraint of internal migration. Or, put alternatively, employment opportunities in agriculture are too restricted to yield a level of personal incomes reasonably comparable with those obtainable from much of industry.

TABLE 70. Distribution of agricultural holdings by size and by total landed property for each size class, 1946 [a]

Size class	Total holdings (per cent)	Total area (per cent)
Dwarf holdings (up to 2 hect.)	83.1	14.0
Small holdings (2–5 hect.)	10.0	11.0
Medium holdings (5–25 hect.)	5.6	19.9
Large holdings (25–100 hect.)	1.0	16.2
Very large holdings (over 100 hect.)	0.3	38.9

[a] Figures based upon a total area of 28.5 million hectares, of which roughly one quarter was wooded or unproductive and nearly a fifth was meadow or pasture. Overlaps in size classes derive from original survey. Distribution of holdings is not equivalent to a distribution of owners, because a given owner may have more than one holding.

Source: (SVIMEZ) Associazione per lo sviluppo dell'industria nel Mezzogiorno, Statistiche sul Mezzogiorno d'Italia, 1861–1953 (Rome: Failli, 1954), pp. 152–155.

The second type of evidence bears directly upon the point. It concerns the distribution of land holdings by size and by extent of total surface for each size class, as shown in Table 70. Note, first, the extremely heavy concentration of dwarf holdings. Even granting that some of these are held in multiple by their peasant-owners, there can be no doubt that many peasant families are dependent upon holdings that are too small to permit them to subsist without supplemental incomes from day labor or other sources. According to Doreen Warriner, the best measure of a "subsistence minimum" is one hectare of arable land per head, a standard used by peasants themselves.[15] Thus a dwarf holding is a convincing symptom of rural overpopulation and of technical and organizational backwardness in agriculture. In this respect, Italy in 1946 was worse off than prewar Czechoslovakia and Bulgaria, since her dwarf holdings absorbed 14 per cent of the agricultural area, as against 7 and 5 per cent in the other two countries respectively. More generally, if we assume that 40 per cent of the population present in Italy in 1951 was rural, then 18.8 million people had to depend upon 13.1 million hectares of arable land, slightly less than 0.7 hectares per capita and seriously short of meeting even a subsistence minimum.[16] Beyond question, the traditional agricultural economy of Italy in 1951 stood badly in need of technical modernization, and abandonment as well as consolidation of many dwarf holdings. But, as always, the slow development of the nonagricultural sector proved a difficult barrier. So, as Wilbert Moore suggests, we have a case of "too many people and too little land." [17] Much can be done to improve agricultural income, to some extent even within the framework of existing institutions, but more rapid industrialization is nonetheless the decisive factor.

The third symptom of dualism exhibited in agriculture is its landless proletariat the group of wage laborers working by the day or on annual contracts. Up to one quarter of all persons economically active in farming in 1936 belonged in this category. Subsisting on daily incomes from one to two-thirds below the earnings of manual workers in advanced industry, and frequently experiencing unemployment for substantial periods during the year, the rural proletariat lay at the bottom of the agricultural structure. In the usual case, it could not hope to acquire land for itself because there was not enough to go around. Nor could most of its members escape to the cities, blocked as they were by legal restrictions against internal migration and by lack of job opportunities in the nonagricultural sphere. So they were caught in a trap —condemned to low incomes and a hopeless existence by a vicious combination of an obsolete agricultural system and relentless population pressure.

The system of landholding and of farm organization in Italy imposes the double handicap of perpetuating backward techniques and of restricting the formation and efficient use of new capital.[18] It does so because it is so heavily dominated by dwarf and small holdings. In consequence, the system dictates very low productivity per active worker and very low incomes per head of rural population. Inevitably, this seriously restricts the entire domestic market for nonagricultural products and services. In turn, this keeps the prices of manufactures high, both by limiting economies of scale and by fostering monopolistic policies because of the small number of possible firms in certain lines of production. Even further, the virtual inaccessibility of manufactured products to much of the farm population reduces the incentive effects, for farm labor supply, of potentially rising consumer aspirations, which also contributes to low agricultural productivity and incomes.

Thus the Italian agricultural system works to perpetuate a large amount of subsistence farming, at the same time slowing the expansion of the nonagricultural sector, although more rapid growth of the latter is imperative for the effective reorganization of the rural economy itself.

Underemployment and unemployment. The last major symptom of dualism is persistent mass unemployment and underemployment, originating in part from the dual wage system and so connecting up with the weak coherence of the entire economy. Underemployment is most acute in peasant agriculture, petty trade and services, and handicrafts, where the family enterprise often involves sharing of work among the members, serving as a haven of refuge in an economy with very limited job opportunities. In fact, many of these small units survive because of the lower level of labor costs inherent to their internal arrangements, owing their very existence to the divided wage system that is one of the hallmarks of dualism itself. During the lengthy period of rapid economic expansion in the postwar years, much progress was made in redistributing the labor force and in cutting down on underemployment. However, the latter problem continues important today.

As for unemployment in the strict sense, it persisted with extreme severity until the beginning of the sixties, when a shortage of industrial workers in the north at last began to appear. This chronic mass unemployment was not cyclical and did not derive from oversaving or investment deficiency. Although its magnitude was made worse by barriers to internal migration, its main causes lay in too high a level of real wages imposed upon the rapidly expanding industrial sector, and in a secular shortage of capital—factors that we later consider in detail.

To sum up the facts as they stood in 1951, economic dualism in Italy asserted itself in a series of sharp contrasts: between forms of productive organizations, between techniques of production, between types of employment, and between types and rates of compensation per earner. Throughout, there is evident a lack of close cohesion among the parts of the whole economy, indicating that Italy did not yet possess a fully unified system.

Furthermore, these contrasts manifested themselves within certain industries, within the cities, between the "advanced" and "backward" parts of the economy, and between town and country. But standing out above all other symptoms of a divided system was—and is—the dichotomy between north and south. To appreciate its full magnitude requires that one go behind statistics of national aggregates, for the south is a special region with its own unhappy history and its own peculiar disabilities as an economy.

CHAPTER XI. GEOGRAPHIC DUALISM: THE PROBLEM OF SOUTH ITALY

Italy, as we have observed many times, is a land of contrasts. The most remarkable of all is that between north and south, for while the north affords some balance between the new and the old, and in general yields impressions similar to those to be drawn from a glance at the civilization of northwest Europe, southern Italy varies mainly only in degrees of poverty and of backwardness. True, it has its full share of the quaint and the beautiful. But behind the sunny towns and orchards of its matchless coastline lie its ancient and impoverished latifundia, its barren uplands, and its rural slums, while within its great cities modern industry has so far found only limited opportunity. To the charm and the beauty to which Norman Douglas so readily responded stand in bitter contrast the squalor and the misery so vividly depicted by Carlo Levi.

Throughout the whole of its vast territory, embracing as it does almost 43 per cent of the national area and nearly 38 per cent of its total population, the southern economic scene is dominated by agriculture, artisan enterprise, petty trade and services.[1] Their counterparts are poverty, stagnation, and backwardness. Clearly, therefore, any explanation of the dualism of the Italian economy must give central place to the persistent gap between north and south.

At the same time, the twofold nature of Italy's economy must be approached with some caution. There is nothing either mysterious or even surprising in the mere intrusion of modern industrialism upon a peasant and handicraft society. This was the common experience of all the lands of northwestern Europe. Its very occurrence is bound to bring about the sharp contrasts described, all of which are manifested at least transitorily in observable gaps in income and in economic development within a nation. Even in the United States today these gaps can be found. The really important questions are different. Why did modern industry find a permanent home in north Italy, but not in the south? Why did the nascent southern industries of 1830–1860 ultimately wither away after unification in 1861? Why have agriculture, petty trades and services continued to dominate the economy of the south, despite the lower returns than the same activities have yielded in the north? And why, in the country as a whole, is the transition to a modern economy so slow?

As was noted in an earlier chapter, the "southern problem," as the Italians themselves have called it for over half a century, is in fact simply a sharply etched illustration of a predicament common to all Italy—a predicament expressed by its low economic ranking relative to the older industrial nations of the West, whatever the measure employed. Within northern and central Italy as well, there are gaps in income and development within industry, within agriculture, within trade, and among localities.

However, it so happens that as one proceeds southward the contrasts disappear and the economic scene acquires a gray and dreamy uniformity of poverty and backwardness, relieved only occasionally by signs of technical advance. In one respect, therefore, the problem of the south is Italy's particular burden and her national tragedy. In another, it is but a symbol of the larger economic difficulties of the country as a whole.

Accordingly, the principal purpose of this chapter is to set forth some origins of the differences between north and south, and to indicate the economic difficulties that have beset the southern region since unification in 1861.

THE PROBLEM

Economic history of the south before 1861. Although it is the fashion today to interpret the facts of economic change in accordance with abstract growth models, it is very doubtful that any one of these intellectual constructions would shed much light upon the causes of the stultified development of the southern economy, let alone its persistence in stunted form for so many generations.

Growth, stagnation, and retrogression are everywhere in the world a phenomenon of history, hence endowed with a time-place setting. Their causes may lie in a peculiar physical environment, in the character of the culture in which they occur, and in the impacts of certain decisive events—among them invasions, occupations, wars, displacement of trade routes, and changes in national economic policies. Economic growth does not occur "by nature," in the Aristotelian sense. It is neither universal nor inevitable. Rather, it is an historical episode calling for explanation, and not an orderly manifestation of mysterious, innate tendencies. Accordingly, one must look to the physical and cultural environment, and to the propulsive role of events, to discover what influences have set the process in motion and have kept it going.

Cases of stagnation or retrogression call for a similar approach. Why have some areas and regions proved unreceptive to modern economic institutions, of which industrialism is frequently a counterpart? Why have others actually undergone decline?[2] Is either predicament attributable to the harshness of nature, to a way of life, to the actions of man, or to a combination of all these? Examination of geographical and historical circumstances will supply the answer.

A glance at a map will reveal that the easiest approaches to southern Italy and the islands are by sea. In fact, the difficulties of overland communications, and, especially for modern times, the great land distances between northern Europe and the Italian south have imposed a maritime character upon the trade of the region, at the same time thwarting the extensive development of its internal markets. In many respects, therefore, south Italy is a maritime culture.

Given this geographical position, it is not surprising that in pre-Christian times, when the civilizations of the eastern Mediterranean were dominant, the littoral lands of south Italy and Sicily would attract settlements from Greece. So emerged Magna Graecia and Sicily in the eighth century B.C.[3] For the same reason, the Phoenicians and the Carthaginians also entered parts of Sicily, with the inevitable wars. By the fifth century B.C., malaria had made its first appearance, coming probably from Asia or Africa, forcing the eventual abandonment of some of the Greek cities and continuing to curse the people of the south with epidemics until very recent times.

During 282–201 B.C., the Romans began a series of wars that ended in their conquest of the lower peninsula, Sicily, and Sardinia. Unfortunately for the inhabitants, the Roman policy was to turn these lands into a granary for Latin convenience, so initiating the spoliation of the southern soil and its formerly productive fruit and wine culture.[4] Rather than assimilate these people under their famous program of cultural diversity, as the Romans did with the Gauls in northern Italy in the same period, they chose to regard the south as a region for exploitative colonial rule.

From the very beginning, therefore, the south was destined to be culturally distinct and politically separate from the rest of Italy, in an isolation permanently favored by the facts of geography.

With the fall of the Roman Empire early in the fifth century A.D., south Italy passed under Byzantine rule, and its separate status continued. After 700, its isolation was again reinforced, when substantial portions of the region were occupied by the Arabs. Wisely following a surprising policy of toleration, they proved able to bring about a notable economic renaissance in Sicily, firmly establishing there a culture whose traces are apparent even today. By orienting southern trade to Africa and the Middle East, the Arabs strengthened the peculiar position of the south in Italian history. Moreover, political separatism found further expression at this time in continued Byzantine rule in Puglia and Calabria, and in the emergence of city republics in Naples, Gaeta, and Amalfi.

By the eleventh century, the Saracen tide finally began to recede. This was also the time when the Normans came to the south, to Aversa, in the Campagna. By 1105, there was a Norman kingdom in south Italy and Sicily, and it brought with it efficient administration and a magnificent cultural florescence. Great prosperity followed, which was probably the origin of the north Italian legend of the great riches of the south. Economic well-being continued under the great King Frederick II of Swabia (1211–1250).[5]

Unhappily, this kind of rule was not to last, and yielded instead to almost five centuries of war and bad government, varied only by the particular foreign house that served as oppressor. Thus at the very time that Florence, Venice, Milan, and Genoa were entering their ascendency with the Italian renaissance, developing banking, the textile industry, and trade with the Middle East and northern Europe, the south fell under the feudal reaction of the Angevin and Aragonese kings. Thus once again the less fortunate half of the peninsula was dominated by outsiders whose interests usually lay elsewhere.

In 1504 the Spanish gained dominion over Naples, south Italy, and Sicily, by defeating the French at Gaeta. So began two centuries of unenlightened rule by a declining foreign power that still cherished dreams of empire.[6]

Within a century, north Italy also entered economic decadence, with the closure of the eastern trade routes and the rise of the cloth trade in England, Holland, and France. But at least the north had had its renaissance, while the south had remained stagnant since Frederick's time.

The evils of Spanish dominion were to end in 1713 with the Treaty of Utrecht, which settled the War of the Spanish Succession by giving Naples and Sardinia to Austria, and Sicily to the Piedmontese house. For the south, this was merely a changing of the guard. In 1735 another bargain between foreign imperialists created the independent Neopolitan Kingdom of the Two Sicilies, ruled by a branch of the Spanish Bourbons, and extending its domain over the lower peninsula and Sicily. Save for temporary dislodgement between 1799 and 1815 during the Napoleonic period, this dynasty was to control the south until unification in 1861. At its beginning, some cultural revival occured, accompanied by the development of handicraft industries in the town and cities. However, the countryside remained backward and impoverished.

The brief period of Napoleonic rule permanently affected Italy. Foremost, it kindled the fires of national unity, igniting movements for independence that ultimately triumphed. Moreover, by the introduction of a uniform coinage and a uniform system of weights and measures, coupled to the abolition of feudal rights and tolls, the promoters of the continental system opened the way to a national economy that was the indispensable counterpart to effective political unity.

For the south, the results of the Napoleonic policies were mixed. The British blockade cut off the French overseas trade and caused Napoleon to create the continental system. Both events had major consequences for the south. On the one hand, the blockade choked off its agricultural exports by sea. On the other, the continental policy meant that the new rulers at Naples were to direct its economy toward the production of cereals, textiles, and extractive materials, to support the French war. To expand the production of cereals and to acquire timber for new ships, the regime of Joseph Bonaparte and Joachim Murat encouraged a reckless policy of deforestation, made fully effective by the high profits occasioned by soaring prices. Long after, the prostrate south was to reap the malign harvest from this disastrous policy—in floods, soil erosion, and malaria. Less evident, the increased resort to cultivation of grain crops on lands inherently unsuited to extensive agriculture was to commit the southern peasantry and landlords to the least productive kind of farming they could possibly adopt.

Partly for ideological reasons and partly to meet the insatiable demands of the French for grain and timber, the regime also undertook a land reform program. Ideologically, its intent was to destroy feudalism by replacing it with small holders. However, the redistribution of land proved largely abortive, while the portions that were divided were handed over to the peasants in such tiny fractions that the result was only to foster the evils of pulverization so readily apparent today.

The end of the Napoleonic wars in 1815 found the Bourbons restored to the throne at Naples, with Austria again dominant in the north. This return to the status quo found favor among the conservatives at the Congress of Vienna, but to the newly awakened people of Italy it was a foreign yoke to be thrown off at the earliest opportunity, and the long and difficult struggle for independence and unification began.

The economic difficulties bequeathed by war to the revived Kingdom of the Two Sicilies were indeed grave and were met with only limited success during the ensuing half-century. Most serious, south Italy was still largely a rural economy resting upon tiny local markets and a backward agriculture composed of small peasant holdings and large estates. In essence it was a precapitalistic society, poor in capital, savings, and natural resources, and above all lacking even the beginnings of a vigorous entrepreneurial class. The cultural climate was hostile to innovation and change, while the Bourbon regime was wholly unprepared, either in ideas or in inclination, to meet the challenge of the times. Instead, it confined itself to a curious collection of policies that largely blended together a mixture of reaction and protectionism. In consequence, agriculture languished in stagnation, while industry could barely gain a foothold.

To counter the competitive effects of the reopening of the

world market, the government turned to protective tariffs, even extending this policy to the internal local markets. Meanwhile, the collapse of the French had ruined the southern export trade in textiles, compelling the hapless peasantry to turn to even more cultivation of cereals. Deforestation accordingly continued, while the switch to grains reduced the livestock population, depriving the south of a promising export trade in meat, cheese, and hides.

After 1825, when economic conditions had reached their nadir, the situation began to change for the better, partly under the pressure of discontent. The government negotiated a series of commercial treaties with other European powers. New industries began to develop, aided by an inflow of foreign capital and technicians. Between 1825 and 1850, the following activities had made a scattered appearance or had developed over much of the south, often through foreign enterprises: metallurgy, machine products, shipbuilding, silk, wool, linen and hemp, cotton, paper, glass, hides, gloves, and soap.[7] According to Cenzato and Guidotti, by the time of the exposition at Florence in 1861, the display of southern products indicated quite notable industrial advance, particularly in papermaking, castings, marine and railway engines, ships, and leather goods. In these activities, at least, the south was comparable to the other industrial countries, although these experts treat with reserve the judgment of Barbagallo and others that on the eve of unification there was no real economic gap between north and south.[8]

It is safer to conclude that even in 1861 the south was the more backward region, despite these surface manifestations of industrial development. Otherwise it is much more difficult to explain the withering away of southern industry during the four decades that followed, even if we accept the often cited withdrawal of protection in the initial liberal period of Piedmontese rule as the underlying cause. If it was, then these nascent industries must have rested upon an exceedingly fragile economic base, unable to withstand the shocks of foreign and northern competition, or the termination of military procurement by the now-extinct Bourbon monarchy.

Consider also that little had been done to remedy the chronic ills of southern agriculture, which retained intact the worst features of the estate system and of peasant holdings alike, and which was far overcommitted to a relatively unproductive grain culture. In addition, the south entered the Italian union with a much poorer endowment of agricultural resources. A larger portion of its area was hilly or mountainous; its soil was generally poorer in yields; its rainfall was irregular; and the land was subject to much more serious flooding and erosion.

Along with its many handicaps, the south lacked an extensive internal market for its industrial products, burdened as it was by very low per capita incomes and decidedly backward land communications. To cite a crude measure of the latter, in 1861 the south had but one fifth of the railway mileage per capita of the north, and one third of the roads and highways.[9] Isolation of the local communities from each other was the rule.[10] Accordingly, custom and tradition continued to dominate social and economic life. There were no effective means for mobilizing what little saving could be had from the low income of the region, which also offered small attraction for foreign capital. At the same time, the south lacked a vigorous commercial and industrial bourgeoisie. All told, therefore, the southern economy was simply in no position even to maintain the slow momentum of advance that it had attained in the last years of the Bourbons. By contrast, the north had already nurtured a healthy new industrialism, stimulated as it was by proximity to northwest Europe and an already well-established tradition of independent private initiative. Thus it had actually won the economic contest with the south even at the very start of united Italy.

A cursory review of the long and tragic history of the south explains both the origins of the region's difficulties and their stubborn persistence into more modern times.

First, its geographic position and its contorted internal topography from the beginning have oriented its trade to the sea, and in particular to trading partners around the Mediterranean basin. Thus the south was certain to suffer from the eventual economic decline of the lands bordering upon the eastern and southern margins of the Mediterranean Sea. Geography also dictated that the south would be settled by colonists from the eastern Mediterranean and North Africa, who were to give to the region its peculiar and mixed array of cultures, which have coalesced in a civilization that has never accepted with enthusiasm the rationalistic materialism and the passion for technical progress of the modern West. Indeed, this civilization has not only proved sectional for Italy herself. It has in fact been localized and parochial for nearly three thousand years, largely because of the isolation enforced by a mountainous terrain and bad overland communications.

When the center of economic gravity began to shift to northwest Europe in later renaissance times, the position of the south was rendered even more distant and more isolated. To be sure, this seismic disruption of the European economic world also invoked the loss of the cloth trade and the ruin of the great cities of the Italian north. But eventually with the *Risorgimento* the very propinquity of these centers to northwest Europe made cultural contacts readily possible, fostering in turn the borrowing, diffusion, and successful adoption of both industrial techniques and of the main tenets of capitalistic enterprise.[11] Thus the north could prosecute its economic revolution, while the south, perforce, was destined to continue in its obsolete ways.

Second, for a great part of its history, the south has lived under the rule of conquerors. These invaders brought ruin and desolation with their interminable wars, imposing their will upon a people too weak and too demoralized to resist. In the pursuit of their ambitions, they turned southern agriculture to grain, stripped the forests, and so fostered the debilitating spread of malaria, the impoverishment of the soil, and the recurrence of disastrous floods. From Roman times they treated the lands of the south as booty to be handed over to a foreign nobility that treated them as an easy means to income and power, with complete indifference to the plight of the local population. Thus in agriculture the contribution of these conquerors was an inefficient estate system, the encouragment of tiny and scattered peasant holdings, and the formation of a rural proletariat. Even by post-Napoleonic times the south had never known a renaissance, while material prosperity had been foreign to the region since the late middle ages. After 1825 a weak form of industrialism finally began to emerge, but most of it was sponsored from abroad and depended upon tariffs and state patronage for its very existence.

Centuries of rule by foreign overlords also had its more subtle effects. Foreign domination inevitably produced a class of local sycophants and go-betweens, interested alike in tax-gathering and enforcement of local regulations, and at the same time in arranging deals for their evasion. Corruption and extralegal "arrangements," so well depicted in Roger Vailland's *The Law,* thus became an integral part of the social fabric. In north Europe respect for the law and adherence to its precepts and processes long since had become a moral imperative, but in the south the law of the conqueror was simply an initial obstacle to be eluded or evaded in one's own private interest, if it could not be turned to advantage.

So emerged a culture whose traditional outlook was selfish, cynical toward government and the commonweal, bereft of much respect for the civic virtues, and rife with preferment and dishonesty. In the extreme version of this malignant system, brigandage, the Camorra, and the Mafia all could flourish, as forms of privately organized violence inspired alike by an evil union of poverty and desperation on the one side, and a ruthlessly exploitative outlook on the other. Thus the spoliation imposed by a long line of conquerors was not limited alone to the lands of the south, but ultimately came to include the people themselves.

This, then, was the unhappy region that was joined to the north in 1861 to make the new Italy. Failing drastic intervention by the state, the south was doomed economically from the start, incapable on its own of even maintaining, let alone closing, the enormous gulf that separated it from its more fortunate northern partner. Surprisingly, too, some forty years had to transpire before the northerners were to lose their illusions and even to become aware of the seriously deteriorating economic position of the south. By 1900 they had begun to realize that they were chained to a dead man. Still, almost another fifty years had to pass before full-scale and sustained action was to be undertaken to bring life to the corpse.

The first forty years of unification: 1861–1901. There is undisputed agreement that economic conditions in the south grew much worse between 1861 and 1901, in agriculture, industry, and trade. As early as 1863, a parliamentary commission of inquiry headed by Giuseppe Massari reported a squalid record of brigandage, corruption, and misery. Its recommendations were appropriate and entirely modern, but they fell on deaf ears: more education, redistribution of land, reclamation of the marshes, reforestation, more roads and railways, and division of the communal lands. Commenting on conditions in the south at this time, the Neopolitan historian, Pasquale Villari (*Le prime lettere meridionali*), decried the irresponsibility of the conservative classes, describing "the enemy" as the mass of illiterates, the bureaucracy, the incapacity of political leaders, the lack of skilled workmen, the patriarchal agricultural system, and "the rhetoric which gnaws our very bones." [12]

The little group of economic liberals who were led by Count Camillo Benso di Cavour and who were to attain political command of the new Italy drew their main support from the emergent professional and commercial bourgeoisie of the north. Well before 1861, they had begun by converting the backward Kingdom of Sardinia-Piedmont to a policy of economic progress through competition and spontaneous private initiative. The culture of Piedmont, with its close ties to France, proved hospitable.[13] With unification, Cavour and his immediate successors sought to extend their liberal economic policy to the south, evidently under the double illusion that the region was basically rich but suffered from torpor and misrule and that unfication under the wise leadership of Piedmont would soon call forth a cultural and economic rebirth. In other words, the gap between north and south was to be overcome by a release of private initiative in the south, stimulated by a wider internal market and increased exports, and aided here and there by well-chosen public works.

There was nothing wrong with the theory in principle. It had already proved its worth in England. The real difficulty was its complete inappropriateness for southern conditions, proceeding as it did from abstract reasoning without regard to the historical circumstances necessary to its successful working.

As a prescription for state policy, the liberal doctrine, in its laissez-faire formulation of that day, was grounded upon a bad diagnosis of the southern problem, if there can be said to have been any diagnosis at all. There was no coiled spring of spontaneous private initiative waiting to be released to give the necessary propulsion to the movement of economic progress. The south had few traders and almost no entrepreneurs; indeed, many areas were still in a subsistence economy and did not even know the uses of money. It lacked capital, saving, and skilled workmen. Most of its people were tied to the soil, demoralized by centuries of poverty, and living without hope. Its markets were local and constricted, often inaccessible to the outside. Its social order lacked credit and marketing facilities, and offered neither security nor opportunity to the aggressive businessman. In short, its ills were ancient, deep-seated, and complex. "Nature's remedy" was inapt counsel and in-ept therapy. Only major surgery could cure the malady, but the new regime was quite unprepared for drastic approaches.

The onset of unification had three initial impacts upon the southern economy, all of them adverse. First, it terminated the protected position of its industries relative both to northern and foreign competitors. Second, it transferred the rather large internal debt of Piedmont to the entire realm. And third, the Piedmontese tax system was extended to the rest of the new nation. Of these three developments, probably the abandonment of protection was the most adverse, given the inherently weak position of southern industries and the already established advantages of industry in the northern triangle. However, Barbagallo contends that within a few years the new tax system almost doubled land rates in the south. In any case, a decline of industry soon set in, from which there was no real recovery for the next ninety years.

In addition, southern spokesmen have complained almost unani-mously that for decades after 1861 the south was consistently neg-lected in national expenditures for education, roads, railways, and port facilities, which, if true, denied the region a variety of exter-nal economies instrumental to the emergence of new enterprise and to the rise of agricultural incomes. However, Clough and Livi contend that the south actually paid less than its proportionate share of the national levies, while its share of public investments exceeded the north's, relative to tax payments to the national treas-ury. Granting the fact, it may still be argued that the plight of the south actually demanded far more than proportional treatment in the allocation of expenditure for public investment, if any real re-dress of the internal economic balance was to be achieved.

The next major development in economic policy began with the modest revenue tariff of 1878, which opened the way to the protec-tionist movement of the eighties, which in turn was to have dis-astrous consequences for the south. This movement drew its support from northern industrialists and large landholders engaged in grain production. The former were beginning to feel the pressure of competitive imports against the relatively new industries, while the latter were inspired by a continuing worldwide fall in grain prices. The movement met with success in the high-tariff legislation of 1887, which brought prompt retaliation from the French and a consequent drastic decline in Italian exports. Within a year the ultranationalist premier, Crispi, seized the opportunity to denounce the French commercial treaty, thereby closing off the French market for Italian wines, cattle, rice, cheese, and silk.

The political intrigues through which Agostino Depretis and his successor, Francesco Crispi, brought these damaging policies into being paid off for the industrialists and big grain producers of the north, though not without injury to other groups in that region. For the south, the results were almost completely disastrous (except for cereals). Increased protection for grains raised the price of bread to the poor. The producers of wine, fruits, and vegetables, whose natural advantage lay in free trade, lost much of their export market and in some cases were ruined. In addition, the southerners now had to pay more for industiral goods, most of which came from the north. For this, all they got in return was the dubious gift of a higher grist tax, which further raised the price of food. Yet so lacking was the south in effective spokesmen for its interests that it acceded to these policies without visible protest.

Because of the constricted and inelastic nature of the southern economy, its people could respond to these new blows only in two ways, both of them signifying desperation. One was resort to increased cultivation of cereals, using the old and obsolete methods. The other was flight from the region itself. According to Coletti, emigration from the south during 1876–1886 averaged 27,911 persons a year, while during 1901–1909 it had soared tenfold, to 278,421 persons a year. By contrast, the annual outflow from the north barely doubled in the same period.[14] Adversity born of economic folly, coupled with a grave increase in population pressure, could no longer be passively tolerated. The only means of protest open to the hapless southerners was to vote with their feet, and they did.

Later history of the southern question: 1951. By 1900, unification had brought few benefits to the south, while adding to its many woes. Probably the adverse impacts were accentuated because of the inherent weaknesses of the southern economy. But whatever the lag at the beginning, there is no doubt that it had increased by the end of the century.[15]

By 1900 the difficulties at last began to command official attention, partly inspired no doubt by rising social unrest throughout the country during the decade preceeding. During 1893–1900, the ministries of Crispi, di Rudinì and Pelloux met the challenge by repressive measures, a policy that ended in obvious bankruptcy by the end of the period.

Beginning with the Zanardelli cabinet of 1901–1903, and continuing with that of Giolitti during 1903–1905, parliamentary inquiry into conditions in the south was undertaken, leading in turn to remedial legislation enacted between 1904–1906. It was found that Naples still retained an industrial complex, sustained mainly by government orders, although the rest of the region had little beyond cottage industries at the time. In 1904 a law was passed establishing an industrial district, new factories, a free zone, public works, and new sources of electric power for the Naples area. In the same year a new statute was adopted for the Basilicata, providing for public works, reforestation, special credit, easier taxes, and emphyteutic contracts.[16] In 1906, similar special legislation was enacted for Calabria, Sardinia, and Sicily.[17] However, all these measures achieved limited results, because they contained more election rhetoric than practical substance, because they were motivated to serve the usual special interests, and because they failed to reach the underlying causes—restricted markets, lack of skilled labor, and excessive men-land ratios and low productivity in agriculture.

The Census of 1911 for the first time permitted some highly revealing interregional comparisons, showing graphically the stunted industrial development of the south. At that time, the region had 36.5 per cent of the population, but only 14.3 per cent of those attached to industry. For establishments involving up to ten persons, the south had 23.1 per cent of the national total, but for those exceeding ten persons its share was only 9.8 per cent. Of leading industries, the south had 23.3 per cent of those in food, 17.7 per cent of those in chemicals, and only 14.4 per cent of these in metal working and metal-using.[18]

These data suggest three major facts: the south was still mainly agricultural rather than industrial; its industry consisted of tiny establishments; and its share of heavy industry was still very small.

No additional major legislation was attempted after 1906, and then the First World War submerged the entire southern question. During the distraught years immediately after the war, the pessimistic view began to grow in intellectual circles that the land and the climate of the south might well make even the noblest efforts quite futile.[19]

With the onset of the Fascist period, the Mussolini Government desired to show its omnicompetence in all fields, and so pessimism yielded to the grandiose schemes typical of dictatorships everywhere. The first of these was the Agro Pontina project to reclaim and settle 60,000 hectares of marshland in lower Lazio. It was a success and remains as one of the few positive achievements of this unhappy period. Other agricultural works were also undertaken, in the Puglian tablehand and in the lower Volturno near Naples. However, these latter projects were left incomplete because the government had now turned to its eventually fatal policy of imperialism and war, much as Crispi had done some forty years earlier. To foster these inflated ambitions, the regime went over to autarchy, part of which involved a program to increase the production of wheat and corn by means of higher import duties and other incentives. Although modern methods of cultivation were encouraged, the scheme served mainly to repeat once again an ancient error in Italian agriculture—resort to extensive cultivation of high-cost grains at the expense of intensive products capable of yielding better returns.

The Fascist regime accomplished little else so far as the south was concerned. It failed to undertake any real reform in the holding and uses of land. It failed to achieve much in reforestation, flood control, or irrigation. It failed to develop a broader nonagricultural economy, hence to widen the internal market. It failed to relieve population pressure, and instead introduced a system of enforced domicile to prevent migration northward and to the cities. And rather than invest the national revenues in extensive improvements and increased education in the south, it chose to squander them in the pursuit of vainglory. The end was defeat and disaster, and here the south suffered worst of all, by reason of destruction occasioned by the Allies' invasion of Sicily and their difficult and protracted advance up the peninsula. Because fixed capital was already much scarcer in the south, the ensuing losses were made all the heavier for the relatively weaker southern economy to bear.

Its economic position by 1951. The economic history of the south since 1861 is dominated by a single fact: the failure of employment opportunities to expand despite an increase of 83 per cent in the population present.

Tables 71 and 72 present the main demographic facts for 1861 and 1951. Over the ninety-year period, the populations in both regions increased by almost the same percentage. Accordingly, the south retained its relative share of the total population. However, the southern totals after 1880 have been much more depressed by net emigration than were those of the north. Moreover, between 1921 and 1951 population present in the south rose much faster, increasing by 32.8 per cent as against 22.0 per cent in the north.

TABLE 71. Population present in north and south, 1861–1951 [a] (in millions)

Census year	North	South	Per cent of national total	
			North	South
1861	16.1	9.5	62.9	37.1
1871	17.3	10.1	63.2	36.8
1901	20.7	12.4	62.6	37.4
1911	22.5	12.9	63.5	36.5
1931	25.8	14.5	64.0	36.0
1936	26.9	15.2	63.9	36.1
1951	29.4	17.4	62.8	37.2

[a] Based upon boundaries of 1951.

Source: (SVIMEZ) Associazione per lo sviluppo dell'industria nel Mezzogiorno, *Statistiche sul Mezzogiorno d'Italia, 1861–1953* (Rome: Failli, 1954), p. 12.

A glance at the balance of births and deaths, as shown in Table 72 will soon show why. Both birth and death rates in the south have consistently exceeded those of the north. While the death rate has dropped sharply since 1881 in both regions and by 1951 was almost identical, the birth rate in the south has fallen much less than in the north. As a result, the natural rate of increase in the south actually rose between 1861 and 1951—from 11.7 per thousand inhabitants to 5.7—while in the north it dropped from 9.9 to 5.5 per thousand. Between 1886 and 1918, these rates were quite close together for both regions, and beginning in 1921 the south took over an ever-increasing lead.[20]

There can be no question that south Italy has long been the focal point of severe population pressure. However, for forty years after 1881 war and emigration did much to relieve the pressure, at the same time holding down the natural rate of increase itself. From 1921 onwards, this pressure has been making itself increasingly felt—and in the least promising economic environment in the whole country.

TABLE 72. Birth and death rates and rates of natural increase, north and south, 1881–1951 [a] (per thousand inhabitants)

Annual average	North			South			Italy		
	births	deaths	excess	births	deaths	excess	births	deaths	excess
1881–85	36.1	26.2	9.9	40.5	28.8	11.7	37.9	27.2	10.7
1901–05	32.0	20.8	11.2	33.4	23.6	9.8	32.5	21.9	10.6
1911–14	30.5	17.8	12.7	33.6	21.1	12.5	31.7	19.1	12.6
1931–35	20.6	13.0	7.6	29.6	16.1	13.5	24.0	14.1	9.9
1936–40	20.2	12.8	7.4	29.1	15.6	13.5	23.4	13.8	9.6
1950–51	15.4	9.9	5.5	25.5	9.8	15.7	19.2	9.9	9.3

[a] Figures for Italy apply to boundaries in force at the time.
Source: *Statistiche sul Mezzogiorno d'Italia, 1861–1953*, pp. 61–62.

Prior to 1936, there are no satisfactory regional emigration statistics, although the mass exodus of 1885–1914 is a well-established fact. Comparing the total balance of births and deaths, SVIMEZ has estimated that during 1936–1938 the south lost 30,333 persons per year, while the north gained 35,304. During 1947–1949, the south's rate of loss rose to 37,134 persons a year, while the north gained 50,385. By 1952, the net movement out of the south was almost exactly 100,000, while the north lost 217 persons.[21] Although emigration from the south is obviously desirable in principle, the rate in recent years has been far too small to be of much significance.

The full extent of the southern population problem can be grasped only by relating it to the movement of economic opportunities since unification. Between 1861 and 1936, the population present in southern Italy rose by 5.7 million. Yet, as Table 73 shows, the active population (including the unemployed and all employed persons of ten years of age and over) increased by only 200,000 persons. Thus between the same dates the economically active portion of the group aged ten and over dropped from 75.7 to 49.6 per cent. In other words, almost the entire increase in the labor reserve—4.1 million persons—went into inactive status instead of productive work. For the rest of the country, the comparative participation ratios for the two dates are 66 and 56.8 per cent. Here the active group rose by 3.6 million, and the inactive by 5.0 million. If the south had expanded pro rata, so that 56.8 per cent of its labor reserve would have been active in 1936, its active group would have advanced by 800,000 more persons, and its inactive group by 3.3 million instead of 4.1 million.

TABLE 73. Economic status of the population, southern Italy and the rest of Italy, 1861 and 1936 [a] (in millions)

Economic status	1861			1936		
	South	Rest	Total	South	Rest	Total
Active population (10 years and over)	5.6	8.9	14.5	5.8	12.5	18.3
Agriculture	3.2	5.1	8.3	3.3	5.5	8.8
Industry and transportation	1.7	2.3	4.0	1.6	4.6	6.2
All other	0.7	1.5	2.2	0.9	2.4	3.3
Inactive population (10 years and over)	1.8	4.5	6.3	5.9	9.5	15.4
Population under 10 years	2.4	2.9	5.3	3.7	5.0	8.7
Total population	9.8	16.3	26.1	15.4	27.0	42.4

[a] Figures for south based on boundaries of 1861; for the remainder, boundaries of 1936.
Source: Statistiche sul Mezzogiorno d'Italia, 1861–1953, p. 39.

This discrepancy in growth of the active population is the essence of the southern economic problem. It demonstrates as sharply as words can possibly do the failure of the south to expand opportunities for its people. The details merely underscore the unfortunate truth. Between 1861 and 1936 the crowded agricultural sector could absorb but 100,000 more hands. Industry and transportation accepted none, but instead actually expelled 100,000. Taken as a whole, the nonagricultural sector was so constricted that it could absorb only 100,000 persons. Yet in the rest of the country agriculture rose by 400,000; industry and transportation, 2.3 million; and all activities outside of agriculture, 3.2 million. If the nonagricultural sphere in the south had expanded at this last rate, adjusted for the south's share of the total population, its increase would have been 1.1 million, or eleven times the tiny gain actually made.

Another way to demonstrate the magnitude of the gap, bearing in mind that per capita incomes were consistently much lower in the south, is to compare the ratios of unproductive persons dependent upon each productive one. For 1861, the southern figure was 0.75. By 1936, it had risen to 1.66, or more than double. For the rest of Italy the figures are 0.83 and 1.16.

TABLE 74. Economic status of the population and attachment by major economic sectors, north and south, 1871–1936 [a] (in millions)

	1871		1901		1936	
Economic status	South	North	South	North	South	North
Agriculture, hunting, fishing	2.98	5.72	3.66	6.01	3.20	5.31
Industry	1.33	1.99	1.37	2.61	1.26	3.90
Transportation	0.12	0.15	0.17	0.25	0.24	0.42
Trade	0.07	0.12	0.25	0.52	0.40	1.02
Other	1.03	1.50	0.51	0.91	0.51	1.30
Total	5.51	9.49	5.97	10.30	5.61	11.95

[a] Figures are for boundaries in force on census date; not comparable with Table 73.
Source: Statistiche sul Mezzogiorno d'Italia, 1861–1953, pp. 40–42.

Table 74 tells a similar story in a little greater detail. Between 1871 and 1901, the southern agricultural sector experienced a modest growth, followed by contraction to 1936. Industry had a negligible gain to 1901, followed by decline to 1936. Over-all, the active population in the south rose by a little over 400,000 between 1871 and 1901, only to shrink by about 350,000 thereafter. By contrast, the north gained 800,000 by 1901 and 1.6 million more between 1901 and 1936.[22]

For both north and south, agriculture has long since ceased to absorb additional productive workers. Indeed, since the war the agricultural labor force has been declining. Obviously, therefore, if employment is to increase along with the labor force, the nonagricultural sphere must expand. And here is the heart of the difference between north and south: the north has been able to expand industry and trade, while in the south these activities actually declined after 1901.

The industrial census of 1911 showed that the south had only 14.3 per cent of the industrial work force, and only 9.8 per cent of those attached to firms with more than ten persons (as against 23.1 per cent of those in establishments of smaller size). Moreover, the industrial workers in the south were mostly concentrated in the food industry (23.3 per cent of the national total attached to this group), chemicals (17.7 per cent), and metal-working and metal-using (14.4 per cent). With rare exceptions, it had little representation in the big industries that had begun to develop in the north by 1880—rubber, steel, cotton and woolen textiles, metal products, and shipbuilding, for example. Despite the limited scale of southern industry in 1911, it was fated to shrink even further by the time of the census of 1937–1940. The only major exceptions were lumber and wood products and food processing—both small-scale industries. By contrast, decline was encountered in metal-working, building, building materials, chemicals, paper, and leather products.[23]

The 1937–1940 Census offers a wealth of detail to document the feeble state of industry in the south. It could claim only 13.8 per cent of the industrial work force; only 10 per cent if artisans are excluded; and only 8 per cent if the count is limited to undertakings using electrical or mechanical motive power. Only in food processing was its share of the national total for that category comparable to its share of total population. Southern industry was dominated by small establishments, often without motive power. In overwhelming proportion it was oriented to local, rather than national and foreign markets—lumber and wood products, building, clothing, and public utilities.

The gap between north and south can also be shown with income statistics, which are presented in Table 75. During a single decade of Fascist rule (1928–1938) per capita income in the south fell 2 per cent, as against a 4.4 per cent increase in the north. For the twenty-year period of 1928–1948, average real incomes in the south fell by almost 25 per cent, while in the north the decline was slightly under 4 per cent. Thus the poorer region suffered the greater loss in average real income. Fortunately, some recovery followed after 1948 for both regions, but as of 1951 the south was still 10.2 per cent below 1928, while the north had recorded a gain of 15.4 per cent.

In relative terms, therefore, the real income gap was actually widening in the decades immediately prior to the introduction of the Cassa per il Mezzogiorno (Fund for the South) in 1950. The same widening disadvantage appears in the south's share of total private net product, which was 24.3 per cent in 1928, when the south had about 36 per cent of the population, and which fell consistently to 21.6 per cent in 1951, when its share of the population was 37.2 per cent.

TABLE 75. Regional distribution of private net national product gross and per capita, 1928–1951 [a] (in 1938 lire)

	Per capita		Regional total		
	South	North	South	North	Share of South in total
Year	(actual)		(millions)		(per cent)
1928	1,819	3,065	25,617	79,587	24.3
1938	1,783	3,201	27,299	88,551	23.6
1948	1,366	2,946	23,113	83,330	21.7
1951	1,633	3,537	28,387	102,781	21.6

[a] "South" here includes the islands.
Source: Statistiche sul Mezzogiorno d'Italia, 1861–1953, p. 683.

To appreciate fully the extent of the income gap, one should consider income differences between the poorest areas of the south—Calabria and the Bastilicata—and the richest ones of the north—Piedmont and the Val d'Aosta, Lombardy, and Liguria, which together comprise the industrial triangle of Italy. Table 76 illustrates vividly the economic plight of the southerners, and its worsening after 1928. Per capita real incomes in Calabria and the Basilicata, already more than 40 per cent below the northern average in 1928, actually fell absolutely between that date and 1951, putting both areas almost two-thirds below the north by the latter year. Equally significant, per capita real incomes rose absolutely in all three industrial areas of the north in the same period. And despite the widening income gap, both absolutely and relatively, population increased by a markedly greater percentage in the two impoverished southern areas than it did in the three prosperious northern ones.[24] Evidently the widening disparity in personal real incomes had failed to induce a massive exodus of population northward, despite the increasing poverty of the southern half of the country during these years. The main reason was that beginning with 1926 statutory restraint of internal migration was introduced. In 1928 it was drastically tightened, and these restrictions were continued in force until 1961.

TABLE 76. Comparative per capita incomes and changes in population, selected areas of north and south, 1928 and 1951 (in 1938 lire)

Region and area	Per capita real incomes			Ratio of area per capita income to north [a]		Change in area popu- lation [b] (per cent)
	1928	1951	Change (per cent)	1928 (per cent)	1951 (per cent)	
South:						
Calabria	1554	1434	−7.7	50.7	40.5	36.0
Basilicata	1751	1489	−15.0	57.1	42.1	34.1
North:						
Piedmont,						
Val d'Aosta	4071	4151	2.0	132.8	117.4	7.4
Lombardy	3717	4719	26.9	121.3	133.4	27.9
Liguria	3784	4353	15.0	123.4	123.1	17.3

[a] Average for entire north.
[b] Applies to change in population present, 1921 to 1951, for boundaries of 1951.
Source: Statistiche sul Mezzogiorno d'Italia, 1861–1953, pp. 12, 683.

Between 1901 and 1951, the economic statistics of the south present a mixed picture of stagnation and decline, depending upon the measure used. What, then, was the position in 1951?

Looking at those actually employed in the nonagricultural sphere in 1951, the fact stands out at once that this critical sector barely increased at all between 1938 and 1951 (roughly, it grew by only 75,000 persons, or 5.7 per cent). By comparison, this sector increased in the north by 388,000, or 8.2 per cent. The special parliamentary survey of September 8, 1952, indicates that 11.3 million persons then in the south fell into the population of working age fourteen–sixty-four.[25] Relating nonagricultural employment to this age group, it appears that approximately only 12 per cent of the south's population of working age could find work outside of agriculture. By contrast, 24.9 per cent of the same age group in the north could earn its way outside of farming.[26]

A glance at Table 77 will quickly show the sharp differences in degree of development of the nonagricultural spheres of south and north. Although the south had roughly 35 per cent of the nation's population of working age in 1951, it could claim only 20.9 per cent of all job opportunities outside agriculture. Even worse, its industries accounted for only 17.1 per cent of total employment in this category. Only in services did its share approach proportionality. Worse still, apart from transportation and communications, which remained relatively unchanged, it lost ground between 1938 and 1951 in its relative shares of all other categories.

TABLE 77. Distribution of employment by major sectors outside agriculture, north and south, 1938 and 1951 [a] (per cent)

Sector	1938		1951	
	South	North	South	North
Industry [b]	18.4	81.6	17.1	82.9
Transportation, communications	26.4	73.6	26.2	73.8
Trade, finance, insurance	25.3	74.7	26.6	73.4
Services [c]	30.9	69.1	33.5	66.5
Total	21.3	78.7	20.9	79.1

[a] Based upon a reconciliation, by SVIMEZ, of the industrial censuses of 1938 and 1951.

[b] Includes extractive industry.

[c] Includes hygiene, barber shops, laundries, legal and commercial services, cultural and recreational activities.

Source: Statistiche sul Mezzogiorno d'Italia, 1861–1953, p. 607.

To bring out the laggard status of the south in greater detail requires examination of the comparative distribution of those attached to industry in 1951—by major groupings such as extractive and manufacturing industry, and within these by specific industries. Bear in mind that, as of 1952, the south had an estimated 35 per cent of that part of the national population within the productive age group. This figure will serve as a useful benchmark for gauging industrial development in the south. However, it should not be taken too literally, for the principle of comparative advantage suggests clearly that there is no a priori reason for any major economic area anywhere to attain strict proportionality in all its industries, in the sense indicated by use of this benchmark. Areas and regions will normally specialize according to relative advantage—by agriculture *vs.* industry, and, within agriculture and industry, by specific forms of such activities.

TABLE 78. Comparative regional distribution of persons attached to industrial sector, by major group and by particular industry, census of 1951

Industry group and industry	Number attached		Share of national total	
	South	North	South	North
Extractive industry:	47,068	67,404	41.1	58.9
Metalliferous minerals	11,115	12,544	46.9	53.0
Nonmetalliferous minerals	35,953	54,860	39.6	60.4
Manufacturing:	556,932	2,938,320	15.9	84.1
Foods and related	171,951	304,323	36.1	63.9
Hides and leather	5,896	33,335	15.0	85.0
Textiles	24,783	617,905	3.9	96.1
Clothing	113,073	293,738	27.8	72.2
Wood and products	76,618	207,902	26.9	73.1
Paper and products	4,703	57,068	7.6	92.4
Printing and publishing	9,459	71,675	11.7	88.3
Primary metals	10,372	131,314	7.3	92.7
Metal products	83,280	776,353	9.7	90.3
Building materials	35,514	164,992	17.7	82.3
Chemicals	18,203	182,625	9.1	90.9
Rubber	722	38,414	1.8	98.2
Unclassified	2,358	58,676	3.9	96.1
Other:	105,788	450,742	19.0	81.0
Building construction	82,876	351,964	19.1	80.9
Equipment installation	2,183	27,812	7.3	92.7
Electricity, gas and water	20,729	70,966	22.6	77.4
Total	709,788	3,456,466	17.0	83.0

Source: *Statistiche sul Mezzogiorno d'Italia, 1861–1953*, pp. 393–394.

However, it must be borne in mind that agriculture in southern Italy, while overweighted relative to industry there, yields lower average returns than in the north. Yet industrial activities have failed to expand to compensate for this deficiency. It may well be that industry there generally offers no comparative advantage relative to agriculture, hence that the only hope lies in revitalizing and modernizing southern agriculture, coupled to a massive exodus of much of the resident population. But this remains to be proved.

In any case, the restricted development of southern industry in 1951 shows plainly in Table 78. Comparatively speaking, mining was the most developed branch of southern industry, reflecting production of lead, zinc, and sulphur. Within manufacturing, the largest shares of the south in the national totals lay in foods, clothing and wood—all local-market activities, generally on a small-scale basis. By comparison, its position in those industries making up the heart of the advanced sector and the main source of production for the national and export markets was dismally small. Thus in textiles the north had an advantage of 24 to 1; in metallurgy (mainly iron and steel, 13 to 1; in metal products, 9 to 1; in chemicals, 10 to 1; and in rubber, 53 to 1. Over-all, the industrial development of the north, also measured by relative numbers attached, was almost 5 to 1.

In agriculture the problem of interregional comparisons is even more difficult, although the generalization is certainly safe that again the south was worse off. The regional figures for 1936 show that agriculture, hunting, and fishng in the south accounted for 36.8 per cent of the national total for those engaged in such activities. Further, they absorbed 57 per cent of the productive population in the south, as against only 44 per cent of the productive population in the north. Failure of the nonagricultural sphere in the south to expand significantly between 1936 and 1951 makes it safe to conclude that in the latter year the south was still predominantly an agricultural economy, despite some major changes now under way.

There is no doubt also about its complexity. Indeed, Manlio Rossi-Doria, Italy's foremost expert on the question, has declared, "Everything about southern agriculture is absurd, and a clear solution cannot be envisioned." [27]

In 1936, the active population in southern agriculture consisted of one third as farm laborers, about 29 per cent as owner-operators, and another third in mixed status as owners, tenants, and/or crop-sharers (Table 79).[28] In the north, the main differences were a considerably larger relative number of crop-sharers (25.7 vs. 11.1 per cent), and a considerably smaller relative number of wage workers (23.1 vs. 33.4 per cent).

A survey of June 30, 1946, shows that 85.2 per cent of holdings of landed property in southern agriculture involved strips of two hectares or less, and that 96.1 per cent of all holdings were ten hectares or less (one hectare = 2.471 acres). In total area of productive agricultural and forest land in the region, 16.1 per cent embraced holdings of two hectares or less, and 35.3 per cent included those up to ten hectares. By contrast, 38.7 per cent of the area belonged in large holdings of 100 hectares and over, although these involved only 0.3 per cent of the total number of holdings. Roughly comparable figures also apply to the north.[29]

TABLE 79. Occupational status of persons active in agriculture, south and north, 1936

	Number		Share of regional total [a]	
Category	South	North	South	North
Operators:	2,087,267	4,284,904	66.5	76.6
Nonfarmers	123,786	129,247	3.9	2.3
Farmers	1,963,481	4,155,567	62.5	74.3
Owners	901,381	1,803,388	28.7	32.3
Tenants	286,287	461,615	9.1	8.3
Crop-sharers	349,311	1,438,290	11.1	25.7
Mixed status [b]	426,502	452,364	13.6	8.1
Workers:	1,048,196	1,292,249	33.4	23.1
Day hands	931,506	885,777	29.7	15.9
Annual laborers	95,159	286,626	3.0	5.1
Mixed status [c]	21,531	119,846	0.7	2.1
Managers, technicians	3,974	13,414	0.1	0.2
Grand total	3,139,437	5,590,567	100.0	100.0

[a] Per cent.
[b] Persons who may jointly be owners, tenants, and crop-sharers.
[c] Persons who may be wage-workers and also crop-sharers.
Source: Statistiche sul Mezzogiorno d'Italia, 1861–1953, p. 140.

Since an operator may own or lease more than one holding, there is no direct way to determine the size-distribution of areas under single control. However, there can be no doubt regarding the existence of two pathological situations in southern agriculture, both of them acute and both of them closely related to the latifundia system. One is excessive fragmentation of many holdings, often scattered, and each of them too small for efficient operation. The other consists of the great estates, either broken up into tiny lease-holds at very high rents, or conducted as plantations under a system of hired labor.

Not all the peasant holdings of ten hectares and less are ineffi-cient. Those devoted to intensive production of fruits, nuts, olives, and wine along the coast are in fact quite productive and afford a tolerable existence. But there are also the barren regions of the interior and of the coastal lowlands, largely devoted to extensive cultivation of wheat on soils of low fertility, vulnerable to flooding, erosion, and malaria. These include the hills of the Abruzzi, upper Puglia, the mountainous Sila in Calabria, the lowlands of the Basilicata, and the Sicilian interior. Here are to be found the rural slums, the poverty, and the misery of southern agriculture, made even worse by relentless population pressure.[30]

Beyond question, a substantial number of the peasant owners, tenants, and those in mixed status subsist in absolute poverty, hardly justifying the statistical labels of "operators" or "farmers." Even below this group in the socio-economic scale are the agricul-tural workers, a true rural proletariat, usually without full-time employment, earning wages far below their industrial counterparts in the north. Their position is hopeless and their politics largely Communist, although their goal is a piece of land, not membership in a collective farm.

Part of the economic problem, but only part, originates in the use and misuse of the land. In 1951, approximately 7,460,000 hectares of southern land were allocated to herbaceous plants. Of this total, 3,022,000 hectares, or 40 per cent, were devoted to cereals. Wheat dominated the list, absorbing 29.6 per cent of all land devoted to herbaceous culture. Barley accounted for 2.4 per cent; oats, 4.2 per cent; and corn, 4.0 per cent. Heat and corn to-gether represent the major problem, since yields per hectare in 1951 were far below those in the north—45 per cent lower for wheat and almost 60 per cent for corn.[31] Obviously, not all this land would be suitable for leguminous or arboreal culture, where returns are much higher, but the very fact that cereal cultivation persists despite such low yields is a measure both of the poverty of southern agriculture and of the lack of alternative ways of making a living in this environment.[32]

Note should also be taken of the position of meadow and pasture lands within the total herbaceous area. In 1951, the south had less than a fifth of the meadowland used in rotation in the north, while the bulk was devoted to permanent pasture, mostly of very poor quality. Looking at the livestock population, the south in that year had only 9 per cent of the cattle, 12.8 per cent of the swine, 27.8 per cent of the sheep, and 37.4 per cent of the horses in Italy, even though it had 42 per cent of the agricultural land and 37 per cent of the whole population. These deficiencies reflect the limited extent of intensive agriculture and also help to account for the low yields.

TABLE 80. Gross value product of agricultural and forest production, per hectare, per person attached, and per person dependent upon agriculture, average for 1948–1951 (in 1938 lire)

Unit	South	North
Hectare	1322	1850
Person attached	4394	5230
Dependent	1964	2586

Source: Statistiche sul Mezzogiorno d'Italia, 1861–1953, p. 263.

The position of the south was much more favorable in the production of fruits and vegetables. Here, in 1951, it contributed two thirds of the gross saleable value product of vegetables grown in Italy, and 58.5 per cent of the fruits. On a very rough calculation, the gross value product per hectare devoted to fruits and nuts in the south was 3.8 times larger than that obtained from cereals, and 4.9 times that from herbaceous culture as a whole. For cereals alone, gross value product per hectare in the north was 2.5 that obtained in the south.[33] Finally, the gross value product per hectare for lands in all productive uses in 1951 amounted to 84,000 lire in the south, as against 143,200 lire in the north—putting the south 41.4 per cent below the north over-all.

What did the lower value productivity of southern agriculture mean for the agricultural population? Using average values for 1948–1951 to overcome sharp annual fluctuations, all expressed in lire of 1938 value, Table 80 shows that gross returns per person attached to agriculture in the south were 16 per cent under the northern figure, while on the basis of returns per person directly or indirectly dependent upon agriculture for a living, the south was almost 25 per cent below the north.

CONCLUDING OBSERVATIONS

However regarded, southern agriculture is poor—in absolute terms and relative to the north. Partly its difficulties stem from nature itself—irregular rainfall, flooding, hilly or mountainous topography of much of the land, and soils generally of lower inherent fertility.

However, most of its troubles are man-made. Much of the land is put to the wrong uses, while some of it should not be used at all. Stripping of the forest cover from ancient times has brought flooding and erosion in its wake, also reducing the already inadequate water supply. Excessive resort to cereal culture, also deriving from ancient times but continuing even into the Fascist period, has steadily impoverished the soil, dooming its dependents to the lowest real incomes in all Italy. Remorseless population pressure has forced excessive fractionalization of holdings, while ruthlessly driving up rents. Persistence of the traditional estate system has fostered an impoverished rural proletariat, while at the same time committing its dependents to crops of low value, usually planted and harvested by obsolete methods. For centuries there has been a dearth of private capital for investment in agriculture, while investment by the state in badly needed public works has, until recently, been sporadic and at all times inadequate.

The people of the south have found a dubious kind of refuge in agriculture for generations, not by choice but because the only escape has been flight from the region itself. For over half a century, the agricultural sector has been hoplessly saturated with people. It simply cannot accept any more.

The cluster of difficulties besetting southern agriculture finds its ultimate expression in per capita real incomes that are simply too low to sustain anything even closely resembling a western style of rural life. This, in turn, has been instrumental in thwarting the development of the nonagricultural sphere. But here lies the paradox of the southern problem: to raise agricultural incomes, large-scale rationalization and renovation are required. Yet this cannot be accomplished without the expulsion of large numbers from the land. Where are they to go, if emigration north and abroad is greatly restricted, and if the nonagricultural sphere cannot expand?

Within agriculture itself, the problem is by no means the deceptively simple one of dividing up the estates. Division and distribution are required in some cases. In others, the problem is the opposite one of consolidating pulverized and scattered holdings to make them efficient enough to sustain families on the land itself. Beyond this, there is the equally formidable task of redirecting the use of land to more productive crops. For the specially depressed areas, there is acute need for a new investment, much of it public, for reforestation, for water storage, and irrigation works, and for mechanization of planting and harvesting. Beyond these areas but also including them, the increase of agricultural incomes depends upon much public expenditure in the nature of "social overheads" —for housing, increased education, technical training in scientific agriculture, improved transport and communications.

Leaving aside the very difficult problems of investment criteria and the estimation of prospective returns, there can be no doubt that the rehabilitation of the rural south is an extremely complex task—all the more so because its successful prosecution cannot be divorced from the removal of many people from the land. Accordingly, the job is linked inseparably to adequate expansion of the nonagricultural sphere. In turn, the growth of nonagricultural activities, while acutely needed in the south in particular, must embrace the whole of Italy. Only then can the problem of surplus population in the south be adequately solved. Moreover, it should not be forgotten that the north, too, has a similar agricultural problem, although not generally so deep-seated—in the depressed areas of the Maremma (western Tuscany), the Po Delta, Emilia, and the upper alpine area.

In any case, the issue is not whether to encourage agriculture or industry—both urgently require attention. Nor is it whether to concentrate upon the south or the north—national policy must include both regions.[34]

With good reason, Molinari and Sylos Labini have compared the Italian south with the commercial and manufacturing capitalism of England in the seventeenth and eighteenth centuries.[35] The south still lacks a genuine industrial bourgeoisie. Its agriculture is still dominated by feudal institutions, and its entire cultural outlook is oriented to the past. Like England, this system is in dissolution. In England, the dissolution brought grave social and economic problems, while the transition to a modern economy was under way. In the south, too, the traditional economy is breaking up, but up to 1951 the change was not accompanied by the offsetting compensations extended by the emergence of a progressive counterpart, which it was England's good fortune to have. Therein lies the explanation for the extremity of its difficulties.

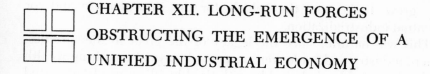

CHAPTER XII. LONG-RUN FORCES OBSTRUCTING THE EMERGENCE OF A UNIFIED INDUSTRIAL ECONOMY

Since the south has so heavy a weight in the statistics of backwardness, and the north in the statistics of advanced industrialism, an explanation of Italy's dual economic structure must account for the sharply divergent records of the two regions after 1861. In turn this requires reference to the enabling and disabling factors peculiar to each. Beyond these, however, we must consider forces operating more generally throughout the country to perpetuate the double system or to delay its eventual consolidation.

THE INHERENT AND ACQUIRED ADVANTAGES OF THE NORTH

The emergence and subsequent concentration of industrialism within the Italian north were not chance phenomena. They were favored from their inception by geographic and cultural circumstance, and by a relatively superior endowment of resources. Industrialism can take root only in hospitable soil. Because the environment there was far more favorable than anywhere else in Italy, the north could become the nodal point for the growth of industry, in a self-sustaining process that was helped further by national policy.

Geography had placed the north in close contact with the older nations of northwest Europe, where modern industrialism found its original home. The bonds were strengthened even more by the political dominion of France during the Napoleonic period.[1] In contrast to the reactionary Spanish influence that dominated the southern scene almost continuously between 1500 and 1861, the French in 1796–1814 introduced into the north the ideals of national independence, strong government, and political and economic liberalism.[2] Here was a culture that could accept the bourgeois style of life, with its doctrines of thrift, competition, and private initiative, and its gospel of hard work and material progress. Thus a middle-class society of farmers and traders gradually grew, to become the vehicle for the *Risorgimento* and for eventual industrialization.

This was natural, since the legacy of the great medieval cities, where industry and trade were respected ways of acquiring wealth and influence, blended readily with the liberalism newly imported from revolutionary France. And it was equally logical that a man imbued with the bourgeois spirit, such as Count Camilio Cavour, should become the leader of Piedmont in 1852 and the chief intellectual force in the founding of united Italy in 1871.

Since the cultural soil of north Italy was receptive, the transplanting of ideas of technology and of business organization from upper Europe was not too difficult. Commercial and agricultural capitalism were already well established. In economic language, the presence of the bourgeois way of life meant that there were a supply of entrepreneurs, a favorable supply curve of effort, a satisfactory propensity to save, and a relatively weak population multiplier.

Moreover, the north could offer a superior resource endowment to emergent industrialism. The Po Valley afforded a large area containing some of the most fertile agricultural land in Italy, much of it in plains, which were easily worked. Thus foodstuffs and agricultural raw materials could be had at comparatively low cost, to supply a growing urban population and developing industrial complex. In turn, the latter could be stimulated by the availability of iron ore in the Val d'Aosta, at Como, and on the island of Elba, while, once the transalpine rail connections were joined to the developing network of upper Italy, coal could be imported more cheaply than into the lower peninsula. Iron and steel production thus became possible, to serve the capital-goods and fabricating industries that emerged in the eighties. Further, timber and hydroelectric power were at hand in the adjacent alpine and subalpine areas. Finally, the north had a more industrious and better trained labor force, derived from its older handicraft and cottage industries, and later augmented by an inflow from its increasingly productive agricultural sector.[3]

The north also possessed, and retains even today, certain locational advantages for industry. Its own regional market was easily the most prosperous and the most rapidly expanding in Italy, hence the largest source of domestic demand for industrial goods. In time this was augmented by a small but growing export market, largely centered in upper Europe. In both cases, delivered costs could be lower than from other potential points of supply within Italy, because transport costs from processing sites were held down by shorter distances. Moreover, shipping costs from points of raw materials production to processing and fabricating plants were generally lower than could be true for manufacturers farther down the peninsula. Finally, the markets of southern Italy and of the Mediterranean basin were simply too small to exert much attraction for potential manufacturing plants. Any savings on delivered costs at such locations would have been more than canceled out by higher access and processing costs at southern Italian sites.[4]

Although the belief is still held in some segments of Italian opinion that the north had no inherent advantages over the south at the time of unification, that subsequent industrial advance in the north was primarily the result of government policies, the facts do not lend this thesis much support.[5] Nonetheless, it can be affirmed that government policy did largely favor the north between 1861 and 1951, both by action and by inaction. Unification opened up the south to the competition of northern handicrafts, quickly eroding much of its nonagricultural tariff policy, shifting its orientation from revenue to protective measures for the benefit of northern cereals, iron and steel. The south had to pay higher prices for its foodstuffs and manufactures, while suffering from retaliatory measures taken by the French against Italian exports. However, the iron and steel tariff also injured the machine-building and fabricating industries of the north, surviving into the late 1950's as a monument to governmental folly.

Beyond tariff policy, there is also evidence that for some decades after 1861 the north enjoyed preferential treatment in railway building and in other forms of social capital.[6] Here it is significant that even now illiteracy is still a major problem and is primarily a southern one. Finally, there is no doubt that the lower peninsula was allowed to languish in neglect and in economic stagnation for ninety years after 1861, save for sporadic and inconclusive "studies" and measures of relief undertaken at the turn of the century and during the Fascist period.

Taken altogether, then, circumstances inherently favored the north, making it the nodal point for industrial growth. The combination of higher productivity, a favorable man-land ratio, and capacity for improvements in the agricultural sector could generate the necessary flow of saving for formation of capital in agriculture and industry, at the same time providing a supply of labor and of cheap food and raw materials for the cities. Agriculture thus supplied the initial impulse for development.[7] Clustering around iron and steel, an industrial complex began to emerge after 1880 centering in machine-building, railway equipment, shipbuilding, metal fabricating, rubber, and chemicals. In the same period, older handicraft industries like textiles were mechanized and expanded, while manufacture of automobiles, office machines, and hydroelectric power followed.[8]

Although these industries had to compete with each other for extremely scarce savings, their joint development in a synchronous and mutually reinforcing process undoubtedly accelerated the expansion of output and industrialization in the north. The secret lay in the pecuniary economies afforded to each of the firms.[9] Net investment in the machine industry would increase capacity, and, through the effects of indivisibilities, bring down unit costs, thus reducing prices to the textile industry. The deriving increase of profits in textiles would foster further investment, lower costs and prices in that field, at the same time reacting to enlarge the demand for products of the machine industry. Further, the expansion of the latter would carry back still another stage as increased demand upon a supplier industry like iron and steel or electric power, generating higher profits and more investment there. Still further, growth in machine manufacturing would have lateral stimulus for shipbuilding or railway equipment, since complementary products supplied to these fields would be available at lower costs, reducing their prices, expanding their sales and profits, and inducing net investment accordingly. Textiles and agricultural raw materials, for example, would benefit on the demand side through increased sales made possible by the rising incomes of workers in the expanding nexus of these industries.

No single one of these activities is "the cause" of the expansion. The process is circular—what goes on in one industry is both cause and effect of what goes on elsewhere. Undoubtedly, too, joint development is promoted further by supportive public expenditures loosely designated as "social overhead capital" or "infrastructure"—education and technical training to provide a suitable labor force, municipal housing for workers, port and transport facilities to reduce shipping costs, civic investments in water supply and sanitation, provision of law and order, and so forth.

This depicts what was actually happening in upper Italy after 1880—the building up of a system of forward and backward linkages among industries, mutually inducing additional investment, increased output, and higher incomes.[10] Economic unification through enlargement and increased interdependence of markets and of activities was thus gradually achieved.

Undoubtedly iron and steel production played a role in the story—to Clough a decisive one.[11] Perhaps it was, at least in fostering the initial spread of industrial activity as such. However, it is also true that the new iron and steel industry, in part dependent upon armaments orders and state subsidy (the works at Terni), soon began clamoring for protection, which was extended in increasing degree between 1878 and 1887 (surely a sign of weakness and plainly an unfortunate turn in state policy). For, as Gerschenkron points out, lack of practically any domestic coal supplies indicated the wisdom of protecting low coal-using industries, such as machine building, rather than the production of ferrous metals.[12] As things actually turned out, steel got the protection in generous degree, while machines and metal products received very little; and even this was reduced after 1887. Thus the far more efficient users of ferrous metals were compelled to pay higher costs for their raw materials—a handicap under which they continued to suffer until the iron and steel tariff was eliminated in 1958 by the program of the European Coal and Iron Community.

The real mistake was one of timing, not the resort to the principle of protection. During the early decades after 1880, development in the north could have proceeded faster with access to cheaper foreign supplies of iron and steel. Once the user-industries had attained substantial size, it would have been strategic to introduce protection for domestic production of ferrous metals, to build it up as an import replacing activity having the prospective domestic demand to permit it to attain an efficient scale.

THE CHRONIC BACKWARDNESS OF THE SOUTH

Since conditions in the south almost perfectly represent the reverse side of the coin, our account can be relatively brief.

The central historical fact, as Cenzato and Guidotti conclude from their exhaustive postwar inquiry, is that an agglomerative process of self-perpetuating industrial growth failed to emerge in the south.[13] There is, of course, no reason to expect the process to appear simultaneously throughout a land as large and diverse as Italy. Nor is there reason to expect manufacturing industry as such to distribute itself uniformly. But granting that some interregional imbalance and diversity are likely, the ever-growing income-gap and the stubborn persistence of peasant agriculture, petty trade, and handicraft production in the lower peninsula and the islands over a period of some ninety years cannot be attributed to chance. The evident failure of the southern economy to modernize itself over so long a time is a problem that demands explanation.

Industrialism can emerge in an old society either by contact and intrusion or at the hands of inhabitants who have had exposure to an industrial way of life in other lands. To take hold and to grow, industrialism must have a favorable environment, such as it came to enjoy in the north—stimulus from agriculture, prevalence of the bourgeois outlook, access to capital and to trained and disciplined labor, and expanding markets.

Prior to 1861, southern Italy as a territorial entity had never known political independence.[14] During the modern period, it was the south's malign destiny to fall under Spanish influence, and Spain was the least progressive of all the nations in Western Europe. Accordingly, the rulers of the lower peninsula lacked either the knowledge or the will to promote economic renovation. On the contrary, their interests lay in perpetuating a feudal agricultural system, and in insulating a backward society from the incursions of change. Leadership in this scattered collection of parochial communities had to depend upon a landed nobility that despised industry and trade, neglected its holdings, consumed or exported rather than saved its revenues, and took no interest in developing nonagricultural activities.

If the newer ideas of business organization and productive technique were to emerge at all in this inhospitable environment, they could come only at the hands of a few ambitious inhabitants, or from outsiders willing to risk their capital in this most unpromising region. As for the former, the feudal nature of the society militated strongly against entrepreneurship—both capital and opportunity were lacking. What little capitalism that could take root before 1861 was destined to be almost entirely commercial in character. Although unification conferred political independence and theoretically opened up the south to development, in fact the heavy overlay of hostile tradition, in particular the obsolete agricultural system, continued to suppress the rise of a strong middle class. Able and ambitious men customarily abandoned their native soil, to seek their fortunes elsewhere.[15]

The region was not attractive to outside capital, either from the north or abroad. Geographic isolation and extremely low and virtually static per capita incomes dictated small and unpromising markets. Local supplies of labor were illiterate, undisciplined, and unskilled. A deeply embedded tradition of violence and corruption denied law and order to prospective businessmen. Since the potential returns from investment were better in the upper peninsula, little domestic capital flowed southward.

Furthermore, the economic resources available in the south were markedly inferior to those of the north. With few exceptions, its agricultural lands are much less fertile, while cultivation is further handicapped by irregular and scanty rainfall, lack of facilities for water storage and distribution, and consequent flooding and erosion. Much of the region is hilly or mountainous, and is remote from efficient transportation. Coupled to the obsolete system of landholding and pattern of farm production, these deficiencies denied to agriculture its customary role as impetus to industrialization.

At the same time, extractive resources were confined to lead, zinc, and sulphur, although postwar discovery of petroleum in western Sicily has brightened prospects somewhat. However, it cannot be denied that, since 1861, extractive activities in the south contributed little to economic development.[16]

Another limitation lay in the labor supply. Opportunities for schooling have always been more restricted in the south. In consequence, illiteracy rates have long been much higher, while those inhabitants who were able to acquire any formal education at all usually did not go beyond the primary grades. Furthermore, lack of modern industry and of vocational schools meant that the labor force could not be technically trained beyond the traditional craft apprenticeships of the artisan trades. The culture of the south, always more Mediterranean than North European, was not the kind to produce workers with aptitude for discipline and efficiency. Not that southerners are inferior, as some north Italians still believe: once transplanted to Milan they soon become as productive as their northern counterparts. Rather, the culture of the south is hostile to the incentives and practices of western rationalism. As Banfield suggests, one cannot "choose" his culture if he wishes to remain an inhabitant. Having chosen it, one thereby acquires an outlook, an environment, and a style of life.

Finally, the list of deficiencies must include lack of capital. Little investment ever flowed in either from the north or abroad, while chronically low per capita incomes precluded significant local accumulation. Until quite recently much of the region even lacked ordinary banking and credit facilities. Accordingly, capital formation after 1861 was wholly inadequate even to begin a transformation of this ancient society.

Since 1861, the southern population rose by almost eight million, of which certainly less than a half-million entered active employment. Up to 1936, this number was divided about evenly between agricultural and nonagricultural activities. Virtually none of it entered modern industry simply because there was no little development of this kind.

Behind the increase in population lay a very high birth rate (40.5 per thousand during 1881–1885, the earliest available figure), which dropped to 25.5 per thousand by 1950–1951; and a high death rate (28.8 per thousand in 1881–1885, which fell rather slowly until after World War I, when it dropped sharply to 9.8 per thousand by 1950–1951.[17]

It is now a commonplace that in countries that have successfully entered into self-perpetuating industrialization and rising per capita incomes, the death rate starts downward before the birth rate, which follows at an indefinite later point under the impact of the "standard-of-living effect."[18] Since both death and birth rates were dropping steadily in southern Italy, one might infer that sustained economic development must have been under way. However, this would be an error.

First, we know that there was almost no expansion of employment in the nonagricultural sphere; that this was not a side effect of highly capital-intensive investment. We know also that agriculture absorbed only a small number of productive workers. Second, although there may have been some over-all rise in per capita incomes during the ninety years after 1861, it certainly must have been small. In fact, the evidence shows a decrease after 1928.

Instead, the fall in the death rate can be attributed to gradual, but still quite modest, sanitation improvements, better medical care, and control of malaria—all primarily exogenous influences unconnected with productivity and incomes within the region. As for the drop in the birth rate, it was a consequence of emigration, concentrated among the younger adult groups. As such, the exodus of over three million people between 1871 and 1936 was a pathological sign, underscoring other undeniable symptoms of social-economic malaise—failure of capital to enter or to accumulate locally, saturation of agriculture, constricted and primitive nonagricultural activities, sharp and persistent decline in the ratio of active to total population, and ubiquitous poverty.[19]

Excluding those lucky enough to have escaped from the region, the bulk of the population increase had to be absorbed on the land. This fact destroyed any private incentives to reorganize agriculture. Consider, first, that the supply of usable land was limited and had long since been taken up. Accordingly, the man-land ratio steadily increased, with little or no rise in capital employed per farm worker.[20] Demographic pressure thus led to more and more labor-intensive farming, to fragmentation of properties under the inheritance system, and to rising money rents for a restricted supply of land. True, there was good economic reason for highly labor-intensive farming, but the evil combination of enforced population growth on the land with the system of peasant ownership or cultivation brought about a rise in the number of suboptimal or dwarf-holdings.

Under this system, there is nothing to prevent the emergence of a hidden labor surplus, whose marginal product would be zero. In this situation, some workers could have been withdrawn without causing a fall in total output, and without requiring collateral substitution of land and/or capital, or reorganization of activities.[21] When cultivation is conducted by peasant families under these circumstances, the basic problem is the lack of work-opportunities sufficient to provide each member with full-time annual employment. Work is then shared. Each able member contributes his positive average product, even though the total work could be performed, and the same total product obtained, with a smaller number working full time. This is the meaning of disguised unemployment. Its origins flow from the peculiarities of family enterprise: pooled income from which each member draws his maintenance, a restricted volume of work, work-sharing, and lack of alternative employment opportunities.

The side-effects of the system were equally bad. Where there is surplus labor, the worker has no incentive to become more efficient, and there is no advantage in increasing capital investment per worker. Laborers are a free good because there is no explicit price or cost attached to them. The head of the family must maintain all members as an overhead expense quite detached from any additional contribution each could make to total product. Thus there is no reason to economize on labor, and every reason to economize on land and capital. Excessively intensive use of labor automatically follows. Because the system lacks incentives for reorganization and improvement, it perpetuates its own effects—low incomes and restricted markets.

Similar evils prevailed in the cities and towns. Here the dominant organizational forms were family enterprise in trade and handicrafts, and self-employment. Within the former excess labor is again typical for the same reasons. Why modernize when capital, rather than labor, is the scarce factor, and when the market is too tiny to permit economies of scale?

Self-employment or "own-account" labor requires no land and little or no capital. Entry is therefore easy, and in consequence returns are flexible and are readily pressed downward. Thus self-employment becomes a natural haven of economic refuge in a stagnant economy for those who cannot afford land, or who have quit the peasant family to seek their fortunes in the city, or who are barred by artificially high and rigid wage rates from competing for jobs with the few modern employers at hand. Again we find overcrowding, idle time, low productivity, and low income—all made worse as population pressure forces more and more people off the land.

One might say that these troubles arise from deficiency of total demand for goods and services, hence for labor. But why is demand deficient? Not because the propensity to save is excessive relative to investment opportunities, but because total output cannot increase. Productivity and incomes permit virtually no saving, while redundancy of family and own-account labor throttles all incentive for capital investment. As a result, southern society became mired in the swamp of economic stagnation: capital stock failed to grow, hence did not check the fall of the marginal productivity of labor; techniques remained traditional; yet population and labor force continued to increase. All the other evils followed— disguised unemployment, underemployment, unemployment, falling productivity and per capita incomes, exodus from the land, and clotting of people in poorly paid activities in the cities and towns.[22]

At this point, the neoclassical economist would properly suggest that labor would have left the south, attracted by higher incomes abroad or in the north; and conversely, that capital would have been drawn to the south to earn higher returns, since it was relatively scarcer than labor in that region.

As we have seen, extensive emigration did occur, but not at a rate sufficient to diminish the population or even to hold it constant. Thus its main effect was to check to an unknown extent the tendency for per capita output and income to fall. Exodus of population was curtailed after 1913 by restrictions abroad, by the labor-retention effect of family enterprise, and by legal restraint of internal migration. This last restriction came from the lack of job opportunities in the progressive industrial sector of the north. Behind it were limitations imposed by the lag in the rate of national saving and investment relative to the rate of increase in population and labor supply, augmented after World War II by the policy of pushing wage rates above the competitive level in the progressive sector.[23] In consequence, these obstacles to population exodus restraints compelled the southern economy to be even more labor-intensive than it would have been if labor could have moved freely.

For a labor-redundant and backward setting such as this, neoclassical theory would predict that capital would have flowed in to capture the higher returns implied by the greater relative abundance of labor there. In turn, this would have raised labor productivity and per capita incomes. However, the economic gap between north and south continued to widen. Neither interregional trade nor mutually opposing labor and capital flows served as the necessary equilibrating forces to bring the two regions together.

On the economic side, the obstacles to capital migration were formidable. About all the south could offer was cheap labor. However, cheap labor does not mean lower production costs when that labor is poorly trained and disciplined. Even more, the south could offer none of the external economies available from sustained growth in the northern triangle, while transport costs at southern sites were undoubtedly higher. Finally, capital investment of the labor-saving type was not attractive under the family-enterprise system. True, massive investment in peasant agriculture might well have paid off if land holdings could have been bought up and consolidated. But these private reforms were inseparable from expulsion of large numbers from the soil, while investment of this kind was simply too risky relative to the alternative of further developments within the northern triangle. As for the nonagricultural sphere, the system of agriculture itself so constricted the local market that it could not offset the other disadvantages of southern manufacturing locations. In short, we have a case of circular causation dominating the whole problem: the traditional system bred poverty, while poverty perpetuated the system.[24]

To clinch the point, the heart of the southern problem lies in a failure of adaptation, a persistence of cultural and economic backwardness entrenched rather than disrupted by the operation of political and economic forces after 1861. What the unification of Italy actually meant was a welding together of two quite distinct social-economic systems, with the north as the dominant political partner in this strange union. If the south were to escape from its traditional status as a subsistence and handicraft economy, it would have had to begin a substantial process of cumulative growth and industrialization.

On the political side, unification exposed the weak handicraft industries of the south to competition from the north. They were quickly undercut. Then, within twenty years tariff policy was turned against the region, raising the costs of its imported food-stuffs and manufactured goods, while curtailing foreign markets for its agricultural exports.

On the economic side, market forces also proved disabling, through the very development of industrial concentration in the northern triangle. What little capital the south could accumulate mostly flowed northward in search of larger and more secure returns. Relatively free internal trade in industrial goods also favored the north. Moreover, the generally superior efficiency of northern agriculture prevented a change in the terms of agricultural trade in favor of the south. In turn, emigration of labor drew off the most efficient age groups, leaving an even larger number of dependents for an almost static number of productive workers to support. Thus in every way the "backwash effects" of burgeoning industrialization in the upper peninsula worked against the southern economy.

RESTRICTED CAPITAL FORMATION

It was pointed out earlier that the incomplete economic unification of Italy is not wholly a geographic problem. Even in the highly industrialized north, peasant agriculture, handicraft industry, petty trade, and menial self-employment can be found. In some cases, modern and traditional forms of production coexist within the same industry. Thus the inherent disabilities of the south do not fully account for the two-sided character of the Italian economy. More pervasive influences have also been at work.

In resuming her career as a national power after a lapse of over fourteen centuries, Italy found herself caught in the predicament of a late arrival as a modern nation—burdened from the outset by an obsolete economy. Given extremely low levels of productivity and income per head, her people had very little propensity to save. Augmented significantly by inflow of foreign funds, which dried up after 1870 but again became important during the brief period of 1885–1890, much of the investment capital available in the first two decades after 1861 was committed to railways and communications.[25] These and other internal improvements prepared the ground for industrialization, but necessarily restricted the availa-

TABLE 81. Net and gross propensity to save, five-year averages, 1861–1915 [a] (in millions of current lire)

Period	Net national product	Net investment	Net propensity to save (per cent)	Gross national product	Gross domestic investment	Gross propensity to save (per cent)
1861–1865	7,374	55	0.74	7,782	463	5.95
1866–1870	8,406	316	3.76	8,874	784	8.83
1871–1875	9,963	423	4.24	10,558	1,013	9.58
1876–1880	10,090	402	3.98	10,707	1,019	9.52
1881–1885	9,803	593	6.05	10,410	1,200	11.53
1886–1890	10,128	404	3.99	10,777	1,053	9.77
1890–1895	10,405	414	3.98	11,076	1,085	9.79
1896–1900	11,079	664	5.99	11,816	1,401	11.86
1901–1905	12,768	1,394	10.92	13,682	2,308	16.87
1906–1910	15,767	1,764	11.19	17,032	3,029	17.78
1911–1915	19,500	1,149	5.89	21,140	2,789	13.19

[a] Calculations were made according to the following definitions: $NNP = C_t + I_n$, where NNP is net national product, C_t is total consumption including public, and I_n is net investment; $I_n = I_g - D \pm X$, where I_g is gross investment, D is depreciation, and X is exports minus imports (X will be negative with an import surplus) and $GNP = C_t + I_g \pm X$, where GNP is gross national product.

Source: Istituto centrale di statistica, Indagine statistica, pp. 260–261, 264–265, and 268–269.

bility of investment for the development of industrial production itself.

Primarily in consequence of limited availability of capital, the mean annual rate of increase in real gross national product during 1861–1897 was only 0.75 per cent (prices of 1938).[26] By contrast, between 1897 and 1913, when industrialization began to accelerate, the average annual rate of increase jumped to 3.06 per cent, fostering in itself much higher rates of saving and investment, both absolutely and relatively. However, Italy did not experience explosive growth until much later—with the reconstruction and development boom of 1947–1961, when the growth rate soared to over 5 per cent.[27]

TABLE 82. Comparative sector contributions to total value added, five-year averages, 1861–1915 [a] (per cent)

Period	Agriculture, forestry and fishing	Industry		Tertiary activities [c]
		Manufacturing	All industry [b]	
1861–1865	57.7	16.9	19.8	22.4
1866–1870	57.3	16.9	19.7	23.0
1871–1875	57.6	16.2	18.9	23.5
1876–1880	55.6	16.0	19.1	25.3
1881–1885	52.0	16.2	20.6	27.4
1886–1890	49.8	16.3	20.8	29.4
1891–1895	50.7	15.1	18.9	30.3
1896–1900	50.3	15.8	19.5	30.2
1901–1905	48.8	17.0	21.3	29.9
1906–1910	44.9	20.6	25.1	30.0
1911–1915	43.8	21.4	25.8	30.4

[a] When combined, the respective sector contributions are gross of an undistributed adjustment that is then deducted to yield gross private value added. Subsequent deduction of depreciation then yields total private net product. The relative shares shown here assume that the adjustment was distributed in the same proportions as the sector shares before deduction. Original data in current prices.

[b] Includes extractive, manufacturing, construction, and utilities.

[c] Includes transport and communications, trade and services, finance and insurance, and real estate.

Source: Indagine statistica, pp. 245–246.

Table 81 shows the role of capital supply in the economic growth of Italy in the early decades after political unification. If we follow current fashion and define self-sustaining growth as starting when gross saving and investment reach a continuing level of at least 10 per cent of gross product, then Italy entered this phase of industrialization during 1896–1900, when this rate attained almost 12 per cent.[28] This conforms very well with Gerschenkron's dating of Italy's "big push," which he places at 1896–1908.[29] Similarly, net capital formation also jumped sharply, to almost 6 per cent of net product during 1896–1900, soaring to over 10 per cent in the decade following.

Further evidence of the constraining influence of limited capital supply on the spread of industrialization appears in the comparative contributions of agriculture, industry, and manufacturing to gross private product during 1861–1915, shown in Table 82. At the outset, agriculture accounted for almost 60 per cent of gross private product, drifting downward slowly but steadily to 43.8 per cent by 1911–1915. By contrast, manufacturing alone held very steadily at one sixth until 1901–1905, when it began its rise to 21.4 per cent by 1911–1915. Dominated as it was by manufacturing, industry as a whole behaved similarly, holding at one fifth until the end of the century, when it started to rise, attaining 25.8 per cent during 1911–1915.[30] Not until 1896–1900 did industry as a whole and manufacturing in particular begin a sustained rise in their relative contributions, again suggesting that the critical phase of industrialization in Italy came only toward the end of the nineteenth century—an influence also strongly supported by the data for net and gross investment presented in Table 81.

Table 83 permits us to carry forward the analysis. Following World War I, the formation of capital in Italy displays a ragged profile until after 1950. The explanation lies in the economic disruptions wrought by three wars, the great depression, and the imperial ambitions of later fascism. World War II brought about a serious consumption of capital, so that by 1945 perhaps one third of capital stock had been destroyed and real gross product had fallen to the level of 1900. Yet it was from this setting of national disaster that the country was to begin its most dramatic period of industrial advance.

The initial years 1946–1950 were ones of recovery and reconstruction, with rates of saving comparable to the last previous "normal" period, 1926–1930. Then during 1950–1960 an investment boom caused the rate of saving to surge upward to heights close to the unprecedented levels achieved by West Germany and the Soviet Union. Beyond doubt, this development has greatly speeded the process of industrialization.

TABLE 83. Net and gross propensity to save, five-year averages and by particular years, 1921–1960 [a] (current prices)

Years	Net national product	Net investment	Net propensity to save (per cent)	Gross national product	Gross domestic investment	Gross propensity to save (per cent)
	(million lire)			(million lire)		
1921–25	107,211	7,427	6.93	117,509	17,725	15.08
1926–30	127,965	10,637	8.31	140,505	23,177	16.49
1931–35	95,485	6,254	6.55	105,730	16,499	15.60
1936–40	140,351	12,977	9.25	155,607	28,233	18.14
	(billion lire)			(billion lire)		
1946–50	5,868	540	9.20	6,420	1,092	17.01
1950	7,694	832	10.81	8,442	1,580	18.72
1955	11,801	1,513	12.82	12,995	2,707	20.83
1960	17,197	2,871	16.69	19,078	4,752	24.91

[a] For definitions see Table 81.

Source: (1955 and prior) *Indagine statistica*, pp. 260–261, 264–265, 268–269; (1960), *Relazione sulla situazione economica del paese*, I (Rome: Istituto poligrafico dello stato, 1962), pp. 61–63.

But aggregative figures can be misleading for a divided economy, because they do not tell where this investment actually went or what form it took, either by region or economic sector. Investment by private industry in Italy is conducted largely through auto-financing from internal earnings, particularly in the large firms that dominate the technically advanced parts of the economy. These firms are heavily concentrated in the northern triangle. With few exceptions, they have continued to center their capital outlays in this region. Moreover, they cluster in already well-developed industries such as chemicals, metal products, transportation equipment, and primary metals. In consequence, investment directed by private choice has not gone mainly either southward or into the more primitive parts of industry. Instead, such outlays constitute a deepening rather than a widening process, both geographically and industrially.

Other evidence points in the same direction. Recent data show that the Fund for the South has been investing roughly 125 billion lire yearly during 1950–1960, and that other sources, both government and private, have contributed up to 125 billion more per annum for southern uses.[31] Putting aside any questions about the productivity of these outlays, at the outside their total scale still represents less than 10 per cent of average annual gross domestic investment during 1950–1960, even though this small share was applied in a region with 37 per cent of total population. This is not to say that the south should have obtained 37 per cent of all capital expenditure, or any other specific portion. But failing a massive exodus of people to the north, the share actually devoted to the southern economy could not be expected to effect the extensive modernization required for a transformation even within a generation after 1945. With the advent of the sixties, both public and private investments have begun to flow south in larger amounts, while restriction of internal migration has been ended. Both developments will do much to hasten the economic unification of the nation as a whole.

There is another way of looking at the constraining influence of investment in the fifties, indicated by Table 84. Modernization of an economy requires the reorganization and technical improvement of the backward parts of both agriculture and industry, with both reinforced by strengthening the surrounding infrastructure—

and all this without bringing to a halt the continuing progress of the already advanced sectors.

The data in Table 84 show that the share of fixed investment devoted to agriculture has held constant at 12 per cent during 1950–1960. By contrast, the share applied to industry and to transport and communications actually fell—from 55 to about 45 per cent. However, commitments to housing and to public works jumped from 27 to 35 per cent. In other words, the thrust of investment was rather sharply redirected in favor of infrastructure at the expense of directly productive investments of the traditional kind. Of course this is not to deny that improvements in roads and sanitation, for example, contribute indirectly to the productivity of market-oriented resources. But it is to say that the gains in national product so derived may be less, and in some cases negligible.

TABLE 84. Changing distribution of gross domestic permanent investment by sectors, 1950–1960 [a] (per cent)

Sector	1950	1955	1960
Agriculture	11.9	13.0	12.1
Industry	37.6	29.6	29.5
Transport and Comm.	17.8	14.8	16.8
Housing	15.2	25.0	24.8
Public Works	11.5	12.6	10.1
Other	5.9	5.0	6.7

[a] Excepting housing and public works, data were taken from the *Relazioni* because the *Indagine* tabulation lacks the necessary detail. For 1950 and 1955, the *Indagine* figures for housing and public works were used because they are later revisions. Original data in current prices.

Source: *Relazione generale*, 1951, p. 28; 1956, p. 49; 1961, I, p. 55; and *Indagine statistica*, p. 265.

In 1960, 568 billion lire were applied to infrastructure.[32] Of this sum, only 11.8 per cent went into directly productive uses—railways, maritime shipping, and telecommunications. By contrast, 18.1 per cent was assigned to public buildings, 13.1 per cent to sanitation, and 33.8 per cent to roads.[33] On the one side, it is a tribute to the energies of a free people and to the fecundity of their economy that Italy could raise gross national product at the impressive and steady rate of 5.5 per cent yearly throughout the fifties, yet divert up to a third of her annual saving to housing and public works. In sharp contrast to the Soviet case, this high rate of saving came about without forcing, and without denying the people the living improvements that infrastructure provides.[34] But, on the other side, the increased division of resources to such ends has delayed the modernization of the market economy.

Disregarding for the moment questions of geographic distribution and duality, there are two direct ways to test the progress of modernization over time. One is to examine the changing structure of the labor force—by sector, status (wage vs. family labor), and occupational skill level. For Italy this is largely foreclosed by lack of adequate statistics. The other is to consider shifts in the relative contributions of the three broad sectors of the market economy—agriculture, forestry and fishing; industry; and tertiary—to total value added to initial resource inputs by productive activities in each sector.[35] In the usual case, one can expect that the advance of industrialization will bring a relative (not absolute) decrease in the contribution of agriculture, a relative increase for industry, and probably a lesser relative increase for tertiary activities (transport, trade, and finance). The reason is that advance brings higher labor productivity all around; this raises labor and per capita real incomes. As the latter increase, the demand for nonagricultural products will rise more than that for agriculture, and even more so if the economy is closed to the world.[36]

As Table 85 shows, during the four decades after 1920 Italy experienced substantial changes in structure of output, and particularly during 1950–1960. To minimize the short-run influences of disproportionate changes in prices and in production among the three sectors, probably the most useful comparison for long-term purposes is between annual averages for 1926–1930 and 1956–1960. Some major shifts in economic structure then become evident. The relative contribution of agriculture fell by 14.5 percentage points, or 40 per cent. Industry gained 15.9 percentage points, or 50.2 per cent. Within industry, manufacturing rose 9.2 points, or 35.4 per cent. Tertiary activities merely held their own, although undoubtedly there was some internal shift favoring modern activities at the expense of family enterprise and own-account labor.

Equally impressive changes in economic structure are evident from long-term comparisons of relative industry contributions to total output of manufacturing. Again, it is useful to employ annual averages for selected five-year intervals, starting with 1901-1905. For reasons noted earlier, these years involve the beginnings of Italy's sustained "big push" toward full industrialization. And to lay bare the underlying structural changes, the available data for the separate industries can be grouped as basic, medium, and small scale. Table 86 presents the results.

TABLE 85. Comparative sector contributions to total value added, five-year averages and by particular years, 1921–1960 [a] (per cent)

| Year | Agriculture, forestry, and fishing | Industry | | Tertiary activities |
		Manufacturing	All industry	
1921–25	40.6	26.7	31.1	28.3
1926–30	36.2	26.0	31.7	32.1
1931–35	30.1	23.0	30.7	39.2
1936–40	29.6	27.6	34.2	36.2
1946–50	35.8	33.0	39.4	24.8
1955–60	21.7	35.2	47.6	30.6
1950	31.7	34.4	41.8	26.6
1955	26.0	35.2	46.5	27.5
1960	19.0	36.0	48.4	32.6

[a] See notes to Table 83.
Source: (1921–55) Indagine statistica, p. 246; (1960) Relazione generale, 1957–1961.

Although not necessarily universal, one of the typical signs of spreading industrialization is the rise of industries producing iron and steel, machinery and transportation equipment, and producers' chemicals—all of which are usually characterized by large-scale plants with substantial fixed investments. Another indicator is the declining relative importance of food production, reflecting Engel's principle that as average real income rises per head for a comparable group, the percentage outlay on food drops. Also, as growth proceeds the comparative importance of very small firms diminishes—those that for technical reasons cluster in handicraft and related industries, such as wood-working, tanning and leather-working.

These phenomena are clearly apparent in Table 85. Over the six decades, basic industry soared from a poor third to an unassailable first-rank position among the four categories of manufacturing. In 1901–1905, it accounted for only 20 per cent of value added, as against almost 53 per cent in 1956–1960. Iron and steel, nonferrous metals, and chemicals were the sustaining centers of expansion, while durable goods (metal products) had completed their big

TABLE 86. The changing structure of industry contributions to total value added in manufacturing production, in selected five-year annual averages, 1901–1905—1956–1960 (per cent)

Industry group and industry	Relative contribution				
	1901– 1905	1925– 1930	1951– 1955	1956– 1960	1960
A. Basic industry:	19.8	38.1	47.3	52.4	53.7
Primary metals	3.1	5.2	8.6	9.4	8.8
Metal products	15.0	27.8	24.8	27.3	29.0
Chemicals	1.7	5.1	13.9	15.7	15.9
B. Medium industry:	32.1	25.6	19.6	17.0	17.0
Textiles	26.7	20.3	12.0	9.6	9.8
Construction materials	3.6	2.8	4.1	4.4	4.4
Paper and rubber [a]	1.8	2.5	3.5	3.0	2.8
C. Small-scale industry:	44.8	33.7	27.6	24.6	23.0
Foods, beverages and tobacco	29.6	24.6	18.8	16.7	15.2
Clothing, leather and wood [a]	15.2	9.1	8.8	7.9	7.8
D. Miscellaneous [a]	3.3	2.6	5.5	6.1	6.2

[a] Data not available for components separately. "Miscellaneous" includes films, records, and small industries n.e.c.

Source: (1901–55) *Indagine statistica*, pp. 212–215; (1956–60) compiled from annual data in *Relazione generale*, 1956–1961.

jump in relative position by the twenties. In contrast, small-scale industry, which contributed 45 per cent of value added in 1901–1905, dropped steadily to less than a quarter by the end of the fifties. Here the explanation is the lessening relative importance of food production. Finally, medium-scale industry, which held a strong second place at the turn of the century by contributing a third of gross output, ended up in a weak third place, producing just over a sixth of the total. Its relative decline is attributable entirely to the textile industry, once the dominant factor in Italian manufacturing. In 1901–1905, textiles contributed more to total product than the whole of basic industry. By the twenties they were already in eclipse, and in the late fifties their share had fallen to less than 10 per cent—below metal products and chemicals, and now only slightly ahead of primary metals and clothing, leather and wood.

CONCLUSION

Since 1900, the growth of industry as a whole relative to agriculture, and the growth of basic industry relative to small-scale production of consumers' goods within manufacturing, have indeed been impressive. At the turn of the century, industry contributed only 0.44 lira of value product compared to each 1.00 lira produced in agriculture. By 1960, this ratio had been dramatically inverted, to become 2.55 : 1.00. Within manufacturing alone, in 1900 basic industry turned out only 0.44 lira for each 1.00 obtained in small-scale production. By 1960, this ratio, too, had been sharply reversed, now standing at 2.32 : 1.00. Within just six decades, Italy had converted from a predominantly agricultural and handicraft economy to an industrial one, while within manufacturing basic industry had become the primary sector of production.

Along with gradual improvement in the quality of the labor force, capital formation was the indispensable practical instrument through which this remarkable transition was accomplished, because it permitted the introduction of new technology and the expansion of productive capacity. In consequence, resource productivities could rise throughout the system, at rates exceeding the growth of population, in turn permitting a steady rise in per capita incomes that fostered the redirection of final demand toward manufactured producers' and consumers' goods. Meanwhile, agriculture was able to increase its resource productivity and its absolute output, despite substantial loss of relative position, and accordingly to release a substantial amount of labor to other uses, particularly after 1945.

However, while Italy has made impressive progress in the transformation of her economy during the first six decades of the twentieth century, that transition is by no means complete. The south and the islands have barely embarked upon modernization, while elsewhere backwardness still prevails in industry, agriculture and trade. The immediate cause is that the accumulation of capital has not been adequate on the whole, nor its geographic and functional distribution favorable, for effecting full economic unification. As a result, serious income gaps remain, while the employment problem continues to be acute.

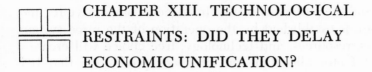

CHAPTER XIII. TECHNOLOGICAL RESTRAINTS: DID THEY DELAY ECONOMIC UNIFICATION?

Although the years following fiscal-monetary stabilization in Italy recorded an unexpectedly high and well-sustained rate of growth in real gross product, a notable improvement in living standards and (until 1962) a strengthening of the foreign exchange reserve, full economic unification remains far from complete. The dual wage and employment system is still prominent. Important segments of agriculture, industry, and trade still await modernization. Furthermore, despite rapid increase of output—indeed, perhaps because of it and because of its changing composition—overt, disguised, and part-time unemployment continued severe throughout the fifties.

In degree and in kind, these continuing signs of incomplete industrialization differ markedly from the symptoms one can observe even in highly advanced industrial countries with similar settings—for example, England and Holland. In a major way, they can be accounted for in Italy by restricted capital formation (including investment from abroad), and cultural, geographic, and locational factors strongly favoring the north. Nonetheless, several expert observers have suggested that perhaps for many decades additional obstructive forces have been at work, among them technology, policies affecting wages and prices, impediments to the mobility of labor, and the structure of final demand. Each of them requires careful analysis and appraisal if the explanation for the still divided economy is to be rounded out.

STRUCTURAL DISEQUILIBRIUM AND THE COMPETITIVE MODEL

Three kinds of structural disequilibrium. In any economy, the distribution of scarce productive factors among competing uses implies both a pattern of goods production and of income distribution. This set of relations identifies the structure of the economy and reflects the level of technology, the relative supplies of capital and labor, and the pattern of wants. In a freely competitive regime, this structure is established by the operation of the price system. Given tastes, resources, and technology, free choice will create a structure of factor allocation and of goods production that balances supplies and demands throughout the system. If the country is open to international trade, then its economic structure will adapt itself to world prices and factor returns, by exports and imports, and by the movement of capital and labor into or out of the territory. Hypothetically, balance can still occur, although it will differ in kind from that of a closed economy, as any protectionist knows.

Of course the histories of the industrial countries do not show convincingly that a comparatively unhampered competitive price system works with such perfection. Because the determining data of the structure—tastes, factor supplies, and technology—all undergo constant and largely unforeseen change in time, complete equilibrium is never achieved, although market forces generally would work toward balance if free to operate. But besides this, none of these countries has ever had a competitive system in the ideal sense. Passing over the usual cases of monopoloid product markets and of doctoring by the state in favor of certain groups, the experience of these nations permits us to identify three major types of structural disequilibrium that can cause serious trouble for domestic policy.[1]

The first is at the factor level when "modern" and "backward" sectors coexist, showing up in agriculture, trade and industry. Here the familiar indicia are those mentioned before—contrasting techniques of production, organizational forms, and incomes per worker. Beneath these is the more subtle fact that ratios of labor to capital per unit of product will also differ sharply. In general, highly labor-intensive coefficients will dominate in the "backward" sector, and capital-intensive ones in the "modern." The crux of the matter is that relative factor prices diverge between the two. Wages are low in one, high in the other, and the rate of interest will show the reverse. In turn, this accounts for the double set of technical coefficients, which are consciously introduced by the two separate groups of producers to adjust the respective marginal productivities of labor and of capital to the two divergent levels of wages and interest rates in effect. If there is intervention to bring up the level of wages in the laggard zones, it will cause unemployment, while attempts to raise capital coefficients will make trouble for the balance of payments.

Second, although dualism need not be important, basic disequilibrium exists because throughout the system prevailing ratios of factor prices generally ediverge seriously from relative factor supplies. In other words, at least one factor is not available at its equilibrium price but in fact is overvalued. The usual example is the price of labor under collective bargaining or state intervention, although any other factor could serve theoretically. Introduction of a supercompetitive level of labor costs will bias technical coefficients toward the capital-intensive end of the spectrum, because, in their effort to maximize returns, employers will economize on labor to bring up its marginal product to equality with its wage.

For the short run, the problem becomes one of partial adaptation. Capital is a stock incapable of much increase, and is mostly fixed and specific in character. As the variable factor, labor will be employed in less than socially optimal amounts; indeed, some establishments may simply close down. Either way, employment contracts. The labor so displaced will have nowhere to go except into unemployment, or underemployment on own-account jobs, or light-works projects undertaken by government, since the distribution of the capital stock is already fixed and offers no openings. On the goods side, capital-intensive products will be under comparatively less cost pressure, and will gain an artificially induced comparative advantage for export and domestic sales. Labor-intensive products will be imported in larger amounts and will suffer greater domestic contraction as consumer substitution exerts its leverage.

In the longer run, the flow of new and freely disposable savings will enlarge the scope for enterpreneurial adaptation, permitting even more substitution of capital for labor. Since labor will probably continue to be overvalued, capital formation will make for still higher capital coefficients all around, and will concentrate in capital-intensive products. The rate of labor displacement will be high, while the rate of absorption will be forced down by the double thrust exerted by both factor and product substitution toward low labor-using coefficients. On top of this, since population will be growing, the available labor force itself must increase, which will compound the problem. In all probability, substitution effects will outweigh the offsetting influence of factor complementarity invoked by growing total output. In consequence, labor will continue to be redundant.[2]

To cope with the problems created by factor price distortions, domestic policy must be stretched or mutilated in Procrustean fashion, in an abortive effort to serve incompatible ends. If full employment is sought, it might be had through expansion of effective demand, but only by inflating costs, increasing imports and decreasing exports, and thereby upsetting the balance of payments. Over the longer run, full employment might be attained by importing capital and exporting labor, adjusting relative factor supplies to their relative prices; or by forcing down real wages to induce the substitution of more labor-intensive methods. But for either of these routes the way is long, hard, and not very promising. If, instead, the immediate goal is equilibrium in the balance of payments, then full employment must go.

The third case is structural disequilibrium caused by factor immobilities. Here the trouble originates from the slow response of capital and labor to a changing pattern of demands. Much capital is embodied in fixed and specific forms, for turning out particular goods, and cannot quickly be shifted to other uses. The counterpart on the labor side involves workers with investments in special skills and with a preference for certain industries or residential locations. Once attached, they do not readily move. Beyond this, workers released by modernization in agriculture are often occupationally immobile for lack of education, requisite skills, and aptitude for the discipline required of industrial employments. In consequence, pronounced demand shifts within the economy will leave as their residue excess supplies of capital and labor, perhaps coterminously with deficient supplies available to other uses. Correcting this kind of unemployment may require a superheated economy of inflationary demand, with adverse results for the balance of payments. Indeed, trouble will arise in the foreign balance in any event if the shift of demand should involve loss of important export markets. And either way factor immobilities imply domestic imbalances in resource allocation, in goods production, and in factor earnings.

Disequilibrium and the competitive model. The competitive model is not tantamount to a photograph of an actual economy. Quite the contrary. It is a methodological device for representing conceptually the equilibrating forces that would come into play under hypothetical conditions of free choice. As such, it is an essential analytical technique for conditional predictions of outcomes and for isolating the effects of various obstructions to competition in practice. Both in its assumptions and in its deductions it contains normative implications as well, but these do not concern us here.

In strict truth, there is no competitive model, but rather a group of them, each dependent upon a common logic of maximization by individual choosers, presuming that choice is free. Divergencies derive from the selection of particular problems—for instance, attainment of equilibrium at various levels from the single consumer to the whole economy—and from the special assumptions introduced—presence or absence of monopolistic elements, degree of knowledge, time allowed for adjustment responses, and so on.[3]

How, then, are we to interpret these three cases of structural disequilibrium from the standpoint of competitive analysis? The fulcrum upon which that analysis turns consists of the assumptions that all prices are flexible, that factors of production are free to move, and that all choosing agents have reasonable knowledge of the alternatives open to them. In turn, these strategic presuppositions lead directly to the concept of substitution, which provides the required thrust to the whole advance toward equilibrium.

In the competitive view of economic behavior, substitution goes on continuously both at the factor and at the goods levels, embracing in the former both resource suppliers (labor, capital) and resource users (entrepreneurs), and in the latter the purveyors of goods (again entrepreneurs) and buyers of goods (entrepreneurs and consumers).

Consider, first, the factor level. Disregarding both costs of movement and varying disutilities among particular employments, labor of homogeneous grade will distribute itself among competing uses so that its wage is equalized among the alternatives. In other words, workers substitute employers for each other in search of maximum returns. At the same time, employers substitute workers for each other, for the same purpose. The same process applies to capital, land, and other factors, effected similarly through resource flows invoked by marginal owners and users in search of best returns. Under the assumptions stated, a single uniform price, and only one, will exist for each class of factor, clearing the market and equilibrating its demand and supply. It will be seen at once that competitive forces, if free to operate, will establish a set of factor price ratios that express the market options open to all entrepreneurs. To maximize returns, they in turn will adopt the technical coefficients consistent with these competitive price ratios. Alternatively put, these data will determine their least-cost combinations, given technology and budget restraints.

Then there is the goods side. Final consumers confront a hierarchy of classes of goods, each with alternative sources of supply. Concurrent substitution by sellers and buyers also invokes a uniform, market-clearing price for each item. Each consumer has a preference system and is given a set of prices at which alternative goods are available, and these together will determine the allocation of his income. More strictly, to maximize satisfaction he will apportion his income in such a way that he equates his subjective marginal rates of substitution with the market rates at which alternative products are available. Thus the processes of substitution here are identical with those in the factor market.

Now let us consider the destinies of the three kinds of structural disequilibrium when competition is effective.

Take, first, the dual economy case, or unequal returns to labor. The double dichotomy in factor price ratios and in technical coefficients could be only temporary at most. Labor would move into the higher wage sector, competing with workers already there, bringing down their wages while bringing up their level in the backward one. It would now pay the employers in the modern sector to shift to more labor-intensive coefficients, economizing on capital; and for those in the backward sector to take the opposite tack, economizing on labor. Twofold factor substitution would be at work—low for high-wage labor, and between capital and labor in both sectors. Factor allocations and goods production would take new and balanced patterns, and full employment would result. Income differences among workers would still remain because of skill differences and the like, but the basic gap would now be closed.

If everything really were this easy, one could hardly call this a case of structural disequilibrium, since the very concept suggests something formidable, intractable, and persistent—and not easily corrected by the beneficent operation of market forces. Cases of this kind are not hard to find in the actual world, and the clue to their explanation lies in impediments to effective competition itself. What really is being talked about here is the failure of market processes to transmit promptly and effectively the methods and outlook of capitalistic rationality to the large, primitive zones of the economy. In this respect, it is almost fatuous to speak of effective over-all competition, because the economy consists of two compartments that are largely sealed off from each other by political, cultural, and geographic barriers. These deny to the backward zone the effective penetration of modernizing capital and entrepreneurship. They also bar the organization of adequately interpenetrating labor markets, hence the transmission of knowledge essential to the emergence of equilibrating labor flows.

By stressing factor immobilities, we seem to be merging the first case of structural disequilibrium with the third. In truth, there is a close bond, except that dualism involves factor immobility of a special kind, one that stems not from *simpliste* concepts of ignorance, transfer costs, and the like—which apply to well-developed systems of wage labor—but instead one that is the built-in consequence of an entire cultural apparatus. What we have in fact are two different societies, with two systems of institutional organization, under the same roof. As Cavour and his colleagues were to find in Italy after 1861, political union and cultural union need not go together. If not, the prospect for economic unification approaches a nullity, without deliberate action toward that end. Indeed, in extreme cases of dualism, market forces themselves can perpetuate division—for example, the backwash effects of geographically concentrated growth, and the incentive problem with a rising man-land ratio in the backward zone. In both cases, the line of causation runs the wrong way.

In other words, there is a profound difference in kind between the industrialization of a comparatively open and newly settled domain (Canada, the United States), and the conversion of an old and tradition-bound society to an industrial system (the European countries, India, and many former colonial lands). The former case is one of development; the latter, one of cultural transformation.

Beyond this, the divergence in wage levels is usually a sign of noncompetitive wage-fixing in the advanced sector, and quite effective competition in the labor markets of the backward one.[4] After all, even against statutory obstacles considerable exodus goes on all the time from subsistence farming. But barring rapid expansion of the progressive sector, there is hope for jobs only if the migrants accept lower wages. If this fails, we can infer that wages are being kept up by anticompetitive forces—trade unions, state intervention, inertia, and so on. Here enters the decisive collateral fact: neither collective bargaining nor state doctoring of labor costs can be of much effect in the soft zones of trade, handicrafts, and services, where family enterprise, tiny firms, and own-account labor dominate. The costs and difficulties of enforcement will be simply too high, for the unions or the state. In consequence, labor flowing outward from the farms will largely end up here and in government light-works projects (at low capital coefficients), or in unemployment. The wage gap will not close, and indeed may widen. This is the meaning of bifurcation of the labor market, both as cause and consequence of economic dualism itself.

The second case, over-all distortion of factor price ratios relative to comparative supplies, and without significant dualism, could not exist if competition were effective. Labor could not be overvalued relative to its equilibrium wage, because forcing the wage level upward requires anticompetitive techniques—trade unionism, minimum wage laws, and statutory social security charges to employers. By assumption, these are all ruled out. In consequence, technical ratios would line up with factor price ratios by adaptation of the former to the latter, and both sets would be congruent with relative factor supplies. Any unemployment would have to be voluntary. That is, some workers would freely elect to withhold some or all of their labor because the ruling marginal real wage falls short of the marginal disutility of work. Over the longer run, if the rate of capital formation outruns the rate of increase in the labor force, the capital coefficient would rise per unit of labor. In turn, this would raise the marginal productivity of labor, and, through this, the level of real wages.

There need be no business cycle and no involuntary unemployment in this model, for three reasons. Each of them underscores its practical absurdity, but a model may be practically irrelevant, yet have high scientific usefulness. First, factor mobilities will be high enough to allow prompt responses to shifts in demands. Further, the range of wants is at all times elastic enough to exclude temporary saturation problems, while the slow rise of capital coefficients poses no difficulties of secular stagnation. Finally, factor and product prices are fully flexible, hence respond promptly enough to assure early return to full employment following any serious initial disturbance. Since deflation is a feasible policy in these strange circumstances, there need be no conflict between having full employment and equilibrium in the balance of payments at the same time.

Last, there is the factor immobility case, already largely anticipated. From the standpoint of competitive analysis, the basic problem is one of time and information. That is, in the real world it takes time to recover capital from declining fixed uses, and time for labor to adapt itself to different employments, often in new industries or locations. Thus, so far as time is concerned, even an effectively competitive economy can suffer from structural maladjustments arising from demand shifts. However, the absence of artificial barriers to entry and of imposed price and wage rigidities makes adaptation faster and more thorough. As for knowledge, competition presumes well-organized markets and free dissemination of information regarding factor and product demands and availabilities. In consequence, there can be no long-run structural disequilibrium involving factor immobilities—only an endless series of short-run adjustments to a shifting pattern of demand.[5]

The problem of fixed coefficients in production. Under effective competition, all prices are flexible, and all factors are free and willing to move. By means of a series of marginal substitutions at both the factor and the goods levels, the economy can advance toward over-all structural balance, although such equilibrium never actually will be attained, because the underlying data are continuously changing.

Against this it has been argued that factor substitution may be foreclosed by a supposed technologically imposed rigidity of required input coefficients per unit of obtainable product. The notion of such rigidity has been developed for different contexts: as a description of factor input relations for the whole economy; or as applicable to each separate product over the entire range; or confined to certain sectors of the economy. In some versions, the concept is modified to allow for greater technological flexibility with increase of adjustment time, or for the possibility of discrete, rather than absolutely fixed or continuously variable, input ratios relative to a given quantity of fixed output. However, in all cases the ruling principle is that technological constraints can obstruct factor substitution, and may enforce a structural imbalance that market forces cannot overcome, even if they are adequately competitive.

The strongest version of the case has been developed for the economywide level in connection with postwar discussion of problems of balanced and sustainable over-all growth. As put forward by Harrod and Domar, growth theory pivots upon a particular kind of general production function, one that relates potential output in the system uniquely to the availability of capital.[6] While labor also enters implicitly, the strategic element is the productivity ratio, which presumes that there is a technically fixed relationship between an increment of product and its required, associated increment of capital. Capacity output at a given moment then becomes determined by the quantity of capital at hand. If, then, capital formation occurs, this ratio fixes the successively higher limits of capacity production in a growing economy, linking them rigorously to the corresponding increments to capital stock.[7]

Here matters can become complicated. If the labor force fails to increase by the "right" amount relative to the increase of capital, or if its productivity fails to expand enough to fill in for the short-fall in labor supply, realized output will not be large enough to make full use of capital stock, although labor itself could be fully employed. By contrast, if labor supply rises more than capital, then since output cannot exceed capacity as determined by the larger capital stock, some labor must be unemployed. Further, if the productivity of labor increases at the same time (less labor being required per unit of output), then the technological unemployment already created will be made that much worse.[8] Note further that the underlying technical constraint precludes effective factor substitution, even if factor prices are free to move. In consequence, structural unemployment of either factor can develop and persist.

Hamberg has approached the problem in a similar way but has made the analysis somewhat more explicit.[9] There are, he asserts, two conceptually distinct required rates of growth in real national income, and these may diverge in actuality. One of them, E, is that rate required to assure full employment of a growing labor force whose productivity is also increasing. The other, U, is the rate required to assure full utilization of a growing capital stock—what he terms "full capacity growth," as distinguished from "full employment growth." If $E / U = 1$, balanced growth occurs, with continuing full utilization of both labor and capital. But if $E / U > 1$, then capital formation falls short of increased labor supply at increasing labor productivity, and there will be technological unemployment. If, instead, $E / U < 1$, labor becomes progressively more inadequate for the growing capital stock, and some capital will be made idle.

However, both discrepancies in comparative required rates of increase in national income become possible only on the assumption of a fixed capital-to-output ratio, O, which determines the potential increase of output for a given increment to capital stock. As in the Harrod-Domar models, then, the decisive element is this peculiar economywide production function, which uniquely relates the quantities of capital and of labor in fixed proportions relative to any given output. Put alternatively, the isoquants in this social production function contain only corner-solutions whose vertices form a straight line from the origin. Abandon this stringent presupposition, and capacity output will depend now upon the initial stocks of labor and capital; net saving and net increase in the labor force during the period; the degree of improvement in labor productivity; and the price ratios prevailing between capital and labor.[10] Full utilization of both capital and labor now become continuously possible, provided that net investment is adequate at all times to absorb all net saving at the rising level of potential output.

As Domar says, there were good methodological reasons for adopting so rigid an aggregative production function, to permit the initial formal development of growth theory. But the idea must be used with care—as an analytical device, and not as a description of reality.[11] Trouble begins because methodological convenience requires strong and potentially treacherous assumptions that can become converted implicitly to empirical necessities, when in fact these necessities need not prevail at all. In truth, it borders upon the absurd to deny all possibility of substitution, either directly as among factors, or indirectly among factors through goods. To do so is to drain all the economics from the adjustment problem, and also to overlook abundant evidence that technical coefficients vary greatly as among goods, and that in the over-all sense they change through time.

In addition to the general case just considered, the notion of fixed coefficients has been applied to lower levels of aggregation, such as single products and sectors within an economy.[12] Although it would be a profitless exercise to review all these cases in detail, they require some consideration because they have been used to extract explanatory hypotheses regarding phenomena frequently observed in underdeveloped or partially developed countries—in particular, the malignant combination of chronic unemployment, high capital coefficients for certain products, and an ever-present threat of inflation and disequilibrium in the balance of payments; all of which describe the Italian case for much of the postwar period. In all instances, the strategic principle in the argument is that technical requirements supposedly obstruct factor substitution. In turn, this leads to structural disequilibrium in which at least one factor is said to be redundant, and for which reduction of its price is declared to be an unlikely corrective. In other words, the trouble derives from technology, and not from market imperfections, although these may make things worse.

Suppose, first, that the goods available in an economy can be produced in variable amounts, but only with fixed proportions of labor and capital per unit of each product; also that technical ratios differ among these alternative goods. In consequence, substitution can operate only at the goods level. Since internal factor substitution is ruled out, the allocation of labor and capital among competing uses will be controlled jointly by the structure of final demand and by the range of technical ratios available. Suppose, next, that these labor-to-capital ratios extend from $1 : 1$ (labor-intensive goods) to $1 : 5$ (capital-intensive). It follows that if demand were concentrated entirely upon capital-intensive goods, far more capital would be required than in the reverse case. If, further, demand conditions dictated that the average ratio for all goods were, say, $1 : 4$, then if labor were to be fully employed, capital supply would have to provide four units for each worker. If capital falls short, some labor will become unemployed. True, if wages can fall, the product price structure can be warped some-what toward labor-intensive goods. Capital then could be stretched over more units of labor, and unemployment would fall. However, it is conceivable that even if the wage could fall to zero, the malign combined effects of demand structure and of technology might still leave some redundant labor. In short, there is a technologically imposed conflict between relative factor supplies and demands, which the market cannot resolve.[13]

The case is extreme and of no practical consequence. Examples of fixed coefficients even for the production of particular products are notoriously elusive in the actual world, a fact conceded by most of those who have examined the problem. Man-shifts can be increased, machinery can be operated continuously, production lines varied in speed, and indirect labor used more or less. Even more dubious is the notion that all goods fall under such technical constraints. Matters simply do not work this way in any actual economy. Man's ingenuity in creating new products, in devising new methods of producing old ones, and in breaking bottlenecks constantly provides the necessary slack to permit the adjustments that substitution provides. Perhaps for this reason, those who approach the problem of factor redundancy from the standpoint of fixed coefficients soon bring market imperfections into their analysis.

Short of this expedient, it is possible to relax the assumption of a single fixed coefficient for each product and to suppose instead that there may be at least two such "processes" available for making each individual product.[14] Each process technically requires a set of fixed factor proportions, but these differ. At one extreme is a capital-intensive process, defined on the production surface as a ray from the origin lying close to the capital axis. At the other is a labor-intensive one, similarly defined but falling much closer to the labor axis. The two rays set the outer boundaries of the field of entrepreneurial choice. If it is impossible to use mixed combinations, then for any given quantity of desired output the choice must be limited to two points, one for each alternative process. In other words, the entrepreneur faces two corner solutions, each representing the required relative quantities of the two factors. Given a factor price ratio, the tangency condition for maximizing returns will dictate which combination will be chosen.[15] Furthermore, if the "distance" separating the combinations is great, it will require a very large drop in the price of the lesser used factor to induce the entrepreneur to shift to the combination that employs it more intensively. Indeed, even if it were technically possible to adopt mixtures of the two processes—meaning that a continuous isoquant with a constant marginal rate of technical substitution now joins the two original points—it will not pay to select a combination along this segment unless the factor price ratio should happen to coincide with it. If not, a solution at one of the vertices would still be adopted.

Everything depends, of course, upon the number of alternative processes for making the product, the "distance" between them for each desired quantity of product, and the possibility of using mixed combinations between the rays that identify each process. The greater the range of choice among available processes, the less important become both the separation problem and its concomitant, the necessity of large changes in relative factor prices to call forth significant factor substitution. Thus even if we retain the assumption that the production alternatives are discrete—which may be more realistic for some industries—we can approach a situation that will approximate the case of continuous variation.

In any event, the practical importance of large technological gaps cannot be determined a priori, but only from evidence that so far is notorious in its scantiness. What is in question, then, is not the logical validity of arguments that presume such gaps, but the empirical truth of their conclusions. Their truth cannot be established simply by pointing to chronic unemployment as a fact. There are other ways to account for the same thing. Hence the choice of hypothesis must be based upon grounds more substantial than casual empiricism.

In a technical tour de force, R. S. Eckaus has extended the gap case to develop a two-sector model for underdeveloped countries with dual economies and overpopulation.[16] His method employs the Edgeworth-Bowley box diagram, which permits him to consider two "goods," each representing the composite product of a "sector." In the first approximation, each sector offers its entrepreneurs a field of choice whose outer bounds are described by one capital-intensive and one labor-intensive process, with the added possibility of mixed factor combinations between these extremes. The two fields partially overlap. Assuming that for any desired quantity of product x we desire the maximum possible associated amount of y, we thereby fix a point on an efficiency locus function. Subject to technical constraints, factor supplies, and the output-maximizing condition, as we progressively increase x and decrease y, we can derive this locus function, which then can be transformed easily into a production-possibility curve. In the nature of the case, this curve will consist of cornered straight-line segments, and will be concave to the origin. If we neglect income-redistribution effects and adopt the expedient of a community indifference curve to express demand structure, tangency of this demand function at some point on the production-possibility curve will then determine the comparative optimal outputs of x and y.

More important, it turns out that at one of the extreme segments of the possibility curve capital will be redundant, and at the other labor will be redundant. If demand conditions fix tangency at a point strongly favorable to capital-intensive goods, then maximizing the value of output will dictate some unemployment of labor. Full employment and maximum output become incompatible ends, while full employment cannot be achieved by inflating effective demand or by reducing the real wage. Still more important, redundancy of either factor is made possible only because the outer limits of the two superimposed fields of entrepreneurial choice on the production surface are rigidly set by technology, and supposedly cannot be widened. This, then, is the crux of the matter.

Using the same technique, Eckaus next assumes that in one sector continuous variation in factor substitution is now possible, while, in the other, factor combinations remain fixed as before. Again labor redundancy can occur at one extreme of the efficiency function, imposed jointly by technological limitations in the fixed sector, and by production-efficiency limits to substitution in the other. Once more, demand conditions may dictate a conflict between full employment and maximum output, for which there is no practical reconciliation. Finally, if market imperfections are now introduced—supercompetitive wages and factor immobilities—these will further narrow the field of choice for input-combinations, at the same time distorting the efficiency function. In consequence, the possibility curve will be thrust further inward toward the origin, meaning that output and income must be less than what technical conditions alone would permit. Moreover, this loss of output can be conjoined to technologically imposed redundancy of labor as well.

The rigor and elegance of this analysis make it undeniably attractive, but it is far from invulnerable in its practical conclusions.

Most of the objections to the theory of a technologically imposed redundancy of labor already have been stated. At most, the notion of fixed coefficients is simply a supplementary hypothesis to that of market imperfections—to help account for chronic unemployment and persistent dualism of economic structure.[17] If an acceptable explanation can be had with the latter tools, aided by adequate recognition of noneconomic factors, it is needless to complicate matters. Instead, Occam's razor ought to come into play.

Beyond this, in order to develop a general theoretical scheme, this procedure risks converting the formal implications of the inner logic of an abstract model into empirical necessities in the real world. At some point, these implications must be tested. It is not enought merely to illustrate them with casually drawn examples, particularly when these accord equally well with simpler hypotheses.

The matter of evidence is decisive.[18] Does the economic world actually behave as the model suggests? The notion that there are fixed outer limits to the choice of processes in any line or sector of production is quite unconvincing. Equally unpersuasive is the supposition that the gaps between alternative processes must be large. Aside from these limits and broad gaps, which empirically can be no more than statistical averages at levels of aggregation above the single establishment, the case for factor redundancy collapses completely.

This collapse is dictated by the facts of economic life. Resourceful entrepreneurs and imaginative engineers are always finding escape from technical constraints, bending technology to their efficiency-seeking objectives by adjusting factor proportions to their changing relative prices. In this, they have the help of the pure scientist, who provides the advances in knowledge that make possible new production functions in all branches of activity. In truth, the very dynamics of industrial progress are fatal to the notion of rigid factor coefficients.

The older, more industrialized countries of northwest Europe long since have achieved well-unified economies. The work of transforming their systems was complex and lengthy. It was prompted by the new outlook of the Renaissance. It was supported in diverse ways by governments, and its practical accomplishment was the joint achievement of scientists, engineers, and entrepreneurs. All these nations experienced, and continue to experience, problems of unemployment and, to some extent, of dualism. However, there is little reason to suppose that the causes of these difficulties lie in purely technical restrictions against factor substitition.

More than this, the record of industrial history suggests no reason to conclude that Italy's case is different in these decisive respects. If production coefficients could be changed elsewhere, they could be changed there. Where Italy does diverge is in her divisions of economic structure, which are far more deeply rooted, and much more resistant to the forces of economic unification. For these problems, there are much more plausible explanations at hand.

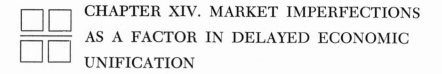

CHAPTER XIV. MARKET IMPERFECTIONS AS A FACTOR IN DELAYED ECONOMIC UNIFICATION

The twin problems of chronic unemployment and perpetuation of substantial divisions within the Italian economy pose the question: to what extent were impediments to effective competition in factor and product markets responsible? The market obstructions in question are two: obstacles to the free movement of capital and labor among alternative employments, and enforcement of non-competitive wages and prices. Obviously, the former in part will flow from the latter.

These obstructions underlie the three types of structural disequilibrium earlier considered in the abstract. As we have seen, disequilibrium in these senses in no way depends upon the presence of fixed production coefficients. At the same time, in some situations structural imbalance itself may be less an independent force than a reflection of other, more fundamental influences—cultural and geographic factors, and a secularly restricted supply of capital. Clearly, its significance will depend upon the extent to which the economic unification wrought by industrialization has proceeded. For this reason, the role of market imperfections in Italian development should be considered within an historical context, although necessarily a brief one.

BEFORE WORLD WAR II

Primitive industrial and social unrest, 1890–1914. In his careful study of industrial growth in Italy during 1881–1913, Alexander Gerschenkron concludes that the "big push" occurred between 1896 and 1908. However, he contends that in comparison with other nations passing through a similar phase, the Italian rate of expansion was lower on geometric average, and also quite irregular. After 1908, moreover, the mean annual rate of advance fell by almost two thirds.[1] Among the factors that would account for this are tariff policy after 1886, the decline of railroad building, and lack of a clear-cut ideology of industrialization. Gerschenkron also emphasizes the tendency of real wages to rise simultaneously with the big push, instead of following as elsewhere. In the background, he suggests, were the political and agrarian disorders of the nineties, which led in turn to Giolitti's conciliatory policy toward the unions, and the strike wave that ensued.

An equally perceptive scholar, Vera Lutz, is even more forthright. In her view, the early union push for higher real wages was "perhaps the most important element" accounting for delayed industrialization. From a lengthier perspective, such delay, she believes, "Probably . . . must be attributed to the early growth of trade union power and the setting of wages above the 'natural' level, and partly to restrictions on internal migration, such as were imposed under fascism." [2]

Certainly the period of 1890–1908 was disturbed. This was when Italy was entering upon the industrial age. With the formation of a market for wage labor, all the issues of labor-management relations became precipitated, in a quite fluid and primitive environment. They found diverse modes of expression: a sharp rise in the strike rate; frequent recourse to the general strike; numerous outlaw strikes and other forms of direct action; formation of many national unions; and emergence of a central union federation. To all this, government's response was erratic, beginning with crude attempts at suppression, and then, with Giolitti's second accession to the premiership in late 1903, efforts to conciliate the unions and to fit them into national life as legitimate regulated associations.[3]

In this turbulent period, the labor movement itself was deeply divided ideologically—into Syndicalists, Marxian Socialists, and the more moderate advocates of straight collective bargaining—a continuing characteristic that it has never lost. In its political life, the nation suffered from similar forms of factionalism, made even worse by reactionary extremism on the right. At that time, the critical weakness, as Giolitti saw with great insight, was the lack of an adequate and responsible middle class, to supply balance and stable leadership to political affairs.[4]

In part, the marked instability of political and economic institutions reflected a trait that is peculiarly Italian. In the main, however, it was the inevitable counterpart of industrialism in its nonage. Older forms of economic life were under increasing strain and were being displaced. But those who were directly affected could only grope toward more suitable responses to new conditions. As the Fascist period was later to show, there certainly were critical, underlying weaknesses in the structure and quality of national life. But the commotion and confusion of those earlier years were less a pathological sign than manifestations of the initial transition to an industrial society.

How important was all this to the delay in the transformation? Did labor unrest and the level of real wages retard the speed of economic change?

The suggestion that labor troubles in these years had the Italian industrialists quaking in their boots has not been proved. Between 1899 and 1908, when the conflicts were most intense, gross real investment rose by the geometric rate of 9.4 per cent a year (Table 87). True, investment fell absolutely in 1902, 1904, and 1908, while the industrial strike rate (measured by numbers involved) jumped in the first and last of these years. But it also soared in 1901, 1906, and 1907, and investment increased in all three, in two of them very substantially. By contrast, a somewhat better case for the general proposition can be made for 1908–1913, when the annual rate of increase in real investment fell to just under 6 per cent, while in three of these years the number involved in strikes was well above average.[5]

Accordingly, the period of 1908–1913 provides somewhat greater support for the thesis. However, to sustain it one must argue either that the shock-effects of conflict in the earlier years took time to reflect themselves in business decisions, or that they were cumulative in their impact.

Also, it must be shown that organized labor was numerically important throughout. While the data are sparse, they are sufficient to justify strong doubts. In 1901 the labor force attached to industry (defined officially as manufacturing, extractive industry, and construction) was 3.98 million persons. At the end of 1902, the nonagricultural membership in national unions was reported at only 240,000. In 1908 the official figure for all union members, including agriculture, stood at 934,000. By 1910, the total had declined to 817,000. According to the 1911 census, the industrial labor force amounted to 4.37 million. Clearly, organized labor could claim only a negligible fraction of the industrial work force throughout these troubled years. Admittedly, many strikes were spontaneous and involved some unorganized workers. Even so, in no single year between 1899 and 1913 did the number of workers on strike in industry and services exceed 385,000 (1913).[6]

TABLE 87. Mean geometric annual rates of change in major series, 1899–1913 [a] (per cent)

Series	1899–1908	1908–1913	1899–1913
Wages (industrial):			
Money (daily)	2.63	3.76	3.04
Real (daily)	1.37	3.06	1.97
Industrial production	6.59	2.40	5.08
Unit labor cost	−3.70	1.30	−1.90
Gross real investment	9.40	5.95	8.20
Real GNP per head [b]	2.31	1.76	2.11
Real consumption per head [b]	2.05	0.096	1.35

[a] The year 1899, rather than 1896, was chosen because it is the initial year for the wage series.

Source: Wages from Antonio Fossati, Lavoro e produzione in Italia dalla metà del secolo XVIII alla seconda guerra mondiale (Turin: Giappichelli, 1951), pp. 631, 634; industrial production from Alexander Gerschenkron, "Notes on the Rate of Industrial Growth in Italy, 1881–1913," Journal of Economic History, XV:4 (December, 1955), p. 362; investment, consumption, and GNP from Indagine statistica sullo sviluppo del reddito nazionale dell'Italia dal 1861 al 1956 (Rome: Istituto poligafico dello stato, 1957), pp. 270–271; population figures from Annuario statistico italiano, 1954 (Rome: Istituto poligafico dello stato, 1955), p. 367.

If labor organizations contributed anything to slowing the growth rate at the time, their influence should show up in the behavior of wages and output. Table 87 presents summary evidence. Again there is little positive showing for the highly disturbed years of 1899–1908, although 1908–1913 points somewhat in the other direction. In the former period, industrial output grew at the rate of 6.59 per cent a year. Money wages in industry rose by 2.63 per cent. Despite this, unit labor cost (money wages divided by output) actually fell at the annual rate of −3.7 per cent. Clearly, gross profit margins in industry could have been under no upward pressure from unionism. Nor did the industrialists respond negatively in their production and investment decisions. Quite the contrary.

The years 1908–1913 stand in some contrast. Compared with the earlier period, money and real wages rose much faster. At the same time, the rate of advance in industrial output slackened by nearly two thirds. Moreover, unit labor cost began rising, by 1.3 per cent a year. If unionism actually were exerting a restraining effect on growth, it was at this time and not before.

Perhaps it did. But the role of unionism must be seen in perspective. The real underlying difficulties for Italian economic development in these years and long afterward were lack of capital, the overwhelming backwardness of the south, and a misguided tariff policy. Foreign capital could have supplemented the low absolute volume of home saving, but there were obvious limits to its availability. As for the south, its renovation would have been a bottomless pit for all obtainable fresh capital for years to come, with little prospect of immediately visible returns—and all this at the cost of virtual abandonment of continued expansion in the north. All that need be said regarding tariff policy is that it retarded the growth both of industry and of real income.

If, then, organized labor also played a negative role, it was after 1908, and it could not have been prominent in this larger context or on its own terms. Its small numbers could have rendered it no more than a make-weight on the adverse side in the balance of the nation's economic fortunes in the decades just prior to the First World War.

Fascist policy toward labor and product markets, 1922–1940. The First World War brought to an end Italy's experiment with market-oriented industrialization. Helped along by the conditions in the protracted demobilization period that followed, which the Fascists themselves helped to inflame with their deliberately cultivated program of violence against the trade unions and cooperatives, the Fascists came to power at the end of October 1922.[7] Thereafter until 1945, the growth of the Italian economy was dominated and distorted by the Mussolini dictatorship.

The economics of fascism are a subject for a book in themselves. Nonetheless, there are three areas of policy that profoundly affected the processes of competition in the market place. They concern the labor market and wages, the control of internal migration, and regulation of investment and market prices. Their consequences were to prove both disastrous and enduring. Considering the fact that since World War II Italy has enjoyed less than two decades of comparative political and economic freedom, the progress she has already made is all the more remarkable.

To the extent that the Fascists had any coherent economic doctrine at the inception of their movement in March, 1919, their aim was to destroy the independent trade unions—a goal that proved understandably attractive to many of the big industrialists and landowners. The Fascists executed this program with diverse and opportunistic methods. Before gaining power, they employed a dual tactic of gangster warfare and the building up of rival unions. After 1922, they continued in this vein, but shifted the emphasis to strengthening their own labor syndicates. By that time, however, they could use the state itself as a weapon, bringing it into effective action once Mussolini had regained his confidence following the Matteotti crisis of 1924. In 1925 the syndicates acquired exclusive power to represent workers before employers, which at one stroke destroyed the functional rationale of the old unions. In 1926 the syndicates became legal creatures of the state.[8] As a result, collective agreements were made by parallel labor and employer syndicates, and required official approval. Boycotts, strikes, and lockouts became illegal. In effect as well as intent, wages ceased to be a problem, so far as union pressure was concerned. They could no longer be pressed upward, and, as events were soon to show, they could not even be held at present levels

Probably more by chance than by design, the destruction of union power was followed within a year by stabilization of the lira (December 21, 1927) at nineteen to the dollar—too high for the internal price level. Severe price deflation and mounting unemployment ensued. Thus an overvalued currency compelled devaluation of industrial money wages, which by state compulsion were deliberately forced down by over 9 per cent between 1927 and 1929. Real wages also declined slightly. Since industrial output rose almost 25 per cent at the same time, unit labor costs dropped nearly 30 per cent. Wholesale prices fell only 8 per cent, although by 1929 they were 22.4 per cent below 1926.

At the close of 1929, the world depression had intervened, and the underlying structural problem quickly was supplanted by an acute cyclical one. Like the orthodox democracies of the western world, the Fascist regime proved neither exempt from the crisis nor particularly original in its response. It, too, practiced deflation, and here its clear intent was to force money wages down, without strikes and political resistance. In sharp contrast to 1908–1913, imperfections in the labor market could be employed to depress wages, since their level was set by the political fiat of a totalitarian government.

Between 1929 and 1932, industrial money wages were depressed another 13 per cent. In fact, they continued to shrink until 1936, when they stood 30 per cent below 1926, and 22.3 per cent under 1929. Purely because the cost of living fell faster, real wages could rise a few points between 1929 and 1932, but by 1936 they were 6.2 per cent under 1929.

Perhaps this ruthless slashing of money wages—purchased at so heavy a cost in broader respects—can account for an otherwise curious fact about the Italian phase of the Great Depression—that the decline of real gross product proved both comparatively brief and mild. The bottom was reached in 1931, at a level only 7 per cent below 1929. But this is deceptive, because the main burden was borne by industry and the industrial workers, whose output fell 22.8 per cent, and continued downward for another year, touching bottom at 27.7 per cent under 1929.[9]

In the final reckoning, these costs cannot be disregarded, and they are by no means the whole story. Here was a government that in fourteen years had depressed the real wages of industrial workers by 12 per cent, smashed their organizations, forcibly subjected them to the rule of an official labor front, and caused unemployment which rose with frightening speed after 1927. And then the regime compounded the crime by resorting to colonial imperialism, autarchy, and finally, to a disastrous world war.

But even this does not complete the trend of repression enforced by Fascist labor policy. It also introduced restrictions upon internal migration. The objectives were to tie the peasant to the land, to hold down visible unemployment, and to check the burgeoning growth of the cities. All three reflected the remorseless pressure of rural overpopulation and the slow growth of the industrial sector. As the system unfolded the regime came to rely upon three major devices: official regulation of changes in residence, which was applied to all citizens; introduction of a "job passport" or labor book (*Libretto di lavoro*), required of all employees; and exclusive state control of the hiring and placement of workers (*Disciplina di collocamento*).

In part, the control of internal migration was the practical consequence of one of Mussolini's favorite themes—that the growth of cities (*urbanesimo*) was a pathological development, which weakened the demographic potential of the nation (the cities had lower birth rates, and the regime was strongly emphasizing the value of a large population), and built up a morally degenerate and potentially subversive proletariat.[10] Behind these shopworn rationalizations —and doctrine was rarely decisive for Fascist policy—lay far more practical considerations. As deflation advanced after 1927, housing programs became more and more difficult for public finance. At the same time, unemployment—largely an urban phenomenon—was becoming more serious. It, too, imposed a growing fiscal burden, while mocking the international pretensions of the regime. Finally, and most important, having introduced a police state, the government early acquired a lively interest in isolating and identifying every citizen, for the simple purpose of gaining control over his daily life.[11]

The regulation of labor mobility was evolutionary, starting in a seemingly innocuous way by decree in 1926, but finding ultimate fulfillment in the drastic law of July 6, 1939 (*Provvedimenti contro l'urbanesimo*).[12] The first step provided for a committee on internal migration to study and recommend measures to encourage the movement of the unemployed from centers of surplus population to less densely settled areas capable of economic expansion.[13] The specific problems at hand were provision of labor for public works projects and resettlement of farm families on newly reclaimed land. Just over a year later (April 21, 1927), the pretentious Charter of Labor was announced, which proclaimed that the state was to control employment and unemployment, and accordingly the placement of workers in new jobs (Articles 22–24). In 1928 these principles became law.[14] By these means, the second step toward full control was taken: private hiring and private labor exchanges were abolished. Placement of the unemployed now was assigned exclusively to the local offices of the various labor syndicates, where those seeking work had to register, and employers to apply for new hands. Although the employer had some power of selection, the rules required him to give preference to members of the Fascist Party. Furthermore, the minister of corporations was put at the head of the whole system. Later, in 1934, the separate local offices—one for each industry, occupation or trade—were merged into one, under what now became a commissariat for internal migration.

But whatever the form of the arrangements, the substance of the scheme had gone unaltered since 1928: the placement offices had been turned into an instrument that gave the Fascists a complete monopoly over jobs for the unemployed. And since employers, too, had to obtain their labor exclusively from this source, the hiring side of the market was also controlled and included employed workers who wished to change jobs.

The third step came in 1935, with statutory introduction of the labor book. Although the *libretto* did not come into general use until 1939, its adoption revealed that the thrust of the system was working toward total control of the labor market. This is clear from the language of the new law. The books were to be issued only to workers who had legally established residences in the locality. To get on the placement register, the unemployed worker had to have a valid book in his possession, which he had to deposit at the labor office. Thus if he lacked legal residence in the province, he could not obtain employment. Moreover, upon entering a job he had to surrender the book to his employer for the duration of his tenure. In turn, the employer had to record various data in the book— wages, occupation, accidents, hiring and dismissal dates, membership in a Fascist labor syndicate. If this information were incomplete or in error, it was illegal for the employer to give him employment.[15]

The iron band of total state control of the labor market finally was welded together with a royal decree law at the end of 1938, which became a formal statute six months later.[16] The right to job placement and job tenure was now firmly joined to the requirement of legal local residence. Placement itself was explicitly declared to be a "public function," to be determined not by the private desires of worker and employer, but by the interests of production and of the state. In other words, the distribution of all workers was to be dominated by the planning requirements of a totalitarian government dedicated to war.

As embodied in statute, the regulations were draconian enough to satisfy the most ardent follower of Il Duce, while at the same time providing ample opportunities for graft to those officials whose commitment to the regime was something more than spiritual.

First, no one was allowed to move his residence to a provincial capital, or to a town of over 25,000 people, or to a designated center of notable industrial importance, unless he already had valid employment, or private means of support and justifiable reasons for the move. Second, no "outsider" could get a job legally without prior approval of the placement office (*Ufficio di collocamento*), which also had to approve the employer's hiring him. Third, no outsider could establish legal residence, hence be registered at the provincial population office (*Ufficio anagrafico*), unless he had legal employment or adequate private means. If not so registered, he could not qualify for poor relief, nor be entered on the job placement list, nor legally rent or sublet living quarters. Fourth, those admitted to such communities on temporary work permits were required to return, or be forcibly returned, to their home provinces when their jobs ended. Fifth, no agricultural worker could be put on the placement register for any other kind of work, even in his own locality, if he had left the land without good reason. Finally, in case of violation, workers, employers, registry officials, landlords, and tenants all were subject to fine or imprisonment, and possible application of the penal code.

The third relevant area of Fascist economic policy concerns investment and commodity prices. The government began to assert an interest in these fields in 1927, at the same time it had begun to intervene in the labor market.[17] Inspired by its anti-urbanization doctrine, the regime issued a decree in late 1927 requiring official consent for location of new plants in communities with over 100,000 persons. Two years later, authority was extended to all new plants, or expansions of existing plants, whose products were related to national defense. Early in 1933, control was extended still further, including all new plants or plant expansions of any kind in any location. The main impetus for this sweeping assumption of power over the direction of industrial investment was to help enforce the price-fixing practices of the several voluntary industrial cartels (*consorzi*), by forestalling the creation of additional production capacity. These cartels had begun to appear by 1928, increasing rapidly in number with the decline in prices thereafter. In 1932, they acquired official sanction, under certain conditions involving compulsory membership of all producers.

Parallel with this program of control over the location and direction of investment in industry, the government embarked upon a similar program for agriculture. Soon after taking power, Mussolini resurrected the old policy of land reclamation, giving it new vigor. In December 1928 land recovery was linked with the Battle of the Wheat (*Battaglia del grano*), to make the country self-sufficient in grains. By 1936, $619 million had been spent on projects involving 2.3 million hectares of land, 7.6 per cent of the present total land area. Yields and total output were sharply increased, and imports greatly reduced. However, the prices of flour and bread rose, because Italian production involved comparatively higher costs. If one looks solely at the increase in arable land, the scheme can be counted a gain, provided one safely assumes that the same investment would not have rendered higher returns in other uses. But precisely because the new lands were committed to wheat, actual returns were below what could have been had elsewhere, even within agriculture. As a result, the blind pursuit of autarchy lowered national income below its full potential.

Conclusions on Fascist economic policy. Viewed as a whole, Fascist labor policy after 1926 introduced two decisive changes into the operation of labor markets: state regulation of money wages, which were severely depressed; and state control over the mobility of labor, which was strongly repressive. Regarding mobility, the effect was to tie the peasantry to the soil, and so to impede the gradual voluntary redistribution of the labor force toward nonagricultural uses. In addition, the system blocked the flow of labor from town to city, and from city to city. Finally, by the late thirties the regime was regulating all uses of labor according to its over-all objectives, which centered upon autarchy and preparation for war.

Both forms of market intervention represented efforts to obstruct the working of competitive forces—efforts that were imposed upon an economy that still was backward in its total bearing. In other words, throughout the lengthy period of Fascist rule, the underlying structural problems were left unsolved. Indeed, the control of internal migration served to petrify the distribution of labor, and so to perpetuate the dual character of the economy.

Superficially, it is easy to interpret the official policy of wage control as at least a constructive attempt to bring the relative price of labor into more realistic balance with its supply, relative to the price and quantity of capital. But there is ample reason to reject this inference. First, the migration controls after 1928 worked counter to any adjustments that lower money wages might have caused. Second, the commitment to a deflationary policy after 1927 aborted the expansion of industrial employment anyway. Prices were forced down along with money wages, partly canceling the fall of real wages to 1929. After that, the price level fell so fast that real wages actually could rise.

Seen as a whole, the Fascist economic program fostered restrictive industrial and trade monopoly, and forced the country's very scarce productive resources into uses that yielded comparatively low returns. In the latter respect, this was the real meaning of the policy against urban growth, the compulsory location and direction of industrial investment, the Battle of the Wheat, the spread of autarchy, and the promotion of war industry. Together with the encouragement of restrictive cartels, these measures retarded the growth of national income. For the same reason, they checked the modernization of the economy. On top of all this, the turn to war absorbed great amounts of national product, and led eventually to disastrous losses of capital. After all the bombast and all the theatrical proclamations of its leader, the end result of Italian fascism was economic ruin.

MARKET IMPERFECTIONS AND CONTINUED OBSTRUCTION OF
ECONOMIC UNIFICATION AFTER WORLD WAR II

Restraint of internal migration. With the fall of Mussolini, it might have been expected that the controls over migration and hiring of labor would have ended. But this did not happen until 1961. In consequence, although political freedom was regained with the destruction of the Fascist system, the worker did not thereby obtain full freedom of choice in employment or place of residence, nor the employer in selection of his employees. For the same reason, the dual wage system was strengthened rather than weakened, while the south continued to suffer a disproportionately heavy burden of unemployment and underemployment.

Although there was some loosening up of the labor controls between 1944 and 1948, they were clamped down tightly again by a new law in 1949. In the meantime, the Communist-controlled CGIL (labor confederation) had seized many of the local placement offices, using the system to favor workers loyal to its cause— an illegal, additional discrimination.

In 1944 the Allied Military Government issued Order no. 28, which abolished all Fascist institutions within occupied territory, but not the underlying Fascist labor legislation.[18] Although the placement offices were transferred to the local governments, after a brief interlude the old controls were reintroduced. When the new republic came into being in 1946, it chose not to repeal *en bloc* the enormous twenty-two year accumulation of Fascist statutes and decrees, because it feared the disruptive effects implied by such breach of continuity, not to mention the tremendous legislative task that would be required to fill the void.[19]

However, the new constitution of January 1, 1948 extended some firm guarantees that seemed to mean doom for the old system of labor control. Article 3 established equality before the laws and required the state to remove all economic and social obstacles to personal liberty and equality. Article 4 proclaimed the right to work, while the very pertinent Article 16 assured to each citizen the right to live where he chose. Article 120 forbade any region within the realm to obstruct the free movement of persons and goods, or to deny any citizen the right to practice his profession or to engage in labor anywhere within the national territory.

Despite the clear-cut intent of these protections for the free geographic mobility of labor, parliament enacted a new restrictive law the following year.[20] In essence, this measure preserved the Fascist restraints of 1931, 1938, and 1939. Internal migration, especially from farm to city, was still blocked. Access to jobs was still an exclusive monopoly of the state, now justified as a job-rationing device for dealing with severe unemployment. Under this statute, the obligation to register for placement was reaffirmed, to be performed only at the placement office in the worker's district of legal residence. To register and to be referred for work, one had to have a valid *libretto* for deposit at the office. Employers had to hire through the appropriate local office, requesting unskilled and semi-skilled workers in numbers only, without reference to proper names. Exception was made for very small employers, which of course encouraged the dual wage system. Most important, the old statutes were not repealed, but actually were tightened: under Article 15 the placement offices were required to give preference in job referrals to local residents.

In consequence, a worker who was laid off, and who had no hope of finding another job in his home province, would find himself trapped. To get a job elsewhere, he first had to get on the placement register at the new location. To register, he had to establish residence at the chosen place. To establish residence, he had to have a job or other adequate means of support. In other words, he either had to hire out illegally, on pain of losing all his social security benefits (the family allowance alone was worth nearly 40 per cent of total earnings), to accept lower wages, and, if discovered, be dismissed with legal penalties; or to remain in his old location, waiting for recall or a new job, either of which literally might require years of idleness.

The consequences of the new law were twofold. First, the movement of the unemployed and underemployed out of backward areas was still largely dammed up. Second, those who did move mostly did so illegally, which promoted clandestine employment at low wages, reinforcing the dual wage system.

In view of the admirable intentions proclaimed by the new constitution, how does one explain the reimposition of restrictions, a little over a year later, which were comparable in severity to those of fascism?

It could be argued (and was argued) that job-rationing was essential in a context of chronic mass unemployment, to protect the rights of the neediest unemployed; also, that prevention of migration was essential to protect the wage standards of workers who were better paid. On the first count, the obvious reply is that job-rationing did less to protect the most deserving than it did to put a premium on persistence, bribery, and even violence.[21] To the second, the short answer is that the supercompetitive wages enjoyed by a minority of the industrial workers were purchased by barring the competition of outsiders. Thereby the outsiders became condemned to badly paid jobs whose wages were made even worse by the very fact of their exclusion from the high-wage citadel. Otherwise they remained unemployed. In short, if the intent of noncompetitive wage-raising were to redistribute income in favor of the poor, its real effect was quite the opposite. Yet that effect was buttressed by the 1949 legislation.

However, there were far more mundane sources of support for this law. The relevant administrative bureaucracy was for it, because it meant jobs, regulations, and influence. The landlords were for it, because it assured a comfortable supply of cheap farm labor. The Communist-controlled CGIL was for it because its strength and its dues revenues lay in the well-paid groups of industrial workers, who wanted no outside competition. The industrialists were half-heartedly for it, for while the regulations were onerous, the employers could escape higher taxes and possible civil disorders. And the local authorities of the larger industrial centers were for it, because a potential influx of migrating poor meant added fiscal burdens to provide temporary barracks, permanent low-cost housing, schooling, sanitation, and relief for the unemployed. In short, almost every interest group that counted politically had much to gain and little to lose from enactment of the measure, while its real victims lacked organizations and spokesmen to express their interests.[22]

At the end of 1954, parliament passed a new statute governing residence, but it did not reopen the question. This law made it a duty to register in the place of regular residence, and allowed changes of residence upon cancelation and reregistration, but without stipulating that the migrant have either a job or means of support upon removal to his new domicile.[23] At the same time, this new statute did not explicitly repeal the Fascist law of 1939 (*Provvedimenti contro l'urbanesimo*). Although it recognized the constitutional right to change one's residence, it did not assure to such persons the all-important right to be entered upon the placement register, hence to have the necessary legal access to new jobs. On the contrary, the 1949 placement law gave preference to local residents.

However, the struggle against the system went on. In 1957 and again in 1958, attempts were made to upset the placement controls in the Constitutional Court (*Corte costituzionale*), by contention that the relevant provisions of the statute of 1949 were in conflict in particular with Article 16 of the constitution. The issue submitted in 1957 attacked the requirements that only those validly on the register in their localities could hire out, and that employers must do all their hiring through the placement offices. In this instance, the issue included all workers, while in 1958 it was limited to apprentices.[24]

In both cases, the court chose to decide the issue on the narrowest possible grounds, avoiding any findings on the constitutionality of the laws of 1931 and 1939. It could do so because the issue was not formally submitted. The court reasoned that there was a clear difference in purpose between the earlier measures and that of 1949. The latter law, the court found, was intended to promote full employment by use of the state placement control system and thus was compatible with Article 16 of the constitution. In consequence, it continued to be lawful to require all those seeking jobs to be properly registered in their home districts, and to require employers to obtain their labor from the appropriate local offices. More than this, the required preference for local residents remained intact, while the right to move was still obstructed in practice by this very barrier.

Despite these adverse decisions, political and economic pressures were now shifting at last in favor of labor mobility. The postwar boom was in full swing, and northern industry was beginning to require new labor reserves. To the still powerful Communist CGIL, the migrants were no longer a threat to wages but had become added cadres to swell its ranks—cadres with plenty of exploitable grievances. In this respect, the CGIL enjoyed substantial advantages over the rival non-Communist union federations, CISL and UIL, which lacked adequate funds and organizers, and feared dilution of their strength under the system of proportional representation in the factories. Beyond these forces, sentiment within influential circles of the public had begun crystalizing in favor of encouraging more emigration from the south, as a lower-cost and economically more promising alternative to still more industrial investment in the region itself. Thus the stage was being set for relaxation of the labor control system.

The first effort came in early March 1960, when the senate passed a repealer that would have abolished the Fascist laws of

1931 and 1939.[25] However, a ministerial crisis supervened, and the Chamber of Deputies failed to take concurring action. Then on February 10, 1961, both houses finally enacted a law that formally repealed the two Fascist statutes, and modified the 1949 measure as well.[26]

Recall that Article 8 of the 1949 law had required that registration for placement be undertaken at the placement office in the worker's residential district. Under the new measure, this provision was changed substantially. He could transfer his registration, without loss of original registration date and without changing residence, to the capital of an adjacent province; or to a place with over 20,000 residents; or to any significant industrial center—in all cases within a radius of up to 150 kilometers. By the same token, the old preference for local residents was modified. However, for movements beyond the stipulated distance, the migrating worker had to sacrifice his original registration date, and start all over again at the bottom of the list. Nonetheless, he could move freely, establishing residence wherever he wished by filling out a form at the local population registry office. To do this, he no longer needed to have a job or other means of support. Equally important, having done so he acquired the right of placement and had to be enrolled at the office of his new district, for legal referral to a job.

The law of 1949 also provided that if a local office could not supply all the workers requested by employers, it would fill out the balance from nearby offices. The new measure required that a "rule of proportionality" be followed in the distribution of unfilled jobs among authorized candidates from adjacent districts.

Under the present arrangements, the *libretto* is still in use, because the law that introduced it in 1935 was not repealed, while Article 9 of the law of 1949 was left untouched in this respect. Moreover, exclusive state control over hiring and placement—initiated in 1928—also survives. With the addition of the 150-kilometer rule, local geographic mobility is greatly loosened. But workers undertaking long-distance moves are still under some statutory handicap, although their formal freedoms to move and to seek jobs elsewhere are at last decisively and realistically united.

In consequence, the wheel of history has turned full circle. The original purpose of state placement had been to improve the efficiency of the labor market, to increase labor mobility and so reduce frictional unemployment.[27] Under fascism, the intent of the system was completely reversed: to eliminate the voluntary migration of workers and to subject them to totalitarian state controls. With the law of 1949, the principle of enforced settlement was strengthened even more, although the aim was to ration scarce jobs among surplus workers by giving preference to local residents. Finally came the residential law of 1954 and the placement statute of 1961, which returned the system to its original purposes once more. With these measures, statutory law was made consistent at last with the rights guranteed by the new constitution, after a dozen years of delay. In result labor mobility could begin to make an effective contribution to the task of welding together a long divided national economy.

The overvaluation of labor in technically advanced sectors. We have reasoned earlier that the rise in industrial real wages was of doubtful significance for the pace of Italian industrialization before the First World War. As for the interwar period of fascism, money wages soon came under direct state control. Along with real wages, they were cut, and cut severely. However, with the return of collective bargaining and political democracy after the Second World War, wage-making was able to take an anticompetitive upward thrust.

Of what significance was this possibility for further advance in the economic unification of the country? Although incomplete, evidence strongly suggests that wage policy was an obstructing force until very recently, when rapid accumulation of capital brought its supply into better balance with that of labor at the relative factor prices currently in effect.

Wages and supplemental labor costs are determined for important sectors by a combination of collective bargaining and state intervention. For reasons that are obvious, labor costs can be enforced upon large and technically advanced firms, but not upon small or family enterprises. This immediately creates the possibility of one form of structural disequilibrium—unequal factor earnings and consequent perpetuation of technological dualism and an incompletely united economy.

If such bifurcation of the labor market and of the wage system is achieved, wage costs would be pushed up in the vulnerable sectors, reducing opportunities for employment there because producers will shift to more capital-intensive methods.[28] In turn, this would slow down the absorption of labor from agriculture and from natural increase of the labor force, diverting the influx variously: into the less advanced parts of the nonagricultural sector (trade, artisan shops, small firms), into government make-work projects, or into outright unemployment.

By contrast, if competition were fully effective for all types of comparable labor, real wages could not rise in the technically advanced centers of expanding output until the available labor reserves had been fully absorbed, apart from frictional residuals. On the contrary, initially real wages would be competed down by the unemployed, which would encourage more labor-intensive methods of production, together with a price-induced shift in final demand for output in favor of high labor-using products. As a result, the real price of labor would eventually balance its demand and supply, after which real wages could rise all around as capital formation outran the natural increase in the labor force. For the same reason, the dualistic phenomenon of making low wages still lower, and high wages still higher, could not survive.

Beyond a general overvaluation of labor within its zone of influence, anticompetitive wage-setting can lead to distortion of the relevant occupational wage structure as well. If the managers of wage policy follow a deliberate equalitarian policy in favor of common labor, they will squeeze occupational differentials, awarding larger increases to the lower brackets. Unskilled labor then becomes overvalued relative to skilled workers. Here the consequences can be particularly severe for those migrating from agriculture or newly entering the labor force, since most of them are without skills and often without experience as well. Presumably the purpose is to improve income distribution in their favor, but in any case the consequences will run in the opposite direction: these workers will have special difficulties in finding good jobs, and will concentrate in low-wage occupations and in unemployment.

To apply the foregoing analysis to the postwar Italian experience, the first step is to examine the over-all changes in employment, and then to place these facts in comparison with the behavior of the technically advanced inner sector of industry. Unfortunately, aggregative employment data are not available in serial form, while the intervening sample studies that might be used suffer from changes of definition that seriously weaken their usefulness. Accordingly, the next best expedient is to put in contrast the figures from the Census of November 4, 1951, with those of a sample survey for 1961, which yields some informative net results but says nothing about what went on during the decade interval. Moreover, this comparison is not wholly satisfactory, because it requires dependence upon the 1961 sample survey, and also necessitates some adjustments in the 1951 data to make them comparable. In the latter respect, the main problem is to exclude from the census totals those workers who were unemployed on November 4, 1951, but who had previously had jobs. Because the figures for registered unemployment are incompletely allocated in detail, unavoidably arbitrary assumptions are required regarding the sectoral distribution of the unemployed manual workers and the division of the unemployed between manual and clerical groups. In consequence, the adjusted sector data will not round out perfectly with the over-all totals. Nonetheless, the results are adequate for the general comparisons required. Table 88 presents the latter in summary form.

These figures indicate a shift of impressive proportions from agriculture into nonagricultural activities, particularly into industry.[29] In fact, the employment of manual workers in industry rose at a compound annual rate of 4 per cent, yielding an increase of almost two million over the decade. Such figures afford no basis for inferring that anticompetitive wage-setting was an obstacle either to industrialization as such or to the rapid expansion of employment, but this is by no means the whole story.

One significant contrary sign is that approximately one million of the almost four-million increase in total nonagricultural employment consisted of family assistants (233,000) and persons going into own-account labor (774,000).[30] As noted elsewhere, activities of these types concentrate predominantly in the relatively backward zones of the nonagricultural economy. In consequence, the mere fact that nonagricultural employment rose at the compound annual rate of 3.3 per cent, while agriculture was sharply contracting, does not constitute proof that economic unification was proceeding rapidly.

Beyond this, we must inquire into the behavior of employment within the technically advanced inner sector of industry—where large firms, comparatively high wages, and effectively anticompetitive control of labor cost per worker all prevail. Unfortunately, the data underlying the several comparisons just presented do not permit detailed industry-by-industry analysis. For such purpose, we must rely upon the monthly statistics collected by the Ministry of Labor from all firms employing at least ten manual workers.

TABLE 88. Comparative employment statistics for 1951 and 1961 [a] (in thousands)

Employment by sector and type	Nov. 4 1951	1961	Net change	Index (1951 = 100)	Geometric rate (per cent)
Total employment [b]	18,367	20,267	1,900	110.3	0.98
Agriculture	7,946	5,907	−2,039	74.3	−2.93
Industry	5,532	8,012	2,480	144.8	3.77
Tertiary [c]	4,889	6,348	1,459	129.8	2.64
Nonagricultural only [d]	10,421	14,360	3,939	137.8	3.26
Manual workers only [e]	8,497	10,127	1,630	119.2	1.77
Agriculture	2,326	1,708	−618	73.4	−3.05
Industry	4,136	6,128	1,992	148.2	4.01
Tertiary [c]	2,035	2,291	256	112.6	1.19
Nonagricultural only [d]	6,171	8,419	2,248	136.4	3.15

[a] The original data for November 4, 1951, derive from the population census, and were compiled from respondents' returns. Besides employed persons, they include employed minors of age ten and over; unemployed who were formerly employed; and formerly employed persons then in military service, in prison, etc. The corrected totals above removed 1.21 million formerly employed unemployed, distributed according to rough inter-sectoral proportions indicated for total registered unemployment in November 1951.

[b] Includes all occupational categories—executive, professional, self-employed, clerical, manual, and family assistants.

[c] Includes transportation, trade, services, finance and insurance, and government.

[d] Industry and tertiary combined.

[e] All of the formerly employed registered unemployed deducted from agriculture and industry were assumed to be manual workers.

Source: Figures for November 4, 1951, from Annuario statistico Italiano, 1956, p. 26; for 1961 from Relazione generale, 1962, I, p. 87. Figures for 1951 were corrected to remove the formerly employed unemployed.

The inner sector consists of extractive industry, textiles, primary metals (iron, steel, and nonferrous), building materials (cement, glass, and so forth), chemicals, rubber, and the metal products group (electrical and nonelectrical machines, and transportation equipment)—the heart of Italian industry. Together, these groups have a weight of almost two thirds in the current official index of industrial production. Between 1951 and 1961, a weighted index of their composite output shows the enormous increase of 137.7 per cent, and a mean annual geometric rate of advance of 9.4 per cent.[31]

Against all this, the ML series for manual employment in the inner sector stands out in glaring contrast. In December 1951 it stood at 1.45 million, rising only to 1.67 million by 1961—a total increase of but 15 per cent, or at a compound annual rate of only 1.4 per cent. On this basis, the inner sector added but 220,000 production workers while it was expanding output by over two and one-third times, and while industry as a whole apparently was taking on nearly two million more production workers.[32] Also of interest, the ML statistics for the same establishments show that the total input of manual-worker hours in the inner sector rose by 21.6 per cent over the decade, indicating that hours per worker were increasing somewhat.[33] More startling, the figures for output and hours together in the inner sector imply that gross productivity per manual-worker hour was rising between 1951 and 1961 at a compound annual rate of over 8 per cent.

Confronted as we are with this puzzling and disappointing behavior of manual-worker employment in the advanced sector, we have two choices: to reject the ML figures as a gross understatement, or to accept them with some reservations. The second alternative is more reasonable.

The ML figures emerge from direct monthly enumerations of the establishments surveyed, collected according to fixed criteria, and yielding detail otherwise not available. However, they do not include overhead labor (executive, supervisory, and clerical). This means that they understate total employment and its rate of increase in the inner sector, where a relative rise in overhead personnel probably is going on.[34] Moreover, the ML tabulations do not cover firms with less than ten manual employees, which leaves out almost entirely whole sectors of industry where small-scale operations predominate—for example, food processing, clothing, and wood. But apart from these deficiencies no reasons have been brought forward for rejecting the ML figures.

Furthermore, in the nature of the case these statistics should reflect accurately the movement of manual-worker employment in the inner sector because it is precisely here that large firms are to be found. For this very reason, we must conclude that a very substantial part of the indicated over-all increase of 1.9 million manual workers in all industry between 1951 and 1961 found employment only in the much less developed branches and firms. This inference will have to stand until better statistics point to the contrary.

To evaluate the influence of wages upon employment within the inner sector and upon the changing over-all distribution of non-agricultural employment, we must consider next the extent of unemployment in the postwar years. For such a purpose, two sets of data are available: the regular ML registration statistics, compiled from the local placement offices; and estimates prepared from various annual sample surveys conducted by the Central Institute of Statistics (ISTAT). The comparative figures diverge seriously and probably cannot be reconciled.[35] However, on either source two facts stand out: overt unemployment was serious until the end of the fifties, but a fairly significant reduction set in after 1958.

Comparing the registration figures with sample estimates for the months in which the samples were taken, we obtain the following general results. Between May 1954 and October 1958 (seasonal variations uncorrected for lack of data), total registered unemployment (formerly employed plus those seeking a first job) fell irregularly from 1.93 million to 1.65 million, while the sample estimates indicate a drop from 1.17 million to 0.93 million. By 1961 (yearly average), the registered total stood at 1.41 million, and the sample figure at 0.72 million. For the formerly employed unemployed alone, the registration statistics show 1.27 million in May 1954, 1.15 million in October 1958, and 0.99 million for all of 1961. On the sample estimates for this group, the corresponding figures are 0.68 million, 0.65 million, and 0.44 million. On either basis, the over-all burden of unemployment was heavy throughout the fifties.[36]

More light can be thrown on the immediate problem by examining the registration statistics for the four northern regions comprising the industrial triangle, which include the cities of Turin, Milan, Genoa, and Venice, along with other important centers. Here attention will be centered upon two decisive categories: the formerly employed (Class I) and those seeking a first job (Class II). The data are summarized in Table 89.

These figures indicate that there was a substantial reserve of experience unemployed right through 1959, although the total began dropping after 1955, and very sharply after 1959. There was available also a smaller reserve of new entrants, whose profile takes roughly the same form. Together these groups varied roughly between 200,000 and 325,000 until the end of the decade. Between 1953 and 1958, the total fell by some 76,000 persons. During these same years, the ML figures for manual-worker employment in the inner sector—whose great bulk is in these localities—increased by only 17,000. This suggests that most of the intervening decrease in

TABLE 89. Movements in categories of registered unemployment, northern industrial regions, 1953–1961 [a]

Year	Class I [b]	Class II [c]	Total	Index for total (1953=100)
1953	241,994	42,843	284,837	100.0
1954	216,147	34,633	250,780	88.0
1955	220,700	35,790	256,490	90.0
1956	195,311	60,869	256,180	89.9
1957	166,014	51,959	217,973	76.5
1958	157,187	51,029	208,216	73.1
1959	229,346	99,596	328,942	115.5
1960	102,714	35,369	138,083	48.5
1961	87,139	30,716	117,855	41.4

[a] Regions include Piedmont, Lombardy, Liguria, and Veneto. Data are for June of each year.
[b] Unemployed who were formerly employed.
[c] Young people under twenty-one and "demobilized" persons seeking a first job. Excludes housewives.
Source: Rassegna di statistiche del lavoro, various issues.

the regional unemployed involved expansion of employment outside the advanced components of industry.[37] However, by 1961 the manual group in the inner sector had jumped to 211,000 over 1953, while the regional registered unemployed had dropped sharply by 167,000 in the same period. In both cases, the big swings came after 1959, when the expansion of employment within the advanced sector at last began to gather force. By the same token, then, this sector had a substantial labor reserve throughout the fifties.

Two other points are of critical importance. First, until fundamental revision of the placement laws was made in February 1961, the registered regional reserve consisted only of legal residents. Outsiders, it will be recalled, could not establish residence and so get on the placement register, since they lacked jobs or private means of support in the usual case. As such, they were made a non-competing group by force of law. In consequence, the regional figures for unemployment grossly understate the real number of potential competitors for the comparatively much better paying jobs within the inner sector. In other words, the effective labor reserve was deliberately being held down by statutory exclusion— mostly at the expense of the southern poor.[38] If these legislative controls had been loosened, in 1949, for instance, it would have been more difficult to force up real wages during the intervening period.

Second, it is in this vital connection that the support of the northern unions for the antimobility law of 1949 gains its real significance: that law strongly reinforced their monopoly power over wages. Indeed, it would be hard to find better circumstantial evidence to support the inference that wage policy in these years was adverse to increased employment in the inner sector. Its beneficiaries wanted it that way. In short, anticompetitive wage-fixing and restrictive placement legislation went hand in hand.

The final step is to consider what happened to wages and labor cost within the advanced sector during the period before 1960, when chronic unemployment was still heavy in the north. Here, *faute de mieux*, the ML data for manual workers must be used, and these are companion enumerations to the hours and employment statistics already cited. Since the basic wage rate has little meaning in Italy by reason of numerous uniform enforced supplements, the proper figure for money wages is a weighted average of gross wages per manual hour. For labor cost, there should be added the hourly equivalent of all social security levies upon employers. However, this should exclude the family allowances, which are already included in the gross hourly wage. Also, the data can be carried back to 1948, which permits division of the whole period into two parts. The facts are presented in Table 90.

It is evident from these data that between 1948 and 1960 the money wages of manual labor in the advanced sector increased at the very high compound annual rate of nearly 6 per cent; also that the speed of increase was considerably higher up through 1953 than thereafter. If we deflate these figures by the national cost-of-living index, then real wages rose throughout the period at a geometric annual rate of just under 3 per cent, and here the difference between subperiods is negligible.[39] Granting that some of the registered unemployed were in noncompeting groups for reasons other than statutory exclusion, the over-all labor reserve through 1959 was big enough to have checked this rise of real wages if it could have forced the gates of the inner citadel. Obviously it could not. Real wages rose rapidly and steadily, by means of a strong and continuing upthrust in money wages. Clearly, anticompetitive wage making was extremely effective within these leading components of industry.[40]

TABLE 90. Comparative behavior of money wages and total labor costs, inner sector of industry, 1948, 1953, and 1960 [a]

Item (hourly)	1948	1953 (lire)	1960	Compound rate		
				1960/48	1953/48	1960/53
Average gross money wage	159.0	230.0	314.8	5.86	7.65	4.59
Employers' social security cost	23.4[b]	47.8	62.0	8.46	15.36	3.78
Total labor cost	182.4	277.8	376.8	6.23	8.78	4.45

[a] Social security costs are from a *Confindustria* estimate, including all regular social insurance items, but after removal of family allowances, which are included in gross wages. Because *Statistiche del lavoro* was not available for 1948, the data were taken from *Rassegna di statistiche del lavoro*, which, as collateral evidence indicates, may understate wages by about 10 per cent, hence overstate slightly the calculated rates of increase.

[b] Based on July 1949, for lack of prior data.

Source: Wages from *Rassegna di statistiche del lavoro* for 1948; from *Statistiche del lavoro* for later dates, various issues. Social security charges from *Rassegna di statistiche del lavoro*, various issues.

However, from the standpoint of employment impacts, the relevant figure is hourly labor cost. It rose by 6.2 per cent compounded for the whole period, although the rate for the earlier subperiod was almost double that of the later one. Even so, the rise after 1953 continued to be very substantial—at just under 4.5 per cent yearly.

But labor cost ought not to be considered alone. It must be related to output per man-hour. The ML data permit this to be done, for manual-worker hours only during 1953–1960. In these years, hourly labor cost per manual worker in the inner sector rose cumulatively by 35.6 per cent; and output per man-hour soared by 74.6 per cent. In result, unit manual labor cost dropped 22.4 per cent, or at a compound annual rate of —3.56 per cent.[41] Unit total cost no doubt fell more slowly, because overhead labor was gaining in relative importance and because raw materials and equipment purchased from other sectors and abroad may have risen to some extent. Nonetheless, there is every reason to believe that after 1953 hourly costs of manual labor exerted no direct upward pressure upon product prices in the inner sector. In fact, as of 1960 (1953 = 100) the aggregate wholesale price index stood at 98.8, while in no category within the relevant nonagricultural products group did the component indexes exceed 100.0. Doubtless gross profit margins were widening within the advanced sector, and very likely net margins as well. Given the context of protected bilateral monopoly in the labor market and monopoloid or oligopolistic structures for the sector's product markets, what was going on was a division of the spoils by private treaty: the savings from rapidly increasing labor productivity were being split up as substantial increases in money wages and as higher profits, with continuous internal reinvestment of the profits to maintain the productivity-generating process itself.

But the absence of upward wage pressure against product prices does not mean that the rapid rise of wage costs had no adverse effect upon the expansion of employment within the inner sector. Quite the contrary. Even oligopolists pay attention to the critical relationship between the marginal value product of labor and marginal labor cost. Both were increasing, the former more rapidly. Politically, a swift advance in labor costs was in the cards. The counterstrategy was obvious: capital-intensive rationalizations of production, to contain the pressure and to leave something over. Absent the strategy, the productivity offset would have been lower and the gain in employment even less. Without the pressure, less scarce capital would have been diverted to socially uneconomic emphasis upon labor saving, and the advance in employment could have been more. At the same time, without the pressure more capital would have been available to the backward sector, where competition of workers for jobs would have been less. In short, as things worked out wage policy—aided by imperfect product markets—helped to perpetuate structural disequilibrium and unemployment throughout the fifties.[42] Furthermore, between 1948 and 1954 common labor progressively was being overvalued relative to skilled, at the very time that the unskilled group was the dominant component in total unemployment. Skilled workers were being hoarded, often for use on menial tasks, while the apprenticeship system was withering away and unskilled labor was clamoring for jobs. Redress of skill differentials became a generally recognized necessity, and was gradually accomplished in the early fifties. Thereafter occupational differentials were in satisfactory equilibrium until 1960–1961, when northern industry again began expressing concern about a shortage of skilled labor.

TABLE 91. Comparative changes in employment, inner and outer sectors of the nonagricultural economy, 1950 and 1957

Sector	1950	1957	Net change	Index (1950=100)
	(thousands)			
Inner [a]	2414	2669	255	110.6
Outer	4643	5765	1122	124.2
Manufacturing only [b]	1560	1780	220	114.1
Services only [c]	3083	3985	902	129.3

[a] Includes extractive, textiles, primary metals, metal products, building materials, chemicals and rubber.
[b] Includes foods, clothing, leather and hides, and wood and wood products.
[c] Includes transportation and communication, trade, finance and insurance, and miscellaneous services.
Source: SVIMEZ, L'aumento dell'occupazione in Italia dal 1950 al 1957 (Rome:Giuffrè, 1959), p. 89.

The overvaluation of labor within the advanced sector naturally poses a collateral problem of high interest: what happened to wages and employment in the "outer" portions of the nonagricultural economy? Although some direct insights can be gained here, reliable data are sparse. Nonetheless, some valuable clues can be had by recourse to the SVIMEZ figures for employment, which also can be related to net product by industry to provide rough but meaningful indication of the wage gap between the inner and outer sectors.

The SVIMEZ data are estimates, not enumerations, but they do include far more activities than the ML figures, and are not restricted to manual employees alone. Unfortunately, they extend only between 1950 and 1957. Nonetheless, they are of extreme interest for our purpose. Table 91 presents the results. In a nutshell, they indicate that while the inner sector accounted for 34.2 per cent of total employment in both sectors in 1950, it contributed but 18.5 per cent of the total increase through 1957. It also had the smallest relative gain—10.6 per cent. By contrast, the miscellaneous sector of services, with its large complement of small firms, jumped by nearly 30 per cent. Here, then, is important supplementary evidence that divergence in wage behavior affected the distribution of employment opportunities. Substantially the same finding derives from the behavior of the outer manufacturing category, where again small firms and generally less advanced technology prevail: it increased employment absolutely by almost as much as the inner group, and relatively by more.

TABLE 92. Average net product per worker attached, inner and outer sectors of the nonagricultural economy, 1950 and 1957 [a]

| | Average net product | | | Ratio to inner | |
| | 1950 | 1957 | Index | | |
Sector	(thousand lire)		(1950=100)	1950	1957
Inner	537	996	185.5	1.00	1.00
Outer	476	647	135.9	0.89	0.65
Manufacturing only	391	539	137.8	0.73	0.54
Services only	519	694	133.7	0.97	0.70

[a] Sector inclusions are the same as in Table 91. Net product data for 1950 rest upon a less reliable base than that for 1957.

Source: Employment data from L'aumento dell'occupazione in Italia dal 1950 al 1957 (Rome: Giuffrè, 1959), p. 58; net product totals for 1950 combined from figures in Annuario statistico italiano, 1952, pp. 153–154; for 1957, Relazione generale, 1958, pp. 16–17, 19.

Although direct wage data are not available to complete the comparison, average net product per worker by sector can serve as a rough substitute, at least to indicate orders of magnitude for the income gaps involved.[43] These figures appear in Table 92.

These figures indicate that the inner sector of industry had a higher gross productivity per employee than did the other main segments of the nonagricultural economy, and that it widened this advantage markedly by 1957. For the same reason, the data suggest that the income-rendering potential to persons employed in the advanced group likewise broadened considerably relative to the other sectors. As of 1957, the gap in actual average incomes per employed person must have been substantial, although it cannot be pinned down quantitatively from these figures.[44]

In any case, the main implication of the bare facts just presented supports the underlying argument here developed: that during the first fifteen postwar years anticompetitive determination of labor costs worked to check the growth of employment in the inner sector, and diverted considerable scarce capital to the introduction of labor-economizing rationalization of production methods in that part of industry. Admittedly, wage-making is not the whole story, but without its inclusion as a factor of ponderate importance, we would have a tale hardly worth the telling.

The cross-effects for the generally less developed sectors also cannot be ignored: reduced availability of fresh investment capital, hence delay in the modernization of production techniques. Moreover, such delay was favored by a division of the labor market that supplied every inducement to the continuation of traditional labor-intensive methods. In consequence, employment opportunities were warped in favor of low-productivity and low-wage jobs. Although unemployment and underemployment were inevitably high in the difficult years immediately after the war, they were kept acute throughout the fifties by the forces that produced this peculiarly unbalanced course of economic advance.

Imperfections in the product market. Three major and highly significant facts emerged from examination of the postwar behavior of the inner sector to 1960. First, money labor costs, money and real wages all were rising at rapid and well-sustained rates. Second, employment expanded with extreme sluggishness, while productivity per manual-worker hour outstripped the rise of unit labor costs by a significant margin. Third, wholesale prices for the products of the sector held almost perfectly constant during 1953–1960, despite the continuing fall of unit labor costs. On the evidence, then, heavy investment in productivity-generating improvements of a highly labor-saving type gave rise to a substantial and continuing "productivity gap" within the sector. More important, the savings emergent from this broadening gap were wholly retained by the sector itself—as internal appropriations for increased money wages and social security benefits to labor, and as higher net profits to capital. Apart from very small variations by specific industries, it is starkly apparent that these savings in the progressive sector were not passed on as lower prices to buyers whose incomes were derived from the other sectors of the economy. In consequence, the less advanced sectors could not share in the gains in labor productivity so obtained.

In this connection, it must be noted that the capital market in Italy is not as well developed as elsewhere in industrialized western Europe. Partly for this reason, retained profits for internal reinvestment are very prominent in the advanced sector. Since the internal savings of, say, the machine-building or automobile industry obviously are not available to rationalize agriculture or the food-processing industry, these latter sectors—along with others —had to depend upon a smaller flow of investible funds, at higher rates of interest, than would have been the case if profits in the inner sector had been paid out as dividends to a larger extent, and so returned in greater part to the capital market to become available for external reinvestment. Alternatively, if productivity gains within the advanced sector had been passed along in some degree as lower prices, then the less developed parts of the system could have acquired more capital goods with the restricted flow of investment funds internally and externally available to them. This was not the case—a handicap of particular importance because the "external" parts of the system experienced generally much lower rates of gain in productivity, hence were less able to create internal savings to effect their own transformation to more modern methods.

Inevitably, therefore, the progress of the less fortunate sectors must have been slowed by the price and income-distribution behavior of the advanced sector. On the very same count, the continuous internal reinvestment of expanding profits within the latter component—both as cause of and as response to wage policy— itself made possible the ever-widening productivity gap, and through this, a continuing disproportionate advance in returns to capital and labor in this well-situated segment of the economy. On the wage side, its unionized workers gained in consumption—at the expense of otherwise greater capital formation in the system as a whole. On the investment side, the sector absorbed more scarce capital than otherwise would have been required to become more competitive in the world and internal markets, while the owners of such capital enjoyed ever higher returns per unit of investment

—at the expense of lower real capital formation to modernize the rest of the economy. Unbalanced development, structural unemployment, increased income inequalities, and retardation of economic unification were the consequences.

In the fall of 1958 Professor Pasquale Saraceno advanced a similiar diagnosis, in a report on Italy to the European Economic Community (EEC).[45] Noting that the nongovernment sphere of the economy was composed of both modern and technically backward parts in greater degree than elsewhere among the Six, he observed that low labor productivity in the retarded segments necessarily restricted the internal markets of the advanced sector. In turn, this fosters technical and economic concentration within the modern zone, thereby favoring its retention of its substantial productivity gains, internal reinvestment of the savings obtained, and an increasing income advantage to its participants. In Saraceno's view, both investment and improvements in factor productivity should be spread more widely over the system, but by incentive rather than compulsion, and without sacrifice of improved competitive strength required by the inner sector to meet the increasing pressures of the Common Market. Also, he declared, union wage demands within that segment were "hardly compatible with a policy of more intense capital formation and higher employment."

Professor Saraceno reiterated this line of analysis in a formal report to the cabinet on June 24, 1959, submitted in his capacity as president of the Committee for the Development of Employment and Income.[46] This highly important document was invoked by the desire of the government to take stock regarding progress toward the aims of the Vanoni development plan for 1955–1964.[47] In Part I, Professor Saraceno remarks that as of 1959 capital formation had not conformed to plan, and had not so far achieved the rapid correction of structural imbalances within the economy. Instead, the report declares, investment had favored higher labor productivity rather than increased employment. In consequence, productivity gains had gone mostly to higher incomes and consumption for the already employed, while the unemployed and underemployed had fallen behind so far as intended improvements in their status were concerned. As pointed out in Parts III and IV of the report, structural disequilibrium had become self-perpetuating, because investment had been so highly concentrated in productivity-generating improvements in the most highly developed sector. By contrast, the committee's view was that faster over-all capital formation should take precedence over more consumption for those in the fortunate sector, and that such investment should be directed in greater measure toward the less developed sectors and regions.[48] For such purposes, the committee suggested the need for a new policy to yield a structure of prices and of income distribution more favorable to the unemployed and the underemployed. Presumably this implies price reductions in the inner sector, connected with some form of wage restraint there also.

Although denunciatory rhetoric is abundant, details are scarce regarding the market structure of Italian industry. Nonetheless, there can be no doubt that for the inner sector the prevailing situations for its products are those of a single seller, or of a few sellers, with or without cartelized arrangements for procurements and/or sales and assignment of market shares. According to the EEC study just considered, technical concentration (comparatively large plants as measured by number of employees) was notable (1951 data) in basic metals, chemicals, mining and extractive industries, metal products, and electric energy—substantially the inner sector as we have defined it. Roughly similar conclusions follow from use of Gini's coefficient, under which inequality of plant sizes becomes greater as the coefficient approaches 1.0.[49]

In addition, an earlier (1947) official inquiry pointed to the market power enjoyed by conglomerate firms such as Montecatini (sulphur, lead, aluminum, marble, industrial chemicals, pharmaceuticals, electricity, and transport); Fiat (Fabbrica italiana automobilistica torinese), a holding and producing company (basic metals, automobiles and trucks, railway equipment, aircraft, radio parts, motor transport, and finance); and Societa italiana Pirelli (tires and tubes, insulated cable, natural and synthetic rubber products, linoleum, and synthetic fibers).[50] Montecatini, which had 60,632 employees in 1958, precedes the First World War and began its rapid growth with that conflict, expanding by internal reinvestment, external acquisitions, and formation of subsidiaries. FIAT (79,930 employees in 1958) dates from 1909 and is a vertically integrated producer, achieving its position primarily by internal expansion, although it now has many subsidiaries. Pirelli (45,000 employees in 1958) is a very old Italian firm that now has important international connections and numerous domestic affiliates. All three of these great enterprises drew much support from government procurement in wartime. Underscoring the diverse scale and still unconsolidated character of most industry, Montecatini, FIAT, and Pirelli are Italy's only entries on *Fortune's* 1959 list of the 100 largest non-American industrial firms, although 46 of these were based in the Common Market countries.[51] Moreover, Italy ranks well below the rest of the Six in development of very large financial complexes of the type common to France and Belgium.

In addition to concentration as such, there is the question of cartelization. It was noted earlier that by 1933 Fascist policy gave official sanction to the formation of cartels (*consorzi*), supporting them by compulsory membership and by direct control of investment either in new plants or in expansion of facilities. The inquiry of the Economic Commission of the Constituent Assembly in 1947 revealed widespread use of the device in agricultural marketing, industrial production, and wholesale and retail distribution—both for joint procurement of supplies and for division of sales. Within the inner sector, one or both forms were found in iron and steel products, aluminum, machines and equipment, wool and cotton textiles, silk, chemicals, construction materials, glass and ceramics.[52]

Another feature of market structure that must be noted is the spotty but sometimes dominant presence of government enterprise. In Italy it has taken three forms. First, there are those traditional activities that are under direct state control and are included within the national budget—the railways, tobacco and salt production. Second, there is the IRI (Istituto ricostruzione italiana) group of banking and industrial houses, formed by Mussolini early in the depression as an Italian counterpart to the American Reconstruction Finance Corporation. IRI's purpose was to save the leading banks from collapse, which was threatened by their close involvement with distressed industrial firms in iron and steel, shipbuilding, and other heavy capital goods. Along the way, IRI began financing the latter undertakings as a third-party participant supplied with government money. In the course of time, the state has become increasingly dominant in these mixed enterprises. Third, there are special purpose government ventures on the U.S. TVA model, of which the best known in ENI (Ente nazionale-idrocarburi). ENI engages in petroleum exploration, development, and production on an international scale, and is largely internally financed. Under the flamboyant, aggressive, and quite competent leadership of the late Enrico de Mattei, ENI soon began to branch out after its formation in 1953, and now is a large conglomerate enterprise, operating with government money, but curiously with considerable independence from cabinet control.

Together, the IRI and ENI groups employed 287,000 workers in 1957, mostly in manufacturing and public utilities. They account for almost all production of electric power (private firms in this field were nationalized in 1962) and natural gas (an ENI statutory monopoly); 60 per cent of all combination vessels under Italian registry); all domestic air services; over half of steel output; 10 to 15 per cent of petroleum production, and 10 per cent of machines and equipment.[53]

Although no antitrust legislation was in force during these post-war years, an interministerial committee was given certain powers to control the prices set by dominant firms—initially to suppress inflation, and latterly as a device to regulate monopoly. Two groups of enterprises are involved: public utilities, and producers of raw materials and of widely used industrial and consumers' goods—solid fuel, petroleum and natural gas, sodium iodine, aluminum, glass, cement, fertilizers and copper sulphate, sugar, and pharmaceuticals.

This review of market structure, although dependent upon quite inadequate data, suggests that within the inner sector there is high concentration—in some cases approaching monopoly—in many leading products, and that sellers' power over prices is frequently buttressed further by diverse cartel arrangements. So far as concentration is concerned, it is no more advanced than elsewhere within the Six, except in its geographic aspect. So far as price behavior is concerned, liberalization of foreign trade before and with adherence to the Common Market probably has been more useful in holding down prices than the direct controls just cited. As for concentration within Italian industry, in both its technical (size of plants) and economic dimensions (product-by-product market occupancy by a given firm) it seems less the consequence of a deliberate intent to dominate than of the economies of large-scale plants serving comparatively small and restricted internal markets.[54] In other words, low productivity and incomes outside the advanced sector constrict the demand for its products, while technology dictates large-scale operations to supply that demand. If the growth and efficiency of the rest of the system could be accelerated, concentration perhaps would become less acute in time.

The stultifying effects of product market imperfections for growth and economic unification have not come from price-raising by monopoloid sellers within the inner sector, for, as we have seen, these price indexes were stable for nearly ten years after the Korean inflation. Rather, their restraining influence derives from the failure of these prices to fall, despite undoubtedly large advances in gross labor productivity in the same period.

The reason for this peculiar phenomenon was a double form of concentration within this strategic sector: in both the labor and the product markets. The former are controlled by highly centralized union syndicates, having impressive and increasing political power. The latter are dominated to a considerable extent by a few powerful firms, that, apart from the IRI group, are closely allied to one another in a central federation—for collective bargaining and other purposes.

The union syndicates set the wage policy for the inner sector. Their aim is rapid increases in wages and supplements for their already employed members. Whatever their public professions, in practice they are not governed by national considerations of increased employment, over-all modernization and development, or a more balanced distribution of factor incomes. Given high economic concentration in many of the sector's product markets, there is extreme interdependence among sellers as to costs and prices. A common wage strategy follows inevitably. It takes the line of least resistance: sharing the gains of higher productivity exclusively with the unionized workers. In this way "destructive" price cutting can be avoided, some increase in profits can still be had, and union political pressure for nationalization can be forestalled. Alternatively put, economies of scale and small markets together foster fewness of sellers. Corespective competition then rules out price cutting. Centralized unionism then enters, effecting a redivision of the savings from increased productivity, invoking at the same time further support for the existing level of prices, ever more capital-intensive methods through internal reinvestment of profits, slow growth of employment within the sector, and enforced retardation of growth in the rest of the system. Thus the root of the problem is both technological and institutional, while the institutional forces have operated so far to perpetuate, rather than to destroy, the structural imbalances involved.[55]

CONCLUSION

It is impossible to assign meaningful weights to the various factors that account for the long delay in the economic unification of Italy, and it would be pointless to make the attempt. Nonetheless, some summary qualitative judgments can be made.

Capital scarcity and the geographic and cultural isolation of the south must rank at the top of the list. Both are long-term and deeply rooted restraining forces, of dominant importance in 1861 and still ponderate a century later. Somewhat more transitory were those adverse impacts of fascism that concerned distortions of investment and wastage of capital in futile wars. Among the more lasting of the evil legacies of that regime were its cartelization policy and the restraints it imposed upon internal migration, both of which continued in force during the postwar period here considered. Finally, for the years between 1945 and 1960 the wage and price policies of the inner sector have exerted a new kind of negative thrust, of such importance that they rank high among the current issues on the government agenda. Indeed, their constructive alteration—if such can be accomplished within a context of private bargaining—is the precedent condition to correction of the still-dangerous structural disequilibrium present in the nation's economy.

CHAPTER XV. ACHIEVEMENTS, PROBLEMS, AND PROSPECTS

This inquiry into the economy of modern Italy leaves certain questions still unanswered. How are we to account for the astonishing postwar renaissance, typified by the magnificent fourteen-year boom? What has happened in the economy since 1961? And what issues and prospects now dominate the Italian scene?

EXPLAINING THE BOOM

Between 1947 and the end of 1961 Italy attained a steady 5.9 per cent annual growth rate, rebuilt much of its industry and its agriculture, recouped its exchange reserve, put its balance of payments in order, became a vigorous international trader, added enormously to its capital, and largely overcame its serious problem of overt unemployment—all this with a comparatively small amount of inflation and with a pronounced improvement in the ordinary standards of life.

Even more remarkable, these accomplishments were erected upon the ruins of an economy bankrupted and ravaged by war, and forever hampered by a poor resource endowment. And beyond these purely physical handicaps lay a much more subtle one: the alienation of a large section of the working class from the institutions and organizations of political and industrial life—a debilitating force that continues to pose problems as acute as they were in Giolitti's time.

The paradox of alienation. Alienation manifests itself in two main directions. To workers of this persuasion, government and politics are and always were a kind of gigantic swindle, operated on the ancient principle, to them that hath it shall be given.[1] At bottom, this cynicism—not unfounded—involves an apolitical point of view, typical of the doctrines of classical syndicalism. In action it finds expression through a massive protest vote—now approaching 40 per cent—for parties whose established stance is

one of uncompromising and permanent opposition. Its consequence, reflecting as it does the numerical weakness of the Italian
middle class and universal extension of adult suffrage, is an enduring propensity for weak cabinets, erected upon fragile multiparty
coalitions—administrations that tend to become paralyzed by
immobilismo, unable to confront basic issues or to discharge
pressing national tasks. True, there have been some notable exceptions to this state of affairs in the postwar years, but the tendency is
there, and it is growing.

Alienation from politics finds its parallel in alienation from the
industrial system as well. Admittedly, this is an international phenomenon but it is particularly prevalent in Italy. For reasons that
go deeply into the feudal past and to prevailing worker and employer ideologies, the gulf separating the two groups remains vast.
In the usual case, the industrial worker senses little or no community of interest with management, according to it the same
cynicism and hostility—often masked by indifference—that he extends to politics and government. Here again "the system" is the
enemy and supposedly is of no benefit to him. If he rationalizes his
opposition, it finds expression in the myth of a socialist revolution
that will miraculously expel all managers and politicians. On the
one hand, alienation of the individual leads directly to weak and
ineffective governments. On the other, it finds issue in poor industrial discipline and enfeebled incentives in production. Over-all it
makes for a divided society, irresolute in its regard for national
interests and purpose.[2]

At this point we encounter another of the paradoxes that make
interpretation of Italian affairs so difficult at times. For we are
going to argue that among the foremost factors responsible for
postwar economic success were the creative energies of the Italian
people. How then do we resolve the apparent contradiction between intense and almost universal efforts and the undeniable existence of a substantial stratum of the population that was and remains uncommitted to the political and the economic system alike?
The short answer is that Italians work for their families, not for the
boss or the nation, and family incentive has at all times proved
strong enough to produce results, in this period astonishing ones.
This principle both the managers and the politicians well knew
and could live with, shaping their policies accordingly.

The advantages of military defeat. Then there was loss of the war, which, as in the other defeated industrial lands—West Germany, Japan, and France—has exerted a peculiarly constructive influence upon national affairs, in several diverse ways. Italy received aid and grants from the victorious powers, which meant the difference between starvation and probable revolution on the one side, and recovery and renewal on the other. Timely and essential as it was, foreign aid was more permissive than decisive for the reinvigoration of national life.

The basic contribution of defeat was that it permitted the overthrow of fascism, opening the way to a "great instauration." By this time the problem of survival had made people so desperate that the need for reconstruction was obvious to all. Despite deep and enduring cleavages in outlook, there existed a broad measure of agreement that the economy had to be rebuilt, to overcome the wastes and the losses that were part of the evil inheritance of fascism. With the return of free discussion and parliamentary rule, it now became possible to examine existing institutions critically, and to debate openly the direction and execution of national policy. Here the early appearance of a very substantial Socialist and Communist vote made those in charge of political and industrial affairs well aware that their survival depended on their ability to produce prompt recovery.

Then, too, ten years of war economy and five years of open struggle had stimulating effects after 1945. Capital destroyed by military operations or neglected for years all had to be replaced. There was also the catch-up and adaptation problem. The program of autarchy had diverted much investment to the production of armaments and food. Enforced isolation of the Italian economy distorted the allocation of its resources, leaving it unadapted to the emerging peacetime structure of domestic and foreign demands. Beyond this, the insatiable needs of the war economy and the interdictions against contact with the enemy denied to industry the opportunity to improve its technology. Thus with the return of peace the industrialists found a great new technological frontier lying before them. Since they were virtually starting from scratch, they were able to rebuild with the latest innovations.

Defeat in the field delivered Italy temporarily into the hands of the Allied powers, who, profiting from bitter experience after 1918, chose this time to play the role of enlightened and compassionate trustees, rather than conquerors. In consequence, the country gained a priceless opportunity to reconstruct its political institutions and to rebuild its broken economy. Inherent in that opportunity was the challenge to renovate national life. The difficulties were enormous, but Italians seized the opportunity with vigor and with courage.

At the same time, the war economy itself bequeathed the country a strange inheritance: a huge backlog of investment opportunities, for capital replacement and development. For years to come, there could be no possibility of oversavings, but only a problem of adequate noninflationary financing to meet the emerging array of investment and consumption demands. Since Italy's principal trading partners all found themselves in the same boat in this respect, it was inevitable that Europe would soon embark upon a protracted capital-formation boom, leading to soaring export demands. American aid, of course, was decisive to all those countries at the initial stage, providing as it did both the raw materials and the equipment for recharging the economic machine, and the convertible foreign balances for financing the revival of international trade.

Rising consumer expectations. There was another powerful stimulus operating on the boom in Italy as well as the other European countries—of much greater intensity than in the postwar United States. It was the insistence of the masses upon breaking through into new territory for consumption, upon attaining modern urban styles of life, American fashion—housing and its accouterments, automobiles and motor scooters, recreation, travel, and all the rest. This continued upsurge in popular aspirations—no less than a revolt against craft-goods in favor of those made by machine—undoubtedly threatens the charm of the traditional Italy. However, at the mundane level of economics it has served the very useful indirect purpose of giving the boom a solid footing in demand, while its collateral assertion throughout Europe has greatly boosted the country's earnings on current foreign account. Moreover, the very slow growth of the Italian population—0.62 per cent a year as against 1.7 per cent in the United States—has had favorable effects for per capita real consumption. Between 1948 and 1961, the latter could rise by an impressive 4.06 per cent yearly, without trenching upon the very high yet increasing rate of saving and investment actually achieved. The explanation was a fortunate combination of little population pressure and rapid advance in resource productivity. Quite literally, the Italians could have their cake and eat it too.

The strength of autonomous investment. It is tempting to explain the boom as the mechanical consequence of the strong support furnished throughout by rapidly expanding consumer demand. This would attribute the even faster growth of investment demand solely to the acceleration effects of growing consumption pressure on productive capacity. No doubt this factor has been at work, but not all by itself. The prospective high returns from long-term investment must be recognized as an independent force, contributing directly to the very high rate of investment, and through the multiplier effects flowing therefrom, fostering expansion of both income and consumer demand. For this has not been a purely consumption-oriented boom. Beyond direct investment to enlarge capacity in the purely quantitative sense, much capital outlay has been applied to qualitative improvements, to the exploitation of technical possibilities, and to the development of new markets. Qualitative upgrading of capital stock has been strongly aided by the postwar opportunity to catch up with the outside world. Comparatively low rates of direct profits taxation have widened that opportunity, by giving progressive firms a chance to carry down large sums to retainable net, for reinvestment in further improvements and developments. Thus the Italian boom has been the joint consequence of an interaction between consumption and autonomous investment, strengthened further by strong export demand and substantial government spending.

Industrial leadership. Before examining the government's role, credit must be given to the high quality of Italian entrepreneurship in these years. It has not shown itself only in a few big concerns, but has proved widespread. Profiting from a tradition of engineering stemming from classical Roman times, and maintaining the role of aggressive traders that reaches back to the beginnings of modern capitalism, Italian industry has been a major factor in postwar economic success. It is recorded in the vigor with which investment opportunities were seized, in the success with which foreign markets were penetrated despite considerable odds, and in the enormous gains in labor productivity that were achieved. There is no whitewashing of monopoloid positions here and there to say that the big firms have not been content with passive exploitation of static markets but have moved ahead to enlarge sales and to improve efficiency. The main weakness has been their failure to pass on large cost-savings in lower domestic prices, a policy that has slowed the modernization of the less developed sectors and regions.

When one considers the alienation from the industrial system of many workers as individuals, the startling gains in their productivity require explanation. In the first place, the incentive to better the material position of one's family is one factor. In the second, management in the leading sector has devoted much effort and capital to making the workers more productive, spurred on by the high and rapidly rising costs of labor. Artificial scarcity of this factor of production has forced industry to economize its use. Here the coefficients of more and better capital per worker on the one side, and improvements in plant organization and managerial technique on the other, have resulted in large gains in output per manhour, without calling for increased personal efforts on the workers' part.

Finally, there is unionism itself, and the manner in which industry has dealt with it. From 1948 onward, the Italian union movement was split into three major groups, which ended exclusive Communist control. In addition, the unions have at all times been strongly centralized as national bodies, with pronounced weaknesses at the plant level, which has favored a strategy of bargaining for standardized wages and supplements, and relatively little emphasis on shop rules.

In consequence, the employers have had a bargaining advantage and an opportunity to concentrate on wages, given the system of proportional representation in force and the influence of centralization upon union demands. Furthermore, slow as Italian management may have been to face up directly to the problems of worker incentive and commitment, it has followed the astute strategy of not attempting to keep all the savings to itself. Prodded by political pressures, by the unions, and by the threat to its survival implicit in an always substantial anti-capitalist vote, big industry has chosen to share these savings with its organized employees. In this way it has kept the unions comparatively quiet, conceding them large gains in wages and benefits, and diverting them from serious attack on the existing system of power.

At the same time, Italian industry has been comparatively untroubled by problems of costly work rules, partly because of the local weakness of the unions, but mainly because it did not have to face a major layoff problem in these years. True, it entered the boom with too many workers whom it could not dismiss. But with the rapid expansion of demand this surplus was soon worked off. Thereafter the very force of the expansion made protection of the work opportunity of little relevance as a goal for union strategy. Further, Italian industry was not cursed with a bargaining structure composed of warring craft unions, and this good fortune has exempted it from the futilities of jurisdictional controversies and the whole dreary apparatus of elaborate work-separation rules.

Admittedly, while it could be defended on grounds both of expediency and of the absolutely low level of real incomes even in advanced industry, the wage policy followed in this sector was not without costs. It blocked the transfer of workers to better-paying opportunities, and it slowed the absorption of the mass of unemployed. For these very reasons it helped to retard the rise of wage incomes in the rest of the economy. At the same time, the rapid advance conceded to labor costs in the advanced segment of industry helped to bolster the prices of capital goods—at the expense of the less fortunate parts of the economy. However, in retrospect this policy toward wages was the only one open to management, since restraint by the unions—hopefully voiced by the government in the Vanoni Plan—never was acceptable to them. If it had been, the government would have found itself in a far better moral position to intervene more vigorously into industrial price-making.

The role of government. What about the contribution of government to the boom? Although hard and fast measurement is not possible, it is quite reasonable to suppose that public spending at all levels of government added something net to total demand during these years. The amounts cannot be determined with precision, because there is no way of knowing the extent to which such expenditures displaced rather than supplemented private outlays. Furthermore, the Italian national income accounts do not include estimates of total government purchases from the private sector.

However, a rough idea of the current government share of GNP can be had by combining the figure for "public consumption" with that for investment at all levels of government, including in the latter figure direct investments in the form of straight public works or of expenditures applied to sectors such as agriculture and transportation, and indirect investments undertaken by state and municipal enterprises. In 1961, these totalled 3482 billion lire, or 16.6 per cent of GNP (20,975 billion lire).[3]

In 1961, total permanent investment (plant and equipment, public works, and housing) amounted to 5058 billion lire. Of this sum, government at all levels accounted for 485 billion applied to public works, only part of which was self-liquidating; 151 billion allocated to improvements in agriculture, transportation and communications; and 558 billion assigned to enterprises controlled or conducted by the central and local governments—for a total government outlay of 1194 billion.[4] This figure represents 23.6 per cent of total fixed investments in 1961. Combining the 558 billion invested by government firms with 151 billion of permanent improvements applied by government to certain sectors—for example, 49 billion for the state railways, which are operated as a regular branch of the central government—yields 709 billion of government outlays for additions to plant and equipment. This accounted for 21 per cent of total outlays in this category. Finally, all forms of government investment represented 21.7 per cent of gross investment (including net foreign).

Thus a little over one fifth of capital formation in Italy in 1961 was undertaken by government at all levels, however one defines total investment—gross, gross fixed, or plant and equipment only. The data are inadequate to permit determination of the steadiness of the rate of absolute increase in government investment during 1948–1961, or changes in government's relative share. All that is certain is that these outlays rose. In consequence, we cannot assert that government so managed its capital expenditures to contribute to the over-all stability in the rate of growth in aggregate demand, although given the remarkable steadiness actually attained we have a priori reason to suspect this. In any case, we can say that because one fifth of investment today is undertaken by government, through decisions that largely are taken independently of changes in the expected profit rate, opportunity for total investment to fluctuate is reduced commensurately, if government expands its capital spending at a steady absolute rate. Indeed, government's current one-fifth share, while not strictly the product of a single central decision, constitutes a lever of some importance for counteracting cyclical movements emerging from the private sector and abroad, if such spending is to be deliberately varied under a discretionary offsetting policy.

In short, the emergence of government as a major channel for investment of the nation's savings affords Italy a steering mechanism—or, as the French say, a "generalized market"—for curbing the swings of a free economy, without sacrificing the benefits of allocation and coordination through the price system.[5] Whether the mechanism will be employed with such wisdom remains to be seen.

Appraisal of the contribution of government takes us onto even more treacherous ground, given the quite controversial nature of the choices made and the impossibility of gauging their results with any precision.

For example, under the leadership of De Gasperi and Einaudi the decision was made in 1947 to bank on the revival of an economy conducted primarily by private initiative and guided mainly by the market mechanism. As these men saw the problem, the first steps were to halt inflation, to restore the will to save, and to rebuild the foreign balance. This led in turn to quite orthodox policies affecting money, the balance of payments, and to some extent fiscal affairs. Implicitly these choices involved resolute rejection of any extension of direct controls, and in fact to firm determination to get rid of those still in effect. Except for embarking upon long-run state intervention into the south, these principles continued to guide government policy throughout the period under review. However, in their execution they were blended pragmatically with a large amount of welfare spending, a good deal of state enterprise in some important industries, and a toleration of monopolistic or quasi-monopolistic structures in leading product and labor markets. Looking at state policy as a whole, the generalization holds that in these years Italy operated an unplanned market economy.

In view of the traditional contempt of Italians for government regulation, and of their equally traditional adherence to the family virtues of thrift, hard work, and attention to ones own interests, the initial decision to stabilize the price level and to let the market do the rest was wise, requiring no larger ideological defense. Direct controls were not a superior alternative and in any event stood no practical chance of success. Beyond this, there existed no common consensus for any radical change—only those deep divisions that continue to plague the formulation of a responsible national policy. In these circumstances, the market approach offered the best possibility, precisely because it requires no broad measure of prior formal agreement on priorities and programs. Its chief agenda are simple, clear-cut, and in good part consist of prescriptions of what not to do. In the main, they were adopted.

The decision to rely on the market began to pay off almost at once, and it continued to do so handsomely throughout the period. In addition to the rich rewards it yielded in rising per capita income, it reopened Italy to foreign commerce, reversing the accumulated inefficiencies bred by autarchy. More than this, it strongly favored the rapid formation of capital, rebuilding and developing the economy, and adding enormously to the productivity of its resources. If the proof of the pudding is in the eating, then the rapidity and the steadiness of the growth rate attained over these fourteen years surely validates the original decision, demonstrating conclusively at the same time that central planning is not a precondition for sustaining high rates of expansion.

The problem of north-south imbalance is of quite another genre. This is not to say that the difficulties of the southern peninsula and the islands were the direct mechanical result of the decentralized market economy that came into being as a national unit in 1861. In truth, this was a factor, but the principal origins of these troubles were deeply rooted in Italian history. Moreover, they were undoubtedly made worse by badly conceived types of state interference long before 1945. However, few would question the postwar need for some kind of intervention if this unhappy region were ever to become a full partner in national union. The issue here is different: the wisdom—or lack of it—of the decision in 1947 to concentrate initially upon resusciation of the badly ailing market economy. In action this meant emphasizing the overriding interests of the system as a whole. In practical effect, the decision stressed the revival of industry, whose focal point lay in the north. Viewed analytically as well as in retrospect, this was the right line for state policy. It permitted recovery first, through this providing the additional scarce resources to afford the government some desperately needed room for maneuver. Within three years it then became possible to introduce the *Cassa* scheme as a costly long-term program. This step is to the great credit of the cabinet of the time, for it implied nothing less than acceptance of a permanent commitment to do something substantial to relieve the plight of the people below Rome. Succeeding administrations also deserve credit for adding to the outlays and widening and extending the plan. All this can and should be counted as a contribution of government to economic advance.

Clearly, the original emphasis upon external economies never won wholehearted assent. However, it continued in full force until introduction of the law of 1957 controlling geographic allocation of investments of state enterprises, and even today supplies decisive guidance to the over-all program. Moreover, it was quite at one with the chosen national policy of 1947, subjoining framework planning of an indirect type to bend the forces of the market toward development, and thus leaving the tasks of commodity production to private initiative. To those who find consistency one of the minor virtues and who look upon the whole approach as quite unsuited to their view of the southern problem, the later shift to experimentation with state-operated plants was welcome, although to some it has not gone far enough. On a quite different plane, it can be urged that if the government really intended to rely upon the forces of the market, then principle as well as interest dictated that it should have abolished the statutory restrictions upon internal migration, instead of tightening them in 1949 and maintaining them in force until 1961. However, one thing is clear: the south needed large-scale fiscal aid, and needed it badly. It was provided on a very costly scale, and it has yielded a substantial absolute improvement in real per capita income, also checking at last the malignant growth of the rural population.

ECONOMIC DEVELOPMENTS AFTER 1961

Wages and money supply. If all stories should have a happy ending, then our account should end with 1961, when the Italian economy finally entered a new *konjunktur*, characterized by inflation and growing difficulties with the balance of payments. With these developments have come some important shifts in policy, all aimed at regaining stability without invoking outright deflation.

Tables 93 and 94 underscore the sea-change in economic affairs after fourteen years of comparatively "steady state" expansion. Relative to trend, the annual rates of growth in real investment and exports during 1962–1963 fell off sharply, while both consumption and imports soared. After almost a decade of stability, wholesale prices began rising in 1962, more than doubling this advance in the year following. Export prices also finally started upward, after an extended eight-year decline to 1961. During 1962–1963, the cost-of-living index—to which the wage level is closely tied—began rising at over double the trend rate of advance for 1948–1961.

Wages also took a dangerously inflationary turn, indicated in Tables 95 and 96. Table 95 shows that the rapid advance of wage rates has spread quite generally over the economy, reaching extreme proportions in the government sector. As Table 96 reveals, hourly earnings within industry rose almost 15 per cent in 1962, and almost 19 per cent in 1963, which stands out sharply against the preceding trend rate of advance of less than 6 per cent yearly. Even if gross output per man-hour had continued to rise by over 8 per cent annually after 1961, a sharp increase in the unit labor cost of industrial goods was inevitable.

The squeeze exerted by soaring labor costs also manifested itself in a marked shift to wages and salaries as a share of net product at factor cost. Between 1950 and 1961, the employees' relative share gradually edged upward from 50.8 to 55.3 per cent, meaning that the percentage share for profits and other property returns was slowly declining. During 1962 wages and salaries rose to 58 per cent, while in 1963 they jumped to 62.2 per cent.[6] In turn the growing squeeze against profits helps account for the pronounced slackening of the rate of increase in real investments and the rapid upswing in the expansion of consumption and imports (Table 93).

In part the sharp upthrust in labor costs was autonomous in origin, deriving from the enhanced political power of the trade unions after 1961, when the Fanfani Goverment embarked upon the *apertura alla sinistra* (opening to the left). This factor is well illustrated by the large rise in government salaries, which advanced 26 per cent in 1963 alone. It also appears in a 46 per cent

TABLE 93. Movements in real output, 1961–1963 [a]

Year	Real GNP		Components of real GNP								Industrial production	
			Consumption		Investment		Exports		Imports			
	Amount	Change	Amount	Change	Amount	Change	Amount	Change	Amount	Change	Index	Change
	(billion)	(per cent)	(billion)	(per cent)	(billion)	(per cent)	(billion)	(per cent)	(billion)	(per cent)	(1953 =100)	(per cent)
1961	18,748	—	13,806	—	4,941	—	3,968	—	3,967	—	202.2	—
1962	20,000	6.7	14,825	7.4	5,344	8.2	4,391	10.7	4,560	14.9	221.7	9.6
1963	20,960	4.8	16,164	9.0	5,563	4.0	4,691	6.8	5,458	19.7	241.1	8.8
Trend, 1948–61	—	5.9	—	4.7	—	9.0	—	13.5	—	—	—	8.8

ᵃ Figures for 1961 differ slightly from those cited in previous chapters because of recent revisions.
Source: Relazione generale, 1963, II, pp. 360–361, 382.

TABLE 94. Movements in prices, 1961–1963

	Wholesale		Cost of living		Consumers'		Imports		Exports		Implicit GNP	
	Index	Change	Index	Change	Index	Change	Index	Change	Index	Change	Index	Change
	(53 = 100)	(per cent)	(38 = 1.0)	(per cent)	(53 = 100)	(per cent)	(60 = 100)	(per cent)	(60 = 100)	(per cent)	(61 = 100)	(per cent)
1961	99.9	—	70.4	—	117.8	—	97.7	—	96.6	—	100.0	—
1962	102.0	2.1	74.5	5.8	123.3	4.7	97.6	−0.1	97.0	0.4	105.6	5.6
1963	107.3	5.2	81.1	8.9	132.5	7.5	99.4	1.8	99.9	3.0	114.3	8.2
Trend, 1948–61	—	—	—	3.1	—	—	—	—	—	—	—	2.3

Source: *Relazione generale*, 1963, II, pp. 149, 153, 185; 381–382.

TABLE 95. Movements in minimum contractual wage rates for married workers, by main sectors, 1961–1963 (1938 = 1.0)

Year	Agriculture		Industry		Trade [a]		Transport		Government	
	Index	Change (per cent)	Index	Change (per cent)	Index	Change (per cent)	Index	Change (per cent)	Index	Change (per cent)
1961	122.5	—	101.2	—	87.3	—	100.0	—	77.0	—
1962	142.7	16.5	109.5	8.2	92.0	5.4	109.0	9.0	87.2	13.2
1963	158.2	10.9	121.2	10.7	103.2	12.2	115.4	5.9	109.9	26.0

[a] Clerical workers only.
Source: Relazione generale, 1961, II, p. 105; 1963, II, p. 115.

jump in 1963 for wages in electric power, an industry that was nationalized in the preceding year and whose employees were already among the highest paid in Italy.

The autonomous wage-raising power of the unions was strengthened futher after 1961 by the approaching exhaustion of the excess labor reserve prevaling throughout the preceding postwar years. Starting with 1.14 million registered unemployed (Classes I and II) in 1961, their numbers fell 245,000 in 1962, and nearly 100,000 in 1963, reaching a postwar low of 1.07 million in the latter year. By

TABLE 96. Increases in average hourly earnings in industry, 1961–1963 (per cent)

Industry	Net earnings [a]		Gross earnings [b]	
	1961–62	1962–63	1961–62	1962–63
Mining	14.1	24.9	13.0	23.0
Foods	15.3	19.1	14.7	17.9
Textiles	23.6	11.6	21.7	12.4
Metal products and transport equipment	11.7	19.2	12.1	17.3
Chemicals	15.0	14.3	13.7	15.1
Miscellaneous	15.9	16.1	15.8	14.9
Electric power	8.0	46.7	8.7	46.4
Over-all	14.7	18.6	14.4	17.6

[a] Excludes certain supplements: family allowance, wage integration, vacation and holiday pay, and Christmas bonus.
[b] Includes supplements cited in note [a].
Source: Relazione generale, 1962, II, p. 105; (1963), II, p. 115.

contrast, throughout the fifties registered unemployment consistently ranged between 1.6 and 1.9 million, without downward tendency until after 1956.[7] During the last three years, Italian industry has lost the advantage of unlimited supplies of labor, and has also experienced falling quality in marginal additions to its work force. Even before this long delayed advent of full employment, the unions were able to impose a substantial wage push. Now they have market forces also on their side, and are taking full advantage of the situation, resisting all official efforts to bring about a "wage pause" in the interests of over-all stabilization.[8]

But the wage push was not the only factor responsible for current inflation. At the same time expansion of the money supply got out of hand, bringing about an increasing excess of over-all demand. Table 97 indicates this influence clearly. Even before 1962 the quantity of money had been rising at a trend rate of over 11 per cent yearly, which was acceleerating after 1958. During 1961 and 1962 it grew by huge amounts—16.5 and 18.4 per cent. Behind this rapid expansion were easy private credit, recourse of the government to central bank financing of its deficit, and increased borrowing by municipalities and special government agencies.[9] Although inflation, capital flight, and a payments deficit were already manifest during 1962, the monetary authority clung to its long-established easy money policies, even reducing the reserve ratio

TABLE 97. The growth of money supply, 1957–1963 (in billions of lire, each December 31)

Year	Money supply	Annual increase	
		Amount	Per cent
1957	5,342	303	6.0
1958	5,911	569	10.6
1959	6,641	730	12.3
1960	7,518	877	13.2
1961	8,759	1,241	16.5
1962	10,369	1,610	18.4
1963	11,680	1,311	12.6

Source: (1957–1960) Table 22; (1961–1963) *Relazione generale* 1962, II, p. 125; (1963), II, p. 450.

required of the commercial banks and allowing the latter to build up a large amount of short-term foreign debt. Not until the summer of 1963 was a program of restraint finally initiated, and then only in a limited way.

The payments deficit. The drastic reversal in the country's economic fortunes shows up clearly in its current international accounts, shown in Table 98. With the single exception of 1958, deficits in the commodity trade had been traditional since 1947. However, those returned in 1962 and 1963 were the largest on record. As for the goods and services account, it showed consistent surpluses for 1958–1961. But in 1962 this advantage was lost, while in 1963 the largest deficit of the postwar period was registered. In consequence the current account as a whole turned negative by the large sum of $636 million. In the first quarter of 1964 alone, the current account deficit was $474 million; however, marked improvement than followed, and preliminary figures for the first half indicate that this deficit has been eliminated at least for the time being.[10]

TABLE 98. Movements in net balances in current international accounts, 1961–1963 [a] (in millions of U.S. dollars)

Year	Commodity trade	Goods and services	Official and private transfers	Over-all
1961	−555.9	236.4	272.1	508.5
1962	−877.5	0.1	293.9	294.0
1963 [b]	−1797.7	−930.3	294.1	−636.2
Average, 1959–61	−440.9	298.3	228.5	526.8

[a] For details regarding these accounts, see Table 19.
[b] Provisional.
Source: International Monetary Fund, *Balance of Payments Yearbook*, (1961) vol. 15; (1962–1963) vol. 16.

Underlying forces in the inflation problem. Before reviewing recent shifts in economic policy, some attempt should be made to account for Italy's economic troubles after 1961. Their source is twofold: demand inflation coupled with a strong autonomous push from the side of wages. After fourteen years of remarkably steady expansion, by the end of 1961 the country finally began to confront a shortage of skilled labor and of real saving. In hopes of maintaining the preceding growth rate in output, the monetary authority allowed the banking system to accelerate credit formation. This inflated the money supply and effective demand.[11] In this respect, the case is the classical one of monetary overinvestment. In consequence, the price level began to rise. By itself excessive demand contributed an upward pull on wage costs. In addition, wages received an autonomous push from the operation of the cost-of-living escalator and from government and trade union policies. Profits were squeezed in favor of wages, and the rapid growth of labor incomes soon made itself felt in soaring consumption and imports, at the expense both of investment and exports. By early 1963, the Bank of Italy faced a clear choice: either surrender control of the money supply to accommodate wage excesses, accepting at the same time open inflation and a dangerous hemorrhage in the exchange reserve; or reduce liquidity in the interest of regaining stability, at some risk of deflation, higher unemployment, and interrupted growth.[12]

The decision actually taken was somewhat hesitant as well as long delayed: to tighten up somewhat on credit formation, but not drastically enough to produce a liquidation crisis. In the summer of 1963 moves were made to slow down bank lending, and in September the banks were forbidden to borrow further from abroad. At the same time, the government began efforts to reduce its deficit, introduced excises on certain luxuries, and—to stimulate private investment—granted tax concessions and more liberal depreciation rules. As Table 97 shows, for 1963 as a whole the rate of increase in money supply was cut one-third below 1962. Real GNP also grew less rapidly than in the preceding year, although it continued to increase.

However, these initial steps were both timorous and inadequate. Early in 1964 they were followed by added increases and extensions in excises, and by large-scale food imports to hold down prices. In March action was taken to shore up the lira to check capital flight: Italy drew $225 million from IMF; arranged for $550 million in swap credits with the United States Treasury and certain European central banks; and obtained $450 million in medium-term credits to finance imports from the United States. Beyond these measures, the government announced that it was considering proposals to slow down the growth of installment credit, to reduce its deficit further, to cut back upon municipal borrowing, to review and postpone certain public investment projects, and to bring about a more moderate wage and salary policy. It is still too early to determine how much has been undertaken— let alone accomplished—in these areas, but, given the many difficulties connected with forming a stable coalition, there is no great room for optimism.[13]

ISSUES AND PROSPECTS

The great boom did far more than reveal Italy's productive potential and her capacity for vigorous growth. It put the country on the road to becoming a strong middle-class nation, uniting in practice the principles of the welfare state with those of modern private enterprise. Even by 1961 this synthesis had proved to be an outstanding success. It had accomplished much in transforming the traditional peasant and handicraft society. It had made possible an impressive long-term program for the development of the south. It had produced large and broadly distributed gains in real income, and it had increased opportunities for employment. Altogether, these achievements implied that Italy at last could begin to enjoy a stable system of parliamentary democracy. Unfortunately, this stability has so far failed to emerge. Instead the actual *dénouement* is of a quite different order, one that justifies concern for the future.

The country is beset today by three great problems—inflation, southern development, and badly enfeebled government. They are tightly interlacing and depend for their common solution upon the emergence of resolute and informed political leadership. Moreover, their nature is complex, their causes deep-seated and difficult to overcome, and their very existence gravely divisive at a time when common concern for the national interest is the critical need of the hour. As it did in 1947, the nation stands again on the threshold of basic decisions. The choices made will be crucial, for the kind of industrial economy and political society that will come into being.

Consider, first, the question of inflation. It will not be possible to end the upsurge in prices without pursuing a policy of monetary restraint. But even if recent moves in this direction prove adequate, monetary policy cannot restore stability all by itself, and it is here that two formidable obstacles immediately appear. One involves wages and the other the scale of public spending and deficit-financing.

The control of wage inflation. The system of wage-making is of critical importance yet is almost exempt from the direct influence of tight money. For it must be admitted that over the years the Italian unions have displayed a consistent pattern of conduct, no different in essentials from that followed by labor organizations elsewhere: regularly recurring insistence upon more money per unit of work performed, without regard for its consequences for employment and prices. Its adverse effects are obvious, as recent events should make perfectly clear. What it means to the monetary managers is that they must suffer the tortures of that familiar Procrustean bed so common to policymakers in the postwar western world: the need to reconcile a stable price level, full employment, and unregulated collective bargaining. Can they bring about stabilization of prices and of the nation's foreign accounts if the wage level is to be left free to rise, say, 15 per cent yearly or more? If not, how can the advance in wages be held to a rate consistent with over-all stability?

The classical cure—deliberate deflation—is both harsh and costly, as well as politically unlikely. Apart from the high costs of imposing a contraction sharp enough to bring wages under control—among them heavy unemployment and sacrifice of a large amount of needed output—the political consequences would be a further spread of that crippling disease of alienation that already has made the task of achieving effective government so difficult to discharge. But will a limited braking action against credit formation be sufficient to accomplish the over-all objectives? A chance for success does exist here, but it requires an extremely delicate maneuver: to slow down the formation of money and credit, to put the still sizeable exchange reserve deliberately at risk to gain precious time, and to attempt without delay to bring into being an incomes policy—the last to effectuate an economically rational behavior for wages.

There are two alternative ways to undertake such a policy, one by statutory enforcement, and the other by consent. Needless to say, either would be extremely arduous in Italy today. Common to them both would be the introduction of standards for the guidance of wage setting consistently with the over-all interests of the nation. In principle, those standards would be the following. The average rate of advance in labor costs per hour worked at most should not exceed the national trend rate of advance in labor productivity. In markets of labor surplus, rates and benefits would be held to a slower rate of advance. In those of demonstrable shortage, they would rise faster than average. Admittedly, practical execution of the scheme would be enormously difficult. However, now that full employment is within the nation's grasp, the setting of wages through the uncontrolled and unguided exercise of comparative group power is causing enormous troubles of its own. The problem is to get wages to behave compatibly with the over-all objectives of economic policy. The need is for wage restraint. To provide for it, a framework of public standards is required. This need not mean the end of private negotiations entirely, but it does mean that their results must be shaped according to broader interests. Organizational laissez-faire has been tried and found wanting.

To introduce this framework by statute is to concede at once the political character of the wage problem, and to impose a formidable new burden upon an already overloaded and stumbling system of government. The alternative is to try the method of consent, by opening up to the power groups involved new and more constructive directions for the exercise of their interests and their policies. The obstacles are not to be minimized, among them the traditional Italian aversion to organized endeavor on behalf of any conception of the national interest. Nor is the implication to be evaded that government would still have to assume new responsibiliies, although much less of a compulsory nature.

If wage restraint is to be attempted through the method of consent, probably the most feasible route would be to adopt the procedure of incentive planning within the framework of the market economy, on the model of the present French system. This approach has three great advantages. It does not rely upon coercion, but on the contrary fully retains private decision-making. It depends upon government investment as a device for controlling fluctuations, hence is specially suited to the Italian case. And it calls for the active participation of all leading interest groups in the constructive task of formulating policies consistent with the over-all imperatives of growth, efficiency, and stability. By assuring unions and employers an over-all market, the system concentrates their attention upon common interests. If successful, it would divert the unions from their endless pursuit of more money at whatever social cost, with its sterile emphasis upon conflict, by bringing them into active responsibility for the making of sound national policies, of which wage guidance would be a part. At the same time, industrial entrepreneurs would be induced to follow a more socially acceptable system of price-making.

For the Italian context, these badly needed changes in wage and price behavior are most likely to be achieved by minimizing dependence upon coercion. But to avoid futile resort to direct controls is not to elude the most pressing problem of all, that of inadequate national consensus, without which these changes themselves are unlikely to be attained. Despite some very real accomplishments, the French themselves have not solved the wage problem, and some would dismiss their system as a romantic illusion. This goes too far and is premature. Perhaps incentive planning is the decisive ingredient required to put Italian society on a sound and enduring basis, consistent with its liberal tradition.

The control of public spending. The other main disruptive force for monetary policy is government spending and deficit-financing. The two go together, because resort to deficits has now become traditional regardless of changing economic circumstances, and this releases spending from the conventional restraint of old-fashioned fiscal policy, in which outlays must be financed by prospective revenues. Now that Italy suffers from excess total demand, the control of public spending becomes decisive for regaining price stability. The problem, then, is to make fiscal operations consistent with the over-all needs of the national economy, instead of having them determined as now in a separate compartment, insulated from the influence of the monetary managers. Either monetary and fiscal policy must go hand-in-hand in the pursuit of common purposes, or fiscal decisions will undermine monetary equilibrium.

The great difficulty in the fiscal field in Italy today is that the pressures for increased public spending have become enormous, deriving as they do from popular demands for more and more aid to the south and for enlargement of the already diverse welfare provisions, and encouraged as they are by the competition of parties for votes. One aspect of the problem is that much of this spending either goes to purely current uses rather than to capital formation, or into investment projects that either produce no direct returns or only offer a prospect of eventual yields after long delay. If the absorption of scarce real resources by public spending gets out of hand, it cuts down upon the improvement of factor productivities, thereby reducing the over-all potential of the economy for growth. In other words, government spending tends to emphasize the expansion of demand for total product, and to neglect the problem of increased supply. The danger is real, because fiscal decisions usually reflect claims in equity, backed up by votes, rather than more subtle considerations of comparative returns.

There is also the financial side. When, as in 1962–1963, total demand for product outruns total supply, monetary policy must be redirected toward bringing demand under control. At the same time, however, political pressures not only make deficits inevitable, but cause them to increase. If they are covered by advances from the Bank of Italy and by additional issues of treasury bills sold to the banks, the reserves of the latter will grow. In consequence the banks have every incentive to increase the supply of money and credit, even when the monetary managers are attempting to slow the process down. Alternatively, if deficits are financed entirely through the capital market, they divert savings from private capital formation largely to current uses or to often less productive public projects. The adverse implications for the growth rate are obvious. If price stability and continued growth are jointly desired, fiscal policy must bring the deficit under control. As with wages, the problem is inherently political, because its solution requires popular consent.

Development of the south. Inflation is but one of Italy's foremost problems today. A second concerns economic policy for the south.

The issues in this very complicated field have not been wanting in attention and concern, nor in astronomical quantities of verbiage. Also, they tend to be formulated at the extremes and in oversimplified ways, given the Latin passion for debates over abstractions. Emphatically, the actual questions are not the following: is industrialization of the south forever impossible; shall all efforts be centered upon agriculture; shall massive emigration be promoted, and the south abandoned to its fate? Extremisms of this kind are the natural products of those impassioned regional advocates, known in Italy as *Meridionalisti* and *Nordisti* (southerners and northerners), who are notorious for their willingness to pose questions in polarized forms.

The real issues are a good deal more subtle, involving matters of degree as well as kind. Is the undeniable interregional imbalance simply the inevitable consequence of the free play of market forces alone, hence correctable only by reliance upon state enterprise,

perhaps augmented by central planning? Should balanced industrial development be sought across the full spectrum of commodities, or should primary attention start with agriculture, food
processing, and light industry? Should subsidies to southern industrial enterprise be stepped up even further, or should their growth
be checked and their distribution be made more selective? Should
the whole region be treated as a common entity in need of vast
development expenditures everywhere, or should there be greater
concentration upon selected sites of demonstrable promise, with
collateral exodus from hopelessly overcrowded and underproduc-
tive rural areas? Should the rate of capital formation in the northern triangle deliberately be reduced, and more savings somehow
be directed southward, or should the rapid expansion of the north
be allowed to continue unabated, to build up the export trades
even more and to absorb additional surplus labor from the lower
peninsula?

Since 1958, these issues have become projected for extensive national discussion as the first decade of the *Cassa* reached its com-
pletion, and reliable statistics of results finally began to become
available. At the core of this mass of data are two central facts,
neither of which is in dispute: the continued widening of the
south's relative income disadvantage, despite the declared aim of
the Vanoni Plan of bringing the south up from a 50 to a 75 per cent
position by 1964; and the very disappointing growth of industrial
production and employment in the region notwithstanding expenditures of over six billion dollars together with many other
measures of assistance. Is it too early to judge results? Does the
trouble lie in not enough outlay, or in misdirection of this already
large-scale spending, or in a supposed culturally imposed want of
entrepreneurial spirit, or in something more fundamental? Is the
continuing broadening of the north's income and industrial advantage primarily the consequence of more than a decade of export
boom, or does it prove that the south is a permanently infertile soil
for industrial development?

In some respects, it *is* too soon to gauge results, simply because
it requires more than a decade of sustained effort to work off the
accumulated legacy of centuries of neglect and downright abuse.
There is also considerable evidence to show that the *Cassa* has
been spreading its expenditures indiscriminately, hence too thinly

at promising locations; and that there has been poor coordination of its efforts with those of the Budget Ministry, the Ministry of Industry, and the Inter-Ministerial Committee for the South—all of which have a finger in the pie. More than this, the whole scheme for intervention has not been wanting in opportunities for pork-barreling, nor in their effective exploitation. Consequently, the claim that not enough has been, or is being, spent is dubious, all the more so in view of limitations on the fiscal resources of the state if over-all growth and stability are not to be impaired. As for lack of entrepreneurs, the contention is quite unconvincing when one recalls the many gifted men that the south has contributed to statecraft, industry, and the professions in the decades after 1861.

In any case, the manner in which the basic issues of southern policy are resolved can be of the highest importance for the future of the Italian economy and the country's political system. Fortunately, although the problems are immense, there does exist some middle ground for effective attack and solution, short of leaving everything to the market on the one side, or all-out central planning on the other.

This strategy of the middle way rests upon a particular conception of the southern problem. It presumes that the commitment to reduce and eventually to wipe out interregional imbalance must and will be honored. And it calls for an approach to resolution of this problem that is consistent with a national policy for development that continues to emphasize a maximum noninflationary rate of growth in real output.

As Mrs. Vera Lutz has shown with great cogency, a substantial emergence of self-sustaining industry in the south depends foremost upon the development of adequate local demand for its products.[14] Given the economic structure of the region, the crucial factor determining demand is the rate of expansion of income-formation in agriculture. In other words, the immediate problem is one of constricted local markets for industrial goods, not a lack of entrepreneurial initiative. If it is true, and convincing evidence to the contrary has yet to be presented, that the elasticity of supply of southern agricultural products is quite low at present, then the need of the hour is to speed up the rise of per capita real income in agriculture. Merely to push investment in regional industry will not turn the trick. The main source of income is still agriculture, and if it fails to grow rapidly, local demand for industrial products will continue to be small. Without an unlikely early and rapid development of northern and foreign export outlets for these products, the newly established plants will suffer losses, and state subsidies will have to grow still more.

There are three main ways to boost productivity and real income in southern agriculture. One is continued improvement of its environment, through provision of infrastructure, credit institutions, and technical assistance, as the *Cassa* is doing. The second is direct investments in farming to improve techniques, raise capital coefficients, and effect shifts in production away from cereals, and into livestock, olive oil, wine, fruits, and vegetables. And the third is to encourage migration of the rural population, both within agriculture to better sites and more profitable lines, and out of agriculture, mainly to the expanding industrial labor markets of the north. With out-migration, the critically important man-land ratio can be reduced, in itself adding substantially to the rise of productivity and per capita income of those remaining in agriculture. As Mrs. Lutz emphasizes, this solution does not mean abandonment of the south, or of all attempts at further industrialization. Nor should one assume that a prosperous but heavily agricultural region is incompatible with an integrated and advanced industrial economy for the whole country. The case of Kansas is sufficient evidence to the contrary. However, it should be clear that this approach does mean a decline from the south's present 38 per cent share of the population, and, with this, acceptance undisturbed of the north's present overwhelming predominance as a center for industrial production and employment, although in time this can be reduced as industry begins to expand in the south.

Collaterally, this position implies some other important considerations. It would leave substantially intact—and this is deliberate —the guidance of the Italian economy primarily by market forces. It would require further concentration of population within the triangle and its immediate ambit. It presumes that the south cannot expect to develop a large export surplus of foods; and it recognizes that Italy as a whole is already a substantial net importer of foods and livestock, that this import surplus will grow, and that to cover it will require a continuing rise in her export surplus of manufactures. Because these exports are so critical, *a fortiori* delivered prices become decisive. Accordingly, because plant location can be vital for processing and transport costs, the north's traditional general advantage must be conceded, hence left undisturbed by efforts at forced relocation of industry. Finally, this policy is designed to reduce the dependence of the south upon subsidies—to lighten rather than to increase over time the heavy fiscal burdens of the state, deploying its expenditures as far as possible to improving resource productivity to protect the growth rate of real national income.

Although not free from all objection, the whole approach opens up an avenue for preserving the liberal principles that were the heart of the De Gasperi-Einaudi experiment, without neglect of the south's very real needs.[15] Indeed, it does not differ in essentials from what Luigi Einaudi himself had long advocated as the "natural solution." It should also be noted that despite legal barriers the south has benefited throughout the postwar period by emigration. Now that the statutory restrictions upon internal migration belatedly have been lifted, the exodus to the north is growing, aided by an increasing shortage of industrial labor in that region. This outflow does not please those neo-Mercantilists among the advocates of unconditional regional primacy. But it is the consequence of the exercise of a newly won dimension of personal liberty, and it promises of itself to contribute much to an unforced solution of the problem of southern imbalance.

However, this general line of policy does require some amendment, and some qualifications. It seems too pessimistic about the locational disadvantages of industry in the south. Newly available sources of energy and means of transport are already working in the opposite direction. What continues to be badly needed is adequate provision of primary and secondary schooling, and vocational training—for investment in human capital is now recognized in its own right as a decisive factor in productivity. Enough has already been accomplished here to reduce significantly the cost disadvantage imposed by lower quality of labor, and expenditures in behalf of this kind of external economy are now rising. Beyond these factors, there is a strong prospect that in time the other lands of the Mediterranean basin will become important markets for Italian products, perhaps altering the traditional 60 per cent concentration of exports in northern Europe. Here the south will acquire a locational advantage of its own.

Furthermore, it would be wise to continue a measure of experimentation with the introduction of a few giant industrial complexes such as Taranto and Gela, and of smaller nuclei in promising southern locations, guided by modern methods of programming. This need require neither over-all central planning of investment and production, nor a swamping of the fiscal resources of the state. But it is a useful way to test what really cannot be decided a priori: the potential of the south as a home for viable industry producing jointly for the local market, the north, and the export trades. Obviously, if these pragmatic ventures yield a significant pay-off, they, too, can absorb rural labor, cutting down on long-distance migration, with its heavy social costs of worker relocation, now borne mostly by the north. In a prudent view, these experiments should not be allowed to get out of hand, but neither should they be forgone entirely. At the same time, the immediate over-all strategy would stress agriculture and would favor internal migration as a decisive ingredient of a voluntary solution.

The real dangers lie elsewhere: in blindly urged schemes for over-all "balanced" industrial development of the south without further delay; in the dissipation of fiscal assistance through parliamentary surrender to constituency pressures; and in doctrinaire demands for central planning to supplant the market.[16] All these routes lead to waste of scarce resources, to reduced growth of national income, and to the formation of armies of bureaucrats whose primary product is an endless series of new "programs," supported by unlimited quantities of empty rhetoric.

It should be obvious by now that the issues of southern development policy, as with those of inflation, are political as well as economic. This brings us to the last of the major problems now dominating the Italian scene, that of political leadership and responsible government.

The problem of political consensus. The perennial predicament of all political leaders in modern Italy has been how to construct a cabinet based on majority consent—in other words, a government capable of governing. During 1919–1922, this very weakness was to issue in a breakdown of the parliamentry system and the rise to

power of Benito Mussolini. For this consummation, the Socialist
Party of that time bore a heavy responsibility, for, divided as it was
between its gradualist and revolutionary wings, it chose not to
collaborate in the formation of a government, and instead to enter
into a futile competition against the Communists through a program of factory seizures and violence. Without the party's participation, an effective cabinet could not be put together, and so the
way was opened to the Fascist dictatorship.

As in those times, the system of proportional representation
nourishes a multiplicity of parties. By spreading the vote so
widely, it makes coalition regimes a regularly recurring necessity.
The task becomes all the worse because over a third of the elec-
torate is alienated from all government, voting as *protestatari per
natura* for any party that stands no chance of participating in these
coalitions. During the postwar years, the two great organizations
of the permanent opposition—the Communists and their long-time
allies, the Socialists—have been the chief beneficiaries of this
negative sentiment.

For reasons of common doctrine regarding the reconstruction
of economic policy and institutions, a view emphatically not
shared by over 60 per cent of the voters, these two parties naturally could assume an opposition role—all the more so because
their basic outlook was shaped around an "ethic of ultimate ends,"
to use Max Weber's distinction, rather than by a readiness to undertake the responsible exercise of power. More than this, a negative role was soon thrust upon them. In May 1947, De Gasperi
brought about a decision by the Christian Democrats, then the
leading party, to break completely with tripartite alliances with the
left, hence not to collaborate further with either the Communists or
the Socialists in the formation of any new cabinets. In principle, this
continued to be Christian Democratic policy until the advent of
the opening to the left early in 1962.

In the earlier postwar period, the Socialists and Communists
were in such close alliance that in 1948 they could run a joint
ticket in the national election. Together they represented a hard
opposition to any government of the day. But beginning with the
mid-fifties the Socialist Party began developing an internal split
that put the alliance itself in question. This rupture was partly traditional, in that the party had always included a moderate faction

that was not hostile in principle to action by the parliamentary rather than the revolutionary route. With the revelations contained in Khrushchev's denunciation of Stalin's rule, together with the shock of the Hungarian revolution and its suppression, the moderates began to gain in strength. At their head, furthermore, was the party leader himself, Pietro Nenni.

At the same time, the ominous growth of the protest vote began posing an increasingly formidable problem for the Christian Democrats. Between the elections of 1948 and 1958, their share of the total vote fell from 48.5 to 42.4 per cent.[17] Substantial economic advance had failed to reduce the number of disaffected voters. This is not surprising. Conditions of life remain hard for many Italians, who have not shared in *la dolce vita* and who resent bitterly those who have. Of special significance have been the personal hardships attendant upon migrating from village to city; the chafing restraints of newly imposed industrial discipline; and the higher margins of unsatisfied aspirations aroused by contact with modern urban life—all of which promote discontent, not acceptance.

To the Christian Democrats, the problem was the simple one of how to stay in power despite the continuing erosion of their political base in favor of the parties of the left. Under the leadership of Giovanni Gronchi and Amintore Fanfani—who later were respectively to become president of the Republic and prime minister—the party's own left wing began urging a new orientation, which was to become the *apertura alla sinistra*. This was natural, for the Christian Democratic left had supported the earlier tripartite popular front strategy of 1945–1947, and in its over-all outlook has strongly favored a powerful central government, surrounded by a complex of functional groups, given its affinity for hostile critiques of market capitalism and individualistic competition.[18] On the doctrinal plane, therefore, this faction's position did not foreclose the possibility of a coalition with the Socialists. With Nenni's own gradual shift away from the Communists, some kind of arrangement began to look more and more feasible.

In the meantime, Fanfani became premier, and with the onset of a cabinet crisis in January 1962 found opportunity at a party congress in Naples at the end of that month to put forward the *apertura* proposal. Despite opposition from the center and right factions, Fanfani obtained a four to one majority for a resolution favoring an attempt by the Christian Democrats to bring about a parliamentary alliance with the Socialists. As posed in the resolution, the party would not invite the Socialists to join a new government, but instead would try to create a parliamentary voting alliance with them, by shaping its program in such a way as to win affirmative Socialist support, or at least their abstention from voting. Accordingly, the problem of parliamentary consent could be solved—or so the Fanfani group thought.

On February 18, 1962, the Socialists formally approved the voting alliance. One week later, Fanfani succeeded in forming a new coalition government, dominated by the Christian Democrats and involving the collaboration of the Republicans and the Democratic Socialists (not the Socialist Party referred to up to now, but a separate group led by Giuseppe Saragat). Giuseppe Pella and Mario Scelba, both former Christian Democratic prime ministers, refused posts in the new cabinet. Also, for the first time the small but important Liberal Party, which is strongly committed to private enterprise, found itself on the outside.

Now that the first step in the *apertura* had been taken, its underlying theory became relevant. It was also simple, resting on the old idea of a leftist popular front, but without its original inventors, the Communists. *Combinazioni* are an ancient and not altogether inspiring story in Italian politics, of which this attempt was only the latest. The immediate tactic was to gain the necessary support in parliament for launching a strong government program. As that program took effect, it was supposed to siphon off votes from the ample Communist reservoir. In time, too, it was hoped that the Socialist Party would change its posture, detaching itself entirely from its traditional postwar alignment with the Communists, ultimately committing itself to full collaboration in the tasks of government.

Naturally the Socialists had a price for the parliamentary alliance, and it was one that the Fanfani group was prepared to pay. It consisted of the following agenda: nationalization of the power industry, increased state enterprise in commodity production, increased government spending, rejection of wage restraint, and further extension of the principle of autonomous regions. For these very reasons, the *apertura* was repugnant to large sections of the

Christian Democratic Party and to the Liberals, all of whom viewed it as a dangerous gamble with fateful implications for the future of the nation.

The rest is now history. Open inflation was already under way when the new Fanfani Government took office. Although the origins of the upswing in prices lay in preceding monetary and fiscal excesses, there can be no doubt that for more than a year thereafter the Fanfani regime did nothing to halt it. And for good reason, for the very terms of its arrangement with the Socialists precluded such action. Then came disaster in the election of April 29, 1963, when the Christian Democrats went down to smashing defeat, with their share of the vote sinking to 38.3 per cent. Soon after, the Fanfani cabinet resigned amidst bitter recriminations regarding the causes of the debacle. Weeks of interregnum followed, after which only a weak caretaker government could be formed. In turn it was succeeded by a new version of the *apertura,* a coalition formed by the Christian Democrats, with Aldo Moro as premier and with the Socialists now in the cabinet. Although the Moro ministry had to be reconstituted once, it has continued in power until the present time (the fall of 1964).

No responsible student of Italian affairs would question the need for stronger government, or deny that major changes are needed in both political and economic affairs. Some way must be found to strengthen the weak cohesiveness of Italian society, which, expressing itself through the neutral mechanisms of universal suffrage and proportional representation, leads to a multiplicity of parties and to so extensive a diffusion of votes that no party is likely to win a majority. In these circumstances, coalition regimes are mandatory. Their consequence is likely to be ineffective governments, unable to deal competently with the pressing issues of the times.

So viewed, the *apertura* is but one more coalition, and one more attempt to cope with the underlying problem of weak cohesion by political means. But there is a difference, for this particular arrangement is intended to convert the protest vote into support for a responsible government, by bringing the Socialists into the unfamiliar role of sharing in the formation of a government and in the making of national policy. On the surface and from a purely mechanical standpoint, this coalition is stronger than most.

The real issue is much more subtle: how is this political power to be used for the governance of economic affairs? The immediate need is to regain stabilization. Given the terms on which the Socialists were induced to enter the coalition, what is the likelihood that the necessary steps will be initiated and firmly carried out? Will the Moro Government actually follow through on its proposals of the spring of 1964, to introduce a responsible wage policy, to bring the deficit under control, and to check the diversion of saving to relatively unproductive public uses? Or will it take the easy way, under the illusion that the Bank of Italy can restore stability all by itself? In short, are the politics of the coalition likely to be subordinated to the economic needs of the hour, or will expediency prove dominant, even if the price be slower growth and continued inflation?

As these questions suggest, the ultimate test of the *apertura* will be its ability to end inflation without sacrifice of adequate growth, and to carry on a long-term program for the development and integration of the nation's backward regions.

To carry out these difficult tasks will require leadership of the highest order, of the quality earlier provided by the two greatest statesmen of modern Italy, Alcide De Gasperi and Luigi Einaudi, who confronted and surmounted a crisis of comparable severity in 1947, and who thereby launched the country upon its greatest period of economic expansion. A careful Italian observer, Ettore Massacesi, foresaw the present situation with unusual insight:

> There are not many men of politics in Italy who are capable in terms of will and of competence of conceiving and bringing about a true policy of development. They will require so much strength, so much courage, so much patience, so much breadth of mind, and so much wisdom—all these together. In short, this is a very difficult matter because against it are the whole of the institutional reality and much of the human reality that characterize our country today.[19]

Leaders with these high qualities exist and will be found, for in her times of need Italy has never lacked for men of disinterested but concerned greatness. Only men of this stature can meet the challenge so well expressed by Paul Valéry, that "nothing is more difficult than to determine the true interests of a people, which are not to be confused with its wishes."[20]

SELECTED BIBLIOGRAPHY

NOTES

INDEX

SELECTED BIBLIOGRAPHY

Ackley, G., and L. Spaventa. "Emigration and Industrialization in Southern Italy: A Comment," Banca nazionale del lavoro, *Quarterly Review*, 61: 196–204 (June 1962).

Agnelli, A. *Il problema economico della disoccupazione: Cause e rimedi.* Milan: Società editrice libreria, 1909.

Albrecht-Carrié, René. *Italy from Napoleon to Mussolini.* New York: Columbia University Press, 1950.

Ambrogi, Francesca. "Le retribuzioni dei dipendenti dell'industria dal 1938 al 1955," *Rassegna di statistiche del lavoro*, special issue IX (December 1955).

——— "Le retribuzioni dei dipendenti dell'industria dal 1949 al 1955," *Rassegna di statistiche del lavoro*, VII:112–122 (March–April 1955).

Ammassari, Giuseppe. *I salari di fatto in Italia: Inchiesta sugli slittamenti salariali.* Milan: Giuffrè, 1963.

Andreatta, N., et al. *Introduzione di problemi del lavoro*, vol. I: *I termini economici*, Istituto sociale ambrosiano. Milan: Capello & Boati, 1952.

Associazione per lo sviluppo dell'industria nel Mezzogiorno (SVIMEZ). *L'aumento dell'occupazione in Italia dal 1950 al 1957.* Rome: Giuffrè, 1959.

——— *Economic Effects of an Investment Program in Southern Italy.* Rome: Failli, 1951.

——— *Popolazione e forze di lavoro.* Rome: SVIMEZ, 1952.

——— *Statistiche sul Mezzogiorno d'Italia, 1861–1953.* Rome: Failli, 1954.

Bacchi Andreoli, Silvio. "La teoria keynesiana in Italia," *Bancaria*, V:941–952 (November 1949); V:1029–1049 (December 1949).

Baffi, Paolo. "Monetary Developments in Italy from the War Economy to Limited Convertibility (1935–1958)," Banca nazionale del lavoro, *Quarterly Review*, 47:399–483 (December 1958).

——— "Monetary Stability and Economic Development in Italy, 1946–1960," Banca nazionale del lavoro, *Quarterly Review*, 56:3–30 (March 1961).

Baldinozzi, Giuseppe. "La cassa integrazione guadagni operai dell'industria," in *La disoccupazione in Italia*, vol. II, part 2. Rome: Camera dei deputati, 1953.

Banca d'Italia. *Abridged Version of the Report for the Year 1961.* Annual. English.

——— *Adunanza generale ordinaria dei partecipanti* (succeeded by *Assemblea generale*). Annual.

——— *Assemblea generale ordinaria dei partecipanti* (successor to *Adunanza generale*). Annual.

Banca nazionale del lavoro. *Quarterly Review.* Bimonthly.

Banco di Roma. *Review of the Economic Conditions in Italy.* Bimonthly.

Banfield, Edward C., and Laura Fasano Banfield. *The Moral Basis of a Backward Society.* Glencoe, Illinois: The Free Press, 1958.

418 | Selected Bibliography

Bank for International Settlements. *Twentieth Annual Report,* April 1, 1949–March 31, 1950. Basle: Bank for International Settlements, June 12, 1950.

Barbagallo, Corrado. *Le origini della grande industria contemporanea,* 2nd ed. Florence: La nuova Italia firenze, 1951.

────── *La questione meridionale.* Milan: Garzanti, 1948.

Barberi, Benedetto. 'Aspetti dinamici e strutturali di un secolo di sviluppo economico dell'Italia," Economia e storia, *L'economia italiana dal 1861 al 1961.* Milan: Giuffrè, 1961.

Bauer, P. T. "The United Nations Report on the Economic Development of Underdeveloped Countries," *Economic Journal,* LXIII:210–223 (March 1953).

Bellacci, Riccardo. "Aspetti economici degli assegni familiari," *Rassegna di statistiche del lavoro,* VII:217–228 (May–June 1955); VII:321–336 (July–August 1955).

Boeke, J. H. *Economics and Economic Policy of Dual Societies, as Exemplified by Indonesia.* Haarlem: H. D. Tjeenk Willink & Son, 1953.

Bowden, Witt, Michael Karpovich, and Abbott Payson Usher. *An Economic History of Europe Since 1715.* New York: American Book Co., 1937.

Bresciani-Turroni, Costantino. "Credit Policy and Unemployment in Italy," Banco di Roma, *Review of the Economic Conditions in Italy,* III:171–178 (May 1949).

────── "Monetary Policy and Internal Financial Stability," Banco di Roma, *Review of the Economic Conditions in Italy,* VI:463–475 (November 1952).

────── "Two Contrasting Opinions Regarding Italian Economic Policy," Banco di Roma, *Review of the Economic Conditions in Italy,* IV:355–364 (September 1950).

────── "Working of the Sliding Scale Applied to Wages in Italy," Banco di Roma, *Review of the Economic Conditions in Italy,* X:519–547 (November 1956).

Bundesrepublik Deutschland. *Statistiches Jahrbuch für die Bundesrepublik Deutschland.* Annual.

Caffè, Federico. "Considerazione storico-bibliografiche attorno al problema della disoccupazione in Italia," *L'industria,* 2:236–248 (1952).

Camera dei deputati, Commissione parlamentare di inchiesta sulla disoccupazione. *La disoccupazione in Italia,* 5 vol. in 15. Rome: Camera dei deputati, 1953.

Capanna, Alberto. "Economic Problems and Reconstruction in Italy," *International Labour Review,* LXIII:607–632 (June 1951); LXIV:24–60 (July 1951).

Carlyle, Margaret. *The Awakening of Southern Italy.* London, New York: Oxford University Press, 1962.

Centro di azione latina, Cassa di risparmio delle provincie lombarde. *Italy's Economy, 1961.* Milan: Giuffrè, 1961.

Cenzato, Giuseppe, and Salvatore Guidotti. "Il problema industriale del Mezzogiorno," Ministero per la costituente, *Rapporto della commissione economica,* vol. II, *Industria,* part 1, pp. 361–417. Rome: Istituto poligrafico dello stato, 1947.

Chenery, Hollis B. "Development Policies for Southern Italy," *Quarterly Journal of Economics,* LXXVI:515–547 (November 1962).

Christ, Carl F. "A Review of Input-Output Analysis," in National Bureau of Economic Research, Studies in Income and Wealth, vol. 18, *Input-Output Analysis: An Appraisal.* Princeton: Princeton University Press, 1955.

Cipolla, Carlo M., ed. *Storia dell'economia italiana,* vol. I: *Secoli settimo-diciassettesimo.* Turin: Edizioni scientifiche Einaudi, 1959.

Clark, C. "The Development of the Italian Economy," Banca nazionale del lavoro, *Quarterly Review,* 30:125–128 (September 1954).

Clark, M. Gardner. "Governmental Restrictions on Labor Mobility in Italy," *Industrial and Labor Relations Review,* 8:3–18 (October 1954).

Clough, Shepard B. *The Economic History of Modern Italy.* New York and London: Columbia University Press, 1964.

Clough, Shepard B., and Carlo Livi. "Economic Growth in Italy: An Analysis of the Uneven Development of North and South," *Journal of Economic History,* XVI:334–349 (September 1956).

Comitato dei ministri per il Mezzogiorno. *La relazione al parlamento del presidente del comitato dei ministri per il Mezzogiorno,* 1960, republished in *Mondo economico,* supp., XV:21 (May 21, 1960).

———— *La relazione al parlamento del presidente del comitato dei ministri per il Mezzogiorno,* 1961, republished in *Mondo economico,* supp., XVI: 20 (May 20, 1961).

Comitato interministeriale per la ricostruzione, Segretaria generale. *Politica di sviluppo: Cinque anni del lavoro.* Rome: Instituto poligrafico dello stato, 1958.

———— Segretaria per il programma di sviluppo economico. *Lineamenti del programma di sviluppo dell'occupazione e del reddito in Italia.* Rome: Instituto poligrafico dello stato, 1956.

Comitato per lo sviluppo dell'occupazione e del reddito, report no. 6. *Riconsiderazione dello "Schema Vanoni" nel quinto anno dalla sua presentazione,* republished in *Mondo economico,* supp., nos. 33–34 (August 22, 1959).

Commissione indagini e studi sull'industria meccanica, Gruppo di consulenza dello Stanford Research Institute. *Problemi economici ed industriali delle industrie meccaniche italiane.* Tivoli: Commissione indagini e studi sull'industria meccanica, 1952.

Confederazione generale dell'industria italiana (Confindustria). *Annuario di statistiche del lavoro.* Rome: Confindustria. Annual.

———— *L'industria italiana alla metà del secolo XX.* Rome. Confindustria, 1953.

———— *Rassegna di statistiche del lavoro.* Quarterly.

Coppola d'Anna, Francesco. "E possibile una politica di 'Full Employment' in Italia?" *Previdenza sociale,* II:132–140 (July–August 1946).

———— "Le forze di lavoro e il loro impiego in Italia," *La disoccupazione in Italia,* vol. IV, part 2. Rome: Camera dei deputati, 1953.

———— "Lo schema keynesiano e il problema della disoccupazione in Italia," *Previdenza sociale,* V:11–17 (January–April 1949).

———— "Lo sviluppo della popolazione addetta ad attività non agricole nell'ultimo cinquantennio," in *La disoccupazione in Italia,* IV:51–76. Rome: Camera dei deputati, 1953.

Curatolo, Renato. "Le statistiche corrente dell'occupazione e della disoccupazione in Italia," part I, *Rassegna di statistiche del lavoro,* XIII:17–39

(January–April 1961); part II, XIII:101–123 (May–June 1961; part III, XIII:213–224 (July–December 1961).

De Benedetti, Rinaldo. *Il problema della popolazione in Italia.* Milan: Edizioni di comunità, 1954.

Despres, Emile, and C. P. Kindleberger. "The Mechanism for Adjustment in International Payments—The Lessons of Postwar Experience," *American Economic Review,* Papers and Proceedings, XLII:332–344 (May 1952).

Dickinson, Robert E. *The Population Problem of Southern Italy: An Essay in Social Geography.* Syracuse, New York: Syracuse University Press, 1955.

Dicks-Mireaux, L. A., and J. C. R. Dow. "The Determinants of Wage Inflation: United Kingdom, 1946–1956," *Journal of the Royal Statistical Society,* series A (General), vol. 122, part 2 (1959), pp. 145–174.

Di Fenizio, Ferdinando, *Le leggi dell'economia,* vol. IV, part 1: *Diagnosi previsioni politiche congiunturali in Italia.* Rome: ISCO, 1961.

Di Nardi, Giuseppe. "La disoccupazione nel Mezzogiorno," *L'industria,* 4:515–534 (1951).

——— "The Program for the Economic Development of Southern Italy," Banco di Roma, *Review of the Economic Conditions in Italy,* VI:99–109 (March 1952).

Domar, Evsey D. "Capital Expansion, Rate of Growth, and Employment," *Econometrica,* 14:137–147 (April 1946).

——— Comment on H. Pilvin, "Full Capacity vs. Full Employment Growth," *Quarterly Journal of Economics,* LXVII:559–563 (November 1953).

——— "Expansion and Employment," *American Economic Review,* XXXVII: (March 1947).

Eckaus, R. S. "Factor Proportions in Underdeveloped Areas," *American Economic Review,* XLV:539–565 (September 1955).

Eckstein, Otto, and Thomas A. Wilson. "The Determination of Money Wages in American Industry," *Quarterly Journal of Economics,* LXXVI:379–414 (August 1962).

Economia e storia. *L'economia italiana dal 1861 al 1961: Studi nel lo centenario dell'unità d'Italia.* Milan: Giuffrè, 1961.

Einaudi, Luigi. *Lo scrittoio del presidente (1948–1955),* vol. I, part 2 of *Opere di Luigi Einaudi,* ed. Giulio Einaudi (1956).

Einaudi, Mario. "The Italian Land: Man, Nature, and Government," *Social Research,* 17:8–34 (March 1950).

Einaudi, Mario, and François Goguel. *Christian Democracy in Italy and France.* Notre Dame, Indiana: University of Notre Dame Press, 1952.

Ellis, Howard S., ed. *The Economics of Freedom: The Progress and Future of Aid to Europe.* New York: Harper, 1950.

European Economic Community, Commission. *Report on the Economic Situation in the Countries of the Community.* Brussels: European Economic Community, September 1958.

Federici, Nora. "Recent Forecasts of the Future Growth of Population in Italy," Banca nazionale del lavoro, *Quarterly Review,* 28–29:58–69 (January–June 1954).

Fellner, William. *Trends and Cycles in Economic Activity: An Introduction to Problems of Economic Growth.* New York: Holt, 1956.

Foa, Bruno. *Monetary Reconstruction in Italy.* The Carnegie Endowment for International Peace. New York: King's Crown Press, 1949.

Fortunato, Giustino. "Il Mezzogiorno e lo stato italiano," *Discorsi politici, 1880–1910*, 2 vols. Bari: G. Laterza, 1911.

Fossati, Antonio. *Lavoro e produzione in Italia dalla metà del secolo xviii alla seconda guerra mondiale*. Turin: Giappichelli, 1951.

Friedman, Milton. "Comment" on Carl F. Christ, "A Review of Input-Output Analysis," National Bureau of Economic Research, Studies in Income and Wealth, vol. 18, *Input-Output Analysis: An Appraisal*. Princeton: Princeton University Press, 1955.

Gambino, Amadeo. "The Control of Liquidity in Italy," Banca nazionale del lavoro, *Quarterly Review*, 52:3–23 (March 1960).

Gerschenkron, Alexander. "Notes on the Rate of Industrial Growth in Italy, 1881–1913," *Journal of Economic History*, XV:360–375 (December 1955).

Gibbs, Henry. *Italy on Borrowed Time*. London: Jarrolds, 1953.

Gilbert, Milton, and Irving B. Kravis. *An International Comparison of National Products and the Purchasing Power of Currencies: A Study of the United States, the United Kingdom, France, Germany and Italy*. Paris: Organisation for Economic Co-operation [n.d.].

Gini, Corrado. "La teoria europea del risparmio e la teoria americana dell'antirisparmio," *Rivista di politica economica*, XXXVII:665–670 (June 1947).

Grindrod, Muriel. *The Rebuilding of Italy: Politics and Economics 1945–1955*. London and New York: The Royal Institute for Economic Affairs, 1955.

Guarneri, Felice. *Battaglie economiche tra le due grandi guerre*, vol. I, 1918–1935. Milan: Garzanti, 1953.

Haberler, Gottfried. "Critical Observations on Some Current Notions in the Theory of Economic Development," *L'industria*, vol. 2 (1957).

———— "Some Problems in the Pure Theory of International Trade," *Economic Journal*, LX:223–240 (June 1950).

Hagen, E. E. "Population and Economic Growth," *American Economic Review*, XLIX:310–327 (June 1959).

Hamberg, D. *Economic Growth and Instability: A Study in the Problem of Capital Accumulation, Employment, and the Business Cycle*. New York: Norton, 1956.

———— "Full Capacity vs. Full Employment Growth," *Quarterly Journal of Economics*, LXVI:444–449 (August 1952).

Harrod, R. F. Comment on H. Pilvin, "Full Capacity vs. Full Employment Growth," *Quarterly Journal of Economics*, LXVII:553–559 (November 1953).

———— *Towards A Dynamic Economics*. London: Macmillan, 1948.

Higgins, Benjamin. "The 'Dualistic Theory' of Underdeveloped Areas," *Economic Development and Cultural Change*, IV:99–115 (January 1956).

———— *Economic Development: Principles, Problems, and Policies*. New York: Norton, 1959.

Hirschman, Albert O. "Inflation and Deflation in Italy," *American Economic Review*, XXXVIII:598–606 (September 1948).

———— "Investment Policies and 'Dualism' in Underdeveloped Countries," *American Economic Review*, XLVII:550–570 (September 1957).

"Il lavoro in Italia in 1954" (unsigned), *Rassegna di statistiche del lavoro*, VII:19–36 (January–February 1955).

"Il nuovo sistema di scala mobile dei salari nell'industria" (unsigned), *Rassegna di statistiche del lavoro*, III:273–281 (May–June 1951).

International Labour Office. *Year Book of Labour Statistics.* Annual.

International Monetary Fund. *Balance of Payments Yearbook.* Annual.

Istituto centrale di statistica (ISTAT). *Annuario statistico italiano.* Rome: Istituto poligrafico dello stato. Annual.

——— *Bolletino mensile di statistica.* Monthly.

——— *III Censimento generale dell'industria e del commercio* (November 5, 1951), 17 vols. Rome: Failli, 1957.

——— *Indagine statistica sullo sviluppo del reddito nazionale dell'Italia dal 1861 al 1956*, series VIII, vol. 9: *Annali di statistica.* Rome: ISTAT, 1957.

Istituto sociale ambrosiano. *Introduzione ai problemi del lavoro*, vol. I: *I termini economici.* Milan: Istituto sociale ambrosiano, 1952.

Kantorowicz, Ernst. *Frederick the Second, 1194–1250.* London: Constable, 1957.

Kaplan, Jacob J. "Economic Stagnation in Italy?" Yale Institute of International Studies, Memorandum No. 32 (May 10, 1949).

Kindleberger, Charles P. *International Economics.* Homewood, Illinois: Irwin, 1953.

Kuznets, Simon. *Six Lectures on Economic Growth.* Glencoe, Illinois: The Free Press, 1959.

Loffredo, Ferdinando Enrico. "L'assicurazione disoccupazione," *La disoccupazione in Italia*, vol. II, part 2. Rome: Camera dei deputati, 1953.

Lutz, Friedrich A. and Vera C. *Monetary and Foreign Exchange Policy in Italy.* Princeton Studies in International Finance, no. 1. Princeton: Princeton University Press, 1950.

Lutz, Vera. "The Growth Process in a 'Dual' Economic System," Banca nazionale del lavoro, *Quarterly Review*, 46:279–325 (September 1958).

——— "Italy as a Study in Development," *Lloyds Bank Review*, n.s., 58:31–45 (October 1960).

——— *Italy, A Study in Economic Development.* The Royal Institute of Economic Affairs. London, New York: Oxford University Press, 1962.

——— "Italy: Economic Recovery and Development," in Howard S. Ellis, ed., *The Economics of Freedom: The Progress and Future of Aid to Europe.* New York: Harper, 1950.

——— "Reply," Banca nazionale del lavoro, *Quarterly Review*, 61:205–219 (June 1962).

——— "Some Characteristics of Italian Economic Development, 1950–1955," Banca nazionale del lavoro, *Quarterly Review*, 39:153–185 (December 1956).

——— "Some Structural Aspects of the Southern Problem: The Complementarity of 'Emigration' and Industrialization," Banca nazionale del lavoro, *Quarterly Review*, 59:367–402 (December 1961).

Luzzatto, Gino. "Il problema della disoccupazione in Italia nei primi settant'anni dell'unità," *La disoccupazione in Italia*, vol. IV, part 4. Rome: Camera dei deputati, 1953.

Mack Smith, Denis. *Italy, A Modern History.* Ann Arbor: University of Michigan Press, 1959.

Malagodi, Giovanni F. "Relazione generale," *La disoccupazione in Italia*, vol. II, part 3. Rome: Camera dei deputati, 1953.

Mariani, Isidoro-Franco. "La revisione della scala mobile dei salari," *Rassegna di statistiche del lavoro*, IX:3–20 (January–February 1957).

Marrama, Vittorio. *Teoria e politica della piena occupazione.* Rome: Edizioni italiane, 1948.

Massacesi, Ettore. "Il dibattito aperto dal secondo articolo di Vera Lutz," *Mondo economico,* XVII (March 10, 1962).

Mazumdar, Dipak. "Underemployment in Agriculture and the Industrial Wage Rate," *Economica,* n.s., XXVI:328–340 (November 1959).

Menichella, Donato. "The Contribution of the Banking System to Monetary Equilibrium and Economic Stability: Italian Experience," Banca nazionale del lavoro, *Quarterly Review,* 36–37:5–21 (January–June 1956).

Miani-Calabrese, Donato. "Indices of the Cost of Living in Italy," Banco di Roma, *Review of the Economic Conditions in Italy,* IX:20–32 (January 1955).

Miconi, Gastone. "Recessions in Italy during the Last Fifteen Years," Banco di Roma, *Review of the Economic Conditions in Italy,* XIV:579–593 (November 1960).

"Migrazione interne e mobilità del lavoro," *Mondo economico,* XV:7–8 (March 19, 1960).

Ministero del bilancio. *Relazione generale sulla situazione economica del paese.* Annual.

Ministero del lavoro e della previdenza sociale. *Statistiche del lavoro.* Quarterly.

Ministero per la costituente. *Rapporto della commissione economica presentato all'assemblea costituente,* vol. II: *Industria,* part 2. Rome: Istituto poligrafico dello stato, 1947.

Molinari, Alessandro. "Necessità dell'industrializzazione in Italia: Compiti e problemi dell'industria," *L'industria,* 4:3–18 (1947).

———— "Occupazione, disoccupazione e sotto-occupazione nei paesi sovrapopolati e nel Mezzogiorno d'Italia," *Statistica,* XV:610–644 (October–December 1954).

———— "Southern Italy," Banca nazionale del lavoro, *Quarterly Review,* 8:25–47 (January 1949).

Mondo economico. Weekly.

Moore, Wilbert E. *Economic Demography of Eastern and Southern Europe.* Geneva: League of Nations, 1945.

Myint, Hla. "An Interpretation of Economic Backwardness," *Oxford Economic Papers,* 6:132–163 (June 1954).

Myrdal, Gunner. *Economic Theory and Underdeveloped Regions.* Bombay: Vora and Co., 1958.

Neufeld, Maurice F. *Italy: School for Awakening Countries.* Ithaca: New York School of Industrial and Labor Relations, Cornell University, 1961.

"Nuova elaborazione di un salario medio nazionale degli operai dell'industria" (unsigned), *Rassegna di statistiche del lavoro,* IV:379–386 (July–August 1952).

Occhiuto, Antonio. "Le leve di lavoro," *Rassegna di statistiche del lavoro,* special issue VI, May 1952, pp. 43–44.

Organisation for Economic Co-operation and Development. *Definitions and Methods,* rev. ed. Paris: OECD, 1960.

———— (formerly Organisation for European Economic Co-operation). *General Statistics.* Monthly.

———— *Italy.* June 1964.

Organisation for European Economic Co-operation. *Basic Statistics of Food and Agriculture.* Paris: OEEC, 1954.

—— *Definitions and Methods*, vol. I: *Indexes of Industrial Production*. Paris: OEEC, 1957.

—— *Europe in 1960*, eighth report, vol. 2. Paris: OEEC, 1957.

Orlando, Giuseppe. "Metodi di accertimento della disoccupazione agricola," *Rassegna di statistiche del lavoro*, special issue VI, May 1952, pp. 22–23.

Papa, Gina. "Compulsory Unemployment Insurance in Italy," Banca nazionale del lavoro, *Quarterly Review*, 23:227–237 (October–November 1952).

Parlamento, Camera dei deputati, Commissione parlamentare d'inchiesta sulla disoccupazione. *La disoccupazione in Italia*. Atti della commissione, 5 vol. in 15. Rome: Camera dei deputati, 1953.

Pilvin, Harold. "Full Capacity *vs.* Full Employment Growth," *Quarterly Journal of Economics*, LXVII:545–552 (November 1953).

President's Committee to Appraise Employment and Unemployment Statistics *Measuring Employment and Unemployment*. Washington: Government Printing Office, 1962.

La relazione al parlamento del presidente del comitato dei ministri per il Mezzogiorno, 1961, republished in *Mondo economico*, supp., XVI:20 (May 20, 1961).

Rienzi, Emanuele. "Il mercato del lavoro," *Rassegna di statistiche del lavoro*, special issue VI, May 1952, pp. 19–20.

Roselli, Enrico. *Cento anni di legislazione sociale, 1848–1950*, vol. I: *Titoli legislativi*. Milan: Editrice Bernabò, 1951.

Rosenstein-Rodan, Paul N. "Programming in Theory and in Italian Practice," *Investment Criteria and Economic Growth*. Cambridge, Mass.: Center for International Studies, Massachusetts Institute of Technology. December 1955.

—— "Rapporti fra fattori produttivi nell'economia italiana," *L'industria*, vol. 4 (1954).

Rossi-Doria, Manlio. *Riforma agraria e azione meridionalista*, 2nd ed. Bologna: Edizioni agricole, 1956.

—— *La struttura e i problemi fondamantali dell'agricoltura meridionale*. Portici, 1951.

Rottenberg, Simon. "The Meaning of Excess Supplies of Labor," *Scottish Journal of Political Economy*, VIII:65–70 (February 1961).

Salvatorelli, Luigi. *A Concise History of Italy from Pre-historic Times to Our Own Day*. Translated by Bernard Miall. New York: Oxford University Press, 1940.

Samuelson, Paul A. "Economic Theory and Wages," David McCord Wright, ed., *The Impact of the Union*. New York: Harcourt, Brace, 1951.

Sanseverino, Luisa Riva. "La politica legislativa italiana per la disciplina del mercato del lavoro," *La disoccupazione in Italia*, vol. IV, part 1. Rome: Camera dei deputati, 1953.

Sapi, Jandi, ed. *Il nuovo codice del lavoro: Legislazione vigente con note introduttive, commenti ed indici*, 1st ed. (to November 30, 1951).

Saraceno, Pasquale. "Italy," European Economic Community, Commission, *Report on the Economic Situation in the Countries of the Community*, pp. 351–420. Brussels: European Economic Community, September 1958.

—— "La mancata unificazione economica," Economia e storia, *L'economia italiana dal 1861 al 1961*, pp. 692–715. Milan: Giuffrè, 1961.

Schmidt, Carl T. *The Corporate State in Action: Italy Under Fascism*. London: Gollancz, 1939.

————— *The Plough and the Sword: Labor, Land and Property in Fascist Italy.* New York: Columbia University Press, 1938.

Scitovsky, Tibor. "Two Concepts of External Economies," *Journal of Political Economy,* LXII:142–151 (April 1954).

Scotto, Aldo. "Influenza sulle occupazioni del sistema della previdenza sociale," *La disoccupazione in Italia,* vol. IV, part 3. Rome: Camera dei deputati, 1953.

Segrè, Claudio. *Produttività e prezzi nel processo di sviluppo: L'esperienza italiana 1950–1957.* Rome: Giuffrè, 1959.

Simpson, E. S. "Inflation, Deflation and Unemployment in Italy," *Review of Economic Studies,* XVII:203–225 (1949–1950).

Solow, Robert M. "A Contribution to the Theory of Economic Growth," *Quarterly Journal of Economics,* LXX:65–94 (February 1956).

Somogyi, Stefano. "Previsioni demografiche sulle forze di lavoro per il 1960," *Rassegna di statistiche del lavoro,* special issue VI, May 1952, pp. 41–43.

Sprigge, Cecil J. S. *The Development of Modern Italy.* New Haven: Yale University Press, 1944.

Tagliacarne, Guglielmo. "Demographic and Social Development," Banco di Roma, *Review of the Economic Conditions in Italy,* special issue, *Ten Years of Italian Economy, 1947–1956* (Rome, 1957), pp. 16–32.

Tarle, Evgenij Viktorovič. *La vita economica dell'Italia nell'età napoleonica.* Translated by Santachiara. [?]: Giulio Einaudi, 1950.

Tremelloni, Roberto. *Storia recente dell'industria italiana.* Milan: Garzanti, 1956.

United Nations, Department of Economic and Social Affairs. *Yearbook of International Trade Statistics.* Annual.

————— Economic Commission for Europe. *Economic Survey of Europe in 1949.* Geneva: United Nations, 1950.

————— *Economic Survey of Europe in 1950.* Geneva: United Nations, 1951.

————— *Economic Survey of Europe Since the War: A Reappraisal of Problems and Prospects.* Geneva: United Nations, 1953.

United Nations, Statistical Office, Department of Economic and Social Affairs. *Demographic Yearbook.* Annual.

U.S. Mutual Security Agency, Economic Cooperation Administration. *Italy Country Study.* Washington: Government Printing Office, 1949.

————— Special Mission to Italy for Economic Cooperation. *The Structure and Growth of the Italian Economy,* by H. B. Chenery, P. G. Clark, and V. Cao Pinna. Rome: 1953.

Valk, W. L. *Production, Pricing and Unemployment in the Static State.* Publication no. 21, Netherlands Economic Institute. London: P. S. King, 1937.

Vannutelli, Cesare. "Cause ed effetti dell'appiattimento salariale," *Rivista di politica economica,* XXXIX:559–564 (May 1949).

————— "Le nuove norme per la rilevazione degli indici del costo della vita ed il sistema di scala mobile dei salari," *Rivista di politica economica,* XLII:516–529 (May 1952).

————— "Occupazione e salari in Italia dal 1861 al 1961," *Rassegna di statistiche del lavoro,* XIII:195–212 (July–December 1961).

————— "Recent Wage Structure and Cost of Labour Changes in Italy," Banco di Roma, *Review of the Economic Conditions in Italy,* IX:129–142 (March 1955).

———— "La scala mobile dei salari," *Rivista di politica economica*, XXXVIII: 322–334 (April 1948).

———— "Social Security in Italy," Banco di Roma, *Review of the Economic Conditions in Italy*, III:417–426 (September 1949).

———— "Topical Aspects and Problems of Italy's Wage Policy," Banco di Roma, *Review of the Economic Conditions in Italy*, XIII:180–206 (March 1959).

———— "Wage Structure and Cost of Labour in Italy," Banco di Roma, *Review of the Economic Conditions in Italy*, VI:385–407 (September 1952).

Vöchting, Friedrich. *Die Italienische Südfrage: Entstehung und Problematik eines Wirtschaftlichen Notstandsgebietes*. Berlin: Dunker & Humblot, 1951.

Wallich, Henry C. *Mainsprings of the German Revival*. New Haven: Yale University Press, 1955.

Warriner, Doreen. *Economics of Peasant Farming*. London, New York: Oxford University Press, 1939.

Welk, William G. *Fascist Economic Policy: An Analysis of Italy's Economic Experiment*. Cambridge, Mass.: Harvard University Press, 1938.

Whyte, Arthur James. *The Evolution of Modern Italy*. Oxford: Blackwell, 1950.

NOTES

CHAPTER I

THE POSTWAR ECONOMY OF ITALY IN PERSPECTIVE

1. Einaudi was governor of the Bank of Italy between January 1945 and May 1947, when he became deputy prime minister and minister of the budget in the De Gasperi government. In April 1948 he took office as the first president of the new Republic of Italy. Menichella succeeded Einaudi as acting governor in May 1947, moving up from the post of general manager. He was named governor in 1948, holding this position until 1960.

2. Law n. 646 (August 10, 1950), *Istituzione della Cassa per opere straordinarie di pubblico interesse nell'Italia Meridionale (Cassa per il Mezzogiorno), La gazzetta ufficiale,* 200 (1950). In 1957, the life of the *Cassa* was extended to 1965. By 1961, the cumulative appropriations for the *Cassa* had risen to $3.37 billion.

CHAPTER II

INFLATION AND MONETARY POLICY, 1945–1949

1. For greater detail on inflation during the war, see Paolo Baffi, "Monetary Developments in Italy from the War Economy to Limited Convertibility (1935–1958)," Banca nazionale del lavoro, *Quarterly Review,* no. 47 (December 1958), pp. 399–417.

2. Baffi puts the Bank's note issue of June 1945 at 370.5 billion. The annual report of the Banca d'Italia, *Adunanza generale ordinaria dei partecipanti, 1949* (Rome: Tipografia Banco d'Italia, 1950) sets the figure at 288.6 billion. If we add 74.9 billion for notes of the Allied Military Government (whose issue was not taken under Bank control), and 54.8 billion for circular checks (partly of Bank origin, and all circulating as currency), the total note issue (excluding a negligible amount of government notes and coins) stood at 418.3 billion. Vault cash at the banks must have been around 18.3 billion (known to be 21.1 billion in December); hence total currency in public circulation would have been about 400 billion in June. Figures for AMG lire and circular checks estimated from year-end values.

3. Price data from *Adunanza generale,* 1945, 1946

4. Exchange rates from *Adunanza generale,* 1946, 1947.

5. Under the Italian system, reserves can be kept either at the Bank of Italy or at the treasury and may include certain government bills placed on deposit. The banks can create reserves by (1) depositing excess vault cash, (2) by purchase and deposit of treasury bills, (3) by rediscounting eligible paper with the Bank, (4) by temporary overdrafts with the Bank, and (5) by loans and advances from the Bank. As of that time, only the commercial banks were required to provide reserves, applicable against total demand and time deposits. In 1958, reserve requirements were extended to the savings banks.

6. A law of 1926 limited bank loans and advances to thirty times net worth, with any excess to be covered 100 per cent by investment in government securities for deposit as reserves. Before the war, the figure was cut to twenty but then was raised to thirty once more. On January 29, 1947, Governor Einaudi reminded the banks of the requirement, but it could not be enforced because net worth had fallen so far behind loans and deposits.

7. Figures compiled from *Adunanza generale,* 1948–1950.

8. These figures refer to all types of investments (*impieghi*)—discounts, advances, loans, and securities. Between the end of December 1946 and the end of September 1947 the ratio of bank investments to deposits rose from 59.9 to 74.7 per cent. *Adunanza generale,* 1947, p. 160.

9. The evolution of monetary policy is discussed in the following sources along with the inflation itself and its causes: Baffi, "Monetary Developments in Italy," pp. 435–437; Bruno Foa, *Monetary Reconstruction in Italy,* The Carnegie Endowment for International Peace (New York: King's Crown Press, 1949), pp. 106–107; Albert O. Hirschman, "Inflation and Deflation in Italy," *American Economic Review,* XXXVIII:4 (September 1948), p. 600; Friedrich A. and Vera C. Lutz, *Monetary and Foreign Exchange Policy in Italy,* Princeton Studies in International Finance, no. 1 (Princeton: Princeton University Press, 1950), p. 13; Donato Menichella, "The Contribution of the Banking System to Monetary Equilibrium and Economic Stability: Italian Experience," Banca nazionale del lavoro, *Quarterly Reivew,* nos. 36–37 (January–June 1956), pp. 15–16; and E. S. Simpson, "Inflation, Deflation and Unemployment in Italy," *Review of Economic Studies,* XVII:44 (1949–1950), p. 208

10. *Adunanza generale,* 1947, pp. 153–156.

11. Menichella's paper well reveals his astute and subtle grasp of both the uses and the limitations of monetary policy for the guidance of a market economy.

12. Decree law n. 691 (July 17, 1947), *Istituzione di un comitato interministeriale per il credito ed il risparmio, La Gazzetta ufficiale,* 175 (1947).

13. Simpson, "Inflation, Deflation and Unemployment in Italy," pp. 215 ff.

14. The authoritative text of the new reserve requirements is available in *Adunanza generale,* 1947, pp. 158–159.

15. Paolo Baffi, "Monetary Stability and Economic Development in Italy, 1946–1960," Banca nazionale del lavoro, *Quarterly Review,* no. 56 (March 1961), p. 8.

16. For detailed analysis of exchange rates, see Lutz, *Monetary and Foreign Exchange Policy in Italy,* pp. 26–32. For discussion of changes in 1947, see *Adunanza generale,* 1947, pp. 63–68.

17. Among these independent factors are: union wage policy, government spending, decisions of the public regarding its desired level of cash balances, investment decisions of private firms, movements in foreign price levels, and policies of other governments toward international trade and currency exchange. For discussion see Menichella, "The Contribution of the Banking System to Monetary Equilibrium and Economic Stability," pp. 6–7.

18. Data for prices and wages from *Adunanza generale,* 1950, p. 136; for interest rates from *Bolletino mensile di statistica,* 1947–1948.

19. Counterpart funds emerging from sale of imports received under foreign aid were sterilized by the government during 1948, which also checked the increase of currency in circulation.

20. Note that the other banks reduced their business loans net by 17.2 billion. In part, this reflects a reduced demand for credit during the first half of 1948, when a brief recession was in course following stabilization.

21. U.S. Mutual Security Agency, Economic Cooperation Administration, European Recovery Program, *Italy Country Study* (Washington: GPO, February 1949), pp. 2–3.

22. United Nations, Economic Commission for Europe, *Economic Survey of Europe in 1949* (Geneva: United Nations, 1950), pp. 70–71. A year later, ECE asserted that credit controls has stopped inflation "at the expense of halting the advance of production and holding it well below the technical limits set by total supplies of manpower and plant capacity." *Economic Survey of Europe in 1950* (Geneva: United Nations, 1951), p. 143. By 1953, ECE was still urging faster expansion for Italy, suggesting that inflationary tendencies might be turned aside "by direct controls such as is done more or less successfully both in northern and eastern European countries." *Economic Survey of Europe Since the War: A Reappraisal of Problems and Prospects* (Geneva: United Nations, 1953), p. 210.

23. Using a reweighted index for manufacturing and mining alone—adding engineering products and excluding electric power and gas, rubber, and petroleum products—the ERP study provides an index that shows February 1948 as the bottom, with a drop of 19.7 per cent. It is not known whether the official index cited in the text above had been improved by the time the figures cited had been published (1951). ERP, *Italy Country Study*, pp. 15 and 65.

24. In ECE's case, the argument was that any ensuing inflation could have been suppressed by reimposing direct controls. ERP suggested instead that the threat could have been turned aside by contracting spending.

25. The nature of the Keynesian analysis and its bearing upon the Italian case are ably considered in Bank for International Settlements, *Twentieth Annual Report*, April 1, 1949—March 31, 1950 (Basle: Bank for International Settlements, June 12, 1950), pp. 78–80. See also Costantino Bresciani-Turroni, "Two Contrasting Opinions Regarding Italian Economic Policy," Banco di Roma, *Review of the Economic Conditions in Italy*, IV:5 (September 1950), pp. 355–364.

26. ECE recognized the problem and proposed direct import controls, although the Italians were striving for convertibility and free trade. In any case, import controls simply would have diverted the increased purchasing power to home markets, adding to inflationary pressure there.

27. Some of those who took this side of the matter also contended that fixity of input coefficients made it impossible to substitute much labor for capital, and that capital stock was deficient relative to manpower—therefore production and employment could not have expanded more. This version of the theory of structural unemployment is too rigid and unrealistic, and is unnecessary for the main argument. For a careful statement of the position, see Simpson, "Inflation, Deflation and Unemployment in Italy," pp. 217–224.

28. Cited in Costantino Bresciani-Turroni, "Monetary Policy and Internal Financial Stability," Banco di Roma, *Review of the Economic Conditions in Italy*, VI:6 (November 1952), p. 466. The members of this committee were L. C. Robbins, E. R. Lindahl, A. W. Marget, M. Masoin, J. Rueff, E. Schneider, and C. Bresciani-Turroni.

CHAPTER III

THE LONG BOOM, 1948–1961: OUTPUT, PRICES, AND INCOME

1. It should be noted that Einaudi left the cabinet to become president in April 1948, while De Gasperi resigned the premiership in August 1953. Despite their departure, the principles of stable prices and free international trade have continued to command quite general adherence in the series of governments that followed.

2. Per head of population present, the over-all increase in real GNP for the period was 103.6 per cent. This figure is more relevant for testing the relationship between internal production and population actually at hand.

3. After the origins and slopes of the exponential trend lines were calculated as linear regressions, the annual trend values were estimated from the equation

$$Y_t^* = Y_0 \, (1 + g)t,$$

which in logarithmic form is

$$\log Y_t^* = \log Y_0 + t \log (1 + g),$$

where Y is any year in the series, t is the number of the particular year in the series, g is the growth rate, and * denotes estimated. The estimating equations obtained are:

Total GNP:	$\log Y_t^* = 3.910517 + 0.024733t$	$(r^2 = 0.9943)$
Industrial production:	$\log Y_t^* = 1.77544 + 0.036652t$	$(r^2 = 0.9927)$
GNP per head:	$\log Y_t^* = 2.244468 + 0.022175t$	$(r^2 = 0.9947)$
Consumption:	$\log Y_t^* = 3.84743 + 0.0199699t$	$(r^2 = 0.9942)$
Investment:	$\log Y_t^* = 3.143428 + 0.03749t$	$(r^2 = 0.9872)$
Exports:	$\log Y_t^* = 2.90781 + 0.05513t$	$(r^2 = 0.9836)$

The coefficients of determination, r^2, measure the proportion of total variation in the dependent variable that is attributable to the independent variable, in this case time itself—hence indicate relative goodness of fit.

4. A recent summary of findings appears in Gastone Miconi, "Recessions in Italy during the Last Fifteen Years," Banco di Roma, Review of the Economic Conditions in Italy, XIV:6 (November 1960), pp. 579–593. In another version, see Ferdinando di Fenizio, Le leggi dell'economia, vol. IV, part 1, Diagnosi previsioni politiche congiunturali in Italia (Rome: ISCO, 1961), pp. 182–193. The dating of the cycles in these two sources is not fully in accord.

5. Miconi, "Recessions in Italy," pp. 589–590, 592–593.

6. The growth coefficient is 1.0233, with a coefficient of determination of 0.9389. The estimating equation is:

$$\log Y_t^* = 1.92243 + 0.010093t.$$

7. Between January and July 1951, import prices jumped 25.8 per cent, and those for exports 15.7 per cent. Thereafter both indexes declined. Ministero del bilancio, Relazione generale sulla situazione economica del paese, 1952 (hereafter Relazione generale), p. 47.

8. *Relazione generale,* 1961, II, p. 415.

9. The implicit GNP deflator for the export component alone shows a drop of 3 per cent in these prices during 1950–1961.

10. The growth coefficient is 1.03128, and the coefficient of determination 0.97644. The estimating equation for the period is:

$$\log Y_t^* = 1.983188 + 0.0133783t.$$

11. *Relazione generale,* various issues.

12. As late as 1948, rents were only 3.66 times their 1938 level, although the cost of living as a whole was then 48.4 times higher. Upward revisions occurred in 1951 and thereafter at irregular intervals.

13. Data for consumers' prices from *Relazione generale,* 1961, II, p. 416.

14. As described more fully in a later chapter, the figures for hours are collected by the Ministry of Labor in a running monthly sample of all firms with ten or more manual workers. Thus they exclude small firms and hours worked by nonproduction workers. For the seven groups considered here, sample coverage is much higher than in other segments of industry, and for iron and steel and nonferrous metals (primary metals) it is complete. These data were taken from Ministero del lavoro e della previdenza sociale, *Statistiche del lavoro,* various issues for 1952–1954 and 1959–1961.

15. Excepting metal products, the output series were taken from the *Relazione generale,* 1961, II, pp. 328–332 (1953 = 100); metal products from Organisation for Economic Co-Operation and Development, *General Statistics,* September 1962, p. 11. Relative group weights were taken from OECD (then OEEC), *Definitions and Methods,* vol. I, "Indexes of Industrial Production" (Paris, 1957), pp. 52–56. The actual Italian weights, rather than the revised ISIC ones, were used, although the metal products category was redefined to include transportation equipment, to make it compatible with the OECD production series. Following are the weights, in per cent: extractive (4.77), textiles (19.07), metallurgical (13.54), metal products (34.42), construction materials (6.91), rubber (3.32), and chemicals (17.96). Together, these groups are 64.97 per cent of the over-all index.

16. If prices paid for industrial raw materials were rising, as may have been true; if the proportion of overhead labor were increasing, as probably occurred; and if net investment per man were also going up with technological deepening, then net margins would have risen less than gross. However, the scale of the productivity offset plus a remarkably level price index warrant the conclusion that net margins were increasing.

Wage data compiled from *Statistiche del lavoro,* various issues. They derive from the same sample as the hours figures.

17. One weakness in the procedure is that the hours categories had to be matched with those for output, which are separately compiled according to unpublished criteria. The other lies in the incomplete nature of the hours data, as noted. Thus the results are only indicative, not final. Until official productivity data are made available, they will have to serve.

18. Lack of man-hour data precludes a parallel investigation for the whole economy.

19. It can be objected that this imputation procedure assumes that average product per man-hour is not affected by the quantity of man-hours used. However, there is no way to allow for this influence.

20. The recorded increase in group net product was 1478 billion lire. Thus

the computed increase accounts for 92.6 per cent of the true gain. The difference is explained by the undistributed cross-products implicit in the process of imputation used.

Data for industry net products (1953) from *Annuario statistico italiano*, 1954 (Rome, 1955), p. 359; (1960) from *Relazione generale*, 1961, I, p. 25. Man-hour inputs from *Statistiche del lavoro*, various issues.

21. This compares with a 5.9 per cent per year trend rate for real GNP for 1948–1961 as a whole. It suggests clearly that productivity was increasing much faster in the advanced sector, since employment there increased much less than proportionately, while in the rest of the nonagricultural economy it expanded in greater proportion relative to the latter's share of the increase in national output.

22. Hollis B. Chenery, "Development Policies for Southern Italy," *Quarterly Journal of Economics*, LXXVI:4 (November 1962), p. 528.

23. The main statute was a decree law of December 14, 1947, no. 1598, "Disposizioni per l'industrializzazione dell'Italia meridionale ed insulare" cited in a special issue of *Mondo economico, Guida al Mezzogiorno*, April 21–28, 1962, p. 58. Other laws supplemented this decree during 1948–1950.

24. The full legislative reference is cited in Chapter I, Note 2.

25. *Mondo economico*, supp., XV:21 (May 21, 1960), p. III.

26. See Repubblica italiana, Comitato interministeriale per la ricostruzione, Segretaria per il programma di sviluppo economico, *Lineamenti del programma di sviluppo dell'occupazione e del reddito in Italia* (Rome: Istituto poligrafico dello stato, 1956).

27. Comitato dei ministri per il Mezzogiorno, *La relazione al parlamento del presidente del comitato dei ministri per il Mezzogiorno* (1960), as republished in *Mondo economico*, supp., XV:21 (May 21, 1960), p. III.

28. *La relazione al parlamento del presidente del comitato dei ministri per il Mezzogiorno* (1961), as republished in *Mondo economico*, supp., XVI:20 (May 20, 1961), p. XVI.

29. Figures for investment in the south from *La relazione al parlamento del presidente del comitato dei ministri per il Mezzogiorno*, 1961, p. XVII; for rest of country, from *Relazione generale*, 1961, II, p. 348.

30. Law no. 634 (July 29, 1957), *Provvedimenti per il Mezzogiorno*, cited in *Guida al Mezzogiorno*, p. 61.

31. The estimating equations are as follows:

South:

Total income: $\log y^* = 3.267446 + 0.0294316t$ $\quad (r^2 = 0.98159)$

Per capita: $\log y^* = 2.024254 + 0.0253409t$ $\quad (r^2 = 0.9768)$

Rest of country:

Total income: $\log y^* = 3.79745 + 0.033213t$ $\quad (r^2 = 0.9884)$

Per capita: $\log y^* = 2.32517 + 0.0311996t$ $\quad (r^2 = 0.99839)$

32. Parliamentary discussion of these issues by representatives of the leading parties is reproduced in *Mondo economico*, supp., XVI:7 (February 18, 1961). This exchange of views came to be known as the "Lutz debate," because of two articles by Mrs. Vera Lutz that questioned southern policy in quite penetrating terms. They are: "Italy as a Study in Development," *Lloyds Bank Review*, n.s., no. 58 (October 1960), pp. 31–45; and "Some Structural Aspects of the Southern Problem: The Complementarity of 'Emigration' and Industrialization," Banca nazionale del lavoro, *Quarterly Review*, no. 59 (December 1961), pp. 367–402.

33. *La relazione al parlamento del presidente del comitato dei ministri per il Mezzogiorno*, 1961, p. XVIII.

34. The figures cited were taken from *Rassegna di statistiche del lavoro*, XV:2 (March–April 1963), pp. 140–141, where the census results have been published preliminarily. As defined here, "north" includes the triangle as such —Piedmont, Lombardy, and Liguria—and also Valle d'Aosta, Trentino-Alto Adige, Veneto, Friuli-Venezia Giulia, and Emilia. "South" includes all seven regions of that part of the country.

35. Both figures are brought down by the survival of much artisan industry, but the 3:1 ratio in favor of the north indicates the much greater relative importance of big plants there.

CHAPTER IV

THE LONG BOOM, 1948–1961: THE FOREIGN BALANCE AND MONEY SUPPLY

1. Excluding drawings on special loan credits (war surplus, Export-Import Bank, IBRD, and so forth), net total official aid to Italy (mostly United States) amounted to $2735.1 million for 1943–1954 inclusive. After 1954, Italy became a net contributor to the world on this account. The largest injections occurred during 1943–1947. Source for these figures: (1943–1946) V. Lutz, "Italy: Economic Recovery and Development," in Howard S. Ellis, ed., *The Economics of Freedom: The Progress and Future of Aid to Europe*, with an introduction by Dwight D. Eisenhower, published for the Council on Foreign Relations (New York: Harper, 1950), p. 303; (1947–1954), International Monetary Fund, *Balance of Payments Yearbook*, issues cited for this period in Table 20.

2. Net earnings from tourism rose from $6.4 million in 1947 to $66.8 million in 1950, while remittances advanced from $34.1 million to $88.0 million.

3. A loss of monetary gold to abroad (credit) is counted as a decrease in foreign assets, because possession of such gold represents a claim on foreign currency or other assets. An inflow of monetary gold (credit) is treated in reverse fashion.

4. No monetary gold was exported net in that year. On the contrary, $27.4 million flowed in, mainly via repatriation of capital after the lira was stabilized and confidence restored. The figure on net capital account is net of this inflow.

5. In an extreme case, "net worth" would increase even if external assets decreased, provided that external liabilities declined by a larger amount. "Net worth" would also "increase" if, as a net debtor, a country reduced its net indebtedness to the world.

6. Figures for foreign investment and net foreign debits of the monetary sector from IMF, *Balance of Payments Yearbook*, vol. 14.

7. Of the 1961 figure, 34.8 per cent was in gold, and 63.0 per cent was held for the Foreign Exchange Office (Ufficio italiano dei cambi—UIC). Data for 1947 from Banco d'Italia, *Adunanza generale*, 1947, p. 232; for 1961, Banca d'Italia, *Abridged Version of the Report for the Year 1961* (Rome: Printing Office of the Banca d'Italia, 1962), p. 108. The OECD reports the official reserve at end 1961 at $3.4 billion.

8. An additional 1.9 per cent came from services and supplies to foreign governments, mostly for military purposes; and 1.4 per cent from returns on

Italian investments abroad. All figures from IMF, *Balance of Payments Yearbook,* vol. 14.

9. United Nations, Department of Economic and Social Affairs, *Yearbook of International Trade Statistics* (1951) (New York: United Nations, 1952), pp. 147–149. These comparisons are rough because of intervening changes in classifications.

10. IMF, *Balance of Payments Yearbook,* vol. 14.

11. UN, *Yearbook of International Trade Statistics,* 1961, pp. 354–356, 360.

12. Data for 1950 from UN, *Yearbook of International Trade Statistics,* 1951, p. 152.

13. The estimating equation for money supply is log $y^* = 3.265697 + 0.04766t$, with a coefficient of determination of 0.8929.

14. On this point, see Paolo Baffi, "Monetary Stability and Economic Development in Italy, 1946–1960," Banca nazionale del lavoro, *Quarterly Review,* no. 56 (March 1961), p. 4.

15. Figure for 1948 from Baffi, "Monetary Stability and Economic Development in Italy, 1946–1960," p. 23; for 1961, from *Abridged Version of the Report for the Year 1961,* p. 62.

16. At the end of December 1947, total primary reserves of the commercial banks stood at 177.6 billion lire. On the same date fourteen years later they had reached 2119 billion—an advance of 1093 per cent. Figures from *Adunanza generale,* 1948, p. 169; and *Abridged Version of the Report for the Year 1961,* p. 53.

17. Figure for 1948 from Baffi, "Monetary Stability and Economic Development in Italy, 1946–1960," p. 23; for 1961 from *Abridged Version of the Report for the Year 1961,* p. 62.

18. For able discussions of these matters, see Paolo Baffi, "Monetary Stability and Economic Development in Italy, 1946–1960," pp. 3–30; Baffi, "Monetary Developments in Italy from the War Economy to Limited Convertibility (1935–1958)," Banca nazionale del lavoro, *Quarterly Review,* no. 47 (December 1958), pp. 475–481; and Amadeo Gambino, "The Control of Liquidity in Italy," Banca nazionale del lavoro, *Quarterly Review,* no. 52 (March 1960), pp. 3–23.

19. Huge increases in note issue and deposit currency in every year after 1957 (see Table 23) caused the banks to become fully "loaned up" by 1961, shown by a slippage in the de facto ratio below 24 per cent in this period.

20. The former governor, Donato Menichella, attributes much importance to these relations. See Donato Menichella, "The Contribution of the Banking System to Monetary Equilibrium and Economic Stability: Italian Experience," Banca nazionale del lavoro, *Quarterly Review,* nos. 36–37 (January–June 1956), p. 20.

21. For further consideration of Italian central banking operations in these years, see the articles by Baffi, Gambino, and Menichella, previously cited.

22. Theoretically, the Bank and the UIC could stop buying inflowing foreign exchange, or even resort to selling from the UIC's holdings. But to persist in this would create a shortage of lire on the exchange market, forcing appreciation of their external value. This in turn would discourage exports, which was not at all thought desirable in these years.

23. Figures for money supply from Table 23; for reserves in 1947, Table 5; for reserves and deposits in 1961, *Abridged Version of the Report for the*

Year 1961, pp. 51, 53; for total deposits in 1947, *Adunanza generale*, 1948, p. 169. The deposit figures in the *Report* for 1961 (p. 51) do not line up fully with those on pp. 53 and 62.

24. Figures for December 31, 1961, from *Abridged Version of the Report for the Year 1961*, p. 62.

25. In fact, inflation did break out, starting late in 1961 and continuing on through 1964. So far, the chief devices used to check the upswing in prices have been (1) tightening of bank lending, mainly through enforced decreases in reserves with the onset of a payments deficit; (2) restriction on short-term foreign borrowing by the banks; and (3) increased consumption excises. So far, both the reserve ratio and the discount rate have been left untouched. These developments are reviewed in Chapter XV.

CHAPTER V

POPULATION AND THE LABOR MARKET

1. Annual rates of increase of over 2 per cent in underdeveloped countries today are considered grounds for serious concern. Rates of 3 per cent and more are rather common in Latin America, the Orient, and the Middle East.

2. ECA, *Italy Country Study* (Washington: GPO, February 1949), p. 11. This survey did not overlook the problem of expansion, although it saw little prospect for growth without large increases in government spending and investment.

3. *Mondo economico*, IX:37 (September 11, 1954).

4. Muriel Grindrod, *The Rebuilding of Italy: Politics and Economics 1945– 1955* (London and New York: The Royal Institute for Economic Affairs, 1955), p. 208. See also Henry Gibbs, *Italy on Borrowed Time* (London: Jarrolds, 1953), pp. 76–77, 104.

5. The difference between these two measures reflects the number of persons temporarily out of the country on foreign travel or for employment abroad. Temporary emigration has long been substantial.

6. Because the figures for population present in Table 26 are adjusted to today's boundaries, they are not comparable with those cited in the text.

7. United Nations, Statistical Office, Department of Economic and Social Affairs, *Demographic Yearbook*, 1961 (New York, 1961). All figures are provisional.

8. Guglielmo Tagliacarne, "Demographic and Social Development," Banco di Roma, *Review of the Economic Conditions in Italy*, special issue, *Ten Years of Italian Economy, 1947–1956* (Rome, 1957), pp. 25–26.

9. *Demographic Yearbook*, 1961.

10. Postwar population was inflated by 487,000 refugees returning from the former colonies. Giovanni F. Malagodi, *in* Camera dei deputati Commissione parlamentare di inchiesta sulla disoccupazione, *La disoccupazione in Italia*, vol. II, part 3 (Rome: Camera de deputati, 1953), p. 317.

11. Francesco Coppola d'Anna, "Le forze di lavoro e il loro impiego in Italia," in *La disoccupazione in Italia*, vol. IV, part 2 (Rome: Camera dei deputati, 1953).

12. Only the ISTAT estimate allows for the effects of net emigration.

13. ISTAT data from Tagliacarne, "Demographic and Social Development," p. 18; other estimates from Nora Federici, "Recent Forecasts of the

Future Growth of Population in Italy," Banca nazionale del lavoro, *Quarterly Review*, nos. 28–29 (January–June, 1954), pp. 68–69.

14. Similar forecasts made by Antonio Occhiuto, "Le leve di lavoro," *Rassegna di statistiche del lavoro*, special issue VI (May 1952), p. 44; and Stefano Somogyi, "Previsioni demografiche sulle forze di lavoro per il 1960," p. 43.

15. For example, Gibbs, *Italy on Borrowed Time*, p. 85, puts the total number of emigrants during 1900–1942 at 13.89 million. For 1901–1942, the official figures yield totals of 19.85 million for gross emigration and 8.51 million net. For 1946–1951, Gibbs puts the total at 608,399; the official figures yield totals of 1.42 million gross and 949,000 net. Grindrod, *The Rebuilding of Italy*, p. 193, says that annual emigration for 1900–1910 averaged 603,000. On a gross and net basis for 1901–1910, the averages are 603,000 and 448,700 respectively. For 1950–1955, the OEEC estimates net emigration at 700,000; Organisation for European Economic Co-operation, Eighth Report, vol. 2, *Europe in 1960* (Paris, 1957), p. 15. The official data yield totals, gross and net, of 1,565,000 and 954,000 respectively.

16. The net total is probably seriously overstated because between 1901 and 1920 no figures were published for repatriates returning after emigration to the European and Mediterranean Basin countries. For periods after 1920 roughly one half of those emigrating to these areas became repatriates.

17. Malagodi, *La disoccupazione in Italia*, pp. 254–266, 313–314.

18. Tagliacarne, "Demographic and Social Development," p. 18.

19. According to Occhiuto, "Le leve di lavoro," p. 44, L. Galvani has estimated that for each 100,000 births surviving for one year, 91,544 will survive to the age of 15 years. Total births for 1941–1945, averaged 875,000 per year; on a survival rate of 91.5 per cent, 800,000 would reach working age each year for 1956–1960. For 1946–1950, total births averaged 989,000 per year; on a survival rate of 91.5 per cent, 905,000 would reach working age during each year of 1961–1965—about 12.5 per cent more than in the previous period.

20. By contrast, the Vanoni Plan projections for 1955–1964 assumed the labor force would expand by an average of 200,000 persons each year, assuming further that net emigration would draw off 80,000 per year from the labor force, which yields an average increase of 120,000 per year. The calculations in the text above suggest net emigration from the labor force of 126,400 per year, using present rates instead of the more conservative Vanoni figure. On the Vanoni assumption, the annual increase in the labor force estimated here rises to 115,000 per year, or very close to the Vanoni estimate of 120,000.

21. Table 20.

22. If the earnings, and hence marginal productivity, of those migrating to north and central Italy are greater, national income is increased. World income is increased in the same way by external migration. Within Italy, however, one must also consider the potential development of the south that is foregone by withdrawal of its most productive people. Potential regional growth, as well as the static rearrangement of the existing labor force, must be considered.

23. For the north and center, these cities are: Bologna, Brescia, Florence, Genoa, Milan, Rome, Turin, Udine, and Venice; for the south: Bari, Cagliari, Catania, Catanzaro, Cosenza, Messina, Naples, Palermo, and Salerno. Figures for 1901 from *Annuario statistico italiano*, 1955, pp. 370–371; (1951), 1956, pp. 20–22.

24. Cited in Grindrod, *The Rebuilding of Italy: Politics and Economics 1945–1955*, p. 208.

25. Tagliacarne, "Demographic and Social Development," p. 20.

26. For 1951–1959, SVIMEZ estimates that 610,000 southerners migrated north, while 743,000 went abroad; thus with a natural increase in population of 2,092,000 persons, the net increase in numbers actually present was only 739,000. Cited in Hollis B. Chenery, "Development Policies for Southern Italy," *Quarterly Journal of Economics*, LXXVI:4 (November 1962), p. 521.

27. Federici, "Recent Forecasts of the Future Growth of Population in Italy," pp. 66–67.

28. SVIMEZ, *Popolazione e forze di lavoro* (Rome: SVIMEZ, 1952), p. 69.

29. *Annuario statistico italiano*, 1956, pp. 20–21.

30. Valuable criticisms of the concept of overpopulation are developed by Wilbert E. Moore, *Economic Demography of Eastern and Southern Europe* (Geneva: League of Nations, 1945), pp. 56–61; and by Doreen Warriner, *Economics of Peasant Farming* (London, New York: Oxford University Press, 1939), pp. 61–72.

31. This issue is more than a question of definition, for it centers attention upon economic growth, rather than diverting it to relatively sterile proposals for increased external emigration or stoic acceptance of a supposed Malthusian determinism. For the world as a whole Malthus may well be proved correct, but his interpretation has limited significance for the Italian case today.

CHAPTER VI

THE LABOR FORCE: ITS GROWTH AND USES

1. The Italian data refer to the "active population" rather than to the "labor force." The principal difference is that those who are unemployed and are seeking their first job are excluded from the active population, but included in the labor force. The active population does not exclude those currently unemployed who were formerly employed, and so it is only an approximate measure of total employment.

2. It is not intended to suggest that either the family enterprise as such, or small business in general, is always inherently less efficient than corporate enterprise or the large-scale plant.

3. Professor Francesco Coppola d'Anna has developed an analysis similar to the one presented here. See *La disoccupazione in Italia*, vol. IV, part 2 (Rome: Camera dei deputati, 1953), pp. 1–73; and vol. IV, part 3, pp. 51–76.

4. Istituto centrale di statistica (ISTAT), *Indagine statistica sullo sviluppo del reddito nazionale dell'Italia dal 1861 al 1956* (hereafter *Indagine statistica*), pp. 251–252.

5. The official labor force sample for 1961 indicates that employment in agriculture shrank drastically after 1951. Disregarding some lack of comparability with the census for 1951, the sample suggests that 5.9 million were employed in agriculture in 1961, compared with about 8.08 million a decade earlier—a drop of 27 per cent. For 1961, the sample indicates that agriculture accounted for 29.1 per cent of all employment, and nonagricultural activities for 70.9 per cent, of which industry supplied 39.5 per cent of the over-all total. *Relazione generale*, 1961, I, p. 85.

6. The active population includes employed juveniles in the ten- to fourteen-

year bracket; also persons in the age group sixty-five years and over who either were employed or who had been employed and were now unemployed. Therefore the working age group (fifteen to sixty-four years) was not the sole source of the active population.

7. The Vanoni Plan projected a decline of agriculture to 33 per cent of the labor force by 1964, which implied a continuing net contraction of roughly 100,000 persons a year. The labor force sample for 1961 suggests that the decline is already well below 33 per cent and has been proceeding at roughly 217,000 per year.

8. A participation rate greater than 100 per cent means that part of the active population was supplied from outide the working-age group—from working juveniles under fifteen years of age and from persons sixty-five years and over. For the same reasons, a rate of 100 per cent does not mean that the entire age group was actually in the active population. Unfortunately for more refined analysis, data are lacking regarding the age structure of the active population.

9. Output data from Table 9; employment from Table 88.

10. Regional data for the active population in 1951 were prepared on the basis of the *resident* population rather than the population present; those for 1871 conform to the statistic for population present. For 1951 the difference in the two population categories is about 357,000 persons—not great enough to invalidate the comparisons made above. However it should be pointed out that the 1951 data for the active population, as presented in regional and global form in the *Annuario* for 1956 do not conform to the results published in global form for the same census in the *Annuario* for 1955 because of this change to a resident population basis. However, regional distributions are lacking for 1951 on basis of population present, although only on this latter basis can over-all comparisons be carried back to 1901. Hence the preceding analysis of 1901–1951 changes in the active population is not strictly comparable with the 1871–1951 regional comparisons here presented.

11. In some of the samples, members of the armed forces, housewives performing occasional labor, and persons temporarily employed abroad have been included; in others certain ones of these groups have been excluded. Some of the surveys have been made in the spring, others in the fall, which introduces seasonal influences. Finally, there is considerable possibility for sampling errors, suggested by divergencies between ISTAT estimates for unemployment in September 1952 and the Ministry of Labor figures for the same month.

12. *Relazione generale*, 1962, II, p. 80.

13. Registered unemployment, Classes I and II, in 1961 averaged 1.4 million, not including housewives, pensioners, or employed persons seeking different jobs. The fact that registered unemployment was double the sample estimate is ample reason for treating the latter with caution.

14. Except for some minor exclusions, the assignment of industries according to advanced and traditional categories follows a classification developed for the census of 1951 by Vera C. Lutz, in "Some Characteristics of Italian Economic Development, 1950–1955," Banca nazionale del lavoro, *Quarterly Review*, no. 39 (December 1956), p. 162.

15. Between 1953 and 1960, physical output of this sector alone rose at a geometric annual rate of 9.7 per cent, as against 8.96 per cent for all industry.

16. The ML sample excludes nonmanual employees and is confined to

establishments with ten or more employees. Coverage is best for larger firms.

17. Associazione per lo sviluppo dell'industria nel Mezzogiorno (SVI-MEZ), *L'aumento dell'occupazione in Italia dal 1950 al 1957* (Rome: Giuffrè, 1959), p. 58.

CHAPTER VII

THE PROBLEM OF UNEMPLOYMENT

1. Federico Caffè, "Considerazione storico-bibliografiche attorno al problema della disoccupazione in Italia," *L'industria*, no. 2 (1952), p. 236.

2. Gino Luzzatto, "Il problema della disoccupazione in Italia nei primi settant'anni dell'unità," *La disoccupazione in Italia*, vol. IV, part 4 (Rome: Camera dei deputati, 1953), pp. 7–10.

3. Caffè, "Considerazione storico-bibliografiche," pp. 239–241. Caffè considers A. Agnelli, *Il problema economico della disoccupazione: Cause e rimedi* (Milan: Società editrice libreria, 1909), to be an expression of the dominant point of view in this period. Theoretical studies by Pareto, Loria, Pantaleoni, and de Viti di Marco also emphasized the cyclical character of the problem.

4. Confederazione generale dell'industria italiana (Confindustria), *Annuario di statistiche del lavoro, 1949* (Rome: Confindustria, 1950), p. 96.

5. *Annuario statistico italiano*, 1955, p. 377.

6. *Annuario di statistiche del lavoro, 1949; Annuario statistica italiano*, 1955.

7. Caffè, "Considerazione storico- bibliografiche," p. 243.

8. These constitutional guarantees, which came into legal effect January 1, 1948, are to be found in Article 4 and Article 36. *Codice civile*, ed. Hoepli (Milan: Ulrico Hoepli, 1958).

9. Keynesian doctrines began to exert much influence at this time. There was a lively controversy over whether Keynes' teachings applied to what had come to be called Italy's "structural problem," as distinguished from the conventional Anglo-American cycle of investment deficiency; also over whether spending and monetary expansion were appropriate remedies for the Italian ailments. These matters are considered in Chapters II and III.

10. A careful evaluation is available in Renato Curatolo, "Le statistiche corrente dell'occupazione e della disoccupazione in Italia," part I, *Rassegna di statistiche del lavoro*, XIII:1–2 (January–April 1961), pp. 17–39; part II, XIII:3 (May–June 1961), pp. 101–123; and part III, XIII:4–6 (July–December 1961), pp. 213–224. Part II, pp. 114–118, deals specifically with matters considered in the text above.

For a brief statement, see also President's Committee to Appraise Employment and Unemployment Statistics, *Measuring Employment and Unemployment* (Washington: GPO, 1962), p. 244.

11. It should also be noted that the ML data cover Classes I and II only. In recent years these have accounted for between 85 and 90 per cent of total registered unemployment. Because of the exclusion of Classes III–V, the ML totals in Table 46 are smaller than those in Table 45.

12. Curatolo, "Le statistiche corrente dell'occupazione," part I, pp. 17–26; *Measuring Employment and Unemployment*, pp. 244–246.

13. To adapt the Italian data to United States practice, the President's Commission deducted these three groups from the labor force, and added the

occasional workers, effecting a net increase of 130,000 in the total for 1960. The commission accepted the view that the ML statistics overstated unemployment, and used the ISTAT figures, but without giving reasons for preferring the latter. *Measuring Employment and Unemployment*, pp. 244–245.

14. Regarding these requirements, see Chapter XIV. For a general discussion of ML procedures, see Curatolo, "Le statistiche corrente dell'occupazione," part II, pp. 101–114.

15. For details, see Chapter XIV.

16. *Measuring Employment and Unemployment*, p. 246.

17. Comparable interregional labor force data are not available. The population figures were compiled from *Annuario statistico italiano*, 1951, p. 24.

18. Satisfactory regional breakdowns of population in 1961 are not available except for the south.

19. Population figure from *Relazione generale*, 1962, II, p. 81. This estimate derives from the ISTAT samples of that year.

20. For a careful discussion of the Italian aspects of some of these problems, see Emanuele Rienzi, "Il mercato del lavoro," *Rassegna di statistiche del lavoro*, special issue VI (May 1952), pp. 19–20.

21. Other examples would include persons on make-work public projects and many members of the inflated government bureaucracy.

22. This case is further complicated by the presence of many self-employed, many independent farmers, and even some family assistants who do earn a very good living from their activities.

23. Schneiter distinguished this case, which he contends applies to Italy, from "effective overpopulation" (unemployment where no further technical improvements are possible), and "apparent overpopulation" (manpower supply is poorly adapted to demand, although over-all labor demand is not deficient and technical advances are possible). These concepts were put forward in a report to the Council of Europe in February, 1955. *Mondo economico*, February 19, 1955.

24. U.S. Mutual Security Agency, Economic Cooperation Administration, European Recovery Program, *Italy Country Study* (Washington: GPO, 1949), p. 10.

25. United Nations, Economic Commission for Europe, *Economic Survey of Europe in 1949* (Geneva: United Nations, 1950), p. 68.

26. Giuseppe Orlando, "Metodi di accertimento della disoccupazione agricola," *Rassegna di statistiche del lavoro*, special issue VI (May 1952), p. 23.

27. *La disoccupazione in Italia*, vol. I, part 2, "Indagini statistiche," pp. 7–218.

28. *Rassegna di statistiche del lavoro*, IX:6 (November–December 1957), pp. 356, 358.

29. For crude data, consider that 34.6 per cent of ISTAT's estimated total for all "occasional workers" (all sectors) who worked less than 15 hours during the survey week of April 20, 1960, and the 12.0 per cent working between 15 and less than 25 hours all were underemployed. For 1960 as a whole, the total number of occasional workers was estimated to be 961,000. Roughly 448,000 thus were unemployed; yet this figure is excluded from the ISTAT estimate for unemployment.

30. The figure for self-employment is an overstatement, for it includes

Wage and Social Security Policy | 441

management officials and clerical labor. Data from *Relazione generale*, 1962, II, p. 86.

31. *Annuario statistico italiano*, 1955, pp. 461–462.

32. Henry C. Wallich, *Mainsprings of the German Revival* (New Haven: Yale University Press, 1955), p. 273.

33. Bundesrepublik Deutschland, *Statistiches Jahrbuch für die Bundes-repubilk Deutschland*, issues for 1955, p. 65; 1959, p. 58; 1963, p. 62. For the same years, net immigration from East Germany alone (included above) amounted to 1.6 million persons. Issues for 1954–1963 inclusive.

34. On July 31, 1957, 18,361 Italians were working in West Germany. By June 30, 1961, their number had jumped to 207,128, which undoubtedly afforded significant relief to unemployment in Italy. It is a curious fact that ISTAT includes in its estimate of employment Italians working abroad. The ISTAT estimate serves as a basis for our 1961 figure, which is not adjusted for this particular factor for lack of data.

Figures for Italians working in West Germany from *Statistiches Jahrbuch*, 1962, p. 149.

35. For the Italian figures, see Table 8, Chapter III, for actual values and their sources. The West German data are from the following sources: industrial production (excluding construction), *Statistiches Jahrbuch*, 1957, p. 234; 1952, p. 238; real gross national product, Organisation for Economic Co-operation and Development, *General Statistics* (September 1962), p. VI.

36. For industrial production, the values for *e* are undoubtedly a serious understatement, arising from the use of total nonagricultural employment as a measure of labor input. However, the Italian data did not permit a more refined breakdown of employment.

37. The reasons for this are discussed in Chapter XIV.

CHAPTER VIII

WAGE AND SOCIAL SECURITY POLICY

1. Figures are worked up by ISTAT from labor force samples in 1962. *Relazione generale*, 1962, II, p. 86.

2. Several elements of the wage bargain are described by law—for example, paid vacations and family allowances. Others flow from agreements negotiated between the parties and between their respective peak associations. For nonunion employers, there is obligation to observe the common terms in effect at the workplace, with disputed questions to be resolved by a magistrate (*Codice civile*, Art. 2099). Formerly, nonunion employers were bound by the norms adopted by the respective Facist corporations. These latter bodies were dissolved toward the end of the war.

3. Pay consolidation was also achieved for the trade sector in July 1954.

4. Strictly speaking, the family allowances are not wages but only one of several welfare supplements. However, they are connected with employment and bulk so large in daily earnings that they can hardly be ignored.

5. Istituto sociale ambrosiano, *Introduzione di problemi del lavoro*, vol. I, *I termini economici* (Milan: Istituto sociale ambrosiano, 1952), pp. 274–277.

6. A law dated August 6, 1940, handed administration of the family allowance fund over to the Istituto nazionale di previdenza sociale (INPS),

which manages it in separate parts for the main sectors of the economy. *Introduzione di problemi del lavoro*, pp. 278–279.

7. Giuseppe Baldinozzi, "La cassa integrazione guadagni operai dell' industria," *La disoccupazione in Italia*, vol. II, part 2 (Rome: Camera dei deputati, 1953), p. 149 ff.

8. C. Vannutelli, "Wage Structure and Cost of Labour in Italy," Banco di Roma, *Review of the Economic Conditions in Italy*, VI:5 (September 1952), p. 401.

9. At year's end, 1944–1945, the surviving Mussolini Government, now known as the Italian Social Republic (the so-called "Salò Republic") was nominally in control of the northern areas occupied by German forces. By the Marchiandi and Spinelli decrees of that time, the attendance bonus was incorporated in base salaries and wages. Francesca Ambrogi, "Le retribuzioni dei dipendenti dell'industria dal 1938 al 1955," *Rassegna di statistica del lavoro*, special issue IX (Rome, 1955), pp. 7–9, 12.

10. South of the Gothic Line a similar supplement was decreed, the *indennità di carovita* or cost-of-living allowance. By mutual agreement on May 23, 1946, this allowance was consolidated in the base pay. Just previously, on February 24, 1945, the territorial bargaining associations in the liberated zones had established a new cost-of-living allowance (*Nuova carovita*), which continued in effect with subsequent changes in method of calculation.

11. Cesare Vannutelli, "La scala mobile dei salari," *Rivista di politica economica*, 3rd series, XXXVIII:3 (April 1948), pp. 322–344; Ambrogi, "Le retribuzione," pp. 7–8, 12.

12. The parallel in principle with the American "Little Steel Formula" of 1942 will be obvious.

13. Istituto sociale Ambrosiano, *I Termini economici*, pp. 268–269; Vannutelli, "Wage Structure and the Cost of Labor in Italy," p. 388.

14. Ambrosiano, *I Termini economici*, pp. 269–270.

15. Vannutelli, "La scala mobile dei salari," p. 389.

16. This budget set food consumption at approximately 2600 calories daily per person and assigned food an expenditure weight of 75 per cent in the budget. C. Vannutelli, "Le nuove norme per la rilevazione degli indici del costo della vita ed it sistema di scala mobile dei salari," *Rivista di politica economica*, 3rd series, XLII:5 (May 1952), p. 518.

17. If, then, prices rose 20 per cent, a 46 per cent increase would be applied to the initial 185 lire daily allowance, raising average total pay from 425 to 510 lire daily, or by 20 per cent.

18. Since the 2.0 female coefficient implied an adverse relative widening of the female global pay differential, it was raised to 2.1 in July 1947. Vannutelli, "La scala mobile dei salari," pp. 218–220.

19. In addition, the local basis on which subsequent increases in the allowance were to be calculated created disparities that also led to discontent with the system.

20. Ambrogi, "La retribuzione," p. 10.

21. The minimum for the top-skill bracket of specialized worker was fixed at 27.5 per cent over common laborer, while clerks in the first category were awarded 118 per cent over those in the fourth. Ambrogi, "Le retribuzione," p. 8.

22. Vannutelli, "La scala mobile dei salari," pp. 331–332; Ambrogi, "Le retribuzione," p. 13. The coefficient of 2.3 (adult males) would then have

to be applied in the same manner as before to maintain the relationship between net recognized price changes and total pay.

23. Ambrogi, "Le retribuzione," pp. 8–10.

24. Cesare Vannutelli, "Cause ed effetti dell'appiattimento salariale," *Rivista di politica economica*, 3rd series, XXXIX:5 (May 1949), pp. 559–560, 564.

25. Vannutelli also notes a concomitant severe decline in the real volume of savings between 1938 and 1948.

26. Ambrogi, "Le redistribuzione," pp. 10–14.

27. Vannutelli "Le nuove norme per la rilevazione degli indici del costo della vita ed it sistema di scala mobile dei salari," pp. 518–519.

28. According to Vannutelli, union pressure for a higher standard of living led to some confusion of objectives: between a pure price index with fixed quantity weights and quality levels, and an expenditure index that would allow changes in quantity and quality of components. In addition, the unions sought breadth in the range of components, also presumably because this would raise the standard of living somehow. Actually, it seems to have sacrificed price sensitivity in the index. Vannutelli, "Le nuove norme," pp. 522, 524, n 5; 526.

29. "Il nuovo sistema di scala mobile dei salari nell'industria" (unsigned), *Rassegna di statistiche del lavoro*, III:3 (May–June 1951), p. 274.

30. Vannutelli, "La nuove norme," p. 525; Ambrogi, "Le retribuzione," pp. 14–15.

31. "Il nuovo sistema di scala mobile dei salari nell'industria," p. 276.

32. Vannutelli, "Le nuove norme," pp. 526–529.

33. By this time, there were three main union confederations, following splits from the Communist-controlled CGIL (Confederazione generale italiana del lavoro) beginning in 1948. They were: the CGIL, the UIL (Unione italiana del lavoro), and the CISL (Confederazione italiana sindacati lavoratori). Each confederation has its affiliated "category associations" for subsectors of industry and for trade, finance, agriculture, and so on. There was also a small fourth confederation, CISNAL (Confederazione italiana dei sindacati nazionali dei lavoratori), formed in 1950 and largely southern in its sources of membership. On the employer side, the peak association for industry was Confindustria (Confederazione generale dell'industria italiana).

34. Ambrosiano, *I termini economici*, p. 273. For discussions of the over-all compensation system, see Vannutelli, "Wage Structure and the Cost of Labour in Italy," pp. 385–407; *I termini economici*, pp. 266–280; and Commissione indagini e studi sull'industria meccanica, Gruppo di consulenza dello Stanford Research Institute, *Problemi economici ed industriali delle industrie meccaniche italiane* (Tivoli: Commissione indagini e studi sull'industria meccanica, 1952), pp. 225–297.

35. Ambrogi, "Le retribuzione," pp. 16–17; Comitato interministeriale per la ricostruzione, Segretaria generale, *Politica di sviluppo: Cinque anni del lavoro* (Rome: Istituto poligrafico dello stato, 1958), p. 466.

36. Cesare Vannutelli, "Recent Wage Structure and Cost of Labour Changes in Italy," Banco di Roma, *Review of the Economic Conditions in Italy*, IX:2 (March 1955), pp. 132–137.

37. Ambrogi, "Le retribuzione," pp. 17–19.

38. Vannutelli, "Wage Structure and Cost of Labour in Italy," pp. 137–140.

39. *Politica di sviluppo*, p. 467.

40. Vannutelli, "Wage Structure and Cost of Labour in Italy," p. 141.

41. For a full discussion, see Isidoro Franco Mariani, "La revisione della scala mobile dei salari," *Rassegna di statistiche del lavoro,* IX:1 (January–February 1957), pp. 3–20.

42. Cesare Vannutelli, "Topical Aspects and Problems of Italy's Wage Policy," Banco di Roma, *Review of the Economic Conditions in Italy,* XIII:2 (March 1959), pp. 180–181, 194–195. This article is of interest in other respects as well.

43. Figures for contributions (1955) from *Rassegna di statistica del lavoro,* X:3 (May–June 1958), p. 122; and (1962) XV:3 (May–June 1963), p. 228. These data come from official sources. Internal national income at factor cost (1955) from *Indagine statistica,* p. 248; (1962) from *Relazione generale,* 1962, I, p. 26.

44. *Problemi economici ed industriali dell'industrie meccaniche italiane,* p. 226; Cesare Vannutelli, "Social Security in Italy," Banco di Roma, *Review of the Economic Conditions in Italy,* III:5 (September 1949), p. 419.

45. *Politica di sviluppo,* pp. 477, 498–499.

46. Vannutelli, "Wage Structure and Cost of Labour in Italy," pp. 420–421, 425–426.

47. *Politica di sviluppo,* p. 478. National income for 1947 from *Indagine statistica sullo sviluppo del reddito nazionale dell'Italia dal 1861 al 1956,* p. 250.

48. The preceding summary was based upon the following sources: *Politica di sviluppo,* pp. 480–496; Vannutelli, "Social Security in Italy," pp. 417–426; Vannutelli, "Wage Structure and Cost of Labour in Italy," p. 404; *Problemi economici ed industriali delle industrie meccaniche italiane,* p. 243; Riccardo Bellacci, "Aspetti economici degli assegni familiari," *Rassegna di statistiche del lavoro,* VII:3 and VII:4 (May–June and July–August 1955), pp. 217–228, 321–336; "Il lavoro in Italia in 1955" (unsigned), *Rassegna di statistiche del lavoro,* VII:1 (January–February 1954), pp. 19–36; Ferdinando Enrico Loffredo, "L'assicurazione disoccupazione," in *La disoccupazione in Italia,* vol. II, part 2, *Relazioni dei gruppi del lavoro* (Rome: Camera dei deputati, 1953), pp. 67–89; Gina Papa, "Compulsory Unemployment Insurance in Italy," Banca nazionale del lavoro, *Quarterly Review,* no. 23 (October–November 1952), pp. 227–237; and Aldo Scotto, "Influenza sulle occupazioni del sistema della previdenza sociale," in *La disoccupazione in Italia* (Rome: Camera dei deputati, 1953), vol. IV, part 3, *Studi speciali,* pp. 497–508.

49. *Rassegna di statistiche del lavoro,* XV:3 (May–June 1963), p. 271.

CHAPTER IX

POSTWAR MOVEMENTS IN WAGES

1. Separate series are available for wages and salaries in industry, agriculture, government, and the services group, in *Rassegna di statistiche del lavoro,* XV:3 (May–June 1963), p. 226. The data were prepared by ISTAT.

2. Data and sources for these estimates appear in Table 87.

3. They could be termed indexes of total wage rates, but not in the sense of base pay, which in Italy is separate from the many supplements ("accessory elements") that must also be paid.

4. In 1950, real clerical salaries exclusive of the family allowance were 7 to

Postwar Movements in Wages | 445

15 per cent below 1938 levels. Including the allowance, they were still well below prewar in industry and government.

5. The compound rates of increase were calculated from the figures in Table 56, hence derive from the same sources. The census weights were computed as relative shares of the total number of manual workers in the four sectors involved. By similar procedure, relative shares of clerical workers in the three applicable sectors were found for a separate total. Weight data are from *Annuario statistico italiano*, 1956, p. 26.

6. See Ministero del lavoro e della previdenza sociale, *Statistiche del lavoro*, XIII:10–12 (October–November–December 1961), pp. 3, 38–39.

7. Log $Y_t^* = 1.970527 + 0.0214716t; \ r^2 = 0.96694$.

8. Figure for 1962 is a monthly average for December 1961 through November 1962.

9. Data for monthly wages from *Rassegna di statistiche del lavoro*, various issues. For interpretive purposes, figures for particular months are less reliable than annual monthly averages because of the uneven incidence of supplements such as paid vacations (mainly June and August), the Christmas bonus, and paid holidays not worked (normally sixteen scattered over the year).

10. Log $Y_t^* = 1.980692 + 0.024471t; \ r^2 = 0.99399$.

11. The gap between job rates negotiated at the level of the firm and the confederation minima can be viewed as an aspect of wage drift. For the first important study of wage drift in Italy, see Giuseppe Ammassari, *I salari di fatto in Italia: Inchiesta sugli slittamenti salariali* (Milan: Giuffrè, 1963).

12. Between 1953 and 1962, the three indexes rose as follows: cost-of-living, 31.8 per cent; implicit price deflator, 21.2 per cent; and consumers' prices, 23.3 per cent. For 1950–1962, the first index rose 53.7 per cent, and the second, 39.0 per cent.

13. Log $Y_t^* = 1.998008 + 0.0110202t; \ r^2 = 0.95652$.

14. Cesare Vannutelli, "Occupazione e salari in Italia dal 1861 al 1961," *Rassegna di statistiche del lavoro*, XIII:4–6 (July–December 1961), p. 211.

15. Total real consumption, including public goods and services, divided by population present. Data for real consumption of market goods alone not available. *Relazione generale*, 1962, II, pp. 362–363.

16. The Confindustria estimates boil down to a method of converting the ISTAT index of changes in industrial wage rates to absolute values in lire per day. For such purpose, the key date is August 1952. The ultimate average is built up from the base rate for male common labor, fixed by peak agreement on that date for the "A" group of industries. The relative labor grade differentials established in 1947 are applied to the common labor rate to obtain a structure of minimum base rates. Each such rate is increased by 5 per cent to allow for piece rate and overtime earnings. The cost-of-living bonus, revaluation quotas, and bread allowance are then added to each grade. The latter are then weighted by relative numbers in 1947, to yield an over-all weighted average for men. A similar procedure is followed for women, and the two weighted averages are then merged according to the sex ratio prevailing in 1947. The resulting figure, in lire per day, is then adjusted again for each month and year by tying it to corresponding shifts in the ISTAT index of minimum wage

rates for industry as a whole, which yields a running average of estimated daily wage rates, tied to 1947 base weights. For details, see "Nuova elaborazione di un salario medio nazionale degli operai dell'industria" (unsigned), *Rassegna di statistiche del lavoro*, IV:4 (July–August 1952), pp. 379–386.

17. The statistical analysis that follows has been modeled in part on two earlier studies, one for the United Kingdom, and the other for the United States. They are: L. A. Dicks-Mireaux and J. C. R. Dow, "The Determinants of Wage Inflation: United Kingdom, 1946–1956," *Journal of the Royal Statistical Society*, Series A (General), vol. 122, part 2 (1959), pp. 145–174; and Otto Eckstein and Thomas A. Wilson, "The Determination of Money Wages in American Industry," *Quarterly Journal of Economics*, LXXVI:3 (August 1962), pp. 379–414.

18. The volume of employment, as a measure of demand for labor, might have been used instead, if adequate data were available.

19. I am greatly indebted to my colleague, Professor Ta-Chung Liu, for valuable technical assistance and criticism of this phase of the study.

20. Wages, unemployment, and man-hours were obtained from *Rassegna di statistiche del lavoro*, various issues. Industrial production and value added (the latter from 1956) were taken from *Relazione generale*, various issues. Value added for 1953–1955 was taken from *Indagine statistiche sullo sviluppo del reddito nazionale dell'Italia dal 1861 al 1956*, p. 246. Total wages and salaries in industry were collected from *Rassegna di statistiche del lavoro*, XV:3 (May–June 1963), p. 226.

21. Causal direction might be established by a far more elaborate econometric model, if adequate data were available; or possibly by introduction of time lags, again if data could be had. However, either technique goes beyond the scope of the present study.

22. This judgment applies to industry as a whole, and does not overlook the possibility of a further shift to profits in the strongest firms.

CHAPTER X

EVIDENCE OF THE DUAL CHARACTER OF THE ITALIAN ECONOMY

1. Boeke originally advanced his ideas in works published in 1942 and 1946, which appeared in somewhat revised form under the title *Economics and Economic Policy of Dual Societies, as Exemplified by Indonesia* (Haarlem: H. D. Tjeenk Willink & Son, 1953).

2. The phenomenon in question is no longer solely one of capitalism or of classical colonialism, for it can occur equally under industrial types of collectivism, even in imperialistic form. Benjamin Higgins, "The 'Dualistic Theory' of Underdeveloped Areas," *Economic Development and Cultural Change*, IV:2 (January 1956), pp. 99–101.

3. "Markedly" because all of the leading industrial nations have some surviving areas or activities where the traditional still prevails—by design, isolation, or neglect.

4. For a valuable discussion of the income gap, see Dipak Mazumdar, "Underemployment in Agriculture and the Industrial Wage Rate," *Economica*, ns, XXVI:104 (November 1959), pp. 328–340.

5. This is not to say that all handicrafts and all peasant agriculture are in-

efficient in the sense that all such small-scale units of enterprise are below optimal size, surviving solely because of a lower level of labor costs. Obviously, the case is mixed.

It is common to conclude that where there is a high proportion of the labor force engaged in trade and services, as against agriculture and manufacturing, we have a well-advanced economy. But this is not so where agriculture remains largely primitive and manufacturing has barely emerged, for then the clotting of people in urban trade and services will be a pathological sign, reflecting flight from agriculture and lack of over-all development. See the remarks of Paolo Sylos Labini regarding South Italy, in Alessandro Molinari, "Occupazione, disoccupazione e sotto-occupazione nei paesi sovrapopolati e nel Mezzogiorno d'Italia," *Statistica*, XV:4 (October–December 1954), p. 639, n 35.

6. The two-sector approach to the dual economy is ably developed in Higgins, "The 'Dualistic Theory' of Underdeveloped Areas," p. 106; Albert O. Hirschman, "Investment Policies and 'Dualism' in Underdeveloped Countries," *American Economic Review*, XLVII:5 (September 1957), pp. 557–560; and Vera C. Lutz, "The Growth Process in a 'Dual' Economic System," Banca nazionale del lavoro, *Quarterly Review*, no. 46 (September 1958), pp. 279–281.

7. For a discussion of the "north-south" problem in general terms, see Hirschman, "Investment Policies and 'Dualism' in Underdeveloped Countries," pp. 557–562.

8. Using the customary production-possibilities diagram, Hirschman provides a model that can readily be applied to this case. Given two alternative processes for producing the same good, the one "industrial" (high capital-intensity) and the other "traditional" (high labor-intensity), and given also lower wages and higher capital costs in the traditional sector, then the economic survival of the traditional method will depend upon lower total outlay for the same amount of product. In turn, this will depend upon labor costs in the traditional sector that are sufficiently lower to offset higher capital costs and any advantages of large size for production units.

However, even short of these conditions, which, strictly viewed, would exclude adaption of the modern process, the two forms may coexist because of incomplete transition, difficulties in obtaining capital, geographic isolation, or deliberate protection of the old producers.

9. Figures obtained by relating 1953 data for arable land to numbers attached to agriculture are shown in Table 63; land figures from Organisation for European Economic Co-operation, *Basic Statistics of Food and Agriculture* (Paris: OEEC, 1954), p. 10.

10. The camparative gross national products have been calculated in U. S. prices, in European relative prices, and as a geometric average. Milton Gilbert and Irving B. Kravis, *An International Comparison of National Products and the Purchasing Power of Currencies: A Study of the United Kingdom, France, Germany and Italy* (Paris: Organisation for European Economic Co-operation, n.d.), p. 22.

11. Summarized from Istituto centrale di statistica, *III Censimento generale dell'industria e del commercio*, November 5, 1951, vol. XVI, "Artigianato," (Rome: Failli, 1957), pp. 9–12.

12. As a matter of social values, there is a case for small business beyond the economic—as a vital ingredient of effective individualism. This philosophy,

which is very strong in France and Italy, in large part is hostile to modern industrialism itself, whatever material benefits the latter alone can yield.

13. This transition would probably invoke unemployment for a time.

14. Calculated from statistics for the economically active in Table 66, and from net product figures in Istituto centrale di statistica (ISTAT), *Indagine Statistica sullo sviluppo del reddito nazionale dell'Italia dal 1861–1956,* series VIII, vol. 9, *Annali di statistica* (Rome: Failli, 1957), pp. 209, 211, 216 (hereafter *Indagine statistica*).

15. Doreen Warriner, *Economics of Peasant Farming* (London, New York: Oxford University Press, 1939), pp. 67–72, 140–145.

16. In 1936, the rural population was 44.7 per cent of the total population present. There are no later figures available. In 1951, arable land represented 13.1 million hectares, which compare with the 27.7 million hectares of total agricultural and forest land to which the holdings in Table 69 mainly apply. Data from Associazione per lo sviluppo dell'industria nel Mezzogiorno (SVINEZ), *Statistiche sul Mezzogiorno d'Italia, 1861–1953,* pp. 135, 139, and 1952.

17. Wilbert E. Moore, *Economic Demography of Eastern and Southern Europe* (Geneva: League of Nations, 1945), pp. 96–98, 104–108. Moore's extensive inquiry led him to the same conclusion as presented here, that there was needed an extensive redesign of the entire agricultural system in the countries studied, including Italy, to revamp both technique and organization.

18. Small holdings lead to low use of variable capital for fertilizers, grading and processing of products, and quite generally to higher than optimal ratios of fixed capital to size of holding.

CHAPTER XI

GEOGRAPHIC DUALISM: THE PROBLEM OF SOUTH ITALY

1. Figures cited are for 1957 and embrace southern Italy proper, including the province of Frosinone and Latina in Lazio, together with Sicily and Sardinia. The entire area covers 12.8 million hectares (out of 30.1 million for the whole nation) and 19.6 million people (out of a national total of 49.9 million on December 31, 1957). Data from Istituto centrale di statistica (ISTAT), *Annuario statistico italiano,* 1958 (Rome: Istituto poligrafico dello stato, 1959).

2. Carlo M. Cipolla, a leading Italian economic historian, has shown that the whole of Italy underwent marked economic decline between 1600 and 1670, following attainment of a fully "matured" economy. The reason lay in the decline of the export trades and the deflation it invoked." Il declino economico dell'Italia," *in* Carlo M. Cipolla, ed., *Storia dell'economia italiana,* vol. I, "Secoli settimo-diciassettesimo," (Turin: Edizioni scientifiche Einaudi, 1959), pp. 605–623.

3. Parthenope (Naples) was settled by Greeks ca. 760 B.C. Paestum and Agrigento offer the best Greek ruins in the world today.

4. Corrado Barbagallo, *La questione meridionale* (Milan: Garzanti, 1948), pp. 22–25.

5. Ernst Kantorowicz, *Frederick the Second, 1194–1250* (London: Constable, 1957), pp. 215–368.

6. Barbagallo, *La questione meridionale,* pp. 42–44, 47–52, 54–58.

7. Giuseppo Cenzato and Salvatore Guidotti, "Il problema industriale del Mezzogiorno," in Ministero per la costituente, *Rapporto della commissione economica,* vol. II, *Industria,* part 1, "Relazione" (Rome: Istituto poligrafico dello stato, 1947), pp. 361–362; Barbagallo, *La questione meridionale,* pp. 58–59.

8. Cenzato and Guidotti, "Il problema industriale del Mazzogiorno," p. 363.

9. Shepard B. Clough and Carlo Livi, "Economic Growth in Italy: An Analysis of the Uneven Development of North and South," *Journal of Economic History,* XVI:3 (September 1956), p. 337.

10. In 1860, 1621 villages out of 1848 in the Bourbon kingdom had no roads at all. Denis Mack Smith, *Italy, A Modern History* (Ann Arbor: University of Michigan Press, 1959), p. 50.

11. Clough and Livi, "Economic Growth in Italy," emphasize this factor strongly, along with cultural receptivity and a resource base that they consider much superior to that of the south; pp. 338–349.

12. Mack Smith, *Italy, A Modern History,* pp. 64–65, 110–112, 134–135, 157–161, 348.

13. Cavour himself was both a free trader and a passionate admirer of English parliamentary institutions. Yet at the time of unification only 500,000 persons enjoyed the right of suffrage, while three quarters of the population was illiterate. Right from the start Italy proved incapable for decades of developing an effective party system, hence a responsible opposition. Instead, cabinet after cabinet was melded together on the principles of *combinazioni* and *trasformismo.*

14. Barbagallo, *La questione meridionale,* pp. 71–74.

15. Cenzato and Guidotti, "Il problema industriale del Mezzogiorno," pp. 366–367.

16. Under the emphyteutic contract the owner of the land retains title while the tenant obtains beneficial possession in exchange for a rent payable in kind, an arrangement that encourages the tenant to increase productivity, while protecting the owner from depreciation of money. Mario Einaudi, "The Italian Land: Man, Nature, and Government," *Social Research,* 17:1 (March 1950), p. 24.

17. Cenzato and Guidotti, "Il problema industriale del Mezzogiorno," pp. 367–372.

18. Figures apply to lower peninsula only.

19. Barbagallo, *La questione meridionale,* pp. 79–82.

20. (SVIMEZ) Associazione per lo sviluppo dell'industria nel Mezzogiorno (SVIMEZ), *Statistiche sul Mezzogiorno d'Italia, 1861–1953* (Rome: Failli, 1954), pp. 62, 72.

21. These estimates also suggest some net movement from farm to city, in both regions, although it is far higher in the north (62,652 persons in 1952, versus 4567 in the south). The lag probably reflects the restricted range of opportunities outside agriculture in the south.

22. Lack of comparability precludes extension of these comparisons to 1951, although analysis will be made later of the economic status of the south for that date.

23. Cenzato and Guidotti, "Il problema industriale del Mezzogiorno," pp. 371–375, 383–394. Figures apply to southern peninsula only and exclude the islands.

24. For the south as a whole, per capita real incomes fell 10.2 per cent

during 1928–1951, while population rose 33.1 per cent during 1921–1951. In the north, incomes rose 15.4 per cent, and population increased only 21.9 per cent.

25. This group constituted 63.9 per cent of the entire southern population, and 35 per cent of the national total for this age group. For the north, the comparable figures are 70 and 65 per cent. The proportion of young people in the south is considerably greater.

26. Admittedly, the employed group includes persons under fourteen and over sixty-four, while the figures for population of working age are derived from an ISTAT sample taken ten months later. Nonetheless, these figures will serve to emphasize the constricted nature of nonagricultural activities in the south. All data from *Statistiche sul Mezzogiorno d'Italia, 1861–1953*, pp. 26, 139, 607.

27. Quoted in Einaudi, "The Italian Land," p. 21.

28. Latest figures available.

29. *Statistiche sul Mezzogiorno d'Italia, 1861–1953*, p. 155.

30. Einaudi, "The Italian Land," pp. 18–22.

31. *Statistiche sul Mezzogiorno d'Italia, 1861–1953*, pp. 147, 210, 212, 217–220, 246–249, 267.

32. In 1951, the south had only 13.3 per cent of the tractors and only 20.8 per cent of the threshers used in Italy.

33. These calculations necessarily assume that all land was exclusively used for the crops involved, in other words, that there were no holdings involving mixed herbaceous and arboreal culture on the same tracts. Source data are from *Statistiche sul Mezzogiorno d'Italia, 1861–1953*, pp. 263, 266 (value product), 135 (area of fruit lands), and 217–220 (area of herbaceous lands).

34. The following additional references are particularly useful for comprehending the manysided southern problem; Manlio Rossi-Doria, *La struttura e i problemi fondamantali dell'agricoltura meridionale* (Portici, 1951); Rossi-Doria, *Riforma agraria e azione meridionalista*, 2nd ed. (Bologna: Edizioni agricole, 1956); Robert E. Dickinson, *The Population Problem of Southern Italy: An Essay in Social Geography* (Syracuse, N.Y.: Syracuse University Press, 1955); Friedrich Vöchting, *Die Italienische Südfrage: Entstehung und Problematik eines Wirtschaftlichen Notstandsgebietes* (Berlin: Duncker und Humblot, 1951); Giustino Fortunato, Il Mezzogiorno e lo stato italiano, "Discorsi politici, 1880–1910," 2 vols. (Bari: G. Laterza, 1911); Giuseppe Di Nardi, "The Program for the Economic Development of Southern Italy," Banco di Roma, *Review of the Economic Conditions in Italy*, VI:2 (March 1952), pp. 99–109; Di Nardi, "La disoccupazione nel Mezzogiorno," *L'industria*, no. 4 (1951), pp. 515–534; Alessandro Molinari, "Necessità dell'industrializzazione in Italia: Compiti e problemi dell'industria," *L'industria*, no. 4 (1947), pp. 3–18; Molinari, "Southern Italy," Banca nazionale del lavoro, *Quarterly Review*, no. 8 (January 1949), pp. 25–47; and Molinari, "Occupazione, disoccupazione e sotto-occupazione nei paesi sovrapopolati e nel Mezzogiorno d'Italia," *Statistica*, XV:4 (October–December 1954), pp. 610–644.

35. Molinari, "Occupazione, disoccupazione e sotto-occupazione nei paesi sovrapopolati e nel Mezzogiorno d'Italia," pp. 636–637, n. 33.

CHAPTER XII

LONG-RUN FORCES OBSTRUCTING THE EMERGENCE OF
A UNIFIED INDUSTRIAL ECONOMY

1. On the one side, the Napoleonic conquest introduced the metric and decimal systems, reduced local trade barriers, and effected land reforms. These achievements were primarily confined to the north, where they could become permanent in Piedmont as the sole remaining independent Italian kingdom after 1815. What little was accomplished in the south was lost with the restoration of Bourbon rule. On the other side, the French occupation occasioned serious temporary disruption of economic life throughout the country.

2. Denis Mack Smith, *Italy, A Modern History* (Ann Arbor: University of Michigan Press, 1959), p. 8; Shepard B. Clough and Carlo Livi, "Economic Growth in Italy: An Analysis of the Uneven Development of North and South," *Journal of Economic History*, XVI:3 (September 1956), pp. 338–343. Admittedly, there was already present a tradition of economic liberalism. Also Napoleon's continental policy temporarily damaged Italian industry.

3. Mack Smith, *Italy, A Modern History*, pp. 153–156.

4. The locational handicap of the south—at least until the Mediterranean lands develop a large-scale industrial market—may well be the dominant reason for the disappointing rate of advance in the south since 1951, despite enormous public expenditures and extensive beneficial legislation. Vera Lutz, "Italy as A Study in Development," *Lloyds Bank Review*, n.s. no. 58 (October 1960), pp. 31–45.

5. The issue was clearly revealed as late as 1947 in the division of opinion of an official economic study commission for industry, cited in Giuseppe Cenzato and Salvatore Guidotti, "Il problema industriale del Mezzogiorno," in Ministero per la constituente, *Rapporto della commissione economica presentato all'assemblea costituente*, vol. II, *Industria*, part 1, "Relazione" (Rome: Istituto poligrafico dello stato, 1947), pp. 407–408. For recent discussions that uphold the view that the plight of the south was invoked by government, see Alessandro Molinari, "Southern Italy," Banca nazionale del lavoro, *Quarterly Review*, no. 8 (January 1949), pp. 34–36; also Paul N. Rosenstein-Rodan, "Programming in Theory and in Italian Practice," in *Investment Criteria and Economic Growth* (Cambridge, Mass.: Center for International Studies, Massachusetts Institute of Technology, December 1955), p. 27.

6. It is sometimes argued that for this class of public expenditure the south got its proper share, proportionate to its share of the population. Since the region was falling steadily behind, however, its "proper" share ought to have been more than its demographic proportion.

7. Commercial agriculture is an old story, whose locus lay almost entirely in the north. The figures for 1812, when both the continental system and the maritime blockade were in force, show that 84.7 per cent of Italian exports consisted of raw and finished silk, cereals and forage crops, foodstuffs, yarn and finished cloth. Manufacturers other than textiles accounted for only 5.1 per cent, and metals and metal products just under 2 per cent.

Before the advent of Napoleon, cereals and silk were the dominant products, with silk the leading manufacturing industry. Even in those times, there is evidence of factories employing "hundreds," but cottage and artisan industry were also prominent. Evgenij Viktorovič Tarle, *La vita economica dell'Italia nell'età napoleonica,* translated from Russian into Italian by Italo Santachiara (Turin [?]: Giulio Einaudi, 1950), pp. 375–376, 379–381.

8. Gerschenkron's index indicates that the growth of industrial output came in two distinct surges: during 1881–1888, when the mean (geometric) annual rate of increase reached 4.6 per cent; and 1896–1908, when it averaged 6.7 per cent. He designates the latter period as the beginning of Italy's "big push" of industrialization. Alexander Gerschenkron, "Notes on the Rate of Industrial Growth in Italy, 1881–1913," *Journal of Economic History,* XV:4 (December 1955), pp. 364–365.

9. "Pecuniary external economies" are defined by J. E. Meade as profits invoked for one firm by the actions of other firms. Scitovsky, who develops the case carefully, expresses the relationship as $P_1 = G\ (X_1,\ L_1,\ C_1\ \ldots\ ;\ X_2,\ L_2,\ C_2\ \ldots)$, where P_1 is profits of the first firm, X_1, L_1 and C_1 its output and inputs; and X_2, L_2, C_2 are outputs and inputs of the second firm, and so on. The examples discussed in the text below are applications of Scitovsky's analysis. Tibor Scitovsky, "Two Concepts of External Economies," *Journal of Political Economy,* LXII:2 (April 1954), pp. 146, 148–150.

10. The concept of "linkages" is Hirschman's. Cited in Benjamin Higgins, *Economic Development: Principles, Problems and Politics* (New York: Norton, 1959), p. 405.

11. Clough and Livi, "Economic Growth in Italy," pp. 339–340. The argument is that the presence of iron- and steel-making served as a magnet to draw in metal-working and metal-using activities. However, while iron-working extends back to the eighteenth century, it was never more than a small regional industry, and not internationally competitive. In any case, it would not follow that the steel-using industries were stimulated by being compelled under protection to substitute a high-cost domestic source for cheaper imports. On the contrary, the effect would be to shrink their markets, not to expand them.

12. Gerschenkron, "Notes on the Rate of Industrial Growth in Italy," pp. 368–370.

13. They were the first experts to pose the problem explicitly in these terms. Cenzato and Guidotti, "Il problema industriale del Mezzogiorno," p. 408.

14. Exceptions were the small maritime republics such as Amalfi, and Sardinia, which was joined to Piedmont.

15. In his very perceptive study of the culture of a southern village, Banfield points to "amoral familism"—preoccupation with the short-run interests of the nuclear family to the exclusion of community concerns—as the key to social organization and incentives. This system regards the state as an outside agency, isolates the peasantry from the larger society, and precludes common action for progressive change, also fostering a cynical view of the law and bureaucracy. Edward C. Banfield, with the assistance of Laura Fasano Banfield, *The Moral Basis of a Backward Society* (Glencoe, Illinois: The Free Press, 1958), chs. 5, 8 and 9.

16. Sulphur is still the dominant product in this field, but is badly handicapped on the world market by competition of richer foreign deposits and by obsolete technical methods of recovery and production. Thus the industry

has survived in Sicily only under protection, and is now noted for the poverty of its workers.

17. In 1881–1885, the excess of births over deaths in the north was 9.9 per thousand, as against 11.7 in the south. By 1950–1951, the corresponding figures were 5.5 and 15.7 per thousand. The perverse rise in the south, although the poorer region, was occasioned by the lag in the decline of birth rates there. In turn, this lag originates in the failure of the standard-of-living effect to assert itself, because per capita income failed to rise.

18. E. E. Hagen, "Population and Economic Growth," *American Economic Review*, XLIX:3 (June 1959), pp. 310–328.

19. Vöchting puts emigration for these years at 3.8 million for south and central Italy together. Dickinson excludes Sicily, the other islands, and Lower Lazio from his definition of the south, and asserts that between 1871 and 1951 emigration was 2.7 million persons. Friedrich Vöchting, *Die Italienische Südfrage: Entstehung und Problematik eines Wirtschaftlichen Notstandsgebietes* (Berlin: Duncker und Humblot, 1951), p. 649; Robert E. Dickinson, *The Population Problem of Southern Italy: An Essay in Social Geography* (Syracuse, N.Y.: Syracuse University Press, 1955), pp. 2, 6.

20. The statistics of those actively employed in agriculture during the period seriously understate the numbers actually used, because peasant-family farming involves no recourse to an external labor market.

21. This point must not be pressed too far: the seasonal nature of some employment, if unalterable, dictates some part-time unemployment. This must be distinguished from a permanent hidden surplus. Simon Rottenberg, "The Meaning of Excess Supplies of Labor," *Scottish Journal of Political Economy*, VIII:1 (February 1961), pp. 65–70.

22. Robert Solow has developed the case theoretically, showing that where input coefficients are variable and population growth depends upon per capita real income, an initial improvement of incomes will induce a rise in population. If, further, the initial ratio of capital stock to labor exceeds an initial equilibrium ratio, but falls short of a higher one, it will be driven back by increase of labor to a stagnant equilibrium level, at which there will be little or no saving and investment. Population and labor force continue to rise, with falling returns, accelerated as land is entirely taken up. Redundant labor then develops.

If, somehow, a major burst of externally supplied investment were injected, per capita incomes could rise, while the rate of population increase would begin to taper off with the standard-of-living effect. A new and higher capital-to-labor equilibrium ratio could be reached, with subsequent balance in the growth rates for both factors of production, yielding self-generating and continuing economic expansion. Robert M. Solow, "A Contribution to the Theory of Economic Growth," *Quarterly Journal of Economics*, LXX:1 (February 1956), pp. 90–91; also Higgins, *Economic Development*, pp. 334–335, 341–343.

23. High-wage unemployment can occur whether one assumes that input-coefficients have fixed proportions, as some writers do, or that these coefficients are variable. If the coefficients are fixed in fact, then noncompetitive wage rates will cause employers to select capital-intensive combinations. Also, capital-intensive industries will expand more rapidly. In any case, overt and disguised unemployment will be made worse all around by making wages noncompetitive.

24. Gunnar Mydral, *Economic Theory and Underdeveloped Regions* (Bombay: Vora and Co., 1958), pp. 28–29, 38–41; H. Myint, "An Interpretation of Economic Backwardness," *Oxford Economic Papers*, 6:2 (June 1954), pp. 132–163.

25. Istituto centrale di statistica (ISTAT), *Indagine statistica* (Rome: Failli, 1957), p. 264.

26. The rate of increase in labor supply and the capital-to-output ratio are other variables affecting the growth rate, besides the rate of saving. Apart from technical quality of labor, labor supply has not been a constraining influence for Italian industrial growth. A priori, there is no reason to suppose that the marginal ratio of capital-to-output was unusually high in these years, and so would have depressed the growth rate. A high ratio would suggest capital-deepening, which seems unlikely for this period.

27. Computed from data in *Indagine statistica*.

28. Note, however, the brief burst of investment during 1881–1885, which was not maintained.

The period 1896–1900 is well behind the dates when the United Kingdom, France, and the United States entered their "take offs," underscoring Italy's laggard status in the industrial world.

29. Alexander Gerschenkron, "Notes on the Rate of Industrial Growth in Italy, 1881–1913," pp. 365–366.

30. During the entire period, manufacturing and the rest of industry were preponderantly composed of very small-scale firms, although some big undertakings began to appear by the eighties.

31. *New York Times*, September 14, 1962.

32. This figure exceeds the 448 billion actually credited to public works in the national accounts, because it includes government outlays not considered to be strictly public works, for instance, railway betterments.

33. *Relazione generale*, 1961, I, p. 57.

34. During 1950–1959, the share of housing in fixed investments in the U.S.S.R. averaged 15.9 per cent on the basis of 1955 dollars, and 21.5 per cent in 1955 planning rubles. The two bases of calculation fix the limits within which the actual share probably exists. The initial level and quality of housing in 1950 were poorer in Russia than in Italy, while the rate of population increase throughout the decade was substantially greater. Computed from data in Central Intelligence Agency, *A Comparison of Capital Investment in the U.S. and the U.S.S.R., 1950–1959*, CIA/RR ER 61–7 (no date).

35. Value added in a sector is its value product net of purchases from other sectors. Net value product is value added less depreciation. Statistics for value added are available in current prices. In years of substantial deflation (1930–1935) or inflation (1940–1945), changes in relative contributions will reflect disproportionate movements of prices among sectors, hence will distort real structural changes. In the longer run, these distortions may be disregarded.

36. Simon Kuznets, *Six Lectures on Economic Growth* (Glencoe, Illinois: The Free Press, 1959), pp. 58–59 ff.

CHAPTER XIII

TECHNOLOGICAL RESTRAINTS: DID THEY DELAY
ECONOMIC UNIFICATION?

1. As developed by Despres and Kindleberger, who were concerned with balance of payment problems in the postwar world, one of these cases involves the "goods" level and the other two the "factor" level. I have modified their "goods" case, interpreting it somewhat more broadly as a problem of factor immobility. See Emile Despres and C. P. Kindleberger, "The Mechanism for Adjustment in International Payments—The Lessons of Postwar Experience," *American Economic Review*, Papers and Proceedings, XLII:2 (May 1952), pp. 338–342; also Charles P. Kindleberger, *International Economics* (Homewood, Illinois: Irwin, 1953), pp. 453–468.

2. The main variables in the long-run employment problem are the comparative rates of increase in labor and in capital stock, the structure and rate of change in final demand, and the rate of increase in real wages. Existing growth theory leaves out the wage variable, and for other reasons as well provides no settled conclusions beyond those just noted.

3. The purest and most stringent version excludes all monopoly and immobilities, and presumes perfect knowledge including foresight, immediate adaptability of specific resources for alternative uses, spaceless conditions, and absence of change in tastes, techniques, and factor supplies. It follows that all adjustments are instantaneous—full equilibrium is achieved at once. The purpose of such rigor, of course, is not to sketch a caricature of the real world, but to lay bare the practical consequences of deviations from these assumptions.

4. If the backward zone is entirely one of subsistence agriculture, there is no labor market in the literal sense. Except perhaps in exotic export economies, labor markets do exist in the towns and cities, for workers employed in the backward sector.

5. For a careful consideration of how factor price rigidity and immobility can affect production, foreign trade, and national income, see Gottfried Harberler, "Some Problems in the Pure Theory of International Trade," *Economic Journal*, LX:238 (June 1950), pp. 223–240.

6. R. F. Harrod, *Towards A Dynamic Economics* (London: Macmillan, 1948); Evsey D. Domar, "Capital Expansion, Rate of Growth, and Employment," *Econometrica*, 14:2 (April 1946), pp. 137–147; "Expansion and Employment," *American Economic Review*, XXXVII:1 (March 1947), pp. 34–55.

7. The full implications are carefully developed by Harold Pilvin, "Full Capacity vs. Full Employment Growth," *Quarterly Journal of Economics*, LXVII:4 (November 1953), pp. 545–552. See also "Comments" by R. F. Harrod and Evsey D. Domar, pp. 553–563.

8. This type of unemployment originates on the supply side, by reason of the capital restraint. Causally, it differs entirely from deficiency of effective demand, which is the Keynesian case.

9. D. Hamberg, "Full Capacity vs. Full Employment Growth," *Quarterly Journal of Economics*, LXVI:3 (August 1952), pp. 444–449; *Economic Growth and Instability: A Study in the Problem of Capital Accumulation, Employment, and the Business Cycle* (New York: Norton, 1956), pp. 157–172.

Pilvin's "Full Capacity *vs.* Full Employment Growth" should be read in this connection.

10. In other words, the isoquants are still convex to the origin, but continuous variation now permits a changing marginal rate of substitution and an infinite number of tangency solutions, from which will be chosen the one that equates with the equilibrium rate of exchange (reciprocal of price ratio) established for the two factors. If innovations occur, they will alter the production surface, but without destroying the formal conditions for full adjustment. Factor immobilities and price rigidities are another matter, but these are market imperfections, not technical constraints.

11. Domar, "Further Comment" (on Pilvin), p. 561.

12. Walras, von Wieser, and Cassel all made important theoretical contributions to this analysis. More recently, it has been developed further by William L. Valk, *Production, Pricing and Unemployment in the Static State*, Publication no. 21, Netherlands Economic Institute (London: P. S. King, 1937), pp. 34–75; P. N. Rosenstein-Rodan, "Rapporti fra fattori produttivi nell'economia italiana," *L'industria*, 4 (1954), pp. 463–470; and R. S. Eckaus, "Factor Portions in Underdeveloped Areas," *American Economic Review*, XLV:4 (September 1955), pp. 539–565.

13. Valk, *Production, Pricing and Unemployment*, pp. 45–46, 61–75.

14. Eckaus, "Factor Proportions," pp. 546–548; Rosenstein-Rodan, "Rapporti fra fattori produttivi," p. 464. Eckaus develops the case at the aggregative level for an economy producing a single good, as a first step in accounting for the redundant factor problem. Rosenstein-Rodan employs it for a single industry, and thinks it shows why a wage reduction might still leave some labor unemployed, or alternatively, why full employment and maximum value of output are perhaps incompatible.

15. If there is a dual wage system, both combinations may be found in the industry.

16. Eckaus, "Factor Proportions," pp. 548–562. He suggests that the model is applicable to Italy, as also does Rosenstein-Rodan, using similar analysis.

17. Here it is of interest that two leading Italian economists, Costantino Bresciani-Turroni and Francesco Coppola d'Anna, while urging that the Italian problem was structural and derived from imbalance between oversupply of labor and shortage of capital, both assert that the basic difficulty was political and social: that correction would require reduction of real wages to intolerably low levels. In other words, the trouble really lay in factor prices. C. Bresciani-Turroni, "Credit Policy and Unemployment in Italy," Banco di Roma, *Review of the Economic Conditions in Italy*, III:3 (May 1949), p. 177; F. Coppola d'Anna, "Lo schema keynesiano e il problema della disoccupazione in Italia," *Previdenza sociale*, V:1–2 (January–April 1949), pp. 13–15.

18. See Paul A. Samuelson, "Economic Theory and Wages," *in* David McCord Wright, ed., *The Impact of the Union* (New York: Harcourt, Brace, 1951), p. 317, n. 3. On the question of evidence, see Carl F. Christ, "A Review of Input-Output Analysis" and "Comment" by Milton Friedman, in National Bureau of Economic Research, Studies in Income and Wealth, vol. 18, *Input-Output Analysis: An Appraisal* (Princeton, 1955), pp. 140–143, 159, and 171–172.

CHAPTER XIV

MARKET IMPERFECTIONS AS A FACTOR IN DELAYED ECONOMIC UNIFICATION

1. Alexander Gerschenkon, "Notes on the Rate of Industrial Growth in Italy, 1881–1913," *Journal of Economic History*, XV:4 (December 1955), pp. 364–366, 368–373.

2. Vera C. Lutz, "The Growth Process in a 'Dual' Economic System," Banco nazionale del lavoro, *Quarterly Review*, no. 46 (September 1958), pp. 322–323; "Italy as a Study in Development," *Lloyds Bank Review*, n.s. no. 58 (October 1960), p. 35.

3. For an excellent detailed account of these matters, see Maurice F. Neufeld, *Italy: School for Awakening Countries* (Ithaca: N.Y. State School of Industrial and Labor Relations, Cornell University, 1961), pp. 316–348.

4. Giolitti ruled by assembling and reassembling *combinazioni* of factions, and so gained a somewhat sinister reputation as a "fixer"—which he was. This method was entirely appropriate to the problem—in fact, the only one that would work in that parliamentary regime.

5. The strike data are from Neufeld, *Italy: School for Awakening Countries*, p. 547, and derive from official tabulations. See Table 87 for source of investment figures.

6. Labor force and strike data are from Neufeld, *Italy: School for Awakening Countries*, pp. 329, 350, 528, and 547. There are no statistics for man-days lost in strikes in this period. However, evidence suggests that most of these strikes were brief demonstrations.

7. For details regarding 1919–1922 and thereafter, see Denis Mack Smith, *Italy: A Modern History* (Ann Arbor: University of Michigan Press, 1959), pp. 321–387; Neufeld, *Italy: School for Awakening Countries*, pp. 367–443; and Carl T. Schmidt, *The Plough and the Sword: Labor, Land and Property in Fascist Italy* (New York: Columbia University Press, 1938).

8. Law n. 563 (March 4, 1926), *La gazzetta ufficiale* 87 (1926).

9. Data for money and real wages and for wholesale prices are from Antonio Fossati, *Lavoro e produzione in Italia dalla metà del secolo XVIII alla seconda guerra mondiale* (Turin: Giappichelli, 1951), pp. 631, 634, and 665; real gross domestic national product calculated from tabulations in Istituto centrale di statistica (ISTAT), *Indagine statistica*, p. 269; industrial production from Confederazione generale dell'industria italiana (Confindustria), *L'industria italiana alla metà del secolo XX* (Rome: Confindustria, 1953), p. 14.

10. In an editorial, "Sfollare le Città," published by Mussolini in *Il Popolo d'Italia* (November 22, 1928), he declared the official purpose to be to "facilitare con ogni mezzo e anche, se è necessario, con mezzi coercitivi, l'esodo dai centri urbani; difficoltare con ogni mezzo e anche, se è necessario, con mezzi coercitivi, l'abbandono delle compagne; osteggiare con ogni mezzo l'immigrazione a ondate nelle città." [Benito Mussolini, *Opera omnia*, vol. XXIII (Florence: La Fenice, 1957)], pp. 256–258.

11. Once his unions had been smashed, the worker was "atomized." The next step was to bring him under centrally organized control—through the syndicates and the migration and placement controls.

12. For more detailed accounts, see Jandi Sapi, ed., *Il nuovo codice del lavoro: Legislazione vigente con note introduttive commenti ed indici*, 1st. ed. (Rome: Jandi Sapi Editori [1952?]), pp. 122, 215–223, and 243; Felice Guarneri, *Battaglie economiche tra le due grandi guerre*, 2 vols., vol. I (1918–1935) (Milan: Garzanti, 1953), p. 297; N. Andreatta and others, *Introduzione di problemi del lavoro*, vol. I, "I termini economici," Istituto sociale ambrosiano (Milan: Capello & Boati, 1952), pp. 122–126; Luisa Riva Sanseverino, "La politica legislativa italiana per la disciplina del mercato del lavoro," *La disoccupazione in Italia*, vol. IV, part 1 (Rome: Camera dei deputati, 1953), pp. 159–161. For reference to applicable decrees and statutes, see Enrico Roselli, *Cento anni di legislazione sociale, 1848–1950*, vol. I, "Titoli legislativi" (Milan: Editrice Bernabò, 1951).

13. Royal decree n. 440 (March 4, 1926), *La gazzetta ufficiale* 66 (1926).

14. Royal decrees n. 1103 (March 29, 1928), *La gazzetta ufficiale* 116 (1928); n. 2874 (November 28, 1928), *La gazzetta ufficiale* 302 (1928); and n. 3222 (December 6, 1928), *La gazzetta ufficiale* 18 (1929).

15. Law n. 112 (January 10, 1935), *La gazzetta ufficiale* 54 (1935); see also M. Gardner Clark, "Governmental Restrictions on Labor Mobility in Italy," *Industrial and Labor Relations Review*, 8:1 (October 1954), p. 7.

16. Royal decree law n. 1934 (December 21, 1938), *La gazzetta ufficiale* 298 (1938); law n. 1092 (July 6, 1939), *La gazzetta ufficiale* 185 (1939).

17. These matters are discussed more fully in F. Guarneri, *Battaglie economiche tra le due grandi guerre*, vol. I, pp. 297–303; Neufeld, *Italy: School for Awakening Countries*, pp. 402–443; and William G. Welk, *Fascist Economic Policy: An Analysis of Italy's Economic Experiment* (Cambridge, Mass.: Harvard University Press, 1938), pp. 159–212, 320–323. Guarneri was minister for exchange control in the later thirties.

18. Sapi, ed., *Il nuovo codice del lavoro*, p. 123. See also Clark, "Governmental Restrictions on Labor Mobility in Italy," pp. 8–9.

19. In labor placement alone, serious problems already had occurred when A.M.G. Order no. 28 wiped out the enforcement agencies for the old controls for a brief period. Employers immediately began hiring privately at the gate. They also began mass layoffs of married workers, replacing them with single persons to cut the cost of bread allowance (*Indennità di caropane*); and began ignoring the intended preferential status of disabled ex-soldiers, ex-soldiers as such, and heads of needy families.

20. Law n. 264 (April 29, 1949), *Provvedimenti in materia di avviamento al lavoro e di assistenza dei lavoratori involuntariamente disoccupati, La gazzetta ufficiale, supplemento ordinario*, n. 125 (June 1, 1949).

21. On this and on most of the arguments, see Clark, "Governmental Restrictions on Labor Mobility in Italy," pp. 13–15.

22. Not entirely, for there were at least two distinguished critics of the system, Dr. Ernesto Rossi, a courageous journalist, and the late president of the republic, Luigi Einaudi. As a lifelong classical liberal, Einaudi was strongly repelled by the repressive features of the placement system, which he termed a form of serfdom (*servitù della gleba*). As president, he could not intervene openly, but he expressed his condemnation privately in 1951 and 1953, and these views have since become public. See Luigi Einaudi, *Lo scrittoio del presidente (1948–1955)*, vol. I, part 2 of *Opere di Luigi Einaudi*, ed. Giulio Einaudi (1956), pp. 575–589.

23. Law n. 1228 (December 24, 1954), *La gazzetta ufficiale* n. 8 (January

12, 1955); see also presidential decree n. 136 (January 31, 1958), *La gazzetta ufficiale* n. 64 (March 14, 1958), which set up the regulations flowing from the 1954 law.

24. *Corte costituzionale, sentenza* n. 53 (April 17, 1957), reported in full, with helpful commentary by Dr. Rosario Flammia, in *Il foro italo*, vol. LXXX (1957), part I, pp. 730–734. For the less important decision of 1958, see *Corte costituzionale, sentenza* n. 30 (April 8, 1958), vol. LXXXI (1958).

25. "Migrazione interne e mobilità del lavoro," editorial in *Mondo economico*, XV:12 (March 19, 1960).

26. Law n. 5 (February 10, 1961), *Abrogazione della legislazione sulle migrazioni interne e contro l'urbanesimo nonchè disposizioni per agevolare la mobilità territoriale dei lavoratori*, *La gazzetta ufficiale* n. 43 (February 18, 1961).

27. Then and now, occupational mobility in Italy is a quite different matter. Today as under the Fascist system, it is regulated in great detail, through elaborate distinctions by sex, by clerical vs. manual work, by sector, by industry, and by skill level—all through the placement offices. In short, the classification so assigned to a job-seeker determines the scope of his opportunity for placement, wherever he may be referred for work.

28. To some extent, these employers may consent to some wage-push, to buy off the unions from making trouble and to stem the pressure of some politicians for nationalization.

29. Although adjustment of the 1951 census totals was made to put them on an *employment*, rather than active population basis, and so to approach comparability with the *employment* estimate of 1961, it is safer to view the net sector changes deriving as orders of magnitude rather than absolute values. SVIMEZ undertook a similar procedure, and obtained almost the same total for industry, and about 194,000 less persons for tertiary activities in 1951. The main difference is in agriculture, where SVIMEZ estimated only 6.8 million employed—1.15 million less than our figure. It is impossible to determine SVIMEZ's procedure with exactitude from its published account, but apparently 170,000 of the difference arises from its deduction of "20–25" per cent of 1.94 million *total* registered unemployed, as against our use of 26 per cent of 1.21 million formerly employed unemployed. The latter figure is more appropriate on the census definitions. Beyond this, SVIMEZ states that it also deflated the agricultural total to reconcile it with estimates from subsequent labor-force sample surveys—but the extent and method of adjustment are not disclosed. Associazione per lo Sviluppo dell'industria nel Mezzogiorno (SVIMEZ), *L'aumento dell'occupazione in Italia dal 1950 al 1957* (Rome: Giuffrè, 1959), pp. 45, 49.

30. These figures derive from the reconciliation of the 1951 data with the 1961 survey, partly presented in Table 88, using the same original sources.

31. Except for rubber and building materials, whose output series were taken from the *Relazione generale* because they were otherwise not available, the production series were taken from Organisation for Economic Co-operation and Development, Statistical Bulletins, *General Statistics* (November 1962). Since the series for rubber and building materials are on a 1953 base, values for 1951 were obtained by splicing to the 1938 indexes. Weights for combining the industry series in an over-all index for the inner sector were based upon the relative importance of the items to each other in the official index. See OECD, Statistical Bulletins, *Definitions and Methods* (Paris, 1960), pp. 52–56.

32. The ML data are tabulated monthly and published at irregular intervals during each year in *Statistiche del lavoro*. They are also republished by the private-industry serial, *Rassegna di statistiche del lavoro*. For reasons of availability, both sources had to be used.

33. Until recently, employers preferred to extend hours rather than to add workers, because it was cheaper in added social security charges, and because of the difficulty of making subsequent layoffs.

34. SVIMEZ estimated 2.45 million persons of all categories employed in the inner sector in 1951—about one million over the ML manual-worker figure. By 1957, the SVIMEZ figure had risen to 2.67 million—or at a compound annual rate of 1.01 per cent (compared to 0.62 per cent of the ML). The SVIMEZ estimates combine several sources, rely considerably upon social insurance statistics, involve methods as yet not fully disclosed, and terminate with 1957. See Associazione per lo sviluppo dell'industria nel Mezzogiorno, *L'aumento dell'occupazione in Italia dal 1950 al 1957*, pp. 55–60.

35. The survey for 1961 suggests that there were 724,000 unemployed in that year, of which 442,000 were formerly employed and 282,000 were seeking a first job. By contrast, the ML registration statistics show 1.6 million total unemployed, and 1.4 million in the two categories just cited (997,000 formerly employed and 410,000 new entrants). A parliamentary committee is now attempting a reconciliation. Although the ML statistics have their frailties—errors, stale registrations, and so forth—they are inherently more reliable than the sample estimates.

36. Registration statistics from *Rassegna di statistiche del lavoro*, various issues; sample figures for 1954 and 1958 from *Annuario statistico italiano*, p. 306, and for 1961 from *Relazione generale*, 1961, I, p. 84.

37. A minor fraction of unknown precise size within the registered unemployed were clerical workers, and undoubtedly part of these also found jobs in the inner sector. Also, part was attached to agriculture, hence competitively somewhat outside the industrial labor reserve.

38. Undoubtedly, there was a clandestine northward migration into illegal employment, perhaps totaling around 75,000 a year—reinforcing the divided economy and the double-wage system.

39. This index has a 1938 base and undoubtedly needs revision. However, it provides the necessary continuity, and will have to serve. Converted to 1948 = 100, it shows a rise to 116.7 by 1953, and to 141.2 by 1960. By contrast, a new index of consumers' prices (1953 = 100) stood at 115.4 in 1960, suggesting that the rise in real wages after 1953 may well have been larger than our estimate. Data for both indexes from *Relazione generale*, 1961, I, pp. 135–136, and prior issues.

40. There was some weight-shift effect with redistribution of employment in favor of higher-wage industries within the inner group, but its statistical influence was small.

Emphatically, we are not arguing against higher real wages as such, but simply are pointing out that bending real wages upward in favor of the already best-rewarded group necessarily lowers the attainable real incomes of the many more who perforce are excluded from such jobs.

41. The weighted index of output for the inner sector (1953 = 100) stood at 191.5 in 1960, while the index of manual hours was 109.7.

42. Concededly, the argument assumes that entrepreneurs had some choice regarding production functions. To hold this is not to insist upon continuous variations in all cases, or to deny that new discoveries were concentrated in

the capital-intensive range of the spectrum. We are merely saying that wages are still a variable in employment determination.

43. These figures should not be interpreted as the literal equivalents of average annual wages and salaries of persons occupied in these sectors, for this would mean that there were no nonlabor factor incomes in any of these sectors. However, they do indicate an upper limit to earnings per head, hence convey some idea of differential average productivities and incomes.

44. The gap referred to originates from institutional bifurcation of the labor market, which permits those anticompetitive wage policies that bring the gap about. Even if competition were fully effective, annual earnings per head employed would differ by industry, because of differences in skill mixes, regularity of employment, and shifts in product demand. However, differences in market power have enlarged the income-advantage of workers in the inner group.

45. Pasquale Saraceno, "Italy," Part E of European Economic Community, Commission, *Report on the Economic Situation in the Countries of the Communty* (Brussels: European Economic Community, September 1958), pp. 353–420.

46. Comitato per lo sviluppo dell'occupazione e del reddito, Report no. 6, *Riconsiderazione dello "Schema Vanoni" nel quinto anno dalla sua presentazione*, republished in *Mondo economico*, supp. nos. 33–34 (August 22, 1959).

47. As noted elsewhere, the Vanoni scheme is a framework plan, not a system of direct central control. It relies upon private enterprise and government-guided market incentives to bring about modernization and unification, development and expansion, and full employment. It rests upon certain econometric measures of the propensities to tax, import, and to save, and of the employment effects of the "investment multiplier"; and it projects certain expected changes in employment, real income, saving and investment. Government investment centers in certain "propulsive sectors" (housing, utilities, and infrastructure), with strong emphasis upon the south. The plan aims also at equilibrium in the balance of payments by 1964 (already achieved), presuming liberalization of international trade and an anti-inflationary monetary and fiscal policy. See Comitato interministeriale per la ricostruzione, Segretaria per il programma di sviluppo economico, *Lineamenti del programma di sviluppo dell'occupazione e del reddito in Italia* (Rome: Istituto poligrafico dello stato, 1956). The Report of the Saraceno Committee in 1959 was inspired partly by the Rome Treaty, which effected Italy's membership in the Common Market, hence committing her to the trade-increasing policies within the Six.

48. The redirection of industrial investment in greater degree toward the south poses some serious issues that cannot be considered at this point.

49. European Economic Community, Commission, *Report on the Economic Situation in the Countries of the Community*, pp. 78–79. This section was part of the general report, and was not prepared by Professor Saraceno.

50. Ministero per la costituente, *Rapporto della commissione economica presentato all'assemblea costituente*, part II, *Industria*, section I, "Relazione," vol. 2 (Rome: Istituto poligrafico dello stato, 1947), pp. 292–299.

51. *Mondo economico*, n. 37 (September 12, 1959).

52. *Rapporto della commissione economica*, part II, *Industria*, section I, "Relazione," vol. 2, pp. 243–286.

53. *Report on the Economic Situation in the Countries of the Community*, pp. 53, 372, 373, 392.

54. Saraceno draws the same conclusion.

55. Claudio Segrè has developed a similar analysis, pointing out that most of the postwar change in the composition of output was achieved not primarily by redistribution of the labor force, but by capital investment. The main labor shift has been from agriculture to trade and the weaker parts of industry, while investment has concentrated in sectors where capital-to-labor coefficients were already very high (in the main, most of the inner sector). Failure of the latter group to pass along its above-average advances in productivity in lower prices, he finds, injured the income positions of those in agriculture, trade, clothing, foods, transportation and communication, and, within the inner sector, textiles and machine products. Claudio Segrè, *Produttività e prezzi nel processo di sviluppo: l'esperienza italiana 1950–1957* (Rome: Giuffrè, 1959).

CHAPTER XV

ACHIEVEMENTS, PROBLEMS, AND PROSPECTS

1. Collateral with this cynicism is loyalty to one's own family nucleus as the sole entity worth working for. See Edward C. Banfield, *The Moral Basis of a Backward Society*, with the assistance of Laura Fasano Banfield (Glencoe, Illinois: The Free Press, 1958).

2. The Communist movement did not create this sense of alienation; it exploits it, deriving strength from it, and strengthening it in turn.

3. Figure for government share is sum of public consumption, public works; sector investments shown separately in public works account; and investments by state and local government enterprises in industry, production of energy, transportation including roads, and other public utilities. *Relazione generale*, 1961, I, pp. 57, 59, and 61.

4. The 558 billion figure for state and local enterprises contains no segregation of fixed investments and accumulation of inventories; it is assumed that all of it was in the former category. National enterprises accounted for 92.1 per cent of the total, and are centered in iron and steel, petrochemicals, metal products, electrical and hydrocarbon energy sources, transport (excluding state railways) and communications. These firms include, among others, the IRI, ENI, and BREDA groups. Of the 558 billion total, 27.8 per cent was invested in the south.

5. See "French Economic Planning," an address by M. Pierre Masse, Commissary-General for Planning and Productivity, before the National Institute of Economic and Social Research, London, April 22, 1961; published in Ambassade de France, *French Affairs*, no. 127 (December 1961).

6. Figures for 1950–1961 from Table 55; for 1962–1963 from *Relazione generale*, 1963, I, pp. 28 and 33.

7. Organisation for Economic Co-operation and Development, *General Statistics* (September 1964), p. 107. The ISTAT sample surveys indicate that in 1963 there were only 504,000 unemployed in a labor force of 20 million, as against 708,000 in 1961. *Relazione generale*, 1961, I, p. 80; 1963, II, p. 92.

8. Part of the price demanded by the Socialists in 1964 for continued collaboration in the government was that there be no policy of wage restraint.

9. In 1962 and 1963, short-term credits rose 1839 billion and 1948 billion lire respectively. During the 1961–1962 fiscal year, the treasury ran a cash surplus of 146 billion lire, but in the fiscal year following it had a deficit of 340

billion, nearly all of which was financed by the Bank of Italy. Organisation for Economic Cooperation and Development, Economic Surveys by the OECD, *Italy* (June 1964), pp. 22–25.

10. In the final quarter of 1962 the official reserve reached a postwar peak of $3.4 billion, falling thereafter to $2.9 billion in the second quarter of 1964. As of July 1964, the commercial banks had a net debtor position abroad of $1.1 billion, against which the official reserve was $2.9 billion. OECD, *General Statistics* (September 1964), p. 109.

11. On January 12, 1962, the Bank of Italy cut the required reserve ratio of the commercial banks from 25 to 22.5 per cent. Then at the end of that year it allowed the banks to resume large-scale foreign borrowing: as of the last quarter of 1961, their net indebtedness on exchange account stood at $70 million. A year later it had jumped to $536 million, while at the end of 1963 it reached $1.36 billion. This foreign borrowing enabled the banks to avoid the deflationary impacts of the payments deficit emerging during 1962–1963. OECD, *Italy*, p. 6.

12. This over-all diagnosis is substantially similar to that put forward by Guido Carli, governor of the Bank of Italy, in his annual report, delivered on May 31, 1963. See his "Considerazioni finali," in *Relazione del governatore della Banca d'Italia*, republished in *Mondo economico*, special supplement no. 23 (June 8, 1963), pp. XIII–XXVII.

13. For details on these shifts in and projections for policy, see OECD, *Italy*, pp. 6–9, and 21.

14. See in particular Vera Lutz, "Some Structural Aspects of the Southern Problem: The Complementarity of 'Emigration' and Industrialization," Banca nazionale del lavoro, *Quarterly Review*, no. 59 (December 1961). For criticism, see G. Ackley and L. Spaventa, "Emigration and Industralization in Southern Italy: A Comment," Banca nazionale del lavoro, *Quarterly Review*, no. 61 (June 1962), pp. 196–204. See also Vera Lutz, "Reply," pp. 205–219.

15. For a temperate, sympathetic, and yet not unreservedly favorable appraisal, see Ettore Massacesi, "Il dibattito aperto dal secondo articolo di Vera Lutz," *Mondo economico*, XV:10 (March 10, 1962). Massacesi is a former southerner who had been involved in the development program.

16. On the demand for planning, see the speech of Antonio Giolitti, now minister of the budget (1964), expressing the position of the Socialist Party on southern policy, rendered in parliament early in 1961, *Mondo economico*, supp. XVI:7 (February 18, 1961). The views of the Liberals and Republicans also appear in this issue, along with a reply for the government by Minister Emilio Colombo (Christian Democrat).

17. The combined share of the Socialists and the Communists is an approximate measure of the protest vote. In 1948 their joint ticket drew 31 per cent of all ballots for candidates for the Chamber of Deputies. In 1953 their separate tickets drew 35.4 per cent of all votes. In 1958 the two parties accounted for 36.9 per cent, while in 1963 they attracted 40 per cent. Data for 1948–1958 from *Annuario statistico italiano*, 1958, p. 143; for 1963, *New York Times*, May 1, 1963.

18. Mario Einaudi and François Goguel, *Christian Democracy in Italy and France* (Notre Dame, Indiana: University of Notre Dame Press, 1952), pp. 70–71.

19. "Una politica unitaria per lo sviluppo equilibrato del paese," *Mondo economico*, XV:47 (November 19, 1960). Freely translated from the original.

20. As quoted by Pierre Masse, "French Economic Planning," p. 20.

 INDEX